POCKET GUIDE TO PUNK

Each *Pocket Guide* tells the story of a musical genre, its roots and how it developed

Accessible enough for the newcomer yet detailed enough for the knowledgeable

MICK O' SHEA

—Introduction

I saw a Facebook post the other day which read something along the lines of: "If punk's dead, what've we all been listening to for the last forty years?" Because, unlike other subcultures, history has yet to settle on a definition of punk.

Punk was about ideas rather than three or four chords. If those musicians who became big names within punk hadn't adopted a "so what?" or "says who?" attitude whenever their supposed lack of musical proficiency was called into question by the boorish social commentators of the day, then rock – as a musical force – may well have disappeared up its own indulgent backside. Punk was simply rock music pared back to its original 4/4 roots. Religious leaders, politicians and editorial writers would echo the fears of their mid-Fifties forebears that punk would have a similar corrupting influence as Elvis, Little Richard, Jerry Lee Lewis and other early rock 'n' rollers. Whatever else, as with rock 'n' roll in the Fifties, it only served to make punk all the more alluring.

Which bands are 'punk' has been the subject of debate for 40 years. The Ramones, Television, and the other that were making a name at CBGBs in New York hadn't started out to spearhead a punk scene. It can be argued they were labelled 'punk acts' simply because they regularly featured in *Punk* magazine. The Sex Pistols certainly hadn't set out with any agenda to revolutionise the UK music business, yet the excitement they engendered was to prove the catalyst for The Clash, The Damned, Siouxsie and the Banshees, The Buzzcocks, The Adverts and many more.

It's said that a multitude of bands formed overnight in the wake of the Pistols' now-legendary teatime tête-à-tête with Bill Grundy on ITV's *Today* on December 1, 1976. This wasn't literally true of course, but 1977 will forever be defined as the year of punk; the 365 when it was truly alive. By the time the Pistols imploded in San Francisco in January 1978, punk was already being assimilated into the musical mainstream. Some saw 'New Wave', which was a broader church than punk, as nothing more than a crass marketing ploy. However, if music was ever going to break free of punk's rigid bondage-strapped restraints it had to happen.

The Clash are perhaps the best example of this changing definition. Putting the cover of Junior Murvin's 'Police & Thieves' to one side, the other 13 tracks making up the track-listing on *The Clash* are rumbustious two-to-three-minute punk rockers that wouldn't have been out of place on any of the first four Ramones albums. Indeed, it's been suggested *The Clash* is the best album The Ramones never made. To follow up with a second album in a similar vein would have no doubt pleased Clash purists but would have stunted the band's development.

There's no arguing the songs on *Give 'Em Enough Rope* sounded far better live than they do on the album given The Clash's onstage intensity. With Epic, The Clash's American label, having refused to release *The Clash* stateside – because of what they saw as shoddy production – it's understandable that the band would acquiesce to their manager Bernard Rhodes' insistence they bring in a seasoned American producer. It's also worth remembering that without *Give 'Em Enough Rope* there would have been no *London Calling,* which *Rolling Stone* would hail as the best album of the Eighties. Nor would we have *Combat Rock,* the album that finally broke The Clash in America.

Punk's tentacles were to spread far and wide, but this book will primarily focus on the three main epicentres of that initial amphetamine-fuelled Seventies heyday: New York, London, and Los Angeles; each of which offered a unique stance..

Not everyone got punk. Not everyone was meant to get punk. But those of us that did get it, got it totally. Forty-plus years may have passed yet my memories of dressing up and messing up and going to gigs remain as stark as they ever did. Here's hoping this *Pocket Guide to Punk* will elicit similar memories for those who were there and for those of you looking at punk through fresh eyes, I hope you enjoy the ride.

Mick O' Shea
— *Still Living the Dream, September 2021*

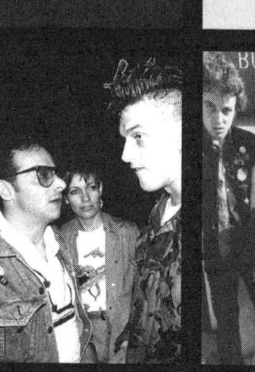

— Of The Street, By The Street, For The Street

"To create an art movement, you have to set something up and then destroy it. The only thing to do is what the Dadaists, the Surrealists, did - complete amateurs who are as pretentious as hell - and just fuck it up the ass. Cause as much bad, ill-feeling as possible... You'll only create a movement when you have a rebellious cause."

David Bowie

The origins of what became known as 'punk' are just as furiously debated today as they were back in the mid-to-late Seventies. Punk didn't spring up overnight, of course. Indeed, its foundation stones can be traced back a decade or so to US garage bands such as The Strangeloves, Count 5, The Seeds, and The Electric Prunes. If truth be told, however, the first instance where punk's DIY ethos was evidenced came with a certain 18-year-old truck driver from Memphis walking into Sun Studios in August 1953 wanting to record a couple of songs for his momma.

That punk started in New York is beyond dispute as *Punk* magazine was highlighting The Dictators, Television, Blondie,

Opposite: Frontage of CBGB OMFUG in New York

The Ramones and other bands operating out of the burgeoning CBGBs scene – whilst careful to show reverence to punk progenitors such as the Velvet Underground, MC5, The Stooges, and the New York Dolls – from January 1976 onwards. The Sex Pistols had played a clutch of dates in and around London by this juncture, of course, but it wasn't until Neil Spencer's now-legendary, "Don't look over your shoulder, but the Sex Pistols are coming" review of their February 12, 1976 show supporting Eddie and the Hot Rods at the Marquee in Soho that the music world began to take notice. While penning his opinion of the Pistols' performance, Spencer likened their playing as being mindful of "Sixties-styled white punk rock".

The origins of the New York punk scene are well-documented; the general consensus being that while Lou Reed's reconfigured Velvet Underground holding court at Max's Kansas City during their nine-week residency from June 24 to August 28, 1970, Patti Smith's poetry readings at St. Mark's Place the following February, and the New York Dolls' securing a Tuesday night residency at the Mercer Arts Center 12 months later, had each played their respective part, it was Hillel "Hilly" Kristal's deciding to give his dilapidated Bowery bar a makeover in December 1973 that proved the ultimate stimulus for everything else that followed.

Kristal, a former US Marine, was a familiar face on the New York music scene. In 1966, he'd co-founded the Rheingold Music Festival with Ron Delsener. His involvement with the festival – staged annually at Wollman Rink in Central Park – would last just two years, however, owing to his switching beer sponsors.

CBGB (OMFUG) – Country, BlueGrass, Blues & Other Music for Uplifting Gormandizers – was located at 315 Bowery, a mile-long thoroughfare running north to south through the eponymous neighbourhood on Manhattan's Lower East Side from St. Mark's Place to Worth Street (one of the city's famed 'Five Points'). Before its gentrification sometime during the early Nineties, the Bowery was home to New York's derelicts and down-and-outs – or 'Bowery Bums' as these unfortunates were colloquially known. Indeed, CBGBs itself was situated directly beneath a flophouse so even upon entering the club one invariably couldn't quite leave the stench of stale urine at the door.

Patti Smith with Robert Mablethorpe around 1970
pictured on the cover of her autobiography

While penning a *History of CBGB* in 1998, Kristal spoke about the advantages of the club's location. The rent was reasonable, most of the neighbours dressed either worse or on a par with the clientele and didn't seem to care about having rock 'n' roll permeating their existence. There were disadvantages, of course. "Within a two-block radius there were six flophouses holding about two thousand men, mostly derelicts," he continued. "I would say most of them were either alcoholics, drug addicts physically impaired or mentally unstable. Some of the men were veterans from the Vietnam war on government disability, and others were just lost in life or down on their luck. The streets were strewn with bodies of alcoholic derelicts sleeping it off after two or three drinks of adulterated wine reinforced with sugar. There were lots of muggers hanging around on the Bowery preying on the old or incapacitated men. When people were let out of jail or institutions, they were very often housed in one of these flophouses by the city, so we had to deal with these crazies trying to come into the club."

The Bowery wasn't the only part of Manhattan in need of serious redevelopment. By the time punk was taking root at CBGBs, New York itself had been on the verge of bankruptcy with NYPD squad cars said to be on standby to serve papers on the city's chief creditors, the banks. Advisors to the incumbent mayor, Abraham D. Beame, went so far as to prepare a statement announcing the city had insufficient funds to meet debt obligations due that day. The statement also set forth a doomsday list of emergency priorities that read like the city's last will and testament. Indeed, it was only through union leaders of the day consenting to the use of union retirement funds to back the loans to the city, that a breakthrough was reached to stave off bankruptcy.

New York boasted other clubs where low rent rockers could usually get a gig such as The Bottom Line, Club 82, the Coventry Club, and Hurrah. Kristal, however, had renamed his club in line with the music he not only liked personally, but intended to feature.

Finding original country, bluegrass, or blues acts was to prove more difficult than Kristal had envisaged, however. Speaking with www.noclass.co.uk, Kristal said he'd been fixing the CBGB awning one day during the spring of 1974 when he espied "three young dudes in torn jeans and T-shirts" ruminating over what the CBGB - OMFUG lettering might stand for. The "three young dudes" in question were Thomas Miller (a.k.a. Tom Verlaine), Richard Meyers (a.k.a. Richard Hell), and Richard Lloyd whose band, Television, had recently made their debut at the Townhouse Theatre – an 88-seat venue located at 120 West 44th Street. The trio struck up a conversation with Kristal – and, according to Verlaine, at least – readily passed themselves off as a country/bluegrass combo.

Another version of the Kristal/Television encounter has

the band's manager Terry Ork descending on CBGBs to cajole Kristal into opening on a Sunday to let his charges play because he whole-heartily believed they were "going to be the hottest thing since John Cage first played a clothesline on stage." (John Milton Cage Jr. was an American composer and pioneer of indeterminacy in the non-standard use of musical instruments. He is perhaps best known for his 1952 composition 4'33", which is performed in the absence of deliberate sound).

Ork, a self-confessed film freak with a penchant for heroin, had arrived in New York several years earlier, landing a job assisting Andy Warhol with his cinematic offerings. His next gig came with managing a film bookstore called Cinemabilia where Verlaine and Hell were also working.

Gender-bending Jayne/Wayne County insists her band, Queen Elizabeth, was the first band to play CBGBs: "I played CBGBs four whole months before Television. It was for a crowd of Hells Angels. They used to hang out there a lot before it became cool and the Ramones and Patti Smith started playing there. In fact, I'm the one who told Dee Dee about CBGBs."

While appearing on Sky Arts' 2019 four-part documentary, *Punk*, renowned rock photographer Bob Gruen told how Kristal had booked Wayne County simply because their name implied they were a country band. Speaking on the same programme Jayne/Wayne said that none of the bands that got their break playing CBGBs had considered themselves a 'punk band'. Indeed, they hated the term because of its negative connotations. They were rock 'n' roll bands doing things a little differently to try and shake their fellow New Yorkers from their "normalcy".

Following on from Queen Elizabeth the Georgia-born County had formed Wayne County and The Backstreet Boys. On dissolving The backstreet Boys, Wayne, together with the band's guitarist, Greg Van Cook, relocated to London where s/he formed The Electric Chairs.

Miller and Meyer's shared love of music, art, and poetry had seen them abscond from Sandford School, a private boarding school in Hockessin, Delaware. They planned to head down to Florida where they would beachcomb and live off the land while fulfilling their literary aspirations in becoming writers or poets themselves. They would get as far as Alabama before being

Jayne/Wayne County claims her band, Queen Elizabeth, was the first to play
CBGBs. her later band the Electric Chairs were regulars at the venue

picked up by the cops for setting ablaze the field within which
they'd built a campfire. They made up some tale about how they
were returning to school in Florida, but the local cops didn't
believe a word of it and duly ran their names against missing
persons. Meyer was collected by one of his mother's relatives
who happened to live in Alabama, while Miller was picked up
by his dad and returned to Sanford. Meyer had no intention of
continuing his schooling and boarded a bus bound for New York.
The rather more utilitarian Millar, however, opted to remain at
Sanford till graduation. He then spent a year in college before
finally hightailing it to the Big Apple.

Hell says he was somewhat piqued at having to plough a lone
furrow while his partner-in-rhyme furthered his education, but
once reunited the two were pretty much inseparable thereafter.
As with every other hipster, they gravitated towards the Mercer

Arts Centre to see the New York Dolls. "The Dolls had a lot to do with me wanting to do a band," he explained. "There was just so much more excitement in rock 'n' roll than sitting at home writing poetry. The possibilities were endless. I could deal with the same matters that I'd be sweating over alone in my room, to put out little mimeographs that five people would ever see. And we definitely thought we were as cool as the next people, so why not get out there and sell it?"

Why not, indeed. Verlaine would take some persuading, however. Although he was writing songs, his only musical moochings up to this juncture came with taking his acoustic guitar along to an occasional hootenanny at one West Village bar or another. Then, just when Hell had all but given up on cajoling his friend into switching from acoustic to electric, Verlaine sat him down and showed him some simple 4/4 rock riffs on bass guitar. "I thought it took some skill to play a musical instrument, and I didn't have any," Hell continued. "But he (Verlaine) showed me and that sealed it. There was the beginning of a band because Tom already knew this drummer from Delaware, and so we started rehearsing together."

The Delaware-based drummer in question was 22-year-old Billy Ficca. Following Ficca's inclusion, The Neon Boys, as the trio had decided on calling themselves, would record a two-track demo: "That's All I Know Right Now" and "Love Comes in Spurts".

Terry Ork was suitably impressed by what he heard and just knew he had to be somehow involved. Following The Neon Boys' subsequent morphing into Television, Ork introduced them to guitarist Richard Lloyd and became their manager. His first order of the day being the band adopt an image to complement their spasmodic musical style.

Although underwhelmed by what he later described as a "terrible, screechy, ear-splitting guitars and a jumble of sounds he just didn't get," Kristal allowed Ork to twist his arm a second time in allowing Television further bookings. "CBGBs was clearly where things were happening from the very first time we played there," Hell reflected. "We were really unique. There wasn't another rock 'n' roll band in the world with short hair. There wasn't another rock 'n' roll band with torn clothes.

Everybody was still wearing glitter and women's clothes. We were these notch-thin, homeless hoodlums, playing really powerful, passionate, aggressive music that was so lyrical."

"Originality was prime, and technique was second place," Kristal reflected on www.noclass.co.uk. "The formula-driven disco music and long-drawn-out solos in much of the rock of the late sixties and early seventies encouraged a lot of disgruntled rock enthusiasts to seek the refreshing rhythms and sounds of simple high energy rock and roll which seemed to take shape at CBGB. We called this music 'street rock' and later 'punk'. Come as you are, and do you own thing rock and roll."

Kristal's son, Dana, insists the kudos for introducing the "simple, high-energy rock 'n' roll" that would subsequently morph into punk at CBGBs belongs to two hitherto unsung heroes. "Bill Paige and Rusty McKenna started punk rock," he told www.tinymixtapes.com in September 2007. "[They] convinced my father to let bands play at Hilly's. And that's really when punk rock started. This was in 1973, right before Hilly's became CBGB. Bill wasn't a musician. He was just a guy who loved crazy acts. One time, I had a bag on my head and Bill said, 'Do that! People will love it!' That was his attitude towards performance.

"Not any of the punk musicians that you read about were ever there when [it] started. It wasn't called 'punk rock' when they started bringing the music in, but it was punk stuff. Tom Verlaine saw them playing and he asked if [Television] could play. I don't know why they don't print that."

Regardless of how Television and Hilly Kristal came to be acquainted, word soon got around the five boroughs that CBGBs was the place where any band could get a gig irrespective of musical proficiency. Within weeks of Television's opening night, Mercer refugee acts such as The Magic Tramps, Suicide, Wayne County, and The Fast had all made their CBGBs debut.

The Mercer Arts Centre was housed within the Diplomat Hotel and located at Broadway and West 3rd Street. When it first opened its doors, the Grand Central Hotel as it was originally called, had been one of New York City's finest hotels. As with much of New York during the Seventies, however, the eight-story building was little more than a crumbling husk in need of a wrecking ball. That it was still functioning at all was due to aspiring theatre impresario, Seymour Kaback, who'd amassed a sizeable fortune from air-conditioning, taking the lease on the hotel's public rooms and catering areas and remodelling them into theatres, drama workshops, and a cabaret known as the Blue Room. "It was effectively a flophouse and the amenities that had once given the place so much glitz had either been repurposed or rented out," says New York Dolls' guitarist Syl Sylvain.

(The hotel would collapse unexpectedly in early-August 1973. While questionable renovations are said to have played their part, it's believed that the winos and derelicts living there pissing where they pleased was primarily responsible for weakening the structure.)

The Dolls had started out playing in the Centre's workshops but their taking to the stage dressed like Harlem hookers and playing a raucous hybrid of Fifties rock 'n' roll and the full-tilt R & B boogie of the Stones was proving such a draw the Mercer's management moved them into the 200-capacity Oscar Wilde Room, and in turn, giving them their now-legendary seventeen-week residency. "We commanded a pretty interesting crowd that were mainly artists and writers," Sylvain continued, "all kinds of outcasts all put together. We were young and screaming our generation's next move."

The Dolls' next move came with a promotional visit to Britain in October 1972. Aside from recording a four-track demo at Escape Studios in Edgerton in Kent ('Personality Crisis', 'Looking For A Kiss', 'Bad Gir', and 'Subway Train'), the Dolls were set to play for a clutch of shows culminating in an appearance at the 8,000-capacity Empire Pool, Wembley, playing alongside the Pink Fairies and The Faces. Future Sex Pistols Steve Jones and Paul Cook were in the audience that night, the duo having gained access by ripping a panel from a side door. The two miscreants even ended up in the headliners' dressing room, gleefully helping themselves to the booze while Ronnie Wood and Rod Stewart supposedly watched on in mild amusement.

The US mainstream music media had dismissed the Dolls as faggots and freaks, but in the UK both *Melody Maker* and the

NME had placed them on their respective front covers despite the band having failed to secure a recording contract. Up to this juncture, only Warner Brothers and Mercury Records had shown any genuine interest in signing the Dolls, but their UK sojourn brought about a bidding war of sorts with Phonogram, Atlantic Records and Richard Branson's newly incorporated Virgin Records. The Stones were also expressing an interest in securing the Dolls to their private label, as indeed was former Move and T. Rex manager Tony Secunda. Indeed, the Dolls' management were meeting with Secunda to negotiate the finer points on a £100,000 deal when word reached them that the band's drummer, Billy Murcia, was dead. The 21-year-old Murcia had suffocated after accidentally overdosing on Mandrex, a powerful and highly addictive sedative that was similar to Quaaludes, and the current drug de jour in rock circles. Had tragedy not struck and the Dolls had signed with Secunda then mid-seventies rock may well have turned a left oblique. As it was, however, the Track contract remained unsigned and the rest of the shell-shocked Dolls were bundled on the next available flight to New York.

A calendar year was to pass before the Dolls next visited the UK. During those twelve months, they'd recruited their pal Jerry Nolan as Murcia's replacement, signed with Mercury Records, and released their eponymously-titled debut album. The Dolls were set to play a string of university dates up and down the country as part of a mini-European tour in support of the album. They would, of course, also make their now-legendary UK TV debut on BBC2's late-evening music show, *The Old Grey Whistle Test*. Unlike the teeny-bop-orientated *Top of the Pops*, which was centred around the weekly UK Singles chart, *The Whistle Test* was regarded as a serious music show catering for serious-minded musos. Having his sedate sanctum invaded by a bunch of wild-eyed New York droogs in hooker's heels – and who were miming to a backing track to boot! - was not to the liking of the show's staid hippie-esque presenter, 'Whispering' Bob Harris. The condescending Harris would churlishly dismiss the Dolls as 'Mock Rock', assuming he'd hear no more of them. Yet those eight minutes of amphetamine-fuelled camp theatrics were to ultimately spark a counter-cultural revolution in Britain.

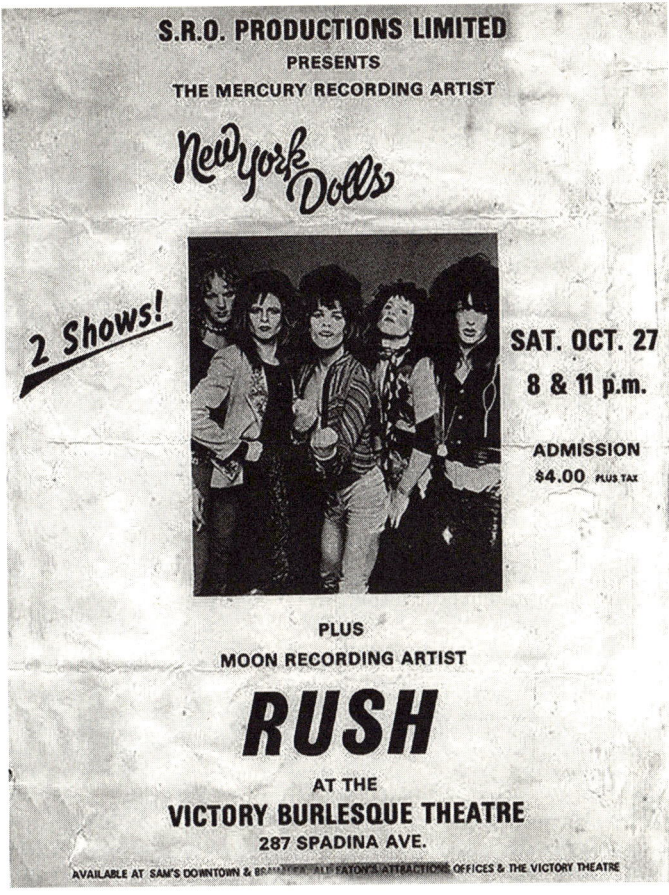

Early appearance by the New York Dolls at the
Victory Burlesque Theatre in Toronto.

The same late-November evening of *The Old Grey Whistle Test* broadcast, the Dolls were strutting their sling-back strut in front of a much more sympathetic crowd at the second of two consecutive shows at the newly opened Rainbow Room at Biba, the ultra-hip Kensington boutique. In the crowd, that night was Malcolm McLaren, a budding 27-year-old impresario, who, together with his 32-year-old school teacher girlfriend Vivienne Westwood was running a fashion emporium called Too Fast To Live Too Young To Die at the unfashionable end of London's

King's Road. The shop had recently undergone a makeover from its original incarnation, Let It Rock.

McLaren and Westwood were already acquainted with the Dolls from their visiting New York back in August where they'd exhibited some of their designs at the National Boutique show at the Hotel McAlpin on the corner of Broadway and 34th Street. Prior to their getting the Dolls up and running, Syl Sylvain and Billy Murcia had built up a thriving knitwear fashion company they'd called Truth and Soul. They'd subsequently sold the company and with his share of the proceeds, Sylvain had spent a couple of months in London buying up the latest fashions and amplifiers. He'd also often visited Let It Rock. Recognising the shop's name adorning the leaflets that McLaren and Westwood had printed up for the exhibition, Sylvain swung by to say hello.

The Dolls didn't have any shows lined up but Sylvain had invited McLaren and Westwood to the band's rehearsal loft to meet the rest of the band. The Dolls' playing style was very much influenced by the Stones and the individual band members' characters weren't all that far removed from Jagger and Co. David Johansen, being the frontman, wasn't only the most voluble but he even bore a passing resemblance to Jagger, while guitarist Johnny Thunders (born John Genzale) had Keith Richards' elegantly wasted chic down pat. Dolls' bassist, Arthur "Killer" Kane, remained riveted in the same spot onstage very much like Bill Wyman, and Sylvain was very much in the Ronnie Wood mould onstage. Indeed, the only stark distinction would be Jerry Nolan's temperament being far removed from that of Charlie Watts.

It was whilst attending a party there that McLaren heard the Dolls' debut album for the first time. Despite his passion for rough and ready rock 'n' roll, McLaren couldn't quite believe what he was hearing. "When I heard it I just fell over backwards," he would subsequently recall. "I thought, my God, this is so bad, how could they make a record like that? I was absolutely shocked, and it made me laugh. It made me laugh so much that I suddenly thought that you can be brilliant at being bad and there were people loving them for it." McLaren, of course, would subsequently rejuvenate his inverted aesthetic as one of his "Lessons" in *The Great Rock 'n' Roll Swindle*.

McLaren's adoration of the Dolls would extend to his flying over to New York in late-January 1975 to assume the mantel of makeshift manager. By now, the Dolls were but a shadow of their former selves. They'd been dropped by Mercury following their second album's desultory showing on the *Billboard* 200 and were in a booze and drug-infused tailspin of their own making. McLaren, however, remained steadfastly convinced the Dolls were still the future of rock 'n' roll. The surviving Dolls have always been quick to play down McLaren's role, but regardless of whatever verbal arrangement was agreed upon at the time, his was the only helping hand offering them a leg up. Aside from taking the lease on a loft space on West 23rd Street (a short walk from the Hotel Chelsea), where the Dolls could store their gear and work up new material, McLaren also took care of Kane's medical insurance and installed him in one of the city's foremost alcohol rehabilitation clinics.

One of the new songs the Dolls had been working on intermittently before McLaren's arrival in New York was called "Red Patent Leather". McLaren's next show of largesse, therefore, came with instructing Westwood to design the Dolls an S&M themed capsule wardrobe incorporating leather, vinyl and rubber of varying reddish hues in time for a four-date booking at the Little Hippodrome at the end of February.

The Little Hippodrome was a 2,000-capacity theatre located on East 56th Street, and those that had been following the Dolls since their Mercer Art Centre days viewed their playing there as a backward step. McLaren, however, remained unmoved by such grumblings. Nor did he pay much attention to the fact that the Dolls' erstwhile management retained complete ownership of the band, other than to issue a press statement – under the banner: What Are the Politics of Boredom? Better Red than Dead – flamboyantly proclaiming the Dolls to have "assumed the role of the 'People's Information Collective' in direct association with the Red Guard." Despite some 58,000 American soldiers having been killed by the Communist-backed NVA in Southeast Asia, McLaren thought it fun to have the Dolls perform in front of a red backdrop bearing a hammer and sickle at the Little Hippodrome. Amazingly, the Dolls went along with it.

"What a lot of people tend to forget is that Malcolm never set out to manage the New York Dolls," Leee Black Childers said in a 2012 interview with the author. "Like many of us, he fell in love with the Dolls. He believed they had the potential to be one of the best rock 'n' roll bands in the world. They already were one of the best rock 'n' roll bands in the world. They were just a little down on their luck, that's all.

"I first met Malcolm while I was over in London in 1971 stage-managing *Pork* at the Roundhouse (*Pork* was an Andy Warhol play based on tape-recorded conversations between Warhol and Brigid Berlin during which Brigid would play him tapes she'd made of phone conversations between herself and her mother, socialite Honey Berlin.) I think Malcolm and Vivienne had just opened their shop in the World's End around that same time. I didn't know him all that well at that time, but I do know that he had no interest in ever managing a rock 'n' roll band. I think Malcolm came to New York simply to give the Dolls a helping hand because, as I say, they were down on their luck at that time."

There's no arguing the Dolls and McLaren made the strangest of bedfellows. Whereas the Dolls were the quintessential bad boy rock 'n' rollers such as Gene Vincent that McLaren had idolised in his youth, he seldom drank to excess, eschewed all drugs, and the opposite sex left him largely unmoved. McLaren was 18-months old when his father left the family home sometime during 1948. He and his older brother, Stuart, were to see precious little of his mother over the coming years as she preferred to while away her time on the French Riviera with her new lover Sir Charles Clore, the Selfridges supremo. Though their mother would eventually remarry, she devoted much of her time in helping her new husband, Martin Levi, with their clothing factory, often accompanying him on lengthy business trips. McLaren was therefore raised by his doting grandmother, Rose Corré Isaacs. He hated school with a passion, and with grandma Rose having a deep-seated mistrust of the British schooling system, it didn't take much badgering on his part to have her brow-beating the local education authority into allowing her to home school him – at least for a time.

McLaren attended several art colleges including Harrow School of Art, where he would befriend Vivienne Westwood's younger brother, Gordon Swire. During his time at Croydon Art School, McLaren and his future Sex Pistols' collaborator Jamie Reid participated in a student sit-in demonstration in support of their Parisian counterparts. Reid, or MacGregor-Reid to give him his full title, hailed from a long line of political activists. His father, John MacGregor-Reid, was City editor of the *Daily Sketch*, while his grandfather Dr George Watson MacGregor-Reid had stood for parliament as one of the first Labour Party candidates.

It was whilst McLaren was enrolled on a film and photography course at Goldsmiths college in 1969 that his non-conformist colours truly came to the fore. Having been inspired by the Stones' recent free concert in Hyde Park, he'd decided to stage his free festival boasting a line-up including The Pretty Things, King Crimson, and William Burroughs amongst others. Whether booking any of the named acts progressed further than McLaren's febrile imagination is anyone's guess, but the 20,000 people that had descended upon Goldsmiths on the day were irked and vented their frustrations by running amok through the college helping themselves to whatever came to hand.

The unrepentant McLaren somehow managed to escape expulsion over the Free Festival debacle. He helped himself to the college's Bolex camera and threw himself into making a conceptual film based on London's Oxford Street and the dehumanising effect of consumer consumption. He would subsequently claim to his having had to abort the project after mislaying the Bolex on the Tube. It's been suggested elsewhere, however, that he sold the camera to fund his and Westwood's first tentative steps into the world of haberdashery at 430 King's Road.

The Little Hippodrome shows were little more than warm-up dates as Sylvain, the only one of the Dolls that could function for any period of time without reaching for a whisky shot or a syringe, had arranged a tour of Florida via his cousin, Roger Mansoeur. (Mansoeur had once played the drums with The Vagrants, a Long Island-based garage rock outfit that had enjoyed a minor hit in 1966 with "I Can't Make a Friend"). "[Roger] booked us a tour of Florida, going all the way from Tampa to Miami," Sylvain reflected. "First we open up at the Little Hippodrome, then we go down to Florida, get really good with the new songs, play all the clubs and get really hot 'cos once we get back to New York, we can't fuck up anymore."

The Dolls would fuck up, of course; the end coming not in New York, but rather in the low-rent Tampa trailer court Nolan's mother ran with her second husband. The $100 they were making per show was barely enough to cover the necessities of keeping the band on the road - and certainly didn't stretch to feeding Thunders and Nolan's collective heroin habit. Following yet another of Johansen's booze-fuelled diva tantrums about how anyone in the band was replaceable – other than himself, of course - Thunders and Nolan took him at his word and flew back to New York to consider their options.

The Dolls' remaining bookings were fulfilled courtesy of future W.A.S.P. frontman, Blackie Lawless, and a jobbing drummer, but the band was now broken beyond all repair. Johansen returned to New York in the hope of furnishing a solo deal, while Kane headed for LA hoping his being an ex-New York Doll might provide an opening. Sylvain was happy to accompany McLaren on an ad hoc road trip to New York via New Orleans in the band's rented station wagon.

As with time and tide, the New York music scene had moved on exponentially by the time of the Dolls' Florida fragmentation. There had been a real groundswell of activity at CBGBs with new and exciting bands such as The Patti Smith Group, Suicide, Blondie and The Ramones all now playing regularly. What made the scene all the more invigorating was that each of these acts brought something different to the mix.

Patti Smith had long been a familiar face on the Bowery, but she was now setting her poems to music. Born to a jazz singer turned waitress and a machinist, she was born in Chicago in late-December 1945. On graduating from Deptford Township High School in 1964, she'd gone to work in a local factory. Within a couple of years, she'd fallen pregnant. Though seeing the pregnancy through to full term, she gave her baby daughter up for adoption and headed for New York City. Within weeks of arriving in the Big Apple, she'd met and fallen for tortured photographer, Robert Mapplethorpe, and the two embarked on a tumultuous affair.

The carefree Smith would subsequently spend some time

in Paris with her sister, busking and doing performance art to supplement their stay in the French capital. Upon her return to Manhattan, she and Mapplethorpe moved into the Hotel Chelsea and fell into the Max's Kansas City scene. Her performance-driven poetry readings soon took on a musical component. In 1971 she began performing with guitarist and critic, Lenny Kaye. Two years later they formed The Patti Smith Group and began performing regularly on the downtown club circuit. Thanks to the largesse of a benefactor from the art world, The Patti Smith Group released a cover of the rock standard "Hey Joe" coupled with Smith's self-penned "Piss Factory" the previous June.

Taking his cue from seeing The Stooges play the New York State Pavilion in August 1969, 31-year-old, Brooklyn-born Alan Vega (born Alan Bermowitz) teamed up with Martin Rev (born Martin Reverby) as Suicide – taking the name from "Satan Suicide", an issue of Vega's favourite comic book, *Ghost Rider*. At the time of their coming together in 1971, Vega was engaged with sculptures and far-flung electronic experiments at the Project of Living Artists, a downtown workshop funded by the New York State Council On the Arts. Rev, a seasoned veteran of avant-jazz ensembles some eight years younger than Vega, literally wandered into the workshop one day to escape a torrential downpour. The two hit it off and began performing together at local galleries. Their second show was entitled "Punk Music Mass", which is widely accepted as being the first time a band used the word "punk" as a means of describing their sound.

When the duo first started out their shared lack of cash limited their ambitions somewhat. They often had to resort to sharing a sandwich per day between them so they might save for proper instruments. In the meantime, they created their avant-garde sounds on Rev's $10 Wurlitzer keyboard, over which Vega would improvise. "For a long time, we didn't have songs as such," Vega revealed. "So Marty would repeatedly kick his keyboard and I'd hit the microphone stand with a broken bottle or make these horrible noises come out of a trumpet. Then I graduated to screaming, and eventually, that led to writing actual lyrics.

"People were looking to be entertained but I hated the idea of going to a concert in search of fun. Our attitude was, 'Fuck you, buddy, you're getting the street right back in your face. And some.' At one of our first shows, there was a guy in the audience who'd brought this trombone. I jumped into the audience, fell over and knocked the slide out of his trombone. These South Americans took real offence to that. So they immediately attacked us with chairs, tables, anything they could get their hands on. That became the norm. I started carrying a bicycle chain on stage, figuring, if you can't beat 'em, join 'em."

Rev says he was convinced Suicide were going to be as big as The Beatles and all the hostility he and Vega faced most nights did nothing to change that. "Even when the violence was going on and the blood was spilling, I'd be thinking that the crowd knew we were doing something from the future. But it wasn't a future they wanted to know about. So the antagonism got stronger and stronger."

By 1975, Rev had acquired a Fifties drum machine, which expanded their musical possibilities exponentially. Vega, in turn, came into possession of a two-track tape recorder, which enabled them to make their first demos.

Whereas Patti Smith had put her daughter up for adoption, Blondie's effervescent Debbie Harry (born Angela Trimble) was adopted during the autumn of 1945, aged just three months old, and relocated to Hawthorne, New Jersey, with her new family. As with many adoptees, young Debbie fantasised about the identity of her biological mother. Not knowing where I came from is a great stimulation to the imagination," she later revealed. "One afternoon while we sat in the kitchen drinking coffee my Aunt Helen said I looked like a movie star, which thrilled me and fuelled another secret fantasy about Marilyn Monroe possibly being my natural mother. I always thought I was Marilyn Monroe's kid. I felt physically related and akin to her long before I knew she'd been adopted herself."

Debbie graduated from Centenary College with an Associate of Arts degree. Determined to live the bohemian life, she relocated to Manhattan, taking an apartment on St. Mark's Place in the East Village. "I went to the Be-Ins in Central Park," she reflected. "They were great – a lot of crazy people tripped out of their minds, dressed great. That was the one thing I liked about hippy nation; everyone was always dressed up. In a way, the Sixties in New York were a larger version of what went on at CBGB in the early Seventies."

In 1966 Debbie took her first tentative steps in the music business, firstly with the Uni Trio, a jazz combo operating out of St. Mark's Place and then with the Tri-Angels. Nothing came of either venture but the following year saw her land the gig as a backing singer in the folk-rockers, The Wind in the Willows. The octet signed with Capitol Records and released an eponymous-titled album in 1968. The album barely scraped into the *Billboard* 200 (#195). A second album was recorded (featuring Debbie's first songwriting credit for 'Buried Treasure') but remains unreleased. The Willows split soon thereafter. She'd undertaken occasional jobs to meet the rent, including at the BBC's New York office, but as the Seventies dawned she was working as a waitress at Max's Kansas City.

Waiting on the weird and wonderful at Mickey Ruskin's celebrity hangout would soon lose its allure and she ran off to San Francisco with a millionaire admirer. Upon her return to New York City, she found work as a Bunny Girl and acquired herself a heroin habit. By her own admission, she was near-permanently stoned for three years or so before encountering a doctor on Central Park South that weaned her off heroin with vitamin shots laced with amphetamine sulphate.

Debbie's return to the spotlight came in 1974 with the all-girl trio, The Stilettoes, alongside Warhol acolyte Edie Gentile. "The Stilettoes were only ever watched by drunks and low-lifes in sleazy bars," says Debbie. "We made no money, but it was fun. The whole early-Seventies period was fun. Sometimes I miss those days." It was whilst playing sleazy bars with The Stilettoes that Debbie met her future Blondie collaborator and long-term boyfriend, Chris Stein.

The Brooklyn-born Stein had been playing guitar in a slew of local bands since the age of 15; having enhanced his playing style at the Leonard Quintano School for Young Professionals, a *Fame*-style academy that groomed its students for careers in the performing arts. The first link in the chain that would bring Stein into Debbie's world came with his befriending The Magic Tramps' Eric Emerson and inviting the band to provide the entertainment at the Christmas party at the New York School of Visual Arts where he was enrolled on a photography course.

The Magic Tramps had formed out in Hollywood as an experimental, instrumental, underground, theatrical rock band called Messiah. "We became the house band for a club on Sunset Blvd. called, Temple Of The Rainbow," says the Tramps' founding drummer, Sesu Coleman on the band's website. "When not performing original material there, we played various blues bars in the Valley under the name Magic Tramps. All material was improvised without lyrics except for some chants. [Our guitarist,] Young Blood, knew Eric from filming *Lonesome Cowboys* in LA for Andy Warhol and thought he would be a perfect fit for our music and theatrical stage show. I, Sesu, was the Indian Warrior; [Violinist] Lary was the classical, dark-ages maestro; and Young Blood was the cosmic neon spaceman. Upon contacting Eric, he came to Hollywood from NYC – a Heat, Chelsea Girls, Lonesome Cowboy, Warhol Superstar, live and in person. He was a natural showman." (Emerson would sadly die as a result of a hit-and-run in May 1975)

Having gained a reputation via a Friday night residency at Max's, the Magic Tramps were offered a slot at the Mercer Arts Centre, having agreed to help Seymour Kaback convert the ballrooms into theatres in return for rehearsal time. Stein would work his way up from the band's ad hoc roadie to occasional guitar and bass slots. Stein accompanied Emerson to see The Stilettoes second-ever show, and it was a cliched case of love at first sight. "I don't know if it was [fate] or it was just sort of apparent that we were supposed to connect up, Debbie recalled. "I know that sounds kind of ridiculous, but I delivered the whole show to him – I couldn't look anywhere else."

"There was a very do-it-yourself aspect to the way she presented herself," Stein told *Vogue* in 2018. "She didn't fit the showgirl motif that was common at that point and she was very casual about it . . . [Her look] wasn't a calculated thing. There was a certain spontaneity about what she did that I think people appreciated."

It was perhaps inevitable that Stein would be invited to join The Stilettoes, even if said invite didn't come from Debbie herself. "We had absolutely no equipment when we started out. We were terrible," says Debbie. "Chris had a little tiny amp thing that was terribly noisy. Everyone was responsible for their own mix so it was all, 'Your amp is on ten so mine's going on ten, too, dammit. Let's watch the singer bleed."

Debbie's first taste of the life awaiting her came with *Melody Maker's* New York correspondent, Chris Charlesworth, reviewing one of The Stilettoes' early shows at Club 82. The review was part of a generic piece Charlesworth was writing about the New York scene, but such was Debbie's luminosity that the paper's sub editor's desk back in London selected one of the shots renowned New York photographer Bob Gruen had taken of her to accompany the piece. Within a couple of weeks of the article appearing in Melody Maker, Debbie met with Charlesworth at a Japanese Restaurant to say she and Chris were leaving The Stilettoes to start their own band. They originally called themselves Angel and the Snake and got as far as playing a couple of dates under that guise before switching to Blondie and the Banzai Babes, and again to the snappier-sounding Blondie. "The street noise was, 'Hey, Blondie! Hey, Blondie!' I'm like, 'Jesus...' Because we were trying to think of a band name and there it was, right in front of me."

Shows were played with varying line-ups but it wasn't until the arrival of Clem Burke (born Clement Bozewski) on drums that Blondie began to coalesce. Burke, who was 20 at the time, had been playing in bands since the age of 14 and was already well known. Debbie and Chris were looking for personalities rather than sidemen, and Clem fit the bill admirably. Burke had no sooner acclimatised himself when Fred Smith decamped to join Television in the wake of Richard Hell's departure. Fortunately, Blondie wouldn't have to look far for a replacement as Burke's roommate, Gary Lachman, just happened to play bass. An ad hoc audition was hastily arranged in a midtown loft where Lachman jammed along to the Stones' 'Live with Me'. On being invited to join the band, Lachman adopted the stage name Gary Valentine.

In early-June 1975, Blondie recorded a set of demos which were financed by *Soho Weekly News* journalist, Alan Betrock. Aside from The Shangri-Las' 'Out in the Streets' they recorded four originals: 'Platinum Blonde', 'Thin Line', 'Puerto Rico', and 'Once I Had a Love (a.k.a. 'The Disco Song')' Though supposedly keen to manage Blondie, Betrock would subsequently throw in his lot with another up-and-coming CBGBs band, The Marbles.

In hindsight, one can hardly blame Betrock for passing on Blondie. Although the band were all very likeable personality-wise, they were woefully ramshackle onstage. Debbie has since admitted she thought of packing it all in and had only persevered because of Chris's unshakable belief that their luck had to change if they kept at it. Blondie would indeed keep at it, the missing piece of the jigsaw finally landing into place with the arrival of Jimmy Destri on piano.

The Ramones were four black-leather-clad delinquents from Queens that had made their CBGB debut the previous August. They'd adopted their name courtesy of bassist, Dee Dee (born Douglas Colvin) from a pseudonym Paul McCartney supposedly used during The Beatles' brief tenure as the Silver Beetles. Their guitarist, Johnny (born John Cummings), and Hungarian-born drummer Tommy (born Tamás Erdelyi) had played together in a high-school garage band called the Tangerine Puppets. "Johnny lived across the street and was friendly to me," Dee Dee revealed. "He worked for a dry cleaners and I would usually see him around, making his deliveries. I thought he was cool because he dressed like he wanted to, even when he was working. I didn't know him that well, but one day [he] and I spoke to each other and both kind of blurted out that we liked The Stooges. I couldn't believe it, because at that time, no one was into The Stooges."

The Ramones began taking shape in early 1974 when Cummings and Colvin invited 23-year-old Jeffrey Hyman to join as their drummer. At the time, Hyman was fronting a glitter punk outfit called Sniper under his alter ago, Jeff Starship. Colvin was singing and well as playing the guitar, Cummings was also on guitar, the fledgling line-up being completed by another friend called Richie Stern on bass. It soon became apparent that Stern wasn't up to the task, so he was let go and Colvin switched to bass leaving Cummings as sole guitarist. Erdelyi was set to become the band's manager and it was at his behest – primarily because Dee Dee was struggling to play and sing simultaneously – that Hyman was invited to take over vocal duties. "I saw Sniper play with Suicide one night, and Joey was the lead singer and he was great," Dee Dee continued. "He was really sick looking.

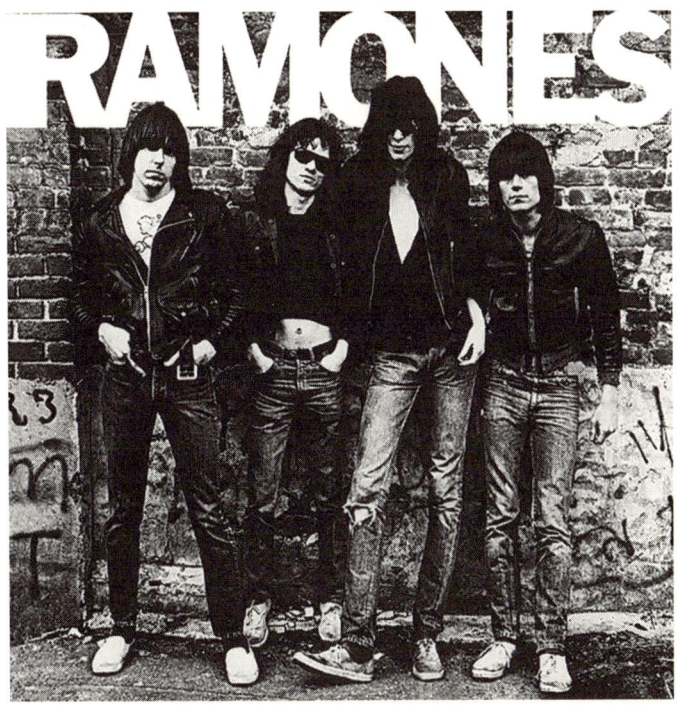

The Ramones made their debut at CBGBs in August 1974

I thought Joey was the perfect singer because he was so weird looking. And the way he leaned on the mic was really weird. I kept asking myself, 'How's he balancing himself.'"

Keeping the beat and singing in unison to Ramones songs was to prove beyond Joey's capabilities, however, so the band began their search for a drummer. "What happened was, they kept playing faster and faster, and I couldn't keep up on drums," Joey later reflected. "It was too fast. Every day in rehearsal it was a little faster. So they asked me to sing. Actually, it was Dee Dee because he'd seen me in Sniper and thought I wasn't like anybody else. Everybody else was doing an Iggy or Mick Jagger."

During the auditions, Erdelyi often sat in to show the prospective candidates what was required. Realising they already had the perfect drummer, Erdelyi became Tommy Ramone.

The Ramones were still honing their haphazard musicianship,

but their dishevelled ripped jeans, beat-up leather jackets, and Converse high-tops style was destined to become the classic punk look – in the US, at least. *Punk* magazine's co-founder, Legs McNeil, was one of the handful in attendance when The Ramones made their CBGBs debut. He subsequently cited the sound emanating from the stage that night as being "just this wall of noise". Nonetheless, by the end of the set, he was hooked. "They looked so striking. These guys were not hippies. This was something completely new."

McNeil had co-founded *Punk* alongside cartoonist John Holmstrom and their publisher buddy, Ged Dunn. The magazine was part-financed by Thomas King Forçade, the larger-than-life cannabis rights activist and founder of *High Times* magazine. Forçade had launched *High Times* on a $20,000 shoestring budget, but such was the magazine's popularity throughout America that the circulation doubled with each issue going on to sell over four million copies a month, grossing an estimated $5million a year. "Tom helped us out several times in very big ways, including advertisers and national distribution," says Holmstrom. "Tom was our biggest fan and a true punk rocker. Keep in mind that although Bob Marley, Blondie, and Johnny Rotten all appeared on the front cover of *High Times*, you never saw the Allman Brothers, or the Grateful Dead, or any other hippie bands on the cover."

Forçade had launched *High Times* in 1974, the same year he'd been indicted over an alleged conspiracy to firebomb the 1972 Republican convention in Miami. "Tom was arrested for 'attempted sabotage' because he was driving a truck that supposedly contained explosives," Holmstrom continued. "Tom was bat-shit crazy alright, but these so-called 'explosives' were actually smoke bombs which were to be used at 'Eat The Rich,' a Yippie rock concert. The charges were eventually dropped, but at the time he had to go into hiding. It was during his exile that he came up with the idea for *High Times*.

"Glenn O'Brien, who was working as an editor at *High Times* back then, claims he was the first person to tell Tom about *Punk* magazine. But since Tom lived near Bleecker Street, which was plastered with 'Watch Out! Punk Is Coming!' posters, I think he was already aware of us. One day in May 1976, Tom came

Cover of *Punk* magazine's first full-length photo comic 'The Legend of Nick Detroit'

storming into our office, sat down at my desk and said, 'I'm going to make you rich and famous!' It was Tom who arranged payment for the printing costs for *Punk #6* ('The Legend of Nick Detroit,' our first feature-length photo comic). *High Times*' parent company, Trans-High Corporation, paid $2,000 for an eight-page mini *Punk* magazine' that appeared in the February 1977 issue of *High Times*. He also gave us remnant advertising space whenever possible. However, this didn't stop Tom from bellowing, 'I gave you $2,000 worth of advertising space' whenever we ran out of money and the rent was due."

The Dictators were by far the most established act on the CBGB scene. They'd been together going on three years and had just released their debut album, *Go Girl Crazy!*, via Epic Records. Prior to the album's March '75 release, The Dictators' brash pedal-to-the-metal style often came under fire for confusing audiences, but in hindsight, they can be viewed as creating the punk rock archetype.

Television were still a huge draw of course, while Suicide and Wayne County were also finding favour at CBGBs. Three Rhode Island School of Design alumni calling themselves Talking Heads were another band beginning to create a stir on the Lower East Side with their funky avant-garde style.

If there was one mistake Malcolm McLaren made during his brief tenure with the Dolls it was his allowing his disdain of both CBGBs and Hilly Kristal to affect his judgement. As with Lou Reed and Iggy, the Dolls were being hailed as the progenitors of this new and exciting scene. Unlike in London where the scene would be contrived to be of the kids, by the kids for the kids and where anyone over the age of 20 would be considered a "boring old fart", their New York counterparts were less elitist. Except for Nolan, the rest of the Dolls were still in their mid-20s and younger than some of those getting up on the CBGBs stage anyway. Debbie Harry and Patti Smith, Tommy Ramone (born Tamás Erdélyi) were all 29, while Suicide's Alan Vega was 37.

McLaren may have had his reservations about CBGBs and Hilly Kristal, but upon his return to New York, he soon found himself following his nose in the direction of the Bowery. Whilst he'd been flogging the Dolls' flatlining corpse down in the Everglades, a musical subculture that was self-generating and reeked of the here and now had seemingly sprung up overnight. Musicianship was of secondary consideration and yet A&R men from several record companies were jostling with each other for pole position to secure the bands' signatures.

The Patti Smith Group were in the middle of a seven-week residency, playing four nights a week, and the word on the street was that they were set to sign with Arista Records. Seeing the reaction of the CBGB crowds reminded McLaren of seeing Buddy Holly and Gene Vincent play the Finsbury Park Astoria (later renamed the Rainbow Theatre) as a wide-eyed

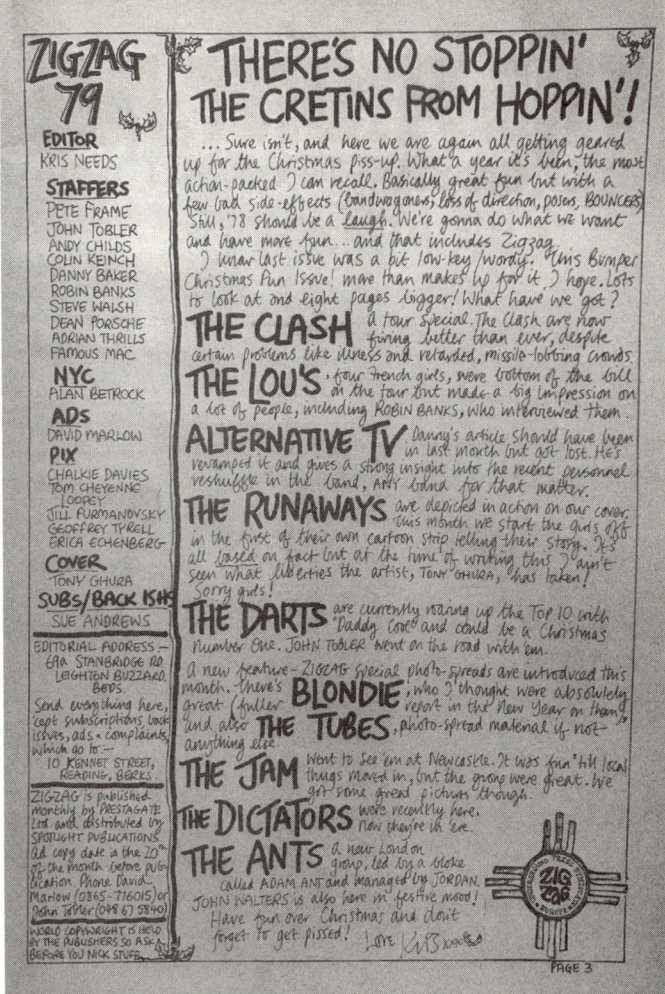

Contents page from the Christmas 1979 issue of *ZigZag* magazine
which had gone punk under the editorship of Kris neeeds

kid barely into his teens. It was his passion for all things rock
'n' roll that had brought about his and Vivienne Westwood's
moving into the backspace at 430 King's Road. And here it was
being reborn before his entrepreneurial eye. Slowly, but surely,
an idea began to form . . .

— Creating A Scene
To Be Seen

"When 430 King's Road reopened as SEX
– another radical overhaul, announced by
three plump pink vinyl letters over the
front door – I knew I had to work there."

Jordan

The New York punk scene had to emanate from a squalid club located on the wrong side of the tracks to give it the necessary credence, but even after four decades it still beggars belief the touch paper to the fabled UK punk explosion of 1976 was lit from within the cramped confines of a fashion boutique situated on the wrongs side of the King's Road. But 430 King's Road was no ordinary fashion boutique, of course. McLaren and Westwood were far from run-of-the-mill couturiers – if only because neither had any formal training in fashion design. Indeed, the closest either had come to qualifying in the field of fashion came with Westwood enrolling on a silversmith and jewellery-making course at Harrow Art School. What makes things even more interesting is there wouldn't have been any punk explosion in London had McLaren not been so hopelessly enamoured with the Dolls that he went off gallivanting to New York leaving Westwood to run the shop and take care of their two boys. Indeed, it was pure happenstance that led to him and Westwood taking over the lease at 430 King's Road in November 1971 in the first place.

Opposite: Storefront of SEX on 430 King's Road, London

The shop was trading as Paradise Garage at the time and run by a happy-go-lucky American called Trevor Myles. Its frontage was decked out in green corrugated iron, with the name spelt out in Hawaiian-style bamboo lettering; an antique petrol pump providing an added touch of kitsch Americana. The interior was decked out like a beach shack and was also awash with bamboo, including bamboo-cages holding exotic love birds which softly cooed to each other while customers rifled through pile after pile of Hawaiian shirts, Oshkosh dungarees, bowling jackets and second-hand Levi jeans that Miles brought over from the US.

McLaren had been making his way through the World's End sporting his beloved powder-blue Teddy boy drape jacket and lurex-threaded drainpipe trousers when the heavens had opened. Desperate not to get his jacket ruined he'd darted inside the public telephone box situated next to the shop. He'd been awaiting the downpour to subside when Bradley Mendelson – an American who was helping out at the shop as a means of funding his stay in London – came rushing out of the shop to compliment him on his look. Mendelson invited McLaren to shelter inside the shop.

By the time the clouds had parted McLaren had accepted Mendelson's offer to sublet the shop's back quarter from where he and Westwood started off selling rock 'n' roll records, refurbished Fifties radiograms and authentic Teddy boy clothing. When Mendelson stopped showing up for work, McLaren, Westwood and their business partner Patrick Casey did what any budding entrepreneur would do under the circumstances and requisitioned the whole shop.

Trevor Myles was over in the US on one of his regular buying trips at the time, and so was blithely unaware of Mendelson's arrangement with McLaren. Business had been rather slow of late, however, so upon his return Myles begrudgingly allowed the interlopers to remain so long as they agreed to share the £80 per week rent. McLaren, Westwood and Casey accepted Myles' proposal without bothering to return their stock to their designated area. But perhaps they had an inkling Myles was on the verge of bankruptcy and about to take a powder of his own.

The change in ownership at the shop brought about a complete overhaul at 430 King's Road, both inside and out. Having dispensed with the bamboo lettering and petrol pump, the corrugated façade was spray-painted matt black with the shop's new name "Let It Rock" in block-red lettering. The front half of the interior was redesigned to resemble a Fifties living room replete with period wallpaper, carpeting, and furniture while the stock was played in Formica cabinets and a glass-panelled sideboard. McLaren and Westwood had the keys to the kingdom but turning a profit didn't appear too high on their list of priorities. Customers would be offered cups of tea and were free to select songs on the shop's jukebox and sit about reading Fifties-era magazines free from the obligation of making a purchase.

"The King's Road was wonderful when I first went there," says Westwood today. "It really was something else, really different and special. Like it is now, it was full of little shops, the side streets as well. Ossie Clark and Alice Pollock had Quorum, and of course, Mary Quant's first shop was there. One of the first ones was Granny Takes a Trip, run by my friend Gene Krell."

By the summer of 1972 (by which time McLaren and Casey had dissolved their partnership), rock 'n' roll was enjoying something of a renaissance in Britain – particularly in London's East End. With Casey out of the picture, however, McLaren and Westwood were struggling to source original Fifties apparel. A fact-finding visit to The Black Raven pub, a rock 'n' roll revivalist stronghold in Bishopsgate had led to the discovery that these latter-day Teddy Boys were having to buy their drapes made-to-measure. Westwood was something of a dab hand with a sewing machine and had been altering her clothes since her mid-teens, but mass-producing drape jackets and drainpipe trousers was beyond her scope. Fortunately, the duo were acquainted with an East End tailor called Sid Green who was happy to undercut the competition.

Let It Rock was already gaining a reputation when McLaren and Westwood were approached to design costumes for Ray Connelly's movie *That'll Be The Day*, a British drama set in the mid-to-late-Fifties starring David Essex and Ringo Starr. A bonus for McLaren coming with his one-time idol, Billy Fury, also appearing in the film. In the August of that same year, Wembley Stadium was the setting for the London Rock and Roll Show, with a line-up boasting Bo Diddley, Bill Haley, Little Richard and Chuck Berry. McLaren and Westwood booked a stall and had hundreds of T-shirts printed up.

The British movie *That'll be the Day* sparked a revival in Fifties fashions

On the day of the show, Let It Rock made the special edition of the *Evening Standard* under the heading "The Teds Are Back". The stall would also feature in Australian film-maker Peter Clifton's 1973 film of the show. Make-up artist, Yvonne Gold, who was herself a frequent visitor to the shop, was co-opted by McLaren to help out on the stall. It's been written elsewhere that despite the crowd being in excess of 50,000, the vast majority of the T-shirts remained unsold. In Clifton's film, however, Gold and McLaren are seen struggling to keep up with customer demand. "We got there quite late and there was a kerfuffle about setting up," Gold reflected. "It was quiet at first until the word got around and then we were overwhelmingly busy – even though there were quite a few of us manning that stall. The T-shirts just flew; we took a lot of money."

That'll Be The Day, the first major British film to take a look back at the Fifties, was released in April 1973, the same year Universal Pictures released *American Graffiti*, starring Richard Dreyfus and Ron Howard. These two films, in conjunction with the West End opening of the smash Broadway musical *Grease*, brought Let It Rock a steady stream of customers. Business was booming but the ever-savvy McLaren and Westwood knew they were living on borrowed time as they couldn't hope to compete once the Fifties revival trend hit the high street and they slowly began diversifying towards the biker element of studs and leather. They also hit upon the idea of baking glitter slogans such as 'Elvis', 'Eddie Cochrane', 'Buddy Holly', 'Triumph' and 'Norton' onto tight-fitting cap-sleeve T-shirts. Other avenues pursued included the 'bike-tyre T-shirt' with strips of old bicycle tyres attached around the armpits, and shirts bearing motifs such as 'Rock 'n' Roll' and 'Let It Rock' from boiled chicken bones which were attached to the shirts with necklace chains. The shop underwent another name change to Too Fast Too Live Too Young To Die (in homage to James Dean). The red-block Let It Rock lettering on the corrugated hoarding vanished beneath another coat of black paint to be replaced by the new moniker in bold white lettering beneath a gleaming skull and crossbones.

In hindsight, it could be said of Too Fast Too Live Too Young To Die that it was the caterpillar betwixt Let It Rock's pupa and the SEX butterfly – as though McLaren and Westwood were grubbing around as yet unsure as to where to focus their creative energies. Let It Rock's reputation had ensured a number of celebrity customers. The Kinks, being dedicated followers of fashion, were familiar faces at 430 King's Road, as were Marianne Faithful, David Essex, Jimmy Page, and Bryan Ferry. McLaren's fascination for the Dolls largely stemmed from their raucous sound harkening back to the halcyon days of rock 'n' roll – or their adding a 'Little Richard drag' as David

Johansen might say. Yet when Iggy Pop and James Williamson swung by whilst The Stooges were in town at CBS's Whitfield Street studio recording *Raw Power* – surely punk rock's ultimate blueprint – McLaren had sneeringly dismissed them as "untidy hippies".

The Janus-like McLaren had one eye affixed to the past and yet his unquenching desire to keep 430 King's Road several steps ahead of the competition brought about another makeover in the spring of 1974 that was to prove fetishistic rather than futuristic. "I just wanted something new," he would subsequently reveal. "I didn't know what, but I couldn't stand the idea of anything retro. Black seemed to be the best colour; where our ideas were the most exciting. I decided to open a shop that was strictly black and design-orientated which would bring out all the sexual clothes that people normally sold as fetish wear."

Westwood had obvious reservations about selling garments one usually associated with the back pages of certain top-shelf magazines and yet despite her being the dominant force in the relationship she nonetheless threw herself wholeheartedly into the venture.

McLaren and Westwood's coming together in early 1967 was hardly what one might describe as being love at first sight. Westwood was some five years McLaren's senior. She'd recently split from her husband and moved into the house in north Clapham that her brother Gordon was sharing with McLaren and several others with her three-year-old son, Ben. She has since admitted she hadn't been remotely attracted to McLaren yet would ultimately succumb to his amorous advances. Their relationship being sealed with the arrival of their son, Joseph, later that same year.

Westwood had never considered herself a beauty in the conventional sense, but she'd come to recognise the power and beauty of clothes whilst growing up in her native Derbyshire. More often than not she'd rush home from school on a Friday afternoon clutching a piece of brightly-coloured material from which she'd fashion a dress to wear at some local dance.

Unearthing specialist suppliers of rubber and leatherwear in the pre-internet age wasn't without its tribulations, of course, but they eventually arrived at the doors of John Sutcliffe at AtomAge in Covent Garden and London Leatherman in Battersea. Whereas the morphing from Let It Rock to Too Fast Too Live Too Young To Die had been done almost overnight, the latest revamping of the shop's interior and exterior was to take several months. The undertaking was further hampered by the ineptness of the builders brought in to carry out the renovations – so much so that McLaren and Westwood ended up overseeing the work themselves.

The walls and ceiling were draped with sheets of peach-coloured surgical rubber and sponge-like grey foam purchased from the Pentonville Rubber Company. The Belle AMI jukebox remained, but its pride of place was usurped by a rusting surgical bed covered with a pink rubber sheet. The wooden rails that had been the mainstay of the interior's fittings were sanded, varnished and bevelled before then being reattached to the walls in the form of monkey bars. The new window displays consisted of the upper torsos of naked headless mannequins suggestively piled one on top of each other. McLaren then set about spray-painting the shop's new womblike interior with slogans and quotations lifted from pornographic literary offerings such as Valerie Solanas' *SCUM* manifesto (Society for Cutting Up Men) and Alexander Trocchi's *School for Wives and Thongs*. To accompany the shop's new line of rubber and leather fetish wear, a salacious array of sadomasochistic accessories ranging from inflatable rubber gimp masks to tit clamps adorned the walls.

The shop's exterior underwent a similar overhaul. The corrugated-iron hoarding was ripped away from its fastenings and sold to a local scrap merchant and replaced with the shop's new identity "SEX" spelt out in three-foot-high Claes Oldenburg-style lettering in provocative-pink padded plastic. On the lintel directly above the door McLaren added his personal pièce de résistance: French philosopher Jean Jacques Rousseau's telling aphorism "Craft must have clothes but the truth loves to go naked".

Purposely attracting a clientele that needed to be dressed head-to-toe in rubber with metal implements attached to their nipples and genitalia to achieve sexual gratification was always going to offend the moral majority. Conversely, however, the shop soon began to attract a coterie of colourful individuals who were desperately seeking something other than what was available elsewhere on the King's Road. Several of these carefree libertines would at one time or another end up working there in one guise or another.

The most recognisable of these, of course, was 19-year-old Pamela Rooke, a curvaceous, kohl-eyed fashion freak who'd taken to calling herself "Jordan" after the fictional character Jordan Baker in F Scott Fitzgerald's *The Great Gatsby*. "Jordan Baker [is] a shrewd golf hustler who knows what really goes down in the clandestine world of the title character's glamorous milieu. Jordan was the name of a sports car that was very popular in Twenties America when the book is set, so it wasn't a sexual definition, it was a brand name. It was inspired – and I took that inspiration and ran with it."

It's often been said that Jordan was the first Sex Pistol. This certainly holds true, for she was indeed the living embodiment of 430 King's Road long before Steve, Paul, Glen and John took to a stage. She'd been experimenting with her appearance since her early teens in her hometown of Seaford in Sussex, having developed her sartorial style in the gay discos of neighbouring Brighton before gravitating to London's club scene. "I'd walk into straight clubs in Brighton and the DJ would clap because I had arrived, whereas in the gay clubs I felt more relaxed and there was better music to dance to," she says in her delightful 2019 autobiography *Defying Gravity*. "There was no threat for a gay man in the early Seventies to have me standing next to him. In fact, the way I looked – dressed in Forties and Fifties skirts, jackets and suits, found in abundance in the second-hand shops of the lanes – they thought it was great.

"The shop at No 430 had previously been Tommy Roberts' Mr Freedom, where I'd bought some of my favourite dancing clothes. A lot of people have said how intimidating they found the new look of the place, like a sex shop mixed with a dentist. But I just walked in and introduced myself to Michael [Collins], who was sitting on the metal medical bed that had become part of the new interior décor. We hit it off instantly and ended up talking for hours. When I left that day, I asked Michael to call me if there was ever a staff vacancy I could fill. It wouldn't be long before I heard from him again."

Indeed, it wouldn't. However, shortly after securing a job at SEX Jordan lost her room in nearby Drayton Place. This meant she was forced to return to her parents' home in sleepy Seaford and commute up to town each morning. Her provocative dress, fastidious make-up and peroxide hair swept up into a beehive would cause the occasional bowler-hatted businessman to shuffle nervously in his seat and tactfully adjust his newspaper.

The shop's teenage clientele had little interest in McLaren and Westwood's fetish line, but rather in their new range of titillating

Jordan, who worked at McLaren's shop SEX, is often seen as being the first Sex Pistol

T-shirts. These crudely-constructed shirts were little more than two squares of material stitched pillowcase-style with openings for the head and arms, bearing wood-block printed images such as Mickey and Minnie Mouse fornicating, a naked pre-pubescent youth suggestively smoking a cigarette, or a simile of the full-face leather mask as worn by the Cambridge Rapist, a serial rapist operating within the Cambridge area and primarily targeting female university students. McLaren is said to have got the idea for the shirt following a visit to 430 King's Road by detectives pursuing information that the rapist had purchased his grim mask from SEX.

The officers were responding to a call from Michael Collins who was working at the shop at the time. "I was sure that one of our customers, this guy from Yorkshire, was the Cambridge Rapist," says Collins. "So I phoned up Scotland Yard and they came to interview me and I wound up in all these newspapers holding this mask, smiling at it. It caused so much publicity that we were inundated by people coming to buy more of them. But Vivienne really hauled me off and told me it was *bad* publicity."

To McLaren's way of thinking there was no such thing as bad publicity and he, in turn, raged at Westwood for not capitalising on the press reaction. "We have to play up things like this," he seethed, "and pretend we really do know the rapist and that we will protect him at all costs."

Speaking about the incident several years later, McLaren explained about the shirt in more detail. "I thought, Hmmm, that's wonderful. I've really got to protect this man, so I thought why don't I associate him with Brian Epstein and the Beatles? So I took this mask that he wore and put it on a T-shirt and put 'Cambridge Rapist' over it in popstar letters. And at the bottom I put a small picture of Epstein and then wrote a few words about him and how the man had not committed suicide but how he died of S&M through loneliness, just to provoke . . ."

Another early design that would bring McLaren and Westwood directly to the attention of the law depicted two cowboys naked from the waist down (except for their boots) and with their flaccid penises almost touching. In July 1975, SEX employee Alan Jones was strolling through Piccadilly wearing the shirt when the police had pounced. He was duly taken to Vine Street station and charged with having "exposed to public view an indecent exhibition".

McLaren was incensed at what he saw as draconian censorship and promised Jones he would have the best lawyers in London defending him in court. Of course, when the case came before the courts the lawyers were nowhere to be seen and the hapless Jones had little option but to plead guilty. That wasn't the end of the matter, however. On August 7, following a police raid on 430 King's Road during which the Two Cowboys shirts and a range of other garments deemed offensive, McLaren and Westwood were arrested and charged under the same archaic 19th-century law as Jones. They were duly fined £100.

At some point during the latter half of 1974 McLaren became acquainted with an unruly gang of miscreants that were treating the shop as something of a second home. They'd recently formed a band and were toying with calling themselves either Swankers or The Strand. Their frontman and self-appointed leader, a 19-year-old semi-illiterate and self-confessed kleptomaniac called Steve Jones, had set about pestering McLaren until the latter had finally agreed to act as their manager. McLaren's first act as manager came with putting Jones in touch with the shop's Saturday lad, Glen Matlock, a happy-go-lucky 18-year-old art student who just so happened to be teaching himself to play bass guitar. Before setting off for New York, McLaren had put down the money on a temporary lease for a rehearsal room at the Covent Garden Community Centre. He also instructed his business associate, the mole-like Bernard Rhodes, to keep an eye on Jones's band.

McLaren and Rhodes had first come into each other's orbit on the early-Sixties Soho coffee bar scene and had remained friends until McLaren hooked up with Westwood. As with McLaren, Rhodes was of Jewish descent. Back in the Fifties, his mother had worked as a seamstress for several Savile Row tailors, including Hawes & Curtis where she was apprenticed by John Pearse, the future founder of Granny Takes A Trip.

Rhodes was running a stall on Chelsea's Antiquarius antiques market, from which he was selling second-hand leather jackets when a chance encounter with McLaren led to his being invited to 430 King's Road. "Malcolm and Vivienne were jealous of me because my second-hand leather jackets were selling as fast as I set them out on the stall," says Rhodes. "They didn't like that, so they brought me in. We tossed some ideas about and they brought me in to help them out by coming up with designs for a new range of T-shirts."

The trio's first collaboration was destined to become the London punk scene's unofficial credo. Titled 'You're Gonna Wake Up One

Morning and Know Which Side of the Bed You've Been Lying On', the polarising design bore a list of 'hates', consisting of antiquated ideals, floundering institutions, fascists, and pompous rockers, and a contrasting list of "loves" championing renegades, outlaws, and other gauche heroes. Tucked away within the shirt's "loves" list is the first-ever printed mention of the band which, over the course of the next three years, was to reshape the musical landscape: Kutie Jones and his Sex Pistols.

McLaren had returned from New York with Jones's band very much in mind. Having witnessed the CBGBs scene where waif-like kids playing second-rate instruments with little or no discernible musical talent were tearing the place up in front of enthusiastic audiences, McLaren had initially hit upon the idea to entice Richard Hell over to London to front Jones's band. It wasn't so much Hell's stage presence but rather his sartorial style that had caught McLaren's eye. Hell was instantly recognisable on the CBGBs scene owing his short dishevelled hair sticking out at all angles. In recent weeks, however, he'd taken to sporting ripped clothes with safety-pins holding them together. There are several versions of how Hell hit upon the look. The one that gets told most often, however, is that an irate girlfriend took a pair of scissors to his sparse wardrobe upon discovering a recent infidelity. As Television had a gig that same night he'd grabbed up the least damaged garments and applied safety-pins to hold them together during the show.

Hell had recently quit Television, but while he was flattered by McLaren's overtures he was in discussion with Johnny Thunders and Jerry Nolan about their putting a new band together. His increasing dependency on heroin proved another reason behind his decision to remain in New York. "I just thought Richard Hell was incredible," McLaren revealed. This was not someone dressed up in red vinyl, wearing bloody orange lips and high heels. Here was a guy all deconstructed, torn down, looking like he'd just crawled out of a drain hole, looking like he was covered in slime, looking like he hadn't slept in years, and looking like no one gave a fuck about him. He was this wonderful, bored, drained, scarred, dirty guy with a torn T-shirt."

While skirting around the issue of whether Hell was utilising safety-pins, McLaren readily acknowledges that he appropriated Hell's look. "There was no question that I'd take it back to London,"

RICHARD HELL
& THE VOIDOIDS

BLANK
GENERATION

McLaren wanted Hell to front the Pistols because of his sartorial style

he shamelessly admitted. "By being inspired by it, I was going to imitate it and transform it into something more English."

During a 2012 house move, Rhodes was sorting through a stockpile of boxes that had been gathering dust for many years when he happened upon the batch of letters McLaren had written from New York. While McLaren primarily focuses on his endeavours with the Dolls, he frequently enquires about what's happening with Jones's band. The majority of these letters being penned prior to the Dolls' break-up is evidence enough that McLaren must have been forming some kind of strategy for Jones's band upon his return to London. With Hell deciding to stick it out in New York, McLaren turned his attention to Sylvain. McLaren had yet to hear Jones's band play, of course, so only had Rhodes' scant progress reports to go off. He nevertheless managed to convince Sylvain that his future lay in London. So much so, the ex-Doll consented to McLaren taking his Fender Rhodes piano and white Gibson Les Paul Custom home with him.

Several months would go by before Sylvain heard from McLaren via a seven-page missive outlining everything the two of them had discussed (McLaren's letter currently resides in the Rock and Roll Hall of Fame in Cleveland). By the time McLaren's letter arrived in Sylvain's parents' mailbox the Sex Pistols were a fully formed unit. Indeed, accompanying the letter were several passport-sized b/w snapshots of his potential future bandmates. McLaren still envisioned Sylvain in the line-up, however. During a transatlantic phone call, he again reiterated his pledge: "You've got to come over .. . we'll send you a ticket . . . we'll get some songs together . . . it's going to be fantastic!"

The plane ticket was destined never to arrive, but Sylvain wasn't left looking anxiously at his watch for long as he and Johansen would cobble together a makeshift New York Dolls line-up for a lucrative tour of Japan. His share of the proceeds would allow him to focus on his first post-Dolls solo project, The Criminals.

During the opening segment of *The Filth And The Fury* John Lydon opines how "the Sex Pistols happened because they were meant to happen." McLaren is on record stating there wouldn't have been a Sex Pistols had he not allowed himself to be seduced by Steve Jones's laddish charm. "It was like Larry Parnes with Billy Fury," he reflected. "You had this marvellous secret eye contact. You didn't have to talk about T. S. Eliot or Gene Vincent, there was just a sense of understanding."

Steve Jones was born and raised in Shepherd's Bush, west London. His father, an aspiring middleweight boxer called Don Jarvis, disappeared soon after he was born, leaving him and his mother Mary to move in with his grandparents in neighbouring Hammersmith. His mother would eventually marry, but Jones's relationship with his stepfather was turbulent from the off. School was to prove equally unsettling. Reflecting on his childhood in his 2018 autobiography, *Lonely Boy: Tales from a Sex Pistol*, Jones says had he been at school today he would most likely have been diagnosed as being dyslexic and/or having ADHD. As it was, his inability to follow what was going in the classroom resulted in his being put back a year.

Whatever Jones lacked in regards to the three Rs was compensated with an abundance of street savviness, and an easy ability to size-up situations. One of his earliest memories is of accompanying his parents on shoplifting forays at the local supermarket. By his early teens, he was well on his way to becoming a seasoned criminal and was also well known to the police. He would subsequently boast of thirteen convictions over a three-year period, the crimes ranging from petty burglary and breaking and entering to stealing cars and driving underage without a license or insurance. One such conviction was to result in a three-week incarceration at Ashford Remand Centre in Kent.

Jones's primary partner-in-crime within the Pistols, Paul Cook, was also Shepherd's Bush born and bred. Indeed, as kids, the two lived just a couple of streets apart and their mothers were acquainted. Whereas Jones was an only child, Cook was the second of three children and the only boy. His father was a carpenter and joiner by trade while his mother worked as a cleaner. Prior to Jones's being kept back a year, Cook was proving a diligent, hard-working pupil. Despite his report cards taking a sharp downturn during his final two years at school, he'd nonetheless secured an apprenticeship as an electrician at the Watney's Brewery in Mortlake. By the time they were starting to put a band together, Jones had moved in with the Cooks, living out of the bedroom recently vacated by Paul's sister, Margaret.

McLaren's fondness for Jones was undoubtedly a key factor in his agreeing to take the nascent Sex Pistols under his wing. And yet the band only came into being because of its unsung hero, guitarist Warwick "Wally" Nightingale. With his parents out at work all day, Nightingale's home in Hemlock Road, East Acton, had been a sanctuary of sorts for Jones, Cook and their fellow Christopher Wren Secondary Modern reprobates, Jimmy Macken and Stephen Hayes. Wally had been teaching himself guitar for the past couple of years, and it was only his constant badgering that brought the others around to the idea of forming a band. Jones elected himself the frontman and begrudgingly agreed to try his hand at learning guitar. Macken, fancying himself as a wannabe Ian McLagan or Brian Eno, announced he'd buy himself a second-hand Farfisa organ, Hayes plumped for bass, leaving Cook the designated drummer. Macken and Hayes would soon fall by the wayside, but Jones, Nightingale and Cook soon began rehearsing in earnest with the latter's new brother-in-law, Del Noones helping out on bass.

"It could have been anybody," says Nightingale in Jon Savage's *No Future*. "Paul was in my class at school; Steve was in the lower class. There were twelve hundred kids there: it was a hard school. I got through the first and second years and by the third year I'd got it sussed out and I'd stopped attending. I started to try to get a band together. I had a guitar and amplifier, a Les Paul copy.

"None of the others would have formed a group. Paul was heavily into an apprenticeship as an electrician. Steve was going to be a petty criminal, as simple as that. Stephan Hayes just ended up being a punk, a weak personality. I was the only one that could play."

As with every other fashion-conscious teenager living in London at the time, the five friends were frequent visitors to the hip and happening King's Road boutiques such as Alkasura, Granny Takes a Trip and City Lights, where Rod Stewart, David Bowie, and Roxy Music all had their stage costumes made up. Jones, however, wasn't satisfied with stealing from these shops so that he could dress like his musical heroes. He and Nightingale took to breaking into their homes as well. A full-length fur coat came courtesy of a nocturnal visit to Ronnie Wood's 18th-century house, The Wick, in Richmond Hill, while inveterate Stone's guitarist Keith Richards' home in Chelsea's Cheyne Walk provided more stylish threads as well as a colour TV.

Jones and Nightingale's thievery would also provide the fledgling band with a surfeit of musical equipment. Targeting the vans of more established local bands supplied a near-complete PA system, a Fender amplifier and precision bass, while a Premier drum kit came courtesy of the BBC. Another raid that has gone down in Pistols' folklore saw Jones grabbing two guitars – including a Gibson Les Paul – from Rod Stewart's house in Windsor. This, however, has since proved a fallacy, if only because Windsor was too far from the guitarist's patch. By far and away the daring duo's biggest coup came at the first of Bowie's Ziggy Stardust farewell shows at the Hammersmith Odeon in July 1973.

Jones says he can no longer remember which night he struck but believes it was most likely after the first show. "That would help explain why D. A. Pennebaker's film of the event had such famously shit sound and picture quality – because we'd nicked most of their

The Sex Pistols formed because of Warwick Nightingale

equipment," he muses in his book. "Either way, after the gig, I had my minivan outside, and I just went in and got as much stuff off the stage as I could fit in the back. I don't recall feeling any compunction about nicking my idol's gear – only the full-on excitement, especially when it was on the news on Capital Radio the next day."

Jones and Nightingale's haul also included several Neumann radio microphones costing around £500 each (at 1973 prices).

The band obtained a practice room at the Furniture Cave, located at 533 King's Road, where they settled into a routine jamming songs easy-to-play numbers such as Rod Stewart's "It's All Over Now" and the Small Faces' "All or Nothing". However, it wasn't until Matlock's replacing Noones sometime during the autumn of 1973 that they began taking the band seriously.

Matlock was born in Kensal Rise in north-west London, the only son of a coachbuilder and a Gas board accounts clerk. Unlike his bandmates he passed his 11-plus and attended the all-boys St. Clement Danes Grammar School where he proved a solid, if somewhat shy student. He was now enrolled in his foundation year at Saint Martin's School of Art on Charing Cross Road. It was whilst he was in his final year at St. Clement Danes that he began working at 430 King's Road. "I can't remember how it came about, but I heard about this shop on the World's End side of the King's Road that was selling brothel creepers. I liked the look of the shop. It was so different from any other shop in London. A guy called Michael Collins was running the shop at the time. I asked him if they needed any casual help on a Saturday. I started just before the shop changed from Too Fast To Live Too Young To Die to SEX. Wally and I were roped into helping with the refurbishment, and I don't remember ever getting paid."

Jones, Cook and Nightingale were initially sceptical when McLaren suggested they try Matlock out on bass. His having attended grammar school automatically disqualified him from ever being considered "one of the lads", while his being tasked by McLaren to thwart Jones's kleptomaniac streak only served to heighten their suspicions. But with no other candidates on the horizon, an audition was arranged when they were at a Thin Lizzy gig at the Marquee and held in Nightingale's bedroom the following afternoon. "Steve, Paul and Wally were Faces fans like me so that gave us something to work from. I'd learned how to play 'Three Button Hand Me Down' that had a pretty intricate bass part. As soon as I saw Steve's jaw hit the floor I knew I was in."

Matlock was indeed in, but Jones was still harbouring reservations that their new bassist would baulk at joining a band that had stolen enough musical equipment to stage the Isle of Wight Festival. Jones had recently snatched a bass from a shop on Shaftesbury Avenue to impress his latest squeeze. He handed Matlock the bass to sell in one of the many music shops on Denmark Street. The shop's owner soon smelled a rat, however, and kept him on the premises until the police arrived. To add humiliation to Matlock's red-faced shame, he was bundled into the back of the panda car in full view of a sizeable number of his fellow Saint Martin's students. Fortunately for him, he would be let off with a caution.

Things clicked into a higher gear during the summer of 1974 when Nightingale's father, a self-employed electrician, secured the contract to replace the wiring at the one-time BBC studios on Crisp Road in Hammersmith. The band had an extra set of keys cut and set up home in the studio's defunct acoustic room, which just happened to be one of the best in Europe. Jones's guitar was in effect little more than a prop, while Cook was still finding his way on the drums. However, with Nightingale and Matlock being on a par musically the quartet steadily built up a raucous repertoire of R&B and Mod classics: The Who's "Call Me Lightning", the Small Faces' "Whatcha Gonna Do About It", the Stones' "It's All Over Now", and Love Affair's "A Day Without Love". They also muddled their way through The Foundations' "Build Me Up Buttercup" - bizarrely renaming it "Proctor & Gamble" after the pharmaceutical company of the same name. The one original song they were working on, "Scarface", came courtesy of a Nightingale riff. ("Scarface" would subsequently evolve into "Did You No Wrong". Following John Lydon's arrival)

It was during the band's time at the BBC studios that *NME* journalist, Nick Kent, was brought in as a second guitarist to bolster their sound. Kent wasn't as proficient on guitar as he liked to think, yet his arrival did at least allow the band to stretch their repertoire to include more intricate songs such as Ronnie Woods' "I Can Feel the Fire" and "Slow Death" by American garage rockers, the Flamin' Groovies. Kent was never considered a member of the band, but his music journo credentials coupled with his being able to get them into The Speakeasy, the renowned rock 'n' roll watering hole on Margaret Street, was enough to ensure a hearty welcome. "Jones's voice was very much like Steve Marriott's, but he didn't know what to do with his hands, so the guitar was a prop," says Kent. "That was the original idea but within six months Steve was playing. After a few weeks, I felt that no one had direction, so I gave them an ultimatum."

Kent's "ultimatum" called for both a change in name and him assuming leadership of the band. McLaren agreed to give it some consideration, but the following day Matlock called Kent with the news that he needn't bother showing his face at rehearsals again. Little could Kent have imagined that his name would come to be forever intrinsically linked with the Sex Pistols owing to Sid Vicious' unprovoked assault at one of the band's 100 Club residency shows on June 29, 1976. Indeed, it was as a result of his bike-chain wielding antics that night that Sid earned his celebrity sobriquet "Vicious".

Sometime in early 1975, the band made their live debut at a mate's

party held in a flat above Tom Salter's Café at 205 King's Road, billed as either Swankers or The Strand. Today, Matlock says he remembers very little about the performance other than they were "onstage" for ten minutes or so and ran through three songs, one of which was "Scarface". Jones remembers those ten minutes being the longest of his life to date. "[It] was just a little party for some coke-taking kids but from how much I was shitting myself, you'd think it was the fucking Royal Albert Hall. Afterwards, Vivienne said I was 'Singing in the back of my throat.' I'm not really sure what that meant but I think she was trying to be kind. [Those ten minutes were] long enough for me to know that being the guy everyone was looking at was not for me. It just ain't my personality."

The gig, if one can indeed call it as such, was to prove Nightingale's only live performance with the band that would soon morph into the Sex Pistols. McLaren had been advising them to ditch Nightingale before his heading over to New York, and Jones and Cook were now reluctantly coming around to the idea. "It was harsh, but we had to do it," says Jones. "He didn't look right, plus he wore glasses which is just not acceptable in a rock 'n' roll guitarist." Once McLaren returned from New York, Nightingale's days were numbered.

Wally Nightingale would slip into obscurity for several years before co-founding Key West (not to be confused with the Irish folk band of the same name) in 1981. They would get as far as submitting a four-song demo to Warner Bros. Records before breaking up in 1983. His being seen as the "Pete Best" of the Sex Pistols took a heavy toll on him. So much so that he descended into drug addiction and ended up in prison for a drug-related offence.

He died of a drug-related illness in May 1996 shortly before the reconstituted Pistols embarked on their Filthy Lucre world tour.

Opposite: Metal Box: Sex Pistols squeeze into an old red telephone box, 1976.
Photo: Ray Stevenson

—We Like Noise It's Our Choice

"In my opinion, rock 'n' roll was getting up there, stepping out and creating the greatest possible imperfection. The music wasn't important. It was just a declaration of intent and an attitude. If you got that, that's what it was all about."

Malcolm McLaren

It's since gone down as part of urban folklore that Britain's perilous economic climate during the early-to-mid-seventies proved a telling component in punk rock coming to the fore; that it was a time of doom and gloom and ever-lengthening dole queues – a *Clockwork Orange*-esque dystopian nightmare. However, this has proved something of a misnomer as Britain was far from being the "failed state" it's usually portrayed. True, the miners' strike of 1974 brought about the three-day working week and power cuts galore, but according to a survey by the New Economics Foundation – based on social inequality indices, investment in public services, levels of pay and other benefits to ordinary workers – 1976 was to prove the "happiest year" since the end of the Second World War.

The reason the British economy was in difficulty had little to do with the welfare state or nationalised industries (which provided a cheap subsidy to underperforming private industry) but rather the ongoing failures of British capitalism. In contrast to what was happening in Europe and elsewhere – with countries such as France, Italy, Germany, and Japan all outstripping Britain in productivity and economic growth - Britain was being badly served by the City and its financial institutions, which prioritised short-term profits, immediate shareholder return and overseas investment and resulted in a steady decline of UK industry.

Inflation rose sharply between 1972 and 1976 but this in the main was due to the Heath government's relaxation of the Bank of England's competition and credit control rules, which had ensured that the ratio of bank deposits to lending should broadly balance out. Without these controls, the banks expanded their "reserve assets" to support massive lending, resulting in an inflation and credit boom. Heath refused to raise interest rates to counter this and by the end of his government, the rate of inflation was rising remorselessly from 10.2 per cent in 1973 to 24.6 per cent in 1975. Although the miners' strike of 1974 was to bring down Heath's government, the strike was nonetheless a lawful industrial action brought forward by the miners' union to ensure its members' pay kept pace with inflation.

Britain's industry may have been in decline, but business at 430 King's Road was thriving. McLaren had returned from New York determined to take advantage of what he'd witnessed at CBGBs to further boost the shop's standing. He'd arrived back in London safe in the knowledge that he had at least six months saving grace before England woke up to what was happening across the Atlantic. Having convinced Jones, Cook and Matlock to give Nightingale the elbow, and gifted the former with Syl Sylvain's Les Paul on the understanding that he concentrated his energies on learning the guitar, the search was now on to find a singer. SEX was already proving a magnet for those dancing to the beat of a different drum, so he simply co-opted Westwood, Rhodes, Collins and Jordan to be on the lookout for prospective candidates that stood out from the crowd.

Over the coming weeks, several such hopefuls were put through their paces at The Crunchy Frog pub in Rotherhithe, south-east London, where the band was now rehearsing. Nightingale's sacking had curtailed their cushy BBC studio set-up. The most promising candidate was 22-year-old Glaswegian Jim "Midge" Ure, whom

McLaren and Rhodes had encountered in a Glasgow music shop, reportedly whilst offloading some of Jones's knocked-off musical equipment. Ure's band, Slik, were on the up, however, having recently switched from Polydor to Bell Records. They would go on to score a UK #1 with "Forever and Ever" in February 1976. Slik would play a part in John Ingham and Caroline Coon's finding common musical ground. "I'd gone up to Glasgow as part of a press package to see Slik and Caroline was there," Ingham explained. "I already kind of knew Caroline because she was friends with Tony Howard, who was the manager of T Rex, and I'd been introduced to her at his place. I actually had a photo of Caroline from a *Life* magazine article about London in 1968 or '69, and there was a big photo of her that I'd cut out and saved."

In early August Rhodes had been making his way up the King's Road towards the World's End when he'd been distracted by a gang of surly-looking individuals making a nuisance of themselves. The most noticeable of the gang had hacked-off green hair jutting out at all angles. What had caught Rhodes's eye, however, was the Pink Floyd T-shirt he was wearing. Green hair had burnt out the band members' eyes and scrawled "I HATE" in biro above the band's logo. When Westwood announced these kids – all of whom were called John – came into the shop on occasion - and that the kid in question was called "Spiky John" - McLaren's interest was sufficiently piqued.

Westwood had her wires crossed, however. "Spiky John", who also answered to "Sid", was indeed a striking and charismatic individual worthy of a second glance. The fates, however, had decreed it wasn't yet his time to step into the spotlight.

John Lydon says he had no aspirations whatsoever of fronting a band when Matlock made his approach in SEX a couple of weeks on from Rhodes's encounter, and yet he immediately recognised an opportunity. "I wanted to be revolting and disgusting but I also wanted the job," he explained in *Anger is an Energy*. "I was working at cross purposes. Now that they'd asked and told me to come back after the shop had shut, I really wanted to be in a band with them."

Lydon, 19 at the time, was the eldest of four boys born to John and Eileen Lydon. As a child, he'd contracted spinal meningitis, which, aside from seriously affecting his schooling, left him with a slight stoop and the menacing thousand-yard stare the world would come to recognise. Upon leaving school in 1972, he'd half-heartedly pursued a higher education to add to his two O levels – firstly at Hackney Technical College where he'd befriended Sid, a.k.a. John Simon Beverley, and later Kingsway College, a further education seminary in King's Cross where he met another future bass playing confederate, John 'Jah Wobble' Wardle.

A meeting was duly arranged later that same Saturday evening at a pub called The Roebuck, which was situated a few hundred further along the King's Road from SEX. Lydon arrived at the appointed hour with another of the 'Johns' – John Gray – providing moral support. "We went back to the shop and I sang to Alice Cooper's '[I'm] Eighteen' and various other records off the jukebox, I really wanted it. I was up for it. I instantly had the mannerisms, the characterisations of the words. That I could do, I just couldn't sing. A minor thing... Fair play to Malcolm, he said, 'We can fix that.'"

Speaking on Steve Jones's LA-based radio show, *Jones's Jukebox*, in 2005, McLaren gave his version of events that fateful evening. "I became very officious and grabbed – I don't know why we had it – a broken shower-head device that could behave like a microphone. I gave it to John and told him to stand at the end of the shop. I remember he began to look like the Hunchback of Notre Dame. He pulled out a handkerchief and blew his nose, he was spitting and coughing and talking about 'sex in the grass is free', I don't know, God knows what he was talking about, but he was trying to imitate and scream along. He was somewhat embarrassed and vulnerable and strange. I laughed because I thought it was really funny and brilliant."

"I'd seen him (Lydon) coming into SEX a few times before the audition and I thought he looked fucking great," Jones added. "He was one of those guys who just have something. It wasn't just John's look that drew you to him, he also had a great face. That set all the other elements off – his excellent bone structure." It was Jones who was to gift Lydon his enduring stage name "Johnny Rotten" on account of his forever hawking up mucus – a leftover from his childhood bout of meningitis, coupled with the perilous state of his teeth.

A full rehearsal was arranged at The Crunchy Frog one evening during the coming week, but Lydon – with John Gray again in tow – was the only one to show. He wasn't best pleased with schlepping across London on a fool's errand. "I felt stupid walking round

Bermondsey Wharf," he later recounted. "It's dangerous down there, particularly the way I looked at the time."

When Matlock called the next day to apologise, Lydon had let rip, threatening him. Evidence of how much Lydon wanted the Sex Pistols gig, however, came with his agreeing to another rehearsal – this time in a room above The Rose & Crown pub in Wandsworth. "Getting John into the band certainly took things up a gear," says Matlock. "He and I got on alright in the beginning. We wrote a lot together. We came up with some new lyrics for 'Scarface', which was renamed 'Did You No Wrong'. John had also written 'Seventeen', and I had 'Pretty Vacant'. We also began to search out cover versions that would help give us an identity."

Said covers included "Psychotic Reaction" (Count Five), "Through My Eyes" (The Creation), "Substitute" (The Who), "(I'm Not Your) Steppin' Stone' (The Monkees), "No Lip" (Dave Berry), as well as the aforementioned "Whatcha Gonna Do About It", which Lydon twisted to suit his own needs: "I want you to know that I hate you baby/I want you to know I don't care".

"They were trying to do early rock 'n' roll, but it weren't right," Lydon reflected. "The notes were wrong, but the patterns were right! The emphasis, the energy on it, was excellent. I loved listening to it, nothing to do with discordancy, or accuracy of notes, and obviously the wrong placement of fingers – it was, the energy was right, and Paul always had brilliant timing. From that point on, I listened attentively to Paul, and I had my anchor."

Lydon had his anchor, but the band were to remain relatively rootless in terms of securing a permanent base until late-September when McLaren put down a £1,000 deposit on a rehearsal space situated to the rear of Denmark Street, accessible from the street via a narrow passageway. (Syl Sylvain maintains a chunk of the £1000 came courtesy of his Fender Rhodes piano). in the heart of Tin Pan Alley. The two-storey rehearsal space was owned by Bill Collins, father of Lewis who would go on to become a household name in the UK playing Bodie in LWT's *The Professionals*. Collins had been involved in the music business since the mid-Sixties, firstly as a roadie with The Beatles before stepping up into pop management with The Mojos and later Badfinger. The ground-floor room was fully soundproofed yet was both dank and dingy; the stench from the clogged-up lavatory adding to the unpleasantness. The band,

however, were happy to have a place they could call their own –
especially Jones who commandeered the upstairs attic space as his
very own W1 bachelor pad.

Within weeks of their moving onto Denmark Street, however,
Cook announced he was quitting the band, citing Jones's
rudimentary guitar style as the reason behind his decision. Matlock
believes Cook was merely stalling for time as he was about to sit his
City & Guilds electricians exam and wanted to get the qualification
under his belt should the band ultimately come to nothing. McLaren
managed to placate Cook by agreeing to bring in a second guitarist.
An ad was duly placed within the "musicians wanted" section in the
Melody Maker seeking a "whiz-kid guitarist no older than 20 and
no worse looking than Johnny Thunders". A 15-year-old Steve New,
who would go on to work with Matlock in Rich Kids was the only
applicant worth considering but was ultimately passed over owing to
his age. Meanwhile, Jones's playing was coming on leaps and bounds.
In the end, it was decided his playing would suffice and the Pistols
remained a four-piece.

Johnny Thunders' being name-checked in McLaren's "whizz-kid
guitarist" ad didn't go unnoticed amongst Dolls aficionados perusing
the *Melody Maker* classifieds. These included 20-year-old art student,
Mick Jones. Jones had played rhythm guitar in a couple of bands,
while his bass-playing compadre – 22-year-old Brunel University
mathematics and computer science graduate, Tony James – was
as yet untested onstage. Before happening upon the ad, Jones and
James had naively believed they were the only aspiring musicians in
London that were hip to the Dolls. Back in early July, the duo had
placed their own ad within the *Melody Maker* classifieds seeking
a lead guitarist and drummer whose musical influences matched
their own – ie the Stones, New York Dolls and Mott the Hoople.
The vital prerequisite for those thinking of applying was that they
possess "a great rock 'n' roll image". One of the first to respond to
their ad was Brian James, a 20-year-old guitarist who'd formed his
own Dolls/MC5-inspired three-piece outfit, Bastard, the previous
summer. Bastard had given up on London in favour of getting a break
on the continent but were barely scraping a living playing low-rent
bars in Brussels when James had espied the ad. "It was like, 'Christ!
Somebody in this country has actually heard of these people,'" says

James. "These were bands I'd been into for a couple of years, and in England, there was nothing like that." Having sailed through his audition with Jones and James, the latter's namesake returned to Brussels to break the news to his unsuspecting bandmates.

Another tried and tested means of unearthing like-minded souls with whom to form or cajole into a band came with checking out London's live circuit. One Saturday in early August 1975, Jones and James went to the Nashville Rooms in West Kensington, ostensibly to catch the Liverpool-based Deaf School showcasing their talents, but also to cast an eye over the audience. By pure happenstance, they'd taken up a position at the back of the room next to an unsuspecting Bernard Rhodes.

Rhodes was no longer involved with the Pistols owing to McLaren's refusal to honour a promise to give him a 50 per cent management share in the band which he'd felt he deserved. Conversely, he and McLaren were still on speaking terms and Rhodes was still a welcome visitor to 430 King's Road. "I loved Malcolm, but he fucked me over on the T-shirts, and he fucked me over on the Pistols," says Rhodes. "I was the one looking after the band while he was over in New York with the Dolls but when he came back to London, he was like, 'It's my band.' I thought right, if that's the way you want to play it, I'm gonna fuck you over. And I did it by planting a bomb with a slow-burning fuse. I knew immediately that John would fuck with Malcolm sooner or later. John was obnoxious with just as big a chip on his shoulder as Malcolm."

Jones and James believed themselves to be the coolest kids in or out of school so the realisation that the diminutive bespectacled figure lurking in their midst was sporting the same "You're Gonna Wake Up One Morning and Know Which Side of the Bed You've Been Lying On" T-shirt as Jones was more than their pride could stand. James sidled across and half-jokingly told Rhodes to "piss off out of it" as he was cramping their style. Quick as a flash, Rhodes retorted that they should be the ones doing the pissing off as he'd designed the T-shirt. In the ensuing sartorial stand-off, Rhodes challenged the two young Turks as to what they had going for them. On hearing Jones and James say they were in the process of putting a band together, which they intended calling "London SS", Rhodes, in turn, told them about his involvement with the Pistols. By the end of the evening, his interest in Jones and James had reached the point where he agreed to be their manager.

Rhodes's first act as manager came with calling his new charges to a meeting at The Bull and Bush on Shepherd's Bush Green, where he proceeded to dump a bag full of SS paraphernalia – swastikas, Iron Crosses, SS daggers etc – on the table in full view of the pub's other patrons. Jones and James were aghast and pleaded with Rhodes to put the Nazi ephemera back in the bag. Rhodes, however, remained undaunted. "I said to them that if they were going to call themselves 'London SS' then they were going to have to deal with everything it entailed, that the name was going to attract people with a fascination for Hitler and the Nazis. Mick said something about how they could say the 'SS' stood for 'Social Security'. I said, 'Yeah, good luck with that one.'"

Rhodes's second act came with introducing Jones and James to McLaren and the Sex Pistols. Also accompanying them to Denmark Street that night were Casino Steel and Andrew Matheson, another of the Warrington Crescent crowd whom Steel had played with in the now-defunct Dolls-esque Hollywood Brats. Rotten was absent, but Jones and James were taken aback at the other Pistols all having short hair. In turn, Jones, Cook and Matlock were bemused at the interlopers' waist-length hair. Eyebrows were no doubt raised at Jones' platform shoes, bell-bottom trousers and frilly shirted attire, but the three Pistols recognised a kindred spirit and duly invited him downstairs for a jam.

Mick Jones's guitar style would impress the three Pistols to the point where it rejuvenated interest in bringing in a second guitarist. McLaren and Matlock would go so far as borrowing the latter's father's car to make an abortive foray to Steel and Matheson's Paddington flat - where Jones was known to stay on occasion - to sound him out about the proposal. The future of UK punk and rock 'n' roll as a whole may have played out somewhat differently had the belligerent Steel not refused to open the door, conversing with them through the letterbox instead.

Realising his new charges would need a permanent base; Rhodes formulated an arrangement with the owner of the Paddington Kitchen café at 113-115 Praed Street for the use of the basement as a rehearsal space and band HQ. For a weekly stipend towards the electricity bill, Jones and the two James's set up home; an added bonus coming with the owner allowing them to stack the jukebox with their favourite records.

On November 6, 1975, the Sex Pistols made their debut in the common room at Saint Martin's School of Art, supporting pub rockers Bazooka Joe & his Rhythm Hot Shots. The admission price was 50p. Bazooka Joe, as they were more commonly known, were co-founded by guitarist John Ellis, who would go on to achieve moderate success with The Vibrators, and of course, featured the soon-to-be-rechristened Adam Ant on bass. Ellis had quit Bazooka Joe by the time of the Pistols date but was in the audience that night. Bazooka Joe are often dismissed as merely being the band that headlined the Pistols' debut. Yet while this has ensured them a footnote in rock folklore, they were an amalgam of talent. Ellis's fellow co-founder, Danny Kleinman, has gone on to achieve recognition as commercial and music video director – particularly with the Bond film franchise - while comedian, actress and writer Annabella Weir of *Fast Show* fame was their occasional backing singer.

Saint Martin's was quite literally a mere stone's throw from the Pistols' rehearsal space so the band walked the gear over from Denmark Street with McLaren, Westwood, Andy Czezowski and his girlfriend Susan Carrington (who would open punk mecca, The Roxy, in Covent Garden at the tail-end of 1976), Michael Collins and Jordan forming what the latter describes as being a "sort of punk Praetorian Guard" trailing in their wake. McLaren was no longer living at the Clapham flat he and Westwood were renting. After one too many of the couple's seemingly never-ending rows, McLaren had moved in with his Goldsmiths ex-girlfriend, Helen Wellington-Lloyd, at her one-bedroom flat on Bell Street in Marylebone.

Bazooka Joe were initially accommodating in allowing the Pistols to soundcheck using their equipment. Jones, however, found the sound unsatisfactory to his needs and returned to Denmark Street for his twin-reverb100 watt Marshall amp. The compact common room was hardly the setting for such a beast and Jones has since likened the Pistols' sound as being akin to a "jumbo jet landing in your living room". Jones was so pumped up on adrenaline that night that he needed a Mandrex tablet to calm himself down. "The Mandy came on during 'Did You No Wrong' and I remember looking at John and leaning on him for a second as we were playing. He kind of pushed me away a little bit and at that moment I was thinking, 'This, right now, is the best thing in the world.' He was the singer and I loved playing in a band with him and the whole thing felt fucking great."

"The Sex Pistols made me think of The Who in 1964 or '65," says Carrington. "There was the same intense energy, but with loads more attitude. They looked amazing, with a charismatic singer. I thought it was great that the students didn't like them at all and that we were all different from them. I certainly believed then that this was going to be a very exciting time."

Andrew Czezowski says the Pistols debut had also reminded him of The Who. "They undoubtedly had the same energy as The Who when they first started out. The invite to Saint Martin's came indirectly as we didn't really socialise with Malcolm and Vivienne. We probably got a phone call from one of them saying the Pistols were playing that night and did we fancy coming along. It's over forty years ago now and the show has taken on mythical status, but whatever's been written and said about that night, I didn't come away thinking I'd witnessed a life-changing event. Having said that, the Pistols were very exciting because they were so different to what was going on at the time."

Not everyone shared Czezowski and Carrington's viewpoint, however. Five songs into the Pistols' set someone from the headliners' entourage brought things to an uncharitable halt by pulling the power. Rotten, in his inimitable style, declared Bazooka Joe to be a "bunch of fucking cunts". Kleinman was so incensed that he pinned Rotten to the wall and kept him there until receiving an apology. Adam Ant later reflected on his being struck by the Pistols' "gang mentality" and Rotten's "don't give a fuck attitude". He also took note of how the Pistols songs were devoid of fancy fills or solos. Kleinman and the rest of Bazooka Joe may have dismissed the Pistols as half-arsed amateurs, but Adam was savvy enough to recognise a change was in the air. He quit Bazooka Joe the very next day and set about forming his own band.

On November 6, 2005, English Heritage erected a blue plaque in the college's common room to mark the thirtieth anniversary of the Pistols' live debut. Not everyone associated with Saint Martin's was in favour of the event, however. Indeed, some of the students mounted a protest, handing out leaflets at the door.

"It wasn't really a standout gig," says Ellis. "I was there to see my

Don't look over your shoulder, but the Sex Pistols are coming

Sex Pistols

MARQUEE

"HURRY UP, they're having an orgy on stage," said the bloke on the door as he tore the tickets up.

I waded to the front and straightway sighted a chair arcing gracefully through the air, skidding across the stage and thudding contentedly into the PA system, to the obvious nonchalance of the bass drums and guitar.

Well I didn't think they sounded *that* bad on first earful — then I saw it was the singer wh'd done the throwing.

He was stalking round the front rows, apparently scuffing over the litter on the floor between baring his teeth at the audience and stopping to chat to members of the group's retinue. He's called Johnny Rotten and the moniker fits.

Sex Pistols? Seems I'd missed the cavortings with the two scantily clad (plastic thigh boots and bodices) pieces dancing up front. In fact, I only caught the last few numbers; enough, as it happens, to get the idea. Which is . . . a quarter of spiky teenage misfits from the wrong end of various London roads, playing 60's styled white punk rock as unself-consciously as it's possible to play it these days i.e. self-consciously.

Punks? Springsteen Bruce and the rest of 'em would get shredded if they went up against these boys. They've played less than a dozen gigs as yet, have a small but fanatic following, and don't get asked back. Next month they play the Institute of Contemporary Arts if that's a clue.

I'm told the Pistols repertoire includes lesser known Dave Berry and Small Faces numbers (check out early Kinks' B sides leads), besides an Iggy and the Stooges item and several self-penned numbers like the moronic "I'm Pretty Vacant', a meandering power-chord job that produced the chair-throwing incident.

No-one asked for an encore but they did one anyway: "We're going to play 'Substitute'."

"You can't play," heckled an irate French punter.

"So what?" countered the bassman, jutting his chin in the direction of the bewildered Frog.

That's how it is with the Pistols — a musical experience with the emphasis on Experience.

"Actually, we're not into music," one of the Pistols confided afterwards.

Wot then?

"We're into chaos."

Neil Spencer

Pistols' Johnny Rotten: it fits.

Neil Spencer's review of the Pistols in NME is one of the first the band received

old band but I don't recall thinking, 'Here's a band that are going to change the world' when the Pistols did their thing. If I remember correctly, it was clear they were trying to create a buzz rather than play anything musically significant. And the argy-bargy between my friend Daniel Kleinman and Rotten has been very overstated historically.

"The big issue for me around the whole punk brand heritage is that unless you were actually there at an event, you don't know what happened so you have to rely on hearsay or faulty memories. Hearsay often comes loaded with an agenda. Let's say you are a 20-year-old Japanese music fan just getting into punk. If your starting point for what to check out are books and magazine articles you will only ever be guided by opinion. Which is why The Vibrators are written out of most of the histories of 'punk', whatever that actually is. And if we're not in the written history, then to all intents and purpose we don't exist. Obviously "I'm not talking about the band as it exists now."

There are those who would have you believe the Sex Pistols burst onto the mid-Seventies staid British music scene like a biblical flash-flood sweeping all before them. This was far from the case, of course, as some thirteen months of hard graft would pass betwixt their Saint Martin's debut and their becoming front-page news following Steve

Ray Stevenson: the art behind him is written with $ bills

Jones's four-letter outbursts on *Today*. But each of their early shows – predominantly on London's college and university circuit – served to polarise the audience.

On February 12, 1976, the Pistols supported current music-media darlings Eddie & the Hot Rods at the Marquee Club on Wardour Street. It was by far and away their most prestigious show to date. *NME* staffer Neil Spencer was there to review the Hot Rods, yet his now-legendary review - Don't Look Over Your Shoulder But the Sex Pistols are Coming – would make no mention whatsoever of the headliners. An altercation with the Hot Rods' management owing to Rotten's wilful destruction of some of their band's equipment would result in the Pistols being banned from the Marquee sine die (though they would be allowed to return the following May to film the promo video to "God Save the Queen"). Spencer's review is best remembered for Steve Jones' quip about the Pistols being into chaos rather than music, but, of course, neither he nor anyone else associated with the Pistols had the slightest inkling as to the level of chaos awaiting them.

It was at the Marquee show that Rolf 'Nils' Stevenson was first introduced to the Pistols live experience. After abandoning art school in 1971, Stevenson had for a time worked for *The Sunday Times's* ballet critic Richard Buckle. He'd been a mod, followed Hendrix in the psychedelic era, and had glammed up in homage of Bowie. He'd been running a stall on the Beaufort Street Market at the time of his befriending McLaren and Westwood and was now socialising with them regularly – more often than not attending sculptor and socialite Andrew Logan's parties at the latter's Shad Thames studio at Butler's Wharf. (Two days on from their Marquee showing the Pistols and their entourage would lay waste to Logan's Valentine's Ball).

Stevenson had been introduced to Jones, Cook and Matlock in the run-up to the Marquee date. He'd found trio likeable enough yet couldn't understand why McLaren was so excited about the Pistols. The Marquee gig proved a gamechanger. So mesmerised was he by Rotten's galvanising stage presence that he'd readily accepted McLaren's offer to become the Pistols' road manager. The Pistols would get two Stevensons for the price of one. Nils's older brother, Ray, a rock photographer of some renown, had been as equally blown away by the Pistols' stage menace at St. Alban's, Herefordshire College of Art & Design on February 19. So much so, he came out of his self-imposed exile, offering to provide his services for free. Over the coming months, Stevenson senior would take hundreds of photographs of the Pistols.

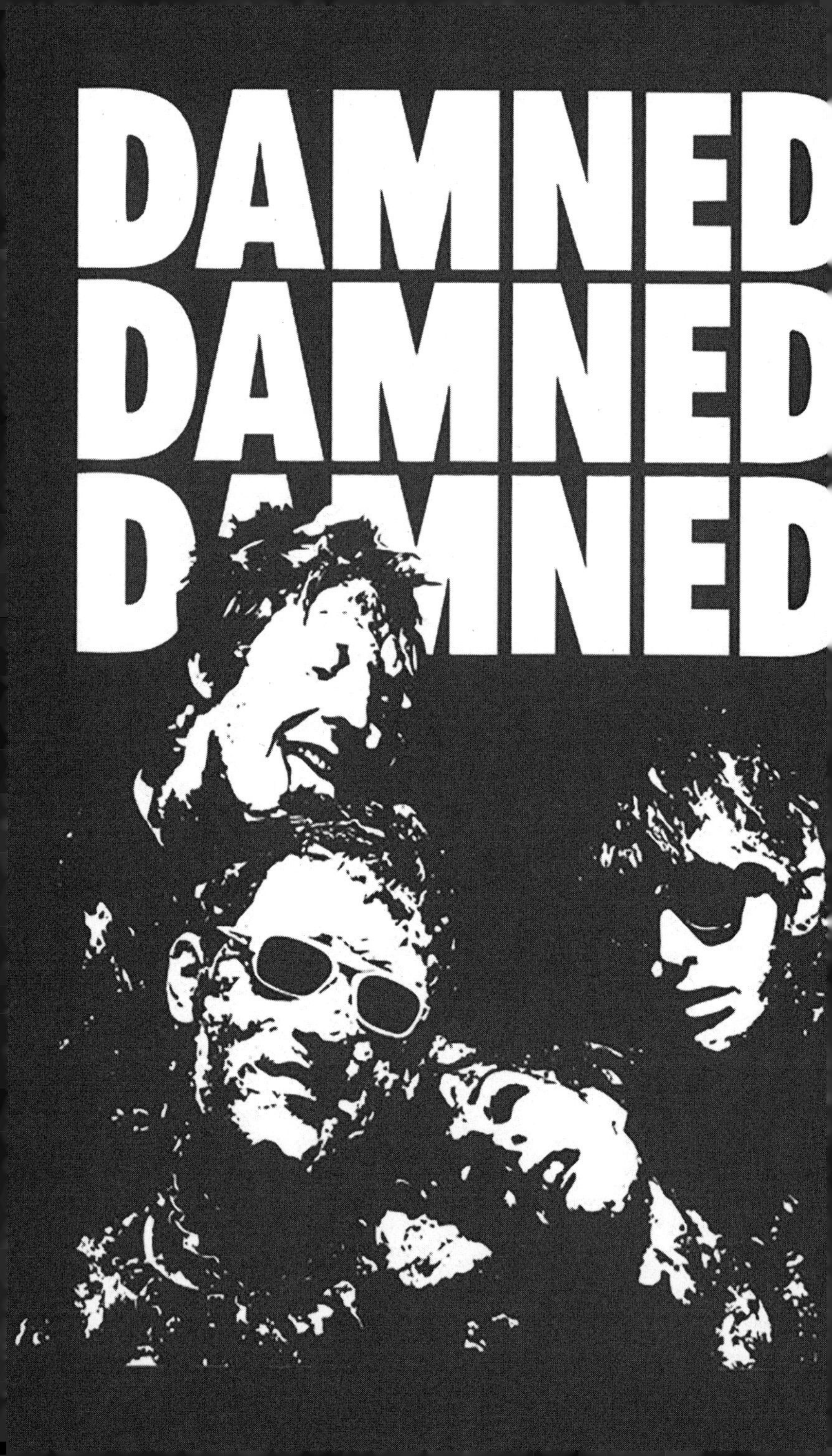
DAMNED
DAMNED
DAMNED

— Brand New Rose
In Town

"People forget awful it was before punk came along. In 1975 we had Little Jimmy Osmond, Emerson, Lake & Palmer and Little Feat. I didn't know what was coming next, but something had to give. Music was so turgid. I thought it was great in the beginning. Every band had a different flavour. The Pistols, The Clash, The Stranglers, The Damned. There was so much variety, that's why it was so marvellous."

Captain Sensible

The British musical landscape of 1975 wasn't quite as bleak as its since been portrayed. While it was undoubtedly true the charts were brimming with disposable pop pap, things were no different in 1977 during punk's highwater mark. It's also worth remembering that 1975 was the year Dr. Feelgood's second album, *Malpractice*, broke into the UK Top 20 – peaking at #17 in early November. The Canvey Island four-piece were at the vanguard of what became known as pub rock, a back-to-basics London circuit scene which was, without question, a precursor to punk. Indeed, Jon Savage would cite the Feelgood's inimitable

Opposite: The Damned make their appearance on Stiff

vocalist and guitarist, Lee Brilleaux and Wilco Johnson as looking like "villains you might see on *The Sweeney*."

"We found aggressive, in-your-face playing worked," says Johnson. "You stare at people, realise you're stirring them up, and do it all the more. It was full of violence. At first, people looked puzzled. Then you'd see them start to laugh. What you wanted was people to enjoy it."

Speaking about his 2009 Dr. Feelgood film, *Oil City Confidential*, with *The Independent* in February of that year, director Julien Temple said how he'd caught the Feelgoods many times during 1974/75 and thought them the "most exciting thing" in London at that time. "But I didn't know how interesting their story was," he continued. "They all came from Canvey, a unique culture where East End villains buried bodies, then came to live. It's the nearest beach to the East End, and this holiday culture coexists with toxic refineries. The Feelgoods had a fantasy about it being Oil City, Essex's version of the Mississippi Delta. And Wilko is the poet of Canvey."

The "poet of Canvey" says he has no hard feelings about the Feelgoods being usurped by punk's Young Turks. "Let's get the record straight – I think it's fucking good that punk has happened," he told *Record Mirror*'s Barry Cain in January 1977. "And the Feelgoods can justifiably take a bit of credit for the whole thing. We showed the record companies you don't need to look at established rock musicians to make music. It can come from anywhere."

BBC 4's three-part series, *Punk Britannia* (first broadcast in June 2012), dedicates much the opening episode to the pub rock scene. American country-rockers, Eggs over Easy, are usually credited with kick-starting pub rock following their arrival in London at the tail-end of 1970 to record their debut album at Olympic Studios in Barnes (with one-time Animals bassist Chas Chandler producing). The recording sessions at Olympic Studios went well enough but escalating problems with the band's US-based backers, Cannon Films, brought the recording to a halt soon into 1971. Rather than return to the US, their manager advised them to remain in London and sing for their supper on the capital's thriving live circuit while he looked for a new deal. The trio played a number of college gigs in and around London, but it was at the long-demolished Tally Ho pub in Kentish Town that they would establish themselves.

In the Seventies the Tally Ho in Kentish Town was a hugely successful pub rock venue

The Tally Ho had a reputation as being a jazz enclave, but the three Americans smooth-talked the landlord into allowing them to play the pub's traditionally slack Monday night slot. Their effortless ability to play any song anyone might shout out saw the band's reputation spread. They began attracting London's homegrown musicians and within no time at all the Tally Ho was staging shows by the likes of Bees Make Honey, Ducks Deluxe and The Amber Squad. Brinsley Schwarz were another of the Tally Ho regulars. The band's bass playing vocalist, Nick Lowe, would produce The Damned's debut single and album.

As the pub rock scene developed, other pubs within London sought to cash in by staging live music. These included The Greyhound (Fulham), The Red Lion (Hammersmith), the Nashville Rooms (West Kensington), The Half Moon (Putney), Dingwalls and The Dublin Castle (both Camden Town), The Sir George Robey (Finsbury Park, where the soon-to-be-famous Johnny Rotten did most of his drinking), and The Hope and Anchor in Islington. By 1975, the pub rock scene was thriving with acts such as Roogalator, Ian Dury and The Blockheads, Elvis Costello, Eddie & the Hot Rods, The Guildford Stranglers, and the Feelgoods, of course.

Another band starting to make a name for themselves on the London pub rock circuit throughout 1975 was The 101ers, a Walterton Road

Joe Strummer was the frontman of the 101ers whose single was released on Chiswick

squat collective featuring future Clash frontman Joe Strummer on lead vocals. Having made their debut at the Telegraph pub in Brixton – billed under their original name El Huaso and the 101 All Stars - The 101ers had accrued a loyal following and their shows were receiving positive reviews in the music weeklies. In early March 1976, they were approached by the co-founders of the recently incorporated Chiswick Records, Ted Carroll and Roger Armstrong, with the view to making a record. Dubliner Carroll was a well-known face on the London music scene. He'd opened his first Rock On music stall on Golborne Road in 1972, primarily selling imported rock 'n' roll and R&B records. A second stall had followed two years later at a temporary market in Soho's Newport Court. He and Armstrong had caught an early Sex Pistols show at the Chelsea School of Art back in December and both had come away mightily impressed by the disorganised yet powerful energy emanating from the stage.

The 101ers took Carroll and Armstrong up on their offer. Selecting what they felt were the three most powerful songs in their repertoire - "Sweet Revenge", "Surf City" and "Keys to Your Heart" - the band headed into Pathway Studios in Canonbury, north London, in early March with Armstrong producing. Further sessions were recorded at Pathway, as well as Chalk Farm Studios in Camden and the BBC studios in Maida Vale. When the dust settled, "Keys to Your Heart" won out as the single's intended A-side, with "Five Star Rock'n'Roll Petrol" on the flipside. As a means of celebrating the arrangement, the band's roadie/factotum, John "Boogie" Tiberi booked a brace of shows at the Nashville Rooms for the following month. The first show was scheduled for April 3, with Carroll's Rock On disco providing the incidental music and with the Sex Pistols as support.

The April 3 Nashville Rooms show was to loom large in the story of The Clash, as Bernard Rhodes, Mick Jones, and the latter's new bass playing sidekick, Paul Simonon, were in the audience that night. As with Jones, the 20-year-old Simonon came from a broken home; his parents having split up when he was eight. Soon after his mother married for a second time, her budding composer husband won a twelve-month scholarship to study music in Sienna, Tuscany, and his new family went with him. On returning to London, the family set up home in Herne Hill, where Paul rekindled his love for reggae and became something of a teenage tearaway. He possessed all the prerequisites needed in a rock 'n' roll frontman: tall, lean, blond, roguishly handsome. He'd only come into Jones's orbit from accompanying a mate to Praed Street that was trying out for the London SS drum stool but was happy enough to step up to the mic for run-throughs of Jonathan Richman and the Modern Lovers' recent release, "Roadrunner". It was obvious to all that singing wasn't Simonon's forte, yet Rhodes would nevertheless file Simonon's name away for possible future use. "There was something about Paul that made him stand out from the idiots Mick was surrounding himself with at the time," says Rhodes. "True, he had no musical ability to speak of and was still hoping to make it as a painter. But you have to remember that Mick was of average ability himself."

In the accompanying booklet to the 1991 *Clash on Broadway* box set Mick admitted to losing heart after Tony James's defection and that Bernard had told him to stop moping after Tony and start a band with Simonon instead. Simonon was amenable to the idea of learning the guitar, but one get-together was enough for Mick to realise Paul might be better suited to the bass. He wasn't initially thrilled as he later revealed: "Mick told me there was an exhibition of paintings at Camberwell Art College by someone called Stuart Sutcliffe who used to be in the Beatles. [Mick said] how he couldn't play the bass either. So after Mick's history lesson, I started to learn." The first step in Paul's musical education came with learning where to put his fingers on the fretboard. To assist him in his endeavours he painted the notes on the relevant frets.

Rhodes's constant hectoring had largely been responsible for James's defecting from the London SS camp to join Gene October's proto-punk outfit, Chelsea. While certain instances, such as his calling James at his parents' home in Twickenham and berating him for not knowing his Sartre were at least constructive. However, his challenging the bassist to forego the turkey and trimmings and instead spend Christmas Day with one of the prostitutes operating out of Praed Street was a push too far. "I don't think I was too hard on Tony at all,' says Rhodes. 'Look what he went on to achieve with Generation X and Sigue Sigue Sputnik? And anyway, he was a bit like Glen (Matlock), forever standing around with an 'anxious to please' look on his face like some girl hoping to be fucked."

London SS were destined to never play a single show yet have gone down in punk folklore for serving as a wellspring for The Clash, Generation X, The Damned and The Boys. Indeed, the closest Jones and James ever came to securing a steady line-up for London SS was with Brian James and future Damned tub-thumper, Chris Millar, a.k.a. Rat Scabies.

The Croydon-based Millar arrived for an audition in early December 1975. His name-checking the MC5 and The Stooges had proved sufficient to get him through the vetting stage, and yet when it came to showing what he could do behind the kit, his prospective bandmates seemed more interested in watching an old war film on the decrepit black-and-white television set in the corner. Determined to get a reaction, Millar had set about pounding the kit for all he was worth. Mick and Tony had nonchalantly continued their gaze on the flickering images, but Brian latched onto Chris's playing and burst into a screeching guitar solo cleverly soundtracking the onscreen aerial dog fight.

Watching from the wings, as it were, Rhodes had noticed how Millar would down sticks and feverishly scratch himself between songs. Upon hearing Millar confess to his having the infectious skin infestation scabies, Rhodes dashed about covering the chairs with sheets of newspaper. Later that evening, after a visit to one of the local pubs, Jones and James walked through the door at Praed Street to find a mouse scurrying across the cellar floor. As Jones looked about for something to scare the mouse back into its hole, James playfully remarked how the rodent reminded him of their ginger-haired prospective drummer. When Millar arrived for a second audition he was greeted with his new, and enduring moniker. "I hated the name at first," Rat confessed to *Uncut* magazine in February 2018. "But I didn't think anybody would like the music, so assuming an alias meant I could stay on the dole. Then, when the bubble burst after three months, I could go back to being Chris Millar and get a proper job as a drummer on a cruise ship."

The quartet knuckled down to working up song ideas such as "Ooh, Baby, Ooh (It's Not Over)", "I'm So Bored With You", "Protex Blue", and "Portobello Reds". The first three were primarily Mick's compositions and would carry over to The Clash ("Ooh, Baby, Ooh (It's Not Over)" would be reworked as "Gates of the West" while "I'm So Bored With You" as "I'm So Bored With the USA". "Portobello Reds", a Tony and Brian composition, would resurface as "Fish" on The Damned's debut album.)

Within a week of Rat's arrival, however, Mick and Tony had concluded that he lacked the all-important "great rock 'n' roll image". For Brian, this was to prove the proverbial final straw. He didn't care one iota what people looked like so long as they could play. He was also tiring of Rhodes' motives. "It was all getting a little bit too much about looking for people who looked right," he explained. "I don't give a fuck what people look like as long as they can play."

Defending his and Tony's sartorial snobbery in a later interview, Mick said it had proved a "very drifting situation" trying to put London SS together: "Sometimes people fitted the bill because they looked right like, and they couldn't play – they couldn't play a note or nothing – they just didn't know nothing about instruments. At one time there was only about two of us who knew how to put a chord together. The rest of them would be just stoned people, just falling all over the drum kit."

Neil Spencer's review of the Pistols' Marquee outing appeared in the *NME*'s February 21, 1976 issue. Brian Southall, EMI's press officer at the time, readily admits to Spencer's review slipping under the radar in his 2007 book, *Sex Pistols: 90 Days at EMI*. He wouldn't be the only music industry insider to neglect his duties that particular week, but the review certainly galvanised 23-year-old Bolton Institute of Technology student, Howard Trafford, into action. "I was already into the Stooges at the time of Neil Spencer's *NME* review and looking to put together a musical project that would be as equally confrontational. And so, reading about a band in London called the Sex Pistols who were into chaos and playing a Stooges song, I thought 'hello that sounds interesting.'" The Stooges song in question was 'No Fun', which features on their eponymous 1969 debut album. Trafford's fellow student and musical collaborator, 20-year-old Pete McNeish, was equally intrigued. Rather than sit looking over their shoulder waiting for the Pistols to sneak up on them, however, the duo borrowed a friend's car and set off for London the following morning (stopping off in Reading to pick up friend, Richard Boon.)

Upon their arrival in London, the trio snapped up a copy of *Time Out*, London's popular 'what's on' guide in the hope of the Pistols playing a show over the weekend. Finding no mention of any forthcoming Pistols shows in the listings they'd telephoned the *NME*'s Carnaby Street offices. As luck would have it, their call was answered by none other than Spencer himself. All Spencer could tell them was that the Pistols' manager had a shop on the King's Road. Their luck was in as the Pistols were playing a Valentine's dance that very night at the Bucks College of Higher Education in High Wycombe, supporting Screaming Lord Sutch, while a second show was scheduled the following night at the Mid Herts College Main Hall in Welwyn Garden City.

Born David Edward Sutch, Screaming Lord Sutch of subsequent Monster Raving Loony Party fame, was one of the more colourful characters within the annals of British rock. During the early-to-mid-Sixties, he'd released several horror-themed singles, the most popular being "Jack the Ripper". His use of such as coffins, daggers, skulls and fake blood as stage props predated the shock rock antics of Alice Cooper by several years, but by 1976 he was largely reduced to trawling London's university and college circuit.

The Pistols had added two new compositions to their set by the time of the High Wycombe show. The first, "New York", was Rotten's withering putdown of the New York music scene – and the New

Sex Pistols held up Lord Sutch

A FOUR MAN group going by the strange name of Sex Pistols stole the show at the Rag Ball on Friday. It wasn't that they were musically good — they just refused to stop playing.

After one song the vocalist shouted at the audience ''That's it we're going home.'' He claimed that something was wrong with the P.A. system and in a stream of language denounced the college, rag committee and the audience.

The audience replied with a slow handclap and jeering. The group stopped playing. Five minutes later they were back and told the audience "We hope you enjoy this because we aren't gonna."

After a couple more tracks the group were asked to finish and the discotheque started.

But the group were not having this and started playing yet again.

During the next song the vocalist decided to lie down on the edge of the college stage and somebody from the audience ran forward and pulled him onto the floor. A small disturbance broke out but the vocalist escaped back to the stage.

Eventually Sex Pistols ran out of songs and left the stage. Members of the Rag Committee later alleged that the group had damaged another performer's equipment.

Before Sex Pistols a new more sombre group called Kites performed. They seemed to be used to abuse from the audience as well, because the Kites vocalist invited the audience to shout at them.

Top of the bill was Screaming Lord Sutch and the Savages. He showed true professional form in the short amount of time left after Sex Pistols had taken up so much.

It was back to the days of nonstop rock and roll and with a few gimmicks such as pretending to set fire to the audience, the rag ended in a happier frame of mind.

Report from *The Bucks Free Press*

York Dolls in particular – while "Submission" which was a tongue-in-cheek jibe aimed at their supposedly S&M-obsessed manager.

The show itself would be marred by violence. Speaking with Jon Savage for *England's Dreaming*, Richard Boon said how the majority of the attendees simply couldn't relate to the Pistols. "They were very disappointed: they were sitting along the front of the stage as Johnny crept along and tousled their hair. One of their mates from the back came running and picked Johnny up and threw him on the floor. The Pistols' friends started piling in and – this was during 'No Fun' – there was this throng of thrashing people."

Midway through the set Rotten's microphone, borrowed from the headliners, suddenly went dead. Rather than call on the rest of the band to stop playing, however, Rotten proceeded to smash the offending mic against the stage. Amazingly, given everyone in the room had witnessed the act, Rotten would deny any culpability for the ruined mic when he came offstage. As far as Trafford and McNeish were concerned, the searing intensity of a Sex Pistols' show more than justified their madcap spur-of-the-moment five-hour drive from Manchester. They now knew in which direction to take their own as yet unnamed musical venture. Their excitement was such they approached McLaren with an offer for the Pistols to play at their college and a date was tentatively set for Friday, June 4.

Another positive to come from the High Wycombe show was Sutch's buddy, Ron Watts, offered the Pistols a slot on "New Band Night" at his sedate subterranean jazz enclave at 100 Oxford Street on Tuesday, March 30.

There are varying opinions as to when punk came into being, but everyone agrees the release of The Ramones' eponymous debut album in late-April 1976 was the gamechanger. The Stones, Eagles, Pink Floyd, Fleetwood Mac et al thought nothing of eating up six-figure budgets on their albums, while spending months on end recording in exotic locations. The Ramones recorded their debut in under a week – reportedly recorded in four days and mixed on the fifth - at a cost of just $6,400. The sleeve's now-iconic shot of the band slouched against a wall directly across from CBGBs was also done on the cheap as Roberta Bayley was paid just $125 for the session. To be fair to Sire, however, both The Ramones and Roberta were relatively unknown quantities at the time. "For that album cover we maybe shot two rolls of film," says Bayley. "It was only something like the twenty-eighth roll of film through my camera. I'd only been taking pictures for a few weeks."

The photo session wasn't meant for The Ramones' album cover but rather for *Punk* magazine. "The session was across from CBGBs, right off 1st Street," says Holmstrom. "Roberta had first tried shooting them in Arturo's loft (Arturo Vega was a Mexican-born graphic designer best known for having created The Ramones' iconic logo.) It didn't work too well so they took them to a playground around the corner. Sire had hired a professional photographer to shoot the cover, but he ended up blowing the $2000 budget without coming up with anything remotely usable. The Ramones hated having their photo taken and were unwilling to have more taken for the cover. Sire were desperate for photos, so they asked to look at the ones Roberta shot for us. They chose the one that ended up on the cover and another one for publicity purposes and paid her $128. That was the deal."

Bayley was acquainted with McLaren and Westwood from her having temporarily helped out at 430 King's Road during the summer of 1973 after relocated to London from her native California soon after dropping out of college. "I only worked at the shop for a couple of weekends," says Bayley. "I remember showing up for my first Saturday at noon and no one was there. I guess I didn't realise things were that casual. I knew Malcolm and Vivienne because they used to come to eat at this vegetarian restaurant I also worked at called the Chelsea Nuthouse on Langton Street in the World's End. Later, I met Gerry Goldstein who was a friend of Malcolm's. Malcolm had hired him to work in the shop, but Gerry couldn't start right away because he was still working at a porno bookstore or something. So I offered to sit in until Gerry could start."

Despite it's now being lauded as the album that changed the musical landscape, *Ramones* failed to crack the upper half of the *Billboard* 200. The attendant singles, "Blitzkrieg Bop" and "I Wanna Be Your Boyfriend" would also both fail to chart. The album consists of fourteen tracks yet has a running time of less than thirty minutes. Even the longest song – "I Don't Wanna Go Down to the Basement" – clocked in at just 2:35. "Doing an album in a week and bringing it in for sixty-four hundred dollars was unheard of, especially since it was an album that really changed the world," Joey reflected. "It kicked off punk rock and started the whole thing – as well as us."

Ramones was produced by Sire's in-house producer, Craig Leon, with Tommy Ramone serving as co-producer. The Miami-born Leon had set about petitioning Stein to sign The Ramones after catching one of the band's CBGBs shows during the spring of 1975. "I saw the Ramones with Talking Heads and loved them," says Leon. "So, I went back [to Sire] and did my little A&R report. Talking Heads seemed a little raw, but I definitely thought I could produce the Ramones. I was more into what they didn't do. Rock was becoming decadent – not in personal morals, the music was decaying. People would listen to long instrumental pseudo-classical solos. The Ramones came on and hit you over the head with what rock 'n' roll was all about. Other bands had done that, like the Stooges and MC5, but the Ramones had a much more commercial pop aspect. Also, they had that very bizarre New York art viewpoint."

Since its 1966 inception Sire had acquired a reputation for introducing progressive UK acts to the US market, releasing albums by the likes of Barclay James Harvest, Tomorrow, and the Climax Blues Band. With Sire having released albums by Sixties proto-punksters, The Deviants, Stein had an ear attuned to what was happening on the Bowery.

Of the other CBGBs bands, Blondie were perhaps making the most headway. After much toing and froing, the band had a settled line-up and by the spring of 1975 were a regular feature both at CBGBs and Max's Kansas City. Though late coming out of the stalls, The Heartbreakers were already being touted as rivals to The Ramones. With Thunders and Nolan having packed away their Dolly trousseau and undergone a punk makeover, ex-Demons guitarist Walter Lure was recruited in time for their live debut at the Coventry in Queens at the end of May.

The Ramones were now being managed by Danny Fields, a well-known and hugely respected figure on the American music scene. Fields, a Harvard dropout, was 36 at the time of his getting involved with The Ramones. Whilst working as a publicist at Elektra Records during the late-sixties he'd worked with The Doors and was solely responsible for bringing both MC5 and The Stooges to the label. He was sacked by Elektra for supporting MC5's insistence in refusing to amend the "Kick out the jams, motherfuckers!" rallying cry to the title track of their debut album. Fields subsequently went to work for Atlantic Records where he would again be shown the door – this time for openly criticizing prog rock dinosaur acts such as Yes and Emerson, Lake & Palmer. More recently, he'd co-edited *16 Magazine* and had also penned a gossip column in the *Soho Weekly News*.

The Ramones may have been packing them in at CBGBs but no one with any influence on the New York music scene was taking them seriously. Back in February, reportedly due to constant badgering by Johnny, Tommy cajoled Fields and *Rock Scene* editor, Lisa Robinson, into attending a Ramones show.

When CBGBs first opened the club had rows of seats bolted into the floor directly in front of the stage. Such a setting was perfect for country, blues and bluegrass acts. It was less suited for punk, of course, and Kristal would ultimately have the obstructive seating removed.

In his forward for The Ramones' 1999 anthology, *Hey Ho! Let's Go!*, Fields singles out Tommy's "relentless" tenacity. "He promoted his band with a fervour that was astonishing. I was a great fan of a certain other group playing frequently at CBGBs – a group the Ramones hated for reasons aesthetic, personal and professional. As I would soon learn, the Ramones hated just about every other band in the world, especially ones that were getting written about in early '75 while they were being ignored – by the press, the music industry, the promoters . . . everybody but Hilly Kristal, who gave them a place to play, because who else would want them?"

Reflecting on his approach to Fields, Tommy said he'd done so simply because he sensed Fields would like their stripped-back approach to playing rock 'n' roll. "We kind of idolised him (Fields) because of his connection to all these famous people. It took a while for him to agree to become our manager. I think it was Lou Reed who finally convinced him. It was like a burden lifted from me."

People were talking about The Ramones, of course, it was just what they were saying was somewhat less than complimentary; the general consensus being that their shows were haphazard affairs more often than not ending with the band bickering on stage because one of them had either come in on the wrong beat, or their gangly, beshaded singer had forgotten the lyrics. As such, Fields and Robinson didn't see much point in their both wasting an evening and – or so the story goes – they flipped a quarter. Fields can no longer remember whether they did indeed bother with fishing for a coin, but whichever way it was decided, it was Robinson that ended up making her way to the Bowery. Fields' belief that he'd won the metaphorical toss would be shattered the following day when an exuberant Robinson called to say he needed to see The Ramones at all costs.

Taking Robinson at her word, Fields checked the CBGBs listings in the *Village Voice* and headed for CBGBs the next occasion The Ramones played. He too would be completely blown away: "I was sitting in front overwhelmed by watching Joey sing 'I Don't Wanna Go Down to the Basement'. It was a great lyric – and you believed him. The song was about primal fear, with an incredible beat, rush and power. I thought, 'This band is great, and that guy is great!'" The moment the band stepped offstage Fields introduced himself to Johnny, offering his services as manager. A deal was then thrashed out whereby the band agreed to Fields' proposal on the proviso he hand over $3,000 to enable the band to purchase a new set of drums for Tommy. Fields wasn't a musician but knew enough to know that a decent set of drums could be procured for a few hundred dollars. However, he didn't care what the band intended to do with the rest of the cash. He didn't have the $3,000 so was forced to ask his mother. It could be said, therefore, that Fields's mother was responsible for not only the rise of The Ramones but also punk rock.

Having presented The Ramones with his mother's cheque, Fields escorted Linda Stein, wife of Sire Records' head honcho Seymour, to see The Ramones play at Mother's on West 23rd Street. "I thought they were amazing," she later reflected. "You'd hear them once and the second time you'd be singing along. I loved the energy, brevity and simplicity. I don't mean simple in a silly way. I loved the fact that there were four of them, the fact they were a band. I loved that they didn't have any sort of costumes, props, make-up and other nonsense."

In late-June, Fields and Stein arranged a private audition for the latter's husband. Seymour was impressed enough by what he heard and offered the band a singles deal on the spot. The Ramones, however, were intent on securing an albums deal, and politely refused. In the coming week The Ramones would audition for both Arista and Blue Sky, but with Linda more or less working alongside Fields in a co-management arrangement – a role that would soon be made official – Seymour was always going to sign The Ramones.

Stein was an aficionado of vintage rock 'n' roll, his passion extending to calling the Memphis operator and cajoling her into duetting Chuck Berry's 'Memphis Tennessee' down the line. With The Ramones, it was merely a case of seeing who blinked first. "I had heard so many negative things about the Ramones and so many positive things that I didn't know what to expect," Stein said in a 2000 interview with *Mojo* magazine. "I certainly expected to see something visually exciting – and it was. I loved their songs. I can sing their songs. I don't know how many artists you can say that about, artists from the mid-seventies onwards. They wrote great fucking songs. It was easy to see their influences were the Beach Boys and, to a certain extent, Abba. I loved them at first sight. Nobody wanted to go down to the Bowery. Nobody. It was a great stroke of luck for me."

Stein is gilding the lily somewhat as he was far from the first music-minded entrepreneur to take a walk on the wilder sides of town in search of something new and exciting. Marty Thau, a 36-year-old university graduate who would go on to form Red Star Records in 1977, had quit his post as head of A&R at Paramount Records to manage the New York Dolls after his inadvertently catching one of their Mercer Arts Centre shows. Indeed, it was Johnny Thunders that gave Thau the heads up about The Ramones. "He (Thunders) told me a new scene was developing at a little [East] Village bar called Mother's and a hot new band called the Ramones were causing all the excitement," Thau reflected. "'You should check them out,' he said, ''cause they're gonna stir some waves.' So I did, and thought, 'Here's a band I'd like to produce.' They had the music, the attitude, the look, and the street smarts to spearhead what was to be known as punk rock ... and they did."

According to Thau's version of history, Danny Fields had yet to commit to The Ramones' cause as they were still on the lookout for a manager. Thau was still the Dolls' manager, but he'd known the writing had long been on the wall for all to see and had raised no objections when McLaren breezed into town with his resuscitation strategy. He'd had more than his fill of playing the peacemaker and assuaging egos within the Dolls. He told The Ramones that while he'd no interest in managing them, or indeed anyone else, he would like the opportunity to get them into a recording studio to record some demos. The Ramones weren't about to pass up such an opportunity and on September 19, 1975, they accompanied Thau into

914 Studios in Westchester to record "Judy is a Punk" and "I Wanna Be Your Boyfriend".

"I discovered the Ramones knew exactly what they wanted: a duplication of their live sound with no added frills, overdubs, or gimmicks," Thau continued. "I wondered if it was because they couldn't play more complex parts but eventually realised they believed less is more and one must keep it honest, keep it pure and never lose sight of the beat. They were striving for good old teen sounds you could dance to, sing along with, and feel way down in your gut, songs with lyrics about sex and love and drugs and [seventies-style] rock 'n' roll that American teens would relate to."

Thau passed the unmixed demos to his good friend Craig Leon, who in turn played them to Seymour Stein. The Ramones signed with Sire Records in January 1976. Though understandably deflated at his not being assigned the role of producer when The Ramones went into Plaza Sound to record their debut album, Thau says he was happy The Ramones were in Leon's hands.

Ramones was greeted with glowing reviews following its release, with *The Village Voice*'s Robert Christgau declaring that as far as he was concerned the album "[blew] everything else off the radio". Despite such heady praise, The Ramones were still struggling to book shows outside of New York. Linda Stein, however, was busy devising a plan to take The Ramones over to London. "[She] was very internationally-minded," says Fields. "She was, I would say, hypnotised, and rightly so, by the lucrative possibilities open to the Ramones in the European market. From the very beginning, she properly sensed that we were likely to find an easier niche in the UK. So from the beginning, we tried to get to England, especially as it seemed less and less likely that we could move beyond New Jersey, the other side of the river."

Three days *before Ramones* hitting the record stores the Sex Pistols again supported The 101ers at the second of the latter band's Nashville Rooms dates. The rest of The 101ers hadn't been overly impressed with the Pistols. Indeed, their drummer, Richard "Snakehips Dudanski" Nother - who would go on to play with the nascent Clash, and later with John Lydon in Public Image Limited – didn't see much difference between the two bands other than the Pistols were younger. Joe Strummer, however, had been captivated by McLaren's attention to detail. During the soundcheck, he'd overheard the Pistols' manager asking his charges what clothes from the shop they'd like to wear onstage. Speaking about that night some years later in a *Melody Maker* 101ers retrospective, Strummer explained the difference between his reaction to the Pistols to that of Dudanski's. "You see, we're talking about a movement of ideas, and [Richard's] talking about a riff onstage. See the difference? I saw it not only as a 'good group' but as a new attitude."

Music scribes Caroline Coon and Jonh Ingham had also come to recognise the "new attitude" at play. The 30-year-old Coon, who would be credited with coining the term 'punk rock', had been writing for *Melody Maker* for several years. Born into a family of wealthy Kent landowners, she'd enrolled at Saint Martin's School of Art to train as a figurative painter. In 1967, her rebellious nature had seen her flying in the face of the establishment by co-founding the drugs agency Release to arrange legal representation for young people that had been arrested for drugs offences.

Coon had caught the Pistols' shambolic March 30 100 Club date, which had come perilously close to proving the band's last show. Matlock and a drunken Rotten had almost come to blows onstage before the latter fled out into the street in a farcical show of hubris. She'd also been in attendance when the Pistols played a sleazy Soho strip club called the El Paradise the following week. Despite her near-constant pleadings, her editor was thus far refusing to countenance a feature on the Pistols.

The Australian-born Ingham had been working at *Sounds* since the previous summer and had interviewed the likes of Jimmy Page, Queen, Roxy Music and the Rolling Stones. By the spring of '76, however, he was "becoming progressively bored with the whole scene."

He was seeing the Pistols for the first time at the El Paradise. Seeing Ray Stevenson setting up umbrella strobes close to the club's postage-stamp-sized stage caused Ingham some initial consternation . . . at least until the lights dimmed and the Pistols arrived onstage. "Filling the stage is a band that sounds and looks like nothing else in music," he says in his 2017 book, *Spirit of 76*. "The songs are short. They are fast. They all sound nearly the same, but not quite. The band all have short hair. The vocalist – he's too primitive to call him a singer – is squirming around in Ben Franklin sunglasses and a too-small red sweater ripped up the side and held in places with safety pins. His hair looks like he cut it himself with his eyes closed. His name is Johnny Rotten, and he doesn't like you."

When Ingham set about trying to convey how the Pistols were operating beyond all existing "rock music tropes" at *Sounds'* offices the following morning, his editor, Alan Lewis, commissioned him to interview the band. "There wasn't much rivalry between the leading music weeklies at the time," says Ingham. "Well, except for the *NME* - they really were the 'enemy'. *Sounds* shared offices with *Record Mirror*, and there was never any problem with *Melody Maker* as Caroline (Coon) and I would often collaborate on features. We'd have coffee meetings and share critiques. Caroline's editor at *Melody Maker*, Ray Coleman, didn't get the Pistols and wasn't remotely interested in allowing Caroline to write a feature about them. When I met up with her at the El Paradise and told her that I there to write a feature on the Pistols for *Sounds*, she said, 'But you can't!' She'd brought the Arrows along with her as she was writing a piece on them. They'd had some pretty big hit singles in 1974 and '75 with 'Touch Too Much", "My Last Night With You" and "I Love Rock 'n' Roll, which Joan Jett subsequently covered, of course. Caroline was writing a piece of them for *Melody Maker*. She liked pop music."

"Malcolm rang our office to tell us about the El Paradise show. Vivien Goldman answered his call, and when I heard her say 'Sex Pistols?' I rushed across, took the phone from her, and said, 'I've been looking for you.' I'd been going to 430 King's Road back when it was Let It Rock. I just didn't know Malcolm was the guy managing the Pistols. Malcolm was always coming up with ideas and usually did most of the talking. Vivienne never spoke much back then and didn't really come into her own until the Pistols had really taken off in 1977. She was just happy making up the clothes. If Malcolm didn't like her designs they'd be scrapped completely. If he liked certain aspects he'd rip away at what he didn't like and leave the strips of material hanging instead of ripping them away completely. That's where the idea for the clothes they sold in SEX came from.

"The Pistols were just incredible at El Paradise. I'd heard so many times about how they couldn't play their instruments, but that was dispelled within the first thirty seconds. I didn't recognise any of the songs but some were clearly better than others. Their playing

'Steppin' Stone' helped provide a reference point. A band should always know where to steal from."

Taking nothing away from the significance of Neil Spencer's Marquee review, the Sounds interview was a major coup for the Pistols so early in their career. "Malcolm being Malcolm, I had to meet with him first," Ingham continued. "It was in a café close to, or maybe even on Denmark Street. It was a surprisingly hot day, as it was still only early-to-mid April, but he was dressed head-to-toe in black leather. Over cups of instant coffee, he laid out his manifesto for the Pistols. It was anti-hippies, anti-drugs, pretty much anti-everything, like the line from the Marlon Brando movie: 'What are you rebelling against? What have you got?' He can't remember if he said anything about the Dolls - at least while we were in the café - but I do remember him saying something about how Richard Hell was going to look through the *Village Voice* and realise the Pistols made him look like a 'dilettante'.

"The interview was in the upstairs bar at the Cambridge pub in Cambridge Circus. When we got there Steve, Paul and Glen were already inside. They were animated but basically rehashing Malcolm's manifesto. Then they started talking about John who was glaringly conspicuous by his absence. John finally arrived with two girls (Debbie Juvenile and Tracie O'Keefe) but completely ignored us. He was wearing the torn red sweater again, only this time a large crucifix is hanging from a safety-pin. So, anyway, Malcolm gets them a drink but then they sit some distance away and carry on with their conversation totally ignoring us. Steve, Paul and Glen continued talking about him in the third person as though he wasn't in the room. If I didn't know better, I would have thought John didn't know them and vice versa. John just carried on sitting there chatting quietly with the girls – all cosy and intimate. Of course, that all changed when I walked over and asked him a direct question.

"It literally was like someone had flicked a switch because he suddenly sprang to life – a face snarling machine gun bullets and a death-ray glare. 'I hate shit! I hate hippies! I hate long hair. I hate pub bands! I'm against people who just complain about *Top of the Pops* and don't do anything. I hate, hate, hate, hate, hate...'"

The 101ers
featuring Joe Strummer.

Five Star
Rock'n'roll

—I Saw Some Passing Yobbos

"I saw Joe play with the 101ers many times. They were nearly at the point of being the best band in London. They were lumped in with the pub rock scene, but they were really a squat band, from the squatting communities. Joe was part of that scene, which was very big in the early Seventies. And we'd seen them many times. We just thought he was the best guy out there. We were looking for a singer and said, 'Let's see if we can get Joe."

Mick Jones

The April 3, 1976, Nashville Rooms show has come to be regarded as the night Joe Strummer realised The 101ers were "yesterday's papers" and decided his future lay with Mick Jones and Paul Simonon under the tutelage of Bernard Rhodes. This, however, is merely a melodramatic oversimplification of a rather more complex situation; with Strummer's complexities adding to the mix.

Strummer was born John Graham Mellor in Ankara, Turkey, in August 1952. Owing to his father, Ronald, being a clerical officer – later attaining the rank of second secretary – in the

Opposite: The 101ers were Strummers first taste of success

foreign service, John and his elder brother David had something of an itinerant childhood flitting betwixt Cairo, Mexico City and Bonn before the family were finally able to put down some home-grown roots of sorts setting up home in Warlingham, Surrey, during the summer of 1960. However, when Ronald received another posting to Iran shortly thereafter, it was decided the boys would remain behind to concentrate on their education. John and David were duly enrolled at the fee-paying City of London Freemen's School in Ashtead Park, Surrey; the government's picking up the tab being one of the perks of their father's working in the foreign office. Once in The Clash, Strummer would subsequently bemoan rarely ever seeing his parents over the next seven years; David's suicide in July 1970 bringing further estrangement.

Deciding to "live, enjoy life and fuck chartered accountancy!'" upon hearing the Stones' February '64 cover of Buddy Holly's "Not Fade Away" on his pocket transistor radio, the precocious John did just enough in the classroom to scrape the three O-Levels necessary to gain a place at art school. He was duly accepted into the Central School of Art and Design, only to drop out during his foundation year. Having taught himself the rudiments of the guitar on a two-quid ukulele, he adopted the name "Woody" in homage of the American folk singer Woody Guthrie before decamping to Newport. Whilst in south-east Wales, John/Woody joined a local band called Flaming Youth, (which he duly renamed "The Vultures") as their singer/rhythm guitarist. When The Vultures fell apart during the summer of 1974, John/Woody moved back to London. Once back in the capital he set about putting his own rock 'n' roll band together while undergoing another name-change to "Joe Strummer".

By the spring of 1976, The 101ers were more than a rock 'n' roll band. Indeed, it could be said they were the rhythmic pulsebeat of the Maida Vale squat community. All those living in the squats on Walterton Road and surrounding environs knew they were on borrowed time before the GLC bulldozers moved in. Should The 101ers secure a recording contract, however, then their plight – and that of squatters elsewhere in London as well as up and down the country – would have a platform from which to air their grievances. So it was unthinkable their frontman would have his head turned by the likes of the Sex Pistols.

The 101ers play the Elgin Arms pub with Joe Strummer (centre).
Photo: Julian Yewdall/Getty

There wouldn't be any approach to Strummer at the April 23 Nashville Rooms show, either - despite Bernard Rhodes, Mick Jones and Paul Simonon all being in attendance. Legend has it that Jones and Simonon - with Glen Matlock in tow – happened upon Strummer on the Portobello Market one Saturday afternoon and supposedly made a tentative approach by lauding his talents and lambasting his band in equal measure. The Clash would subsequently immortalise the occasion in the song 'All the Young Punks (New Boots and Contracts)', the closing track on *Give 'Em Enough Rope*. The reality, however, is that the fabled encounter never happened.

Another enduring punk parable regarding the birth of The Clash that did occur came with Jones and Simonon finding themselves standing in line together with Strummer at the Lisson Grove dole office. Conscious that he was being eyeballed, Strummer assumed Jones and Simonon were plotting to jump him once he got outside and relieve him of his giro. This was the last thing on their minds, however, as Jones revealed: "He had seen us out a few times, either at his gigs or in the dole queue. We were in the dole queue looking across at him – glaring – and he thought we were gonna start a fight with him. But we were actually looking in awe because we'd seen him play the other night! So we'd seen each other before, but he had obviously noticed us as well."

Just as they had at the Marquee, the Sex Pistols would steal the limelight at the Nashville for the chaos rather than the music. The Nashville's policy of placing several rows of foldaway chairs in front of the stage was hardly conducive for a rocking atmosphere, but the Pistols – Rotten in particular - appeared subdued and simply going through the motions. Indeed, the performance was in danger of descending into normality when Vivienne Westwood ratcheted up the intensity levels by getting into an altercation with the guy whose chair she'd appropriated whilst he'd popped to the bar. McLaren and Vicious both came rushing across with their arms swinging, while Rotten, Jones and Matlock would all jump in to extend the mêlée.

"It was my fault, I did start it," Westwood has since admitted. "I didn't start it on purpose, but this bloke told me to get off his seat. He'd gone to the bar and I'd sat down on his seat. He'd come back from the bar and I'd thought, 'Come on, this is punk, I don't get up off my seat for you, it's all part of the Establishment. I wouldn't get up and this man tried to lift the chair and tip me over, and as soon as he did that the band were there. Steve Jones stopped playing in order to protect me, and Sid, who was in the audience, took his belt off and hit this man round the head. It was dreadful."

"It was all Vivienne's fault," Matlock reiterates. "She'd taken a seat in front of the stage and, when she went off to get a drink, some bloke just sat down in her seat not knowing it was hers. When she came back with her drink she wanted her seat back.

"'You can't reserve seats here,' he said. And got jumped for his pains. Because it was Vivienne all the kids who hung out in the shop joined in on her side. I felt really sorry for the poor bloke because he was getting a right hammering. It was something like eight on to one. Even Malcolm joined in – like some action man, leaping over people's shoulders to get his punches in. Sid was caught steaming in by a photographer. You can see the real madness in his eyes in that picture. The retinas look like they're on fire as he 'defends' Vivienne."

Order was quickly restored, but not before Joe Stevens and Kate Simon had captured the free-for-all in their lens. The incident making all three leading music weeklies. The Nashville's promoters were understandably less enthralled by the Pistols and banned them indefinitely - although the band would return just six days later under the pretext of it being a private function.

Jones and Simonon were again in the crowd when The 101ers played the Red Cow in Hammersmith on May 12, 1976. Glen Matlock was definitely with them on this occasion, but again no approach was made. Mick was now sharing a room at a squat on Davis Road in Acton Vale with his girlfriend, future Slits' guitarist Viv Albertine. Another frequent visitor to the one-bedroom upstairs maisonette was 18-year-old Keith Levene who, like Jones, had taught himself to play the guitar. Levene had also accompanied Rhodes and Co. to the second Nashville show.

Levene was born in Muswell Hill and grew up in Finsbury Park within the extended shadow of the Benwell Estate where John Lydon grew up. From an early age, Levene had shown a keen interest in music, his eclectic tastes ranging from The Beatles to a Prokofiev's "Peter and the Wolf" and anywhere in-between. "Sitting there in the cold in north London listening to 'Peter and the Wolf'; that was where it was fucking at as far as I was concerned," the guitarist later reflected. "I didn't care about the rest of the shit. I was just this weird kid, but in these sounds, I sensed a strange vocabulary I could understand. This sound emanating from the speakers was what it was all about."

For a time Levene served as a roadie for prog-rockers, Yes, and would subsequently boast to his being given guitar lessons by Steve Howe. Though he was another that had been enamoured by The Ramones – and to this day regards them as being to punk rock what Roy Orbison or Buddy Holly were to fifties rock 'n' roll – Levene insists he didn't allow their frenetic 4/4 style to influence his playing. He was already acquainted with Mick Jones from the Warrington Crescent scene and so was familiar with his precocious talent. "I met Mick and got on really well with him. The main thing we had in common was we knew we really wanted to get a group together.

That was it." In Simonon and Levene, Mick Jones now had the nucleus of a band. The bonding that all bands need coming with the three of them buying gaudy ladies car coats from a second-hand stall on the Portobello Road Market one Saturday afternoon.

Given that Strummer didn't at least acknowledge Jones and Simonon at the Lisson Grove Labour Exchange suggests he was as yet blithely unaware of their intent to poach him away from The 101ers. In hindsight, it's a wonder Jones and Simonon thought they stood any chance in getting their guy. Strummer was far from famous, of course, but he was still two years of hard slog further along the line musically. As such, there was no logical reason for him to quit a band on the cusp of signing a record deal with Chiswick to start grubbing about for gigs again in a band that was as yet without a drummer and had a bassist that was still finding his way.

Jones, Simonon and Levene couldn't possibly know that Strummer had been so galvanised by the Pistols that he sought to steer The 101ers in that direction. He also started showing up at the Pistols' Tuesday night 100 Club residency dates, the second of which (May 18, 1976) was the day The 101ers signed with Chiswick. Rival bands showing up to check out the competition was nothing new, of course, but Rhodes says he sensed something in Strummer's demeanour that told him the time was right to make his approach. Said approach came at the Pistols' third residency date on May 25. Yet while Strummer listened to what Rhodes had to say and gave him his phone number, things were left hanging in the air. "The rest of the 101ers sensed a change in Joe's behaviour since the Nashville dates," says Rhodes. "One or two of the band must have had an inkling as to what I was up to. When I called the squat [in Orsett Terrace] where Joe was living, one of them (101ers' bassist, Dan Kelleher) picked up the phone and pretended to be Joe. He was obviously looking to join the dots for the others, but I knew instantly that it wasn't Joe and put the phone down."

Rather than wait to see how the situation developed, Rhodes decided the time had arrived to grasp the nettle. When The 101ers played the Golden Lion pub in Fulham Road on May 30, Rhodes went along, taking Levene with him. The two waited until after the show before asking Strummer to accompany them outside. While Levene kept a watchful eye on the pub door, Rhodes edged Strummer over towards the bus stop and the delivered his ultimatum. "You could say it was an ultimatum of sorts," says Rhodes. "I said to Joe that I was in the process of putting a band together to rival the Pistols Was he in or out?" When Strummer continued to vacillate, Rhodes put him 48 hours notice to make up his mind.

Rhodes is the first to admit that patience has never been one of his virtues. The following day he called Strummer asking for his decision. Strummer had done plenty of soul-searching since their clandestine meeting outside the Golden Lion, but rather than ask for the remainder of his allotted 48 hours he saw little point in delaying the inevitable. He was in. On his being introduced to his prospective bandmates the following afternoon at Davis Road the four began rehearsing in earnest. Various band names would be mooted over the coming weeks such as the Psychotic Negatives and The Weak Heartdrops before finally settling on The Clash.

Howard Trafford and Pete McNeish were proving as equally industrious as The Clash in putting their Pistols- influenced band together. The "GET A BUZZ, COCK!" tagline to a *Time Out* review of ITV's BAFTA-winning musical drama series, *Rock Follies,* had provided them with a name for their band, and they too had both adopted stage names. Trafford was now Howard Devoto (Devoto being Latin for "Bewitching"), while McNeish was now calling himself Pete Shelley, (Shelley being the name his parents had chosen should he have been born a girl).

Buzzcocks made their debut at Bolton Institute of Technology's 'Textile Students' social evening on April 1, 1976. Their set that night comprised of covers and a couple of Shelley's compositions: "Get on Our Own" and "No Reply", both of which would subsequently feature on Buzzcocks' 1978 debut album *Another Music In A Different Kitchen.* It was Devoto's first time onstage, but Shelley had started playing guitar whilst at grammar school, first with Kogg, and later with Jets of Air which featured Buzzcocks' founding bassist Garth Smith (a.k.a. Garth Bass) in the line-up. Since making their debut, however, Buzzcocks had lost both Smith and their drummer and were desperately trying to find a replacement for the Pistols' June 4 show. To add to their woes, the Student Union at their college vetoed their application to hire the hall for June 4. The refusal, however, had nothing to do with the Pistols being banned from both the Marquee and the Nashville Rooms, but rather because the union simply hadn't heard of the Pistols.

An alternative venue was found in the Lesser Free Trade Hall, a 400 all-seat-capacity room situated above the more illustrious Free Trade Hall on Peter Street. The Free Trade Hall was built during the 1850s to serve as a permanent monument to commemorate the repeal of the Corn Laws and stands on the site of the Peterloo Massacre of August 1819 when 18 people were killed and hundreds more injured during a cavalry charge to disperse the crowd. The Hall was the scene of a more recent – and some would argue a more despicable charge – when a member of the audience at Bob Dylan's now-legendary May 17, 1966 show dared to accuse Dylan of being a "Judas" for betraying his unplugged acoustic folk roots and going electric.

The Pistols' June 4, 1976, Lesser Free Trade Hall show was to have a seismic effect on Manchester's music scene. Indeed, the "Madchester" scene of the late Eighties and early Nineties can be traced back to that night. One-time *NME* journalist, Paul Morley, who was in attendance on the night, is certainly in agreement with this assertion. "Funnily enough, I've often done it for practice. Everything that happens is still a fall-out of the Sex Pistols coming to the Lesser Free Trade Hall. There's no doubt about it. You can draw it all back to that little explosion at the Lesser Free Trade Hall. It's not hard at all."

Buzzcocks' failure to find a replacement rhythm-section would force Devoto to call upon an old work acquaintance's prog-rock outfit, Solstice, to open for the Pistols. Devoto and Shelley were understandably frustrated at Buzzcocks not being able to play on the night, but they would be compensated in encountering 20-year-old Steve Diggle, whose name, of course, has since become synonymous with Buzzcocks. What makes their coming together all the more momentous is that Diggle was at the Free Trade Hall waiting to meet up with a guy from another prospective band while Devoto and Shelley were expecting to meet a prospective bass player who'd responded to the ad they'd placed Manchester's version of *Time Out*. McLaren had only approached the unsuspecting Diggle in the hope of coaxing him inside. On hearing Diggle say that he was a guitarist, McLaren confused the situation further by dragging him inside to meet Shelley who was manning the ticket booth. "Back then

The Buzzcocks Pete Shelley (left) and Steve Diggle playing at Eric's in
Liverpool in September 1977. Photo: Kevin Cummings/Getty Images

Manchester was a sea of flat-cap grey and beige flannel," says Diggle.
"I was only there to meet some bloke and then we were planning to go
to Cox's Bar (a popular pub situated close to the Free Trade Hall) and
to this day I can still remember seeing Johnny Rotten, Steve Jones
and Nils Stevenson come out of the lift at the Lesser Free Trade Hall.
They were dressed like nothing I'd ever seen. I knew straight away
that something was definitely gonna happen for them." The ever-
savvy Diggle readily volunteered his services as a bassist and agreed
to an audition at Trafford's place the following afternoon.

The Lesser Free Trade Hall would need to have been the size of
Manchester United's Old Trafford stadium to house all those who
"swear they were there" at the June 4 show. In reality, the crowd
numbered less than fifty. Within that number, however, were future
Joy Division/New Order stalwarts Bernard Sumner and Peter Hook,
(Joy Division's frontman, Ian Curtis, would be similarly captivated
by the Pistols' July 20 return to the venue), The Fall's Mark E.

Smith, Eddie Garrity, who would go on to front Ed Banger and the Nosebleeds, and 15-year-old future Smiths frontman, Steven Morrissey.

"Ever since a young age I've been an avid reader of the music papers and my escape during work was reading them," Hook told the *Manchester Evening News* in June 2016. "I was reading about all these heavy metal bands, Led Zeppelin and Deep Purple, but I never felt inspired by it - it seemed so untouchable. I kept reading snippets about this group called Sex Pistols and all they seemed to do was fight at their gigs. I saw the advert in the *MEN* and said to Barney (Sumner), 'We've got to go and see this band, they do nothing but fight'. There was a lot of football violence then, it felt like the working-class world I was used to as a lad from Ordsall and Salford. I walked out of that gig as a musician. I came home with a guitar and told my dad, I'm a punk musician now', and my father said, 'You won't last a week' [yet] here I am forty years later."

Factory Records supremo, Tony Wilson, would also claim to have been at "Gig One". At the time of the Pistols' Manchester debut Wilson was one of the main anchor on Granada TV's long-running regional news programme, *Granada Reports,* and also hosted the station's late-night arts show *So It Goes.* In the lead-up to the show, Devoto had sent Wilson a cassette tape containing three Pistols' songs – "Problems", "No Feelings" and "Pretty Vacant" – that the band had recently recorded at Mickie Most's Majestic Studios with Chris Spedding producing. Shelley believes that Wilson was only at the second Pistols' show as he doesn't recall seeing him come past the box office. Hook and Sumner have also poured scorn on Wilson's claim as they only remember bumping into him at the July 20 show. Regardless of which show Wilson attended, he was to prove instrumental in "putting the Pistols on the telly" in cajoling his bosses at Granada to allow them to perform live in the studio on *So It Goes* later in the year.

Looking at photographs from the June 4 show it's easy to understand Steve Diggle's comment about the Pistols "being dressed like nothing" he'd ever seen. While the guys in the audience are dressed in double-breasted jackets, kipper ties flared denim, cheesecloth shirts and knitted tank-tops, the Pistols do indeed look out of this world. Matlock is sporting his customised "Jackson Pollock" paint-splattered straight-leg black jeans – a look the nascent

Clash would prove quick to appropriate. Jones is dressed in a navy-blue boiler suit, whilst Rotten is in a natty sleeveless yellow top that looks as though like it's come out second best to a kiddie's scissor class, a ripped black T-shirt and tapered Oxford bags. McLaren cut an equally outré figure to the Mancunians, dressed as he was in black leather jacket, trousers and winkle picker boots

Sunday, July 4, 1976, was to prove another standout date on the punk rock calendar. Linda Stein had made good on her promise to bring The Ramones over to England and "Da Bruddas" as the leather-clad quartet were now colloquially known, marked their nation's bicentennial playing the first of two London dates at The Roundhouse in Chalk Farm, supporting the Flamin' Groovies. That same day would see The Clash mark their UK debut supporting the Sex Pistols at the Black Swan in Sheffield. A second Ramones' date was scheduled for July 5 at Dingwalls on Camden Lock. "England was amazing," Tommy would recall. "In New York, they hardly knew we existed, and in England, we were treated like stars. We sold out Dingwalls and the Roundhouse, it was really exciting – meeting the up-and-coming English punk bands that came to our soundcheck at Dingwalls, members of the Pistols, the Clash, the Damned, Chrissie Hynde of the Pretenders . . . It happened so quickly it was a blur."

"There's a comic book called *Gabba Gabba Hey* that talks about the Ramones trip to London and how we were so concerned about the economic conditions, the UK depression, unemployment, children out of work," says Fields. "In truth, we were there for three days and the last thing anybody was thinking about was whether the British state was unfair to unwed mothers. They only thing they were worried about on the flight over is whether we had enough T-shirts to sell and what if nobody speaks English."

The Roundhouse was the perfect setting for The Ramones – a run-down industrial shed from the bygone steam locomotive age. Its facilities were primitive; the interior charred, poorly lit and ill-kept. Originally built in 1847 by the London and North Western Railway as a roundhouse (a circular building containing a railway turntable), it served as a warehouse and inevitably fell into disuse before being made a listed building in 1954. Since the turn of the decade, however, the Roundhouse had become one of the hippest venues in London as it transitioned from a theatre and counter-cultural centre to the epicentre of London's rock music scene. Each Sunday, DJ Jeff Dexter compared Implosion, an iconic series of shows that ran from 3:30 till 11:30 p.m., with artists ranging from Black Sabbath, Soft Machine, Elton John, The Who and David Bowie. The Clash would play The Roundhouse in early September 1976.

According to the *NME's* Max Bell, The Ramones reduced the Roundhouse to the hottest, sleaziest garage ever while succeeding in dividing opinion into believers and open ridicule. Indeed, the ceiling would soon be dripping from the generated steam heat emitting off the sweaty massed ranks at the front of the stage, obliging the more brazen young ladies in the crowd to dispense with their upper attire – much to the delight of the guys.

Somewhat surprisingly, given the waves the Pistols were beginning to make on this side of the Atlantic, Bell makes no mention of them in his review. Proceedings got off to a shaky start owing to problems with Dee Dee's microphone, which persisted throughout. Unsurprisingly, The Ramones' 14-song set consists primarily of their debut album's track-listing with a couple of covers thrown in: Joe Jones' "California Sun" and Chris Montez's "Let's Dance". What's interesting about The Ramones' visit to the UK is that Danny Fields and Linda Stein didn't think to suggest inviting the Pistols onto either the Roundhouse or Dingwalls bill.

McLaren had tried getting the Pistols onto The Roundhouse bill, only to thrown down the stairs for his show of impertinence by the venue's promoter, John Curd. The Ramones may or may not have been aware of the Pistols at this juncture, but *Punk* magazine was certainly following the band's progress. "We got to hear of the Sex Pistols pretty early into their career," says John Holmstrom. "We had a clipping service at *Punk*. We paid a small fee for each clipping and in return, we received a 'tear sheet' from a newspaper or magazine article whenever 'punk' was mentioned. At first, the service was inexpensive as there were few mentions of punk rock in the media in 1976."

The Ramones' Roundhouse show is now viewed as the night punk went overground, yet Rat Scabies believes the New York band's influence on UK punk was open to question. "We were rehearsing, the Sex Pistols and Clash were doing the odd gig," he told *Uncut* magazine. "But I remember listening to the Ramones debut album with Paul Simonon and we thought it was great as it was exactly

Soo Catwoman on the cover of the incredibly rare Pistols Anarchy fanzine

what we were all about, three-minute pop songs about life. We felt an immediate connection and it was confirmation: we realised we weren't the only ones doing it. What was important isn't 'Who came first?' It was the fact the same thing was happening in different parts of the world. It was the next generation getting angry. It made us realise we weren't alone."

19-year-old Devonian, Gaye Black, who was in the process of putting The Adverts together with her boyfriend Tim Smith, was also at the show. "Joey came down the side at the end and of the gig and was handing out these miniature baseball bats. I'd never heard of the Flamin' Groovies before and it seemed strange the Ramones were supporting them. The Ramones were amazing. You wouldn't have known the lyrics from the gigs! Thirty seconds into the track and you would realise which song it was, and then the song was over. I've still got my toy baseball bat. It shares pride of place in my living room with the dog collar Iggy gave me."

It's odd to think that McLaren had spent the last few months striking to keep the Pistols away from playing pubs, yet on the night UK punk was said to have come out of the shadows he would book the band a date at the Black Swan in Sheffield, a regular venue on the pub rock circuit, colloquially known as the 'Mucky Duck'. That The Clash were making their debut owed more to Rhodes making what was to prove the first of several misguided shows of solidarity with McLaren over the coming months rather than his charges desperation to get up onstage. Indeed, there's every chance all five band members would have all been at the Roundhouse been given the choice. (Terry Chimes, who'd also auditioned for London SS had recently been recruited on drums.)

Though ostensibly a public house, the Black Swan's interior was more in keeping with a reception room where one might stage a wedding reception or birthday bash: ceiling tiles, plastic chairs, flock wallpaper, naff carpet etc. The acoustics more than made up for the poor ambience, however. Not that this was much in evidence when The Clash took to the stage. Simonon missed his cue on the opening song, 'Listen', and things didn't much improve from there. Indeed, an anonymous review which appeared in the following week's *NME* cited The Clash's performance as being a "cacophonous barrage of noise" and dismissed the band as being a "second rate Dr. Feelgood". For Strummer, who'd enjoyed an enthusiastic reception whenever The 101ers had played the Black Swan, the stinging critique would have been hard to ignore. Little wonder he and the rest of the band retreated behind closed doors at Rehearsal Rehearsals to work on their stage act.

The Stranglers shared support duties with The Ramones at both The Roundhouse and Dingwalls. Despite their sub-Doors sound receiving a much more positive response from the audience than when they'd supported Patti Smith at the latter's Roundhouse shows back in May, there were those within the UK music press that viewed them with suspicion on account of their age and musical virtuosity – a view shared by the Sex Pistols and their clique.

"The other bands were a bit pissed off that we had been chosen to represent London at the July 4 bicentennial gig," opines The Stranglers' long-serving bassist, Jean Jacques Burnel. "We were the first to play with the Ramones and Patti Smith and that pissed a few people off. We were out of the inner circle after that. That did us immense favours in the long term. We evolved on our own as if we had been in Australia for millions of years, like weird animals."

After the Dingwalls show Burnel got into an altercation with his opposite number in The Clash, thinking Simonon had spat at him. The two bassists headed out into the courtyard followed by their respective bands and a coterie of hangers-on. The situation was soon defused, most likely owing to Burnel being adept at karate. The two bassists wouldn't speak again for thirty years but ended up shaking hands after happening on each other at a traffic light whilst out riding on their prized Triumph motorbikes.

Their being kept at arm's length by the punk cognoscenti wouldn't stop The Stranglers' frontman, Hugh Cornwall, from offering his opinion to *Record Mirror* in January 1977. "The Sex Pistols opened the floodgates and must be credited with that. The Damned are a bit lightweight but they've got a couple of really good numbers. The Clash are really exciting. I saw Queen on TV at Christmas and they were crap. Give the Pistols their equipment and they could come across with the goods."

It wasn't only London's emerging musicians that latched onto The Ramones's anyone-can-do-it approach, of course. 18-year-old bank clerk, Mark Perry, had already latched onto the pub rock scene when he discovered what was happening over in New York via the *NME* and *Melody Maker*. Perry attended both of The Ramones' July London dates and came away even more enthralled: "I met other like-minded kids such as Shane MacGowan and Brian James. Brian told me about his new group, the Damned. I began to realise that these people were starting to call themselves punks and I felt that I was becoming a part of it, part of something big."

One of Perry's preferred hangouts around this time was Ted Carroll's Rock On record stall in Newport Court. Perry says he was aware of *Punk* magazine but was hoping there might be one or two

Mark Perry was in Ted Carroll's Rock On store when someone suggested he start a punk fanzine. He went straight home and started writing issue 1 of *Sniffin' Glue*

London-based magazines covering what was happening over in New York. Carroll, or whoever was manning the stall that day, tongue-in-cheekily suggested he should start up his own magazine. "It was said more of a joke than anything else," says Perry. "I obviously took his idea seriously because I went straight home and typed the first words of my fanzine, 'Sniffin' Glue and Other Rock 'N' Roll Habits'. I put the magazine together with the same 'back-to-basics' approach as the music that I was to feature. It was raw, to say the least, but it put across the punk message perfectly. I was identifying punk as a scene separate from the rest of rock music, but because of my openness it could include reviews of my old favourites Blue Öyster Cult alongside the obvious ravings about the Ramones."

Having got his girlfriend to print up 50 copies of the inaugural issue of Sniffin' Glue on the Xerox machine where she worked, Perry took them along to Rock On. To his astonishment, the stall bought all 50 copies and gave him the cash to have another 50-copy run printed up in a proper copy shop. Rock On then helped with distribution to other outlets such as Compendium in Camden Town and Bizarre in Paddington. "Once people started seeing Glue displayed in the shops, they had no trouble selling it," Perry continued. "It seemed there were plenty of fans, like me, who were eager to read about the emerging punk scene. It was still small but it was growing all the time."

Two days on from The Clash's Mucky Duck debut, The Damned announced their arrival on the scene supporting the Pistols at the 100 Club; having worked up their repertoire playing the previous four consecutive Saturdays at a Lisson Grove gay club in preparation for their debut. Their eleven-song set featured their soon-to-be-released debut single, 'New Rose', the aforementioned 'Fish' and other punchy self-penned compositions such as 'Fan Club' 'Feel the Pain' and 'So Messed Up' interjected with covers such as The Stooges '1970' and The Beatles' 'Help!'.

Since breaking from Mick Jones and Tony James, Brian James and Rat Scabies had recruited the latter's zany guitar-playing work colleague at Croydon's Fairfield Halls, Ray Burns, the soon-to-be-rechristened Captain Sensible. With money surprisingly provided by McLaren, the trio brought in Chrissie Hynde and booked a couple of days of rehearsal time – tentatively toying with calling themselves either Mike Hunt's Honorable Discharge or Masters of the Backside. "Malcolm was good to us: he gave us money and talked sense," Sensible reflected. "[He] came down with Helen (Wellington-Lloyd) and Rotten and all these people, and they sat down watching us, laughing and told us to fuck off. No commercial possibilities. Chrissie left [and] we started playing ourselves. Brian and Rat had

Vivienne Westwood on stage during the Pistols set at
Notre Dame Hall in London, 1976. Photo: Ray Stevenson

met Vanian at the Nashville – they thought he looked good. (Sid Vicious responded to the band's singer wanted ad but would fail to show for the audition). The name The Damned was Brian's idea. We were damned really: everything that could go wrong did."

"[Brian had] seen me in the audience at some shows and told me, 'You look like a singer,'" adds Vanian. "Before it became all torn clothes and spiky hair, punk was about individuality. I wore winkle-pickers and was going for that Twenties Rudolph Valentino look. I'd seen a few Hammer horror films, too, and decided I wanted to live in Baron von Frankenstein's castle. So, I left my gravedigger job to join The Damned and everything started moving very fast."

The defining indication that a new musical movement was coming to the fore – no one as yet was calling it punk – came with the Pistols accruing an eclectic following that would come to be known as the 'Bromley Contingent'. With Candy Sue Ballion their uncrowned queen, this trendsetting collective, while respectful of Bowie and Roxy Music, were eschewing the jaded musical heroes of yesteryear and openly seeking something that would allow them to dress up and mess up while striking a pose in the spotlight. Amongst their clique was 20-year-old Billy Broad, who would soon reinvent himself as Billy Idol. The Pistols were hugely appreciative of their support and would come out and talk to them after shows. In return, the Bromley set introduced the Pistols to Club Louise, an exclusive lesbian enclave located on Poland Street where the band could unwind after their oft-frenetic shows away from obtrusive eyes. "Madam Louise looked like Marlene Dietrich at the age of 80, with fantastic jewels and furs," says Shane MacGowan. "Every single guest was greeted personally with a kiss and a hug. She particularly loved her little punk boys. I was one of her favourites. Louise's slung out around four in the morning and then we used to hang around the streets of the West End in all-night coffee bars doing pills."

Another striking female on the scene, of course, was Soo Catwoman (a.k.a. Susan Lucas). She would spend hour upon hour sculpting her shorn hair and applying her make-up until her metamorphism into a feline femme fatale was complete. Indeed, it could be argued that Soo was the true iconic face of the London punk scene. McLaren certainly thought so as Ray Stevenson's now-iconic photo of Soo Catwoman would adorn the front cover of the inaugural issue of the Pistols' *Anarchy in the UK* fanzine released later in the year.

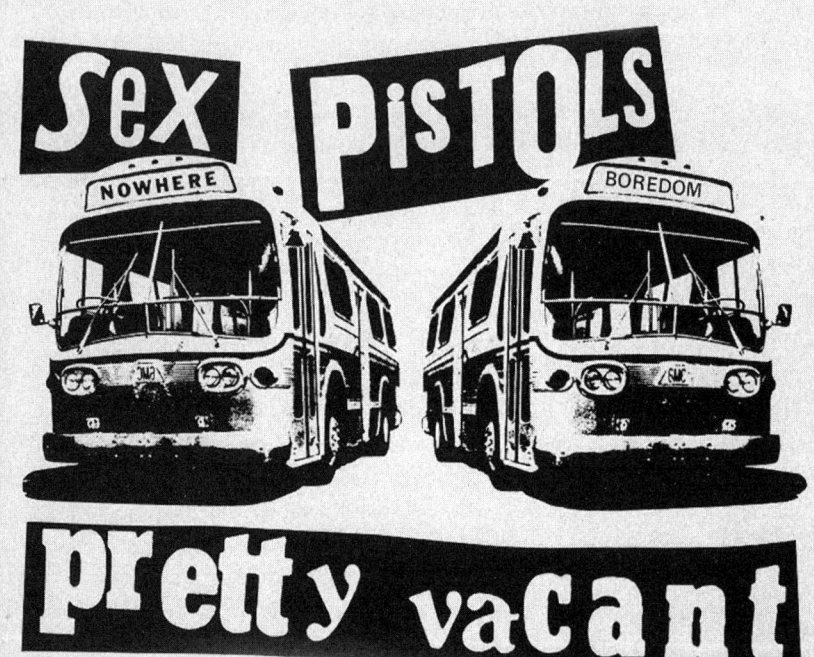

— No Elvis, Beatles Or Stones...

"The atmosphere in the club is feverishly high-pitched. This is the band everyone's been waiting for. Not everyone, however, is happy about the Pistols' growing success and notoriety. The private party is over. The band is public property. It had to happen. But with mixed feelings, the band's throbbing nucleus of fans are holding their breath as their champions start a steady climb to the ethereal reaches of stardom and rock immortality. Will the businessmen spoil them? is the anxious question."

Caroline Coon

To reach the "ethereal reaches of stardom and rock immortality" the Sex Pistols would need a recording contract. With this in mind, McLaren arranged a showcase at a friend's cinema, the Screen on the Green in Islington, on August 29, with The Clash and Buzzcocks providing support. Betwixt bands the audience was treated to two Kenneth Anger films: *Kustom Kar Kommandos* and *Scorpio Rising*. An added

Opposite: Jamie Reid's artwork made the Pistols work instantly recognisable

feature came courtesy of Candy Sue Ballion's fishnet and fetish ensemble – including a risqué e peek-a-boo bra from She an' Me (a marital aids shop). Billed as the "Midnight Special" – the doors opened at midnight and the frolics continued till dawn.

The Clash had already performed a private showcase at their Camden rehearsal space for a select number of invitees a couple of weeks earlier. While a few booking agents were in attendance at the showcase, only three of the music journalists on Rhodes' invitation list proved willing to give up their Friday night – Caroline Coon, Jonh Ingham and the latter's colleague at *Sounds,* Giovanni Dadomo. Rhodes made sure everything was just so on the night – down to the décor. In doing so, he inadvertently gave The Clash an identity. "By the second gig we had skinny ties and semi-smart jackets,' Mick Jones would recall. "We'd gone through the painting thing. Paul made the connection between Jackson Pollock, and our spritzing the paint on ourselves while giving the rehearsal room a lick of paint."

Infinitely more comfortable than they had been in Sheffield the previous month, The Clash put on a display to leave those in the room in little doubt they were a force to be reckoned with. Indeed, Dadomo would bring his critique of The Clash's Rehearsals roustabout to a close by declaring them "the first band to come along who'll really frighten the Sex Pistols shitless."

"The invite to watch the Clash showcase at Rehearsals came via Caroline," says Ingham. "Rehearsals felt a bit like being in a church. It was all whitewashed walls with Paul's cityscape fresco behind an altar of painted pink amps. Bernard Rhodes was hovering in the corner like an Alfred Hitchcock cameo. The Clash's clothes were splattered with paint like Jackson Pollock paintings. They plugged in and counted off – a cannonade of rat-a-tat rhythm. Their action-painting clothes are a superb metaphor for the overwhelming delirium of pinball-frantic music and motion. I wasn't entirely sure what it was I was seeing; the Clash weren't doing anything new but it was another new band and I just knew I wanted more of it.

"As with the Pistols' early shows, certain songs stood out on the night. Keith was still in the Clash at the time, so there were the five of them playing on this cramped makeshift stage. Keith was running up the wall going mad, but it was too busy, too much going on musically. Keith's leaving allowed the band to develop and they got better very quickly. They were great at the 100 Club Punk Festival.

Midway through the set, Mick broke a string. While he was replacing the string, Joe plucked a transistor radio from his pocket and began running through the stations. He happened upon a political debate about the Troubles in Belfast. It was perfect – not at all contrived. When I saw them play the Tiddenfoot Leisure Centre in Leyton Buzzard the following month they were just fantastic. When they finished their set, Joe came rushing over shouting, 'John, John, the promotor is really pissed off with us because we're contracted to play an hour and we've only been on for thirty minutes and we've no songs left. I said, 'Why you asking me? Just play 'White Riot' again and keep playing it.'"

It's doubtful McLaren would have ever admitted to paying Dadomo's review much heed, yet he nonetheless resorted to the time-honoured ruse of sabotaging The Clash's sound at the midnight special. Buzzcocks' set suffered similar problems throughout. Though Dadomo would lambast Buzzcocks for sounding "rougher than a bear's arse" he pointedly blamed the shoddy sound for The Clash's poor showing. The *NME*'s Charles Shaar Murray was somewhat less magnanimous, famously suggesting The Clash be "returned to the garage . . . preferably with the engine left running." When the time came for the Pistols to go on, of course, the problems had magically disappeared, and they gave one of their best-ever performances; Rotten's accidentally chipping a tooth on the mic serving to add extra menace.

For the past month or so McLaren had been touting a set of demos – with accompanying press packs – that the Pistols had recorded with their resident soundman Dave Goodman at Denmark Street on the latter's four-track tape recorder. The 25-year-old Goodman and his partner Kim Thraves had operated the sound at the first of The 101ers/Pistols Nashville Rooms dates. They were so impressed by the Pistols that they'd approached McLaren to offer their services. Of the seven tracks recorded at Denmark Street, "Anarchy in the UK" was deemed to be the strongest. The Pistols had debuted the song that was to become their clarion call at the second Lesser Free Trade Hall show on July 20. "Hearing 'Anarchy' for the first time still sticks in my mind," Pete Shelley later reflected. "I remember turning to Howard and saying, 'Yep, that's the single.'"

Speaking on the 2007 documentary, *Never Mind the Sex Pistols: An Alternative History,* McLaren would confess to his not wanting the

Pistols to make a record, and that he'd only acquiesced because of mounting pressure from the band. The only record company to have expressed any genuine interest in the Pistols to date was Polydor. Having caught wind the Pistols on the industry grapevine, the label's head, Freddie Hine, tasked his newly appointed head of A&R Chris Parry with checking the band out. "Freddie was a bit of a wild boy, but he was the boss, the ultimate boss, for Polydor at the time," the New Zealand-born Parry told *www.rnz.co.nz* in April 2019. "And he said I have just come back from a club and there's this weird band called the Sex Pistols, check them out." Parry had travelled up to Middleborough to catch the Pistols supporting one of Polydor's acts, Doctors of Madness, at The Crypt. While the Pistols had impressed him musically, Steve Jones' rifling the headliners' pockets while they were onstage had left Parry with mixed feelings.

The Screen on the Green showcase failed to garner any firm interest amongst those A&R reps that had deigned to attend. McLaren remained undaunted, however. If the mountains wouldn't budge then he was happy to play Mohammed and keep plugging away till one of them crumbled. With McLaren always insisting that EMI was at the top of his list of record companies, it stands to reason that theirs was the number he called most often – especially in the run-up to the much-vaunted 100 Punk Festival, which to all intents and purposes was nothing more than McLaren's second bite at the recording contract cherry. Unfortunately for him, Nick Mobbs and the rest of EMI A&R department always had warning as to who was calling and were content to let his calls go unanswered. There was one A&R staffer at EMI, however, happy to listen to McLaren's spiel

28-year-old physics graduate Mike Thorne had landed a job in EMI's A&R department at the beginning of 1976 and readily admits finding the record business 'alien territory' – despite his having worked at De Lane Lea Studios and written/edited articles on pop and classical music. "Record companies had always seemed bright, bouncy places with intimidatingly beautiful receptionists doing their nails loudly and impenetrably. However, A&R had fallen into some unadventurous routines by the mid-seventies, which I tried to follow after looking around in a desperate newbie attempt to figure out how to fit in. The old boy network was cosily in place, and most hard work seemed to be lifting drinks at the Marquee or the Speakeasy.

"Although obsessed with music, I never listened to radio and rarely read the 'comics', as the *NME* and the other leading music weeklies were known in the industry, so I hadn't even seen the front-cover *Melody Maker* picture of the Pistols, which had impressed the business but hadn't moved them towards appreciating the group's music and stance. But I was the one who picked up the phone to Malcolm McLaren and was impressed enough by what he said to my agreeing to go along to the now-legendary 100 Club two-day 'festival' of punk rock.

"It just so happened that EMI's latest acquisition, Giggles, were playing the Marquee that night, and the 100 Club was only a couple of blocks away. Giggles were an energetic - although rather contrived - pop band; their style of delivering simple, direct, non-sentimental songs was not too removed from the Pistols. I tried cajoling my colleagues to accompany me to see the Pistols but they weren't interested. The Pistols were on 'home ground' so to speak, but they were immediate and challenging. It was obvious something was happening because the 100 Club was packed. Because I was younger than the other guys at EMI, I was one of the very few A&R men to actually connect with what the Pistols were doing. Everybody now claims they were there at the 100 Club that night, but it wasn't true."

Sensing he had an ally at Manchester Square, McLaren handed over a cassette tape of the demos the Pistols had recorded at Denmark Street with Dave Goodman in July. "The demos weren't very well done but the Pistols were convincing musically so I arranged for the band to record a new set of demos at our in-house eight-track studio at Manchester Square. It was a Saturday as I remember. The Pistols were definitely 'handle with care', and there were fun and games on the day of course, but it was a good solid session. On the Monday, after taking a deep breath, I gave a copy of the demos to Nick (Mobbs). Nick didn't take much convincing. He was an inveterate hippie, culturally one of the prime targets for the new punks. But Nick had seen new, changing music emerge first-hand when founding Vertigo and then Harvest Records (the latter within EMI). He knew the symptoms. He knew 'new' and understood well that it didn't depend on hairstyle or past affiliation."

According to Chris Spedding, however, when he visited Mobbs at EMI's offices in Manchester Square and told him about the Pistols' Majestic Studios demo recordings, Mobbs had brazenly declared he "wouldn't touch the Sex Pistols with a ten-foot barge pole."

If that were true, then it would seem the road to Damascus passed through Manchester Square . . .

Two days on from the Midnight Special, the Pistols played another of their Tuesday night residency shows at the 100 Club with The Clash and Birmingham's Suburban Studs in support. The previous afternoon, Strummer, Simonon and Rhodes – together with Strummer's squat mate Pat Nother (brother of Richard) – got caught up in the Notting Hill Carnival rioting. The carnival had been inaugurated in 1959 as a means of improving morale within the capital's various West Indian Communities following the Notting Hill race riots of the previous year. In recent years, however, mounting tensions between the police and the local black youth had seen a steady increase in police numbers. The spark that would light the riotous flame of rebellion came with a black teenager being arrested near Portobello Road on suspicion of pickpocketing. The teenager's friends pelting the arresting officers with bricks and the ensuing scuffle quickly escalated to the point where riot police mounted a charge. Within a matter of minutes, the peaceful carnival descended into carnage. By nightfall some 350 police officers had been injured, scores of buildings and cars had been looted or destroyed, and 68 rioters were in custody.

The Clash posse managed to survive the melee with nary a scratch between them, the only anxious moment coming with Strummer and Simonon being targeted by a gang of black youths demanding they turn out their empty pockets. On returning to the Davis Road squat the duo regaled everyone with what they'd witnessed – the tale no doubt being further embellished with each telling. Football hooliganism was endemic in mid-Seventies Britain, with so-called supporters of London clubs West Ham United and Chelsea being some of the worst offenders. This, however, was the first time a section of the community had risen against the Establishment. Thinking about how the blacks were prepared to shake a fist in the face of oppression while their more docile white counterparts remained subservience to the state, Strummer committed his musings to paper. The following afternoon at Rehearsals, Jones would set the lyric to an incendiary riff. Later that same day 'White Riot' was unveiled at the 100 Club.

'White Riot' was to become as synonymous with The Clash as

'Anarchy in the UK' was with the Pistols. For Levene, however, the song's simplistic A/D/A/D chorus was more anathema than anthemic. "Mick was always 'Rock 'n' Roll Mick' [and] I didn't realise then just how much I despised rock 'n' roll," he later said. "Any numbers I got together they didn't really understand."

Levene would subsequently reveal that he'd approached Rotten backstage at the Black Swan with a view to their putting a band together. "Neither of us was happy with our band situation that night and John was looking ahead to quite different ideas from the other guys in the Pistols. So right off, me and John understood each other. There was a hatred, a cynicism, a kind of darkness, a nihilistic energy, but also a lot of mad humour. We both wanted to see the death of rock 'n' roll, and to kick the ghost of rock in the arse once and for all; give the ghost a shove as he fell into the grave."

Bernard Rhodes would surprisingly lend a sympathetic ear to the guitarist's plight. "Keith wasn't musically satisfied as a member of the Clash; one particular day he wanted to talk to me privately about something really bugging him. It was a few days after the Roundhouse show – Keith's final show with the Clash. We walked from my studio along Chalk Farm Road towards Marine Ices talking all the way. Acknowledging the music equipment store across the road, Keith stressed that his unhappiness was caused by musical restrictions imposed while working with Mick."

Marine Ices was a particular favourite café of Rhodes's during his time managing The Clash. Unlike every other Camden café, Main Ices served proper cappuccino. Whilst running an eye over the latest record/gig posters plastered along the Roundhouse wall opposite, he would plan his campaigns to outmanoeuvre the competition. "Keith wanted to be more free and experimental adopting new technology," Rhodes continued. "He was especially keen to introduce the latest form of keyboards/sequencers/drum machines etc. into the group's sound but Mick and Joe wouldn't have any of it. Keith obviously had a residue commitment to prog-rock due to his past musical experiences. I knew Lydon and Keith wanted to leave their respective groups because they felt restricted musically. Although Keith liked the guys in the Clash, Lydon thought he was with a 'bunch of thickos' – his words – in the Pistols. He particularly didn't respect Steve Jones. So over coffee, I suggested Keith go and see Lydon to form a totally fresh group. I explained to him that now was the time to catch the concept hot. Otherwise, the opportunity would be gone."

"It was quite possible for it to be Mick's and my band from my point of view," Levene said in another interview, "but it was not possible from Mick's point of view. So, therefore, it had to be Mick or me, and I decided, let it be Mick."

Everyone involved with The Clash at the time has given their version surrounding Levene's departure from the band. Strummer's account has him telling Levene to "fuck off" when he bemoaned having to rehearse "White Riot". Terry Chimes says how Strummer, Jones and Simonon mooted Levene's worth in the band and that he was told he was out when he arrived at Rehearsals. Levene says the decision was put to a vote with him, rather bizarrely, having the casting vote. He told them that he didn't like the musical direction the band was taking and that he was leaving. However, he also told them that if they realised they'd made a "bad move" he'd be willing to return so long as they came in line with his own thinking. Whatever the true turn of events, The Clash were now a four-piece.

The first telling indication that the London scene was being taken seriously came with the Sex Pistols, The Clash and The Damned being invited to appear at the inaugural European Punk Rock Festival at the Arenes de Plumaçon bullring in Mont-de-Marsan in southwest France on August 21. The festival was the brainchild of French promoter and co-founder of Skydog Records, Marc Zermati.

At the time of his co-founding Skydog in 1972, Zermati was running the Rock On-esque Open Market, primarily selling imported records by US and British acts. His partner, Michel Esteban, ran a music magazine called *Rock News* and sold rock 'n' roll merchandise. According to Zermati, Paris boasted a thriving punk scene long before it started taking root in London. "The real punk movement started in New York and Paris came before the UK because we were really connected to New York (through Esteban). It was exciting because we thought we were conspiring against the establishment."

"Marc was putting on a festival at a bullring in Mont de Marsan," says Andy Czezowski, who was managing The Damned at the time. "It was supposed to be a punk rock festival but the majority of bands on the bill were what we considered to be old pub rockers. At the last minute, one of the acts dropped out and the Damned were added to the line-up alongside the Pink Fairies and Nick Lowe. It was a bit

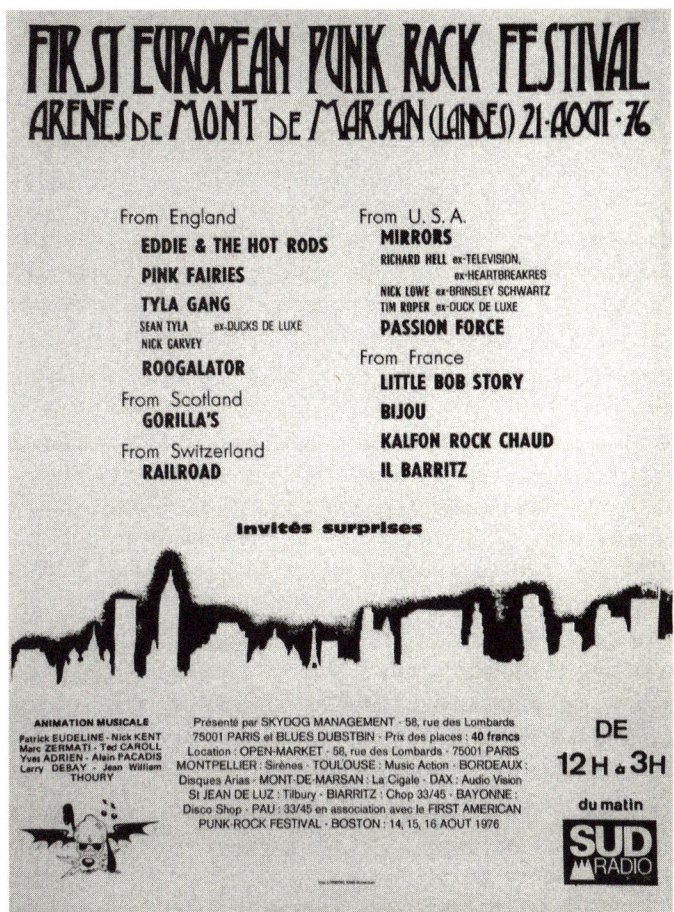

FIRST EUROPEAN PUNK ROCK FESTIVAL
ARENES DE MONT DE MARSAN (LANDES) 21·AOUT·76

From England
EDDIE & THE HOT RODS
PINK FAIRIES
TYLA GANG
SEAN TYLA   ex-DUCKS DE LUXE
NICK GARVEY
ROOGALATOR

From Scotland
GORILLA'S

From Switzerland
RAILROAD

From U.S.A.
MIRRORS
RICHARD HELL ex-TELEVISION,
                        ex-HEARTBREAKRES
NICK LOWE ex-BRINSLEY SCHWARTZ
TIM ROPER ex-DUCK DE LUXE
PASSION FORCE

From France
LITTLE BOB STORY
BIJOU
KALFON ROCK CHAUD
IL BARRITZ

invités surprises

ANIMATION MUSICALE
Patrick EUDELINE - Nick KENT
Marc ZERMATI - Ted CAROLL
Yves ADRIEN - Alain PACADIS
Larry DEBAY - Jean William
THOURY

Présenté par SKYDOG MANAGEMENT - 58, rue des Lombards
75001 PARIS et BLUES DUBSTBIN · Prix des places : **40 francs**
Location : OPEN-MARKET - 58, rue des Lombards - 75001 PARIS
MONTPELLIER : Sirènes · TOULOUSE : Music Action · BORDEAUX :
Disques Arias - MONT-DE-MARSAN : La Cigale · DAX : Audio Vision
St JEAN DE LUZ : Tilbury · BIARRITZ : Chop 33/45 · BAYONNE :
Disco Shop · PAU : 33/45 en association avec le FIRST AMERICAN
PUNK·ROCK FESTIVAL · BOSTON : 14, 15, 16 AOUT 1976

DE
12 H à 3H
du matin

SUD RADIO

The Damned ended up playing at Mont de Marson while
The Clash pulled out after the Sex Pistols invitation was rescinded
due to pressure from headliners Ediie and the Hot Rods

funny as the Damned were the only ones anywhere near being a
punk band."

Zermati and Esteban had since rescinded the Pistols' invitation
partly owing to the reputation they were gaining for violence at their
shows, but mostly because of pressure from headliners Eddie and
the Hot Rods' management. The Clash pulled out in another show
of solidarity to the Pistols. The Damned felt no such compunction,

of course, and stood in bleary-eyed line beside the Hot Rods, the Gorillas, Nick Lowe, Roogalator and the Pink Fairies at Victoria Coach Station awaiting the coach to ferry them to Dover. The French acts set to appear at the festival included Shakin' Street, Il Baritz, Kalfont Rockchaud and Passion Force.

It was during the ride to Dover that Ray Burns received his enduring moniker. "We was driving down to Dover to catch the ferry to Calais when I started mucking about pretending to be the pilot. You know, shouting things like, 'It's alright' everything's under control.' Just having a laugh really. But 'cos I was wearing some cheap second-hand shirt that had epaulettes, some wag shouted out, 'Who the fuck do you think you are, Captain Sensible?' Well, it kinda stuck as at the time everyone was giving themselves silly punk names, weren't they? I thought it was a laugh at the time and maybe, I dunno, cause a bit of confusion down the dole office. But here I am forty years on and still 'The Captain'. You'd think I'd have had a promotion by now, though."

Caroline Coon was accompanying the ragtag assortment of English bands on the two-day coach ride to Mont-de-Marsan for *Melody Maker*. She describes the venue as being white and chocolate brown with tiers of concrete seating and a vast expanse of clean, bright orange sand. There wasn't a black leather jacket. Nor was there any more evidence of anything unique or untoward occurring. "It made a perfect rock venue," she continued, "and about three hundred rock fans, mostly dressed in patched denims, were enjoying the space."

The bullring could hold an estimated 5,000. Whether Zermati and Esteban's decision to pull the Pistols off the bill had any bearing on the poor turnout is, of course, a matter of conjecture. The Damned went on mid-afternoon – the so-called 'punishment spot'. They opened their eleven-song set with 'New Rose', but their usual zany onstage camp theatrics are somewhat stilted owing to the oppressive ninety-degree heat. The denim-clad locals meandered down from the stands for a closer look but remain largely unimpressed.

The Damned may have left the stage to stilted applause, but Coon says they were by far the highlight of the festival: "Their music may not be tidy, technically polished or complex, but it is an authentic expression of a lifestyle with poetry and motion inspired by a forward-looking present rather than a rapidly fading past. Their music is exciting because of the band's intense commitment to it, a refreshing change from hearing bands who have been onstage so often they have it all down pat and have forgotten the fundamental quality needed to make anything creative – the element of risk."

On Friday, September 3, the Sex Pistols flew to Paris to play the opening night at the Club de Chalet Du Lac, a trendy new discothèque located on the French capital's upmarket Bois de Vincennes. McLaren supposedly came up with the idea to play the club as a means of compensating the band for having missed out on appearing at the European Punk Rock Festival. Several of the Bromley Contingent made the trip to Paris in Billy Broad's GPO Morris van. Once again, Candy Sue Ballion caused a stir in her peep-hole bra and swastika armband ensemble. It wasn't so much her nipples being on display that caused consternation amongst the young Parisians but rather her wantonly brandishing a Nazi totem on the anniversary of the day Britain and France had declared war on Germany and thus precipitating World War II. "We were walking to the club and suddenly these guys jumped out with knives, really hassling us," Simon Barker explained. "When we got to the club, Sue got punched by this guy who tried to grab her tits, and then it got so bad that we were moved to another part of the club for our own protection. We just waited in the dressing rooms until the promoter said it was safe for us to leave."

The Pistols were delayed at Heathrow airport owing to McLaren forgetting to bring his passport along. He'd also neglected to arrange a carnet – the customs license required for the temporary transportation of goods across certain borders; ie the band's equipment. Despite the enforced delay the club still wasn't ready, and the Pistols were obliged to carry out their soundcheck while staff and workmen rushed about arranging the decor. In accordance with Parisian tradition, the club's opening night was 'entrée libré' and was soon packed to its freshly painted rafters.

The Pistols emerged onto the futuristic neon-lit glass stage with Rotten sporting McLaren and Westwood's latest fashion statement, the bondage suit: a shiny sateen-ensemble, replete with buckles D-rings and zips - one of which ran from the crotch to coccyx. The suit was also festooned with straps across the chest, as well as the knees to restrict the wearer's movements. He'd worn the upper half of the suit on the flight to Paris and had almost brought the airport to a standstill. As it happened to be Jones's twenty-first birthday, McLaren treated him to a prostitute.

With the Pistols scheduled to play a matinee show on the Sunday, Caroline Coon suggested the band and their entourage hang out at the Les Deux Magots in the Saint Germain des Prés. The café was enjoyed the reputation as being the rendezvous of the city's literary and intellectual élite with Jean-Paul Sartre, Albert Camus, Simone de Beauvoir, James Joyce and Ernest Hemingway all enjoying its patronage. It was under the sightless gaze of the two Chinese mandarins (the "Magots" that gave the café its name), that McLaren first mooted the idea of staging a punk rock festival at the 100 Club.

Upon the band's return from Paris, McLaren set to work laying the foundations for the proposed festival. To aid him in his endeavours he enlisted Jamie Reid's girlfriend, Sophie Richmond, as his PA. She'd worked with Reid at the Suburban Press after leaving Warwick University in 1972 but had been living in Aberdeen when McLaren offered her the job.

The 100 Club Punk Festival was staged over consecutive nights on Monday, September 20, and Tuesday, September 21. The primary problem facing McLaren, of course, was that the London scene didn't have enough punk bands to warrant a festival under that name. If he was to avoid being left with egg on his face he would have to cast his net further afield. Indeed, the original A3 posters advertised the two-day event as a "punk special" rather than a festival.

"The word 'festival' was used totally inappropriately, with a huge sense of fun, and by no means meant to be taken as seriously as it has been ever since," says John Lydon today. "Calling it a festival was a hoax on ourselves, definitely tongue-in-cheek. The reporting at the time – and ever since – saw it as a deadpan, serious, dour affair, rigidly adhering to the cause. No, nonsense! It was a bunch of bands having fun, being entertaining, and somehow being informative."

The punk special/festival wasn't intended so much as a celebration of London's burgeoning punk scene but rather another attempt by McLaren to secure the Pistols a recording contract. Time was now a factor, however, as The Damned had recently signed to Stiff Records.

Stiff was a newly incorporated independent label founded by Pub rock enthusiasts Jake Riviera (aka Andrew Jakeman) and Dave Robinson courtesy of a £400 loan from the Feelgoods' frontman,

Lee Brilleaux. In accordance with the label's name – 'stiff' being the music biz idiom for a failed record – their debut single, Nick Lowe's 'So It Goes', disappeared without a trace. The follow-up, release, however, The Pink Fairies' 'Between the Lines' fared rather better. So much so, that Riviera and Robinson were now in a position to get The Damned into a recording studio. If that were to happen, The Damned would supplant the Pistols as the scene's trailblazers leaving Riviera and Robinson to reap the rewards while McLaren's hard work over the past year or so would count for nought. He was determined at all costs to avoid the humiliation of seeing his charges usurped by a band that had only been together for a couple of months. Signing to an independent such as Stiff was anathema to McLaren's way of thinking. If the Pistols were intent on getting a record deal, he was equally resolved that it would be with one of the majors.

With the Pistols scheduled to play the Top Rank in Cardiff on the twenty-first, they would headline Monday night's bill. The Clash, together with Rhodes' latest acquisition, the recently formed Subway Sect, and French punksters Stinky Toys making up the running order. Tuesday night's bill was to be headlined by The Damned with Buzzcocks and The Vibrators (with Chris Spedding guesting during the second half of their set) making up the numbers. It's unlikely Spedding's playing with The Vibrators at the festival played any part in Mickie Most's thinking, but they signed a singles deal with RAK Records the following month.

McLaren still felt another band was needed to bolster the Monday night billing. He would find one in the unlikeliest of settings. He, Rhodes and Sophie Richmond were holed up at Club Louise on Poland Street discussing where they might find a band at so late in the day when Candy Sue Ballion volunteered her as yet non-existent band for the vacant Monday night slot.

The following day found Ballion seeking three like-minded souls to serve as her backing band from amongst her friends. Billy Idol was the first to be approached, if only because he had a basic understanding of the guitar, while fellow Bromley Contingent stalwart Steve Havoc (aka Steven Bailey) and Sid Vicious agreed to serve as bassist and drummer respectively – despite neither of them having the first clue as to how to play their intended instruments. Broad would reconsider the folly of going on stage with three novices and instead teamed up with Tony James in Chelsea. Ballion

Sex Pistols on stage at the 100 Club Punk Festival in 1976. Photo Hulton Deutsch/Corbis

remained undaunted and cajoled Soo Catwoman's friend and SEX habitué, Marco Pirroni, into taking Broad's place. A band name presented itself later that same day with the Hammer film, *The Cry of the Banshee,* being screened on TV. Ballion changed the spelling of her name and Siouxsie and the Banshees were born (billed as "Suzi and the Banshees" on the festival poster).

While The Clash and the other acts on Monday night's bill went through their respective soundchecks, the four Sex Pistols accompanied McLaren to the offices of his newly hired solicitor, Steven Fisher. Fisher was also to be a co-director of Glitterbest, the Pistols new management company – bought off the shelf for £100 and incorporated on September 23, 1976. The contract was to last for three years, with options for the next two years. In return for his services, McLaren – through Glitterbest – was to take 25 per cent of the band's pre-tax earnings and 50 per cent of all future merchandising. The contract also contained covenants covering every aspect of the band's professional lives. Tucked away within Fisher's carefully worded legal jargon was Clause 14, which stated the name "Sex Pistols" had been created by the manager and therefore belonged to – and was owned by – Glitterbest.

In *Anger is an Energy* Lydon holds his hands up, cautioning his readership never to sign a legal document without first seeking legal representation. At the time, however, he blithely refused to read the document placed before him. Nils Stevenson was also in attendance and says that on his being called upon to witness the contract he'd advised the band to seek independent legal counsel. Matlock was the only one of the four to cast his eye over the terms, but obviously couldn't be expected to understand most of the legalese - or 'mumbo jumbo' as he put it.

Back at the 100 Club, a row was brewing over Ballion's homemade Nazi armband. The Clash had consented to allow the Banshees the use of their equipment but Siouxsie's stubborn refusal to remove the armband – coupled with Sid calling Bernard Rhodes a "mean old Jew" – led to the offer being rescinded. Just when it seemed the Banshees would have to forego the pleasure of wailing in front of their peers, McLaren stepped in to save the day by allowing them to use the Pistols gear.

Subway Sect were set to get the festival underway. The Mortlake-based quartet were content building up an R&B repertoire until their singer Vic Goddard and guitarist Rob Simmons saw the Sex Pistols play the Marquee back in February; the pair having wandered in off the street. The Pistols as a whole had left them unmoved, but Rotten's chair-throwing antics had left an impression. Bernard Rhodes had since taken them under his wing and a daily rehearsal schedule was arranged between them and The Clash.

The Subways' friend/roadie, Barry 'Baker' Glare, who would go on to become The Clash's long-serving factotum, says that whenever the band were awaiting the Clash to finish rehearsing they would often take a stroll to George's Café over by Camden Lock. "There was another closer greasy spoon café right opposite Rehearsals, but everyone used George's, not just because it was more agreeable but because of the owner's daughter, a doe-eyed teenager, Gabby, who we fantasized over constantly," says Glare today. "She worked in the café and we would watch her out of the corner of our eye, trying not to make eye contact. A hush would come over the table as she approached and fetched our orders."

As the day of the 100 Club Punk Festival drew closer, rehearsals for both bands noticeably intensified. "The Clash had about a ten-song set by then, although we only heard snatches of it as we came and went through the studio," Glare continued. "Their rehearsals were conducted at a driving pace and there never seemed to be much in the way of inactivity. In contrast, the Subways had put together a short five-number set of manically fast, dissonant, jarring numbers."

Though people could sense something was happening with the Pistols, the rest of the bands on the bill were still relatively unknown quantities. Seeing a queue some 600-strong stretching along Oxford Street was indisputable evidence that punk rock was taking root.

Melody Maker photographer, Barry Plummer, snapped several shots of the bands loitering with intent awaiting their turn to soundcheck once the PA and lighting rig was in place. With it being their first show, Vic Goddard and the rest of Subway Sect were sat huddled around a table watching on as the club became a hive of frenetic activity. Sid Vicious wandered across to share a few jokes with them while Rotten, to his credit, offered a few words of encouragement. Meanwhile, the ever-mischievous Simonon sat across the room taking occasional potshots at them with a small pellet gun.

Glare says that problems with the PA put things behind schedule which meant there was only time for one of the bands to soundcheck. Ordinarily, this would be the headliners, but with the Pistols deciding they wouldn't bother it fell to The Clash to put the PA to the test.

"They strolled on stage, plugged in and immediately fired straight into 'White Riot' at top volume," Glare continued. "Well! I'd heard of the term 'wall of sound,' but this was like being hit by a sledgehammer over and over again! Played at breakneck speed and full volume it was as if an earthquake had erupted (the emptiness of the club probably contributed to the effect).

"We sat looking at each other, eyebrows raised, and without a word knew we were all thinking the same thing, 'What the hell had we gotten ourselves into?' The number finished on a shout and the room was silent except for feedback and crackling, buzzing electrical connections. It was at if we had been confronted with a force of nature and everyone present seemed speechless by the explosion they had just witnessed, most of all us."

Though nervous, Subway Sect would acquit themselves with aplomb. They were dressed in monochrome grey to suit their utilitarian sound. They stalked purposefully onto the stage and without making eye contact with the audience enter into what Caroline Coon describes as a "lengthy, foot-finding, tuning type warm-up." Their opening number, 'No Love' was generously received, which proved sufficient to coax Goddard from his shell if only a little.

Goddard's stage act at the festival was unashamedly early Rotten-esque, but his pausing to pluck handfuls of nuts from his trouser pocket and gobble them down betwixt lyrics was deemed original enough to be worthy of comment by Caroline Coon. The A&R reps gathered at the bar remained collectively undecided as to the Subways' merits, however.

The Banshees initially decided they would learn John Barry's 'Goldfinger' theme from the 1964 James Bond movie of the same name for their supposed one-off performance. The idea would soon be abandoned in favour of a meandering twenty-minute Velvet Underground-orientated dirge over which Siouxsie intoned lyrics from Bob Dylan's "'Knockin' on Heaven's Door' and The Beatles' 'Twist and Shout' interspersed with snippets of 'Deutschland Uber Alles' and 'The Lord's Prayer'.

Pirroni, however, says he was under the impression they would be playing the Velvets' 'Sister Ray' on the night. "Well, I hadn't really discussed it with the others," he revealed. "I just thought we were doing 'Sister Ray' and that made sense to me. We were all influenced by the Velvet Underground, but I didn't know that Sid, Siouxsie and Steve were all as in love with them as I was. I could have guessed, probably. We just knew, whatever it is that you've got, we don't want it. Like Groucho Marx: whatever it is, I'm against it."

The Banshees had enough friends in the audience to ensure an enthusiastic response, but ten minutes or so into the dirge the smiles faded and silence descended as the crowd tried to decipher whether they are the ones being played. The Banshees were now playing for playing's sake as they'd assumed someone would pull the plug within the first couple of minutes. Finally, however, Pirroni decided they were coming perilously close to wearing out their welcome. On his nod, Vicious abruptly stopped playing and the Banshees departed the stage.

The Clash opened with 'White Riot', which, as with the soundcheck, was again belted out at a blistering pace. They certainly didn't appear to be suffering any hangover following Keith Levene's departure. If anything, his absence has given The Clash an added dynamic as Simonon now has the freedom to express himself onstage. Their eleven-song set included a brand-new composition called 'Deny', which may or may not have been written with Levene in mind. Mick Jones's 'I'm So Bored With You' had since been amended to 'I'm So Bored With the USA'. In the accompanying booklet to *Clash on Broadway,* Strummer would assert that the change came about solely because he'd misheard Mick's title during the initial get-together at Davis Road. Speaking with ZigZag magazine several months on from the festival, however, Vic Goddard, was insistent that Strummer co-opted the title from a Subways song called "USA".

The festival was the Pistols' tenth appearance at the 100 Club all told. Those that have followed them since the start of their residency couldn't help but notice a seismic change within the band – especially Rotten who rarely ventured away from the microphone. His once youthful exuberance is still evident on occasion but is now largely buried beneath a haughty veneer; his playful bantering with the audience between songs has given way to an icy stare. Once again, he's wearing McLaren and Westwood's sateen bondage ensemble. Jones, Matlock and Cook appear more self-assured; as though they've finally begun to believe in their destiny. This was certainly evident of Cook, as he's quit his apprenticeship at the brewery to focus on the band.

Taking the Banshees' novelty value out of the equation, both Subway Sect and The Clash readily earned the kudos being afforded them. However, it was the Pistols that everyone was here to see. After some last-minute checks to the tunings, they thundered into the now telltale G/F/Em/D/C intro to "Anarchy In The UK". This is quickly followed by "I Wanna Be Me", Rotten's acerbic rant against the "typewriter gods" that were still churlishly slating the Pistols at every turn. Caroline Coon is not of that ilk, of course. Indeed, she is now considered one of the Pistols' confidants. When penning her *Melody Maker* review she lauds the Pistols' for being "Frightening in their teenage vision of world disintegration" yet "refreshing in their musical directness and technical virtuosity."

The second night of the festival was to prove a somewhat more demure affair. The atmosphere was still spirited, but the audience was marginally older, longer-haired and more prudently dressed; denim and cheesecloth in place of leather and PVC. First up were Stinky Toys, their having been held over from the previous evening. This was said to be due to time restrictions but in reality, it was the French band's refusal to go on with 95 per cent of the audience having headed for the exit once the Pistols had departed the stage. Their singer, Ellie Medeiros, was so distraught at the prospect of playing to an empty house that she dashed out onto Oxford Street and came uncomfortably close to being hit by a passing bus. Medeiros was easy on the eye, but the French quintet's Stones/Dolls-cloned set was greeted largely with apathy.

Stinky Toys signed with Polydor in 1977. Their debut single 'Boozy Creed' (b/w 'Driver Blues') was met with largely unfavourable reviews, however. Polydor would ultimately abandon the release of the band's eponymous debut album outside of France.

Somewhat surprisingly, The Damned were up next. Dave Vanian, who up until the band's signing to Stiff had been digging graves rather than scenes, took smug satisfaction announcing 'New Rose' was set to be their debut single. A heartbeat later, Rat Scabies tore into the song's thunderous drum pattern intro. Next up was 'Comfort', which will later be reworked as 'Alone' and feature on the band's second album, *Music for Pleasure*. The Damned's camp theatrics was proving popular with the crowd, but one disgruntled audience member expressed his displeasure by hurling his beer glass at the stage. The glass shattered against one of the support pillars, one of the shards supposedly blinding a girlfriend of Vanian's in one eye.

The injured girl has never been named. Though it was her choice whether to go public, it still beggars belief that the tabloids – especially during their post-Grundy muck-racking anti-punk rock smear campaign – didn't search her out and plaster her disfigured face across the front page.

It's since become set in stone that Sid Vicious threw the glass. After all, he was convicted of the crime and subsequently incarcerated in Ashford Remand Centre. Caroline Coon, who was arrested for trying to prevent the arresting officers from bundling Vicious into the back of a police van (and subsequently given an absolute discharge), still believes him to be innocent.

Jonh Ingham is another who still maintains Sid's innocence. What's more, he says Vicious was purposely set up by an undercover copper. Ingham was standing next to Vicious when he espied several uniformed officers descending the stairwell with Ron Watts. He was astonished when the officers made their way directly over to the bar and grabbed Vicious and bundled him out without bothering to first question him or anyone else. Ingham then asserts that within seconds of Caroline Coon's arrest, some guy in a T-shirt, jeans and spiky hair was thrown in the back of the van with her and Vicious. The pretend punk had proceeded to try and pass himself off as one of the audience, but Coon had years of experience dealing with the police through her involvement with Release and soon sniffed him out for what he was.

However, Steve Havoc/Severin says he was standing right beside Vicious at the bar and is as adamant now as he was at the time that Sid was the culprit. Pirroni says he and Severin headed out to the nearest public phone box to call McLaren and give him the news of Vicious' arrest. In shades of Alan Jones's arrest the previous summer, McLaren assured Pirroni he would do everything within his power to secure Vicious' release. Again as with Alan Jones, McLaren did nothing to intervene.

There is no reason as to why McLaren should have thought to involve himself in Vicious' troubles simply because he worked occasionally at SEX. His travails with Vicious lay in the future, of course. Of more immediate concern to McLaren was the 100 Club's decision to ban all punk rock-associated acts sine die. This included the Pistols despite their being some 150 miles away in Cardiff that night.

The mood was even more subdued when The Vibrators arrived onstage. Their story started in the early sixties with frontman, Knox (a.k.a. Ian Carnochan), playing in a band called The Renegades while still at school. Following on from there, Knox formed his own band, Knox and the Nightriders, performing Cliff Richard and the Shadows' numbers. He'd then played with an eclectic mix – including a three-piece called Lipstick and an Irish show band with what he describes as a "strange Nazi transvestite jazz organist" before entering John Ellis's orbit. The Vibrators' bassist, Pat Collier, was also in attendance at the Pistols/Bazooka Joe show, while their drummer John 'Eddie' Edwards was serving as the latter band's roadie.

"The band was started by Eddie in February 1976 and was essentially four friends," Knox explained in a 2002 interview. "It did its first gig supporting the Stranglers at part of Hornsey Art College in March 1976. The band played lots of gigs, and the material was a mixture of pub rock classics – basically so we could get out there and play without a lot of rehearsal – and our own heavier material we were introducing, songs such as 'Whips & Furs', 'Sweet Sweet Heart', 'She's Bringing You Down' etc. which I'd been playing in three bands before The Vibrators – something most people don't know. For me, the thing which really put punk on the map was the 100 Club Punk Rock Festival [when we] backed legendary guitarist Chris Spedding near the end of our set.

"The Vibrators got lots of work through Eddie and Pat driving round to venues and asking if we could play. We had gradually been playing faster as both us and the audience liked it better; and we were then included under the press umbrella term of punk rock with several other bands, as people must have sensed that there was some kind of movement happening."

In an interview in March 1977, Pat Collier said how Spedding was "more or less dragged into it by the scruff of his neck against his will." Indeed, the bassist had never before met Spedding before the 100 Club collaboration. Collier would inadvertently shoot himself in the foot in telling Caroline Coon how The Vibrators didn't "really go along with the punk rock thing" and were only doing so because it was "the fashion".

The Vibrators' punchy R&B was more to the Tuesday night crowd's liking than any of the other acts on the bill – especially as their set is peppered with souped-up sing-along covers such as 'Jumpin' Jack Flash", "Great Balls of Fire" and "Let's Twist Again". Spedding joins them onstage midway through and, unsurprisingly, the first song up is the guitarist's September '75 UK Top 20 hit, "Motor Biking".

It's been written elsewhere that The Vibrators supported the Pistols a month or so before the Punk Festival but John Ellis says this isn't so. "See what I mean about hearsay and inaccurate history? We only played on the same bill as the Pistols and that was at the punk festival. We missed their performance as we had a gig on the first night if I remember correctly. When we got to the 100 Club to do our show on the Tuesday, Spedding strolled up and said, 'I need a band for my show,' which was going to happen in a couple of hours, so we went into the manager's office and learned the material he wanted to do. Our show was very well received by the people who matter - I.e. the punters. I think we played okay. I can't remember much else about it really other than Mick Jones telling me the Vibrators should not have been playing a punk festival when he walked past me in the loo. But I would like to point out that the band they all loved to hate is still touring and making records when nearly all of the rest have disappeared."

For Buzzcocks' second London showing, Howard Devoto has dyed his hair orange and has tacked a homemade patch bearing the Circle-A anarchy symbol. Just as they had at the Screen on the Green they opened with "Breakdown", which will subsequently feature on their groundbreaking January 1977 self-produced EP, *Spiral Scratch*. Their set includes other original numbers such as 'Orgasm Addict', 'Time's Up', 'Oh Shit' and 'Boredom'. Devoto says little between songs, as though he – and indeed, the rest of the band – are overwhelmed by the occasion. They end their set, and the festival as a whole, with their cover of Captain Beefheart's 'I Love You, You Big Dummy'.

—To Many People
Had The Suss

"I had a bunch of riffs I'd written when I was in a band called Bastard. When I played 'New Rose' to Rat, his drumming set it on fire. We signed to Stiff to do a single, and Nick Lowe produced us in a tiny eight-track studio. We spent more time in the pub round the corner than we spent recording, but Nick captured how wild we sounded. We thought we were a fast rock 'n' roll band, but the journalist Caroline Coon coined the term 'punk rock' so suddenly 'New Rose' was 'the first British punk single'"

Brian James

While McLaren continued with his wooing of EMI, The Damned went into Pathway Studios in Newington Green, north London, with Nick Lowe to record "New Rose". There was no immediate rush as far as the band were concerned as they'd yet to iron out the kinks in their live set. Riviera and Robinson, however, were keen to grab the kudos of Stiff releasing the first bona fide punk single in the UK – while also cocking a snook at

Opposite: Nick Lowe captured an amazing sound with The Damned

McLaren and the Pistols. Ironically, it's only because of Steve Jones's four-letter outbursts on *Today* at the start of December 1976, and the subsequent release of 'God Save the Queen' the following spring that cemented punk's standing in the British media. Had McLaren returned from New York with no intention of ever involving himself with a rock 'n' roll band again, London would still have spawned an exciting scene but it would have most likely soon been diluted to the less-threatening "new wave" as it was in the US. And being the band that released the first bona fide new wave single in the UK doesn't have quite the same ring.

Brian James had come up with the incendiary D5/B5/E5/A5/ F#5/G#5/E5 riff to 'New Rose' whilst still with Bastard. "When I played 'New Rose' to Rat his drumming set it on fire," he told *The Guardian* in March 2018. "Nick Lowe produced us in a tiny eight-track studio [and] we spent more time in the pub round the corner than we spent recording, but Nick captured how wild we sounded. We thought we were a fast rock 'n' roll band, but Caroline Coon coined the term 'punk rock' so suddenly 'New Rose' was the 'first British punk single'. Contrary to belief, 'New Rose' isn't a love song. The words were just imagery to go with the riffs. However, some lines did express my excitement about the early punk scene. It was everything I'd ever dreamed of. And there I was in London with everyone going crazy for it."

In a separate interview, James spoke of the pride he felt upon first hearing Nick Lowe's finished mix. "I remember getting the test pressing and thinking, 'It sounds so good. If it all stops now, I'm a happy man. My band sounds great, my song sounds wonderful.' It wasn't until 'New Rose' that I had anything that sounded right."

"I don't think Brian gets enough credit for what an instrumental figure he was in punk," says Scabies. "He was into avant-garde jazz, so was coming from this free-form mentality, but also got the whole thing about three-minute pop songs. He was the first one with short hair and nobody played like him. His philosophy on music was that it should be free, and it should have energy. The relationship with Jake was the turning point. Jake was clued up he knew who the Stooges and MC5 were and just wanted to get on with it. We had a song and studio, so we went and recorded it."

"'New Rose' was a raw, visceral, classic three-minute pop song,"

Back cover of The Damned's debut album
Damned, Damned, Damned and the first Stiff LP

Vanian chimed in. "My famous spoken intro – "Is she really going out with him?" – is from the Shangri-La's 'Leader of the Pack', which I adored. I'd just been clowning around, but everyone liked it, so we kept it. We recorded a whole album – *Damned Damned Damned* – in two days flat. In those days, there was never much food around. We were fuelled by amphetamine sulphate and cider.

"Sometimes the tape would stop, and we'd hear some weird folk thing coming out of the speakers. To save money, it turned out, we were recording over someone else's tape. There were no rules. It was also a celebration of life. If you saw us onstage or in the dressing room, it could be chaos. Most of the wild stories are true and the worst ones have never been told. Roadies tried to imitate us and ended up in hospital or asylums. You'd think, 'My God, how can this band get anything done?' But it was a different story in a studio."

'New Rose' b /w 'Help!' was released October 22, 1976. A promo video was filmed in the basement of the Hope & Anchor in Islington, a short walk from Pathway studios.

Television and The Ramones had already released singles by this juncture, of course, but telling evidence that punk was becoming a global tableau came the same month as the 100 Club Punk Festival, with Australian rockers, The Saints, releasing their debut single 'I'm Stranded' (b/w 'No Time') on their own Fatal Records label. The single was issued in the UK via the short-lived London-based Power Exchange label. When reviewing 'I'm Stranded' for *Sounds,* Jonh Ingham would declare it "Single of this and every week." This would prove sufficient for EMI's head office in Manchester Square to contact the label's offices in Sydney, directing them to initiate negotiations with The Saints. The quartet signed a three-album contract with EMI and relocated to the UK. "I wasn't thinking this was the start of something global because the Saints were in Australia," says Ingham. "The record was just so good that I couldn't stop playing it. I must have driven the rest of the guys in the office because I did literally play it over and over again."

The newspapers of Friday, October 8, 1976, made for particularly grim reading – especially for James Callaghan's ailing Labour government. In a desperate attempt to halt Britain's headlong descent into financial meltdown Denis Healey had gone cap in hand to the IMF (International Monetary Fund) and borrowed its maximum entitlement of $3.9billion (£2.3billion). The headlines that day announced the Bank of England was raising its minimum lending rate from 13 to 15 per cent. Polydor's Chris Parry certainly had a spring in his step, however. Having spent the past few weeks arguing his case, he'd finally succeeded in getting Freddie Hine to agree to sign the Sex Pistols to a £20,000 deal (with an additional £20,000 to be set aside for recording costs and other sundries). Such was Parry's confidence that the deal was as good as inked that he'd booked the Pistols into Polydor's DeLane Lea Studios in Soho to begin working on 'Anarchy in the UK' as their debut single.

Parry's exultation was to prove short-lived, however. When he called McLaren the following day to see how the recording session was going, the latter blithely informed him the deal was off as the Pistols would now be signing with EMI.

McLaren's deciding to favour EMI over Polydor wasn't a monetary one as both companies were more or less offering the same deal. He'd also had to negotiate several hurdles during his negotiations with Nick Mobbs. Mobbs had eventually caved in under Mike Thorne's unrelenting persistence and cut short a trip to Venice to see Paul McCartney's Wings so that he could catch the Pistols play the Outlook Club in Doncaster on September 27. "We took the train up to Doncaster: the Leeds Pullman, very pleasant," says Mike Thorne. "The Pistols played/jammed to about one-quarter capacity at the Outlook Club. The audience reaction varied between wild enthusiasm, tepid applause and irritation at any interrupted lager consumption. But the Pistols did their energetic thing, alternately working and antagonising the crowd. After the show, I took Nick backstage, made brief, formal introductions and agreed to meet back in London the following week. Nick's boss, Bob (Mercer), was very enthusiastic as EMI hadn't had as much fun in years. The reaction to the Pistols within EMI Records was every enthusiastic – in total contrast to the suits higher up who were anxious about their OBEs melting away.

"There were only two record companies seriously interested in the Pistols at the time: us and Polydor. Malcolm played us off against each other brilliantly, ultimately forcing EMI's legal department to sit down uncharacteristically quickly and finalise the contract over a long afternoon. There was, as he pointed out, no earthly reason why contracts should take so long to be formalised, even though they always did. Malcolm made EMI feel as if they were just getting in under the wire ahead of Polydor. The deal was done, and the Pistols' sessions at Lansdowne Studios the following weekend were promptly confirmed.

"Unfortunately, the Lansdowne sessions weren't the Pistols' sessions. They certainly weren't EMI's sessions, either. They were Polydor's sessions. Chris Parry treated me to one of the most outraged phone calls I have ever experienced. Not only had we snatched the Pistols from under his nose, we'd heisted his booked sessions as well."

Despite his having been given approval by his boss, Bob Mercer, to sign the band, Mobbs remained unconvinced as to whether EMI was the right label for the Pistols: whether the band's rough and ready sound would translate onto vinyl. McLaren had simply refused to allow Mobbs' personal tastes to enter into the equation, however.

He'd told the A&R man that if he wasn't prepared to sign a hot new act that was being offered to him on a plate then EMI was living in the past and the label might as well shut up shop. Having succeeded in convincing Mobbs, McLaren refused to leave his office until the contract had been drawn up.

The Pistols' contract was signed, sealed and delivered in a single day making it the fastest-ever signing in EMI's illustrious history to date. The contract was a two-album deal over an initial two-year period with two further one-year options (exercisable only by the label). The group, or rather Glitterbest - as per Clause 17 of the managerial contract - received a £40,000 non-returnable advance, £20,000 of which was paid upon signing with the remaining £20,000 to be paid on the corresponding date in 1977. EMI would also shoulder reasonable recording costs to be recuperated from future royalties. Glitterbest would have record sleeve approval, as well as a say in the choice of producer – which EMI would also pay for. The Pistols had already secured a £10,000 publishing deal with EMI's publishing arm. Although EMI Records and EMI Publishing carried the same company logo, the two companies were entirely separate entities operating from offices located at either end of Oxford Street.

EMI (Electric and Musical Industries) had formed in 1931 following the merger of Britain's oldest record company, the Gramophone Company (His Masters Voice) and the Columbia Graphophone Company. That same year EMI opened its legendary Abbey Road recording studios. Over the ensuing decade, EMI built up a roster of artists such as Arturo Toscanini, Otto Klemperer and Sir Edward Elgar of "Land of Hope and Glory" fame. The label's subsequent acquisition of leading acts of the day such as Cliff Richard, The Beatles and Pink Floyd had seen EMI become the most successful recording company in the world.

EMI had also built up a sizeable portfolio of restaurant, cinema and hotel chains, but as its name suggests, it was also at the cutting edge of electrical technology - notably providing the BBC with its first television transmitter. The company had made significant investment in its radical CAT (Computerised Axial Tomography) brain scanner which would enable doctors to examine the inner workings of the human brain without the need for surgery. It was also developing radar equipment and guided missiles at its Laboratories in Hayes, Middlesex.

The ever-cagey McLaren had kept his charges in the dark over his dealings at Manchester Square. Right up to the eleventh-hour the Pistols had believed they were set to sign with Polydor. Within 24 hours of putting pens to paper, the Pistols went into Lansdowne Studios in Holland Park with Dave Goodman to record 'Anarchy in the UK'. EMI had wanted 'Pretty Vacant' as the debut single, if only because of its being more radio-friendly than 'Anarchy'. Matlock had also thought it the more sensible option, but both he and Mobbs had been shouted down by McLaren and the rest of the band.

Unfortunately for all concerned, over the coming days, Goodman would waste reel after reel of expensive tape trying to emulate Nick Lowe's applications to 'New Rose' to capture the Pistols' live energy on vinyl. The standard process for recording a single took around three weeks, but Goodman's ongoing failure to deliver forced EMI to push back the original November 19 release date. With other EMI acts booked into Lansdowne, the Pistols and Goodman had little option but to relocate to Wessex Studios in Highbury New Park. When the change in venue failed to bring about a reversal in fortunes, Goodman was summoned to Manchester Square to be informed his services were no longer required. (Goodman's version of 'Anarchy In The UK' wouldn't surface until its inclusion on *The Great Rock 'N' Roll Swindle* film soundtrack in March 1979).

"Seeing as the Pistols had played 'Anarchy' so many times onstage and in extreme circumstances and seeing as the song's arrangement seemed absolutely fine to me as it was, I'd assumed that recording the single would be a straightforward process. I was comfortable that Dave Goodman was handling the production process. What I found when I arrived at Lansdowne, however, was lost and directionless, creating nothing but an expensive pile of two-inch tape in the corner. Dave had apparently said to the band that it was great tactics since we could reuse it later. I thought it was rather an expensive way to acquire tape. I would have appreciated a finished stereo recording.

"The aimless drifting continued for several more session days, transferring to Wessex Studios, and then we had to stop. The Pistols were so lost they couldn't get a handle on a three-minute song they could play in their sleep. Malcolm called up a few days afterwards. He said Dave had had his chance and he now had someone else in mind."

The producer McLaren had in mind was Wessex's affiliate

producer, Chris Thomas. Since cutting his teeth working on The Beatles' *White Album* (on which he'd also contributed musically: playing the harpsichord on "Piggies", the Mellotron on "The Continuing Story of Bungalow Bill", and piano on both "Long, Long, Long" and "Savoy Truffle"), the 29-year-old classical violin-trained Thomas had worked with the likes of Procol Harum, John Cale and Pink Floyd. However, it was Thomas's having produced Roxy Music's *For Your Pleasure* that earned him sufficient kudos within the Pistols' camp – notably Jones and Cook.

Malcolm and I turned up at Chris' house in Ealing with the roughs-so-far" says Thorne. "Off we all went to Wessex Studios where Chris listened to the multi-tracks. He agreed to take the job but said he preferred to re-record rather than deal with the story so far. Bill Price, one of London's most established rock 'n' roll engineers and a thoroughly grounded EMI alumnus, was hired. Chris and Bill worked efficiently and relatively quickly, mostly at Wessex but partly at Ramport Studios in Battersea. The sessions went smoothly enough but they weren't completely free of tension. I remember one evening at Ramport when Rotten, in brutal form, was mercilessly torturing *Sounds* journalist Jane Suck. The end result, however, was a more energetic and forceful version of the arrangement the Pistols played live. The only awkward turn was when Chris instigated a curious, jittery, meandering and unfocussed guitar solo to replace the rhythm break after the second chorus. The choppy original was reinserted after my corporate objection.

"The sessions created quite an interest at Manchester Square: why was such a raucous and apparently unpolished group getting such treatment? While we were at Wessex I remember seeing Queen's Brian May standing in the doorway. He was looking very non-punk in his light brown fur coat, but he, like many others, got the plot. There was a considerable groundswell of support for what the Pistols were doing. I was pleased with the finished master. At the weekly A&R presentation meeting I confidently pronounced, 'I'll put my shirt on this one.' The room fell deathly silent, but Nick liked the master. It could have been a real horror show, but he saved me."

"There was an infamous early version of 'Anarchy' that was such a balls-up," says Lydon. "It never got released at the time and thank Christ for that. It put our tails between our legs because we all felt ashamed at just how awful it was. So the next outing to record it, with Chris Thomas, was bang on – you know, 'Get this tight, get this right.' And you could do that with bum notes, it wasn't about that – it's about the timing of the thing."

Indeed, it was. Having won the battle with Rotten to have him enunciate his lyrics, Thomas eradicated a discrepancy with the timing on Cook's snare drum by splicing two backing tracks together. It was also Thomas's idea to create a sonic shutdown by cutting "Anarchy" dead immediately after the "get pissed . . . Destroy" coda, whereas Goodman's four-minute-and-counting version subsided into wave upon wave of meandering feedback.

Goodman would have the last laugh, however. Due to an oversight at EMI, Chris Thomas would be credited as producer on "I Wanna Be Me" (B-side to "Anarchy"). The version that ended up on the single was culled from the Denmark Street demo sessions. Within days of the record's release, Goodman instructed his solicitor to pen a letter to EMI's legal department threatening an injunction on the single whilst also demanding the label send out notices to the media and all other interested parties admitting their error and regretting any embarrassment the oversight had caused. EMI had readily complied with Dave Goodman's instructions and a compromise was reached that after the initial 15,000 pressing with the incorrect labels had been sold, all future copies would carry the correct credits.

While the Pistols were making heavy going of recording their debut single at Lansdowne The Clash emerged from their shadow to play their first headline date at the Institute of Contemporary Arts on October 23. Billed as 'A Night of Pure Energy', the show has gone on to become one of the cornerstones of The Clash legend owing to their uber-fan, 'Mad Jane' Crockford, getting herself into such a frenzy that she supposedly threw herself at future Pogues frontman Shane MacGowan, tearing a chunk from his right earlobe. "We were biting each other's arms until they bled," says MacGowan. "It was a kind of tribal, primaeval, love-hate violence ceremony; extremely painful, but we were getting off on the sadomasochistic ritual. Then she broke a bottle and slashed my ear open, causing loads of blood to splatter all over the place before cutting her wrists. At this stage, the bouncers intervened and dragged her out."

Patti Smith happened to be in the crowd as she was in town playing the Hammersmith Odeon. When Smith jumped up onstage and started gyrating in time to the beat, Simonon came close to swinging a boot at the punk poetess until realising it was she. The bassist was somewhat fortunate to be onstage himself as Bernard Rhodes subsequently revealed: "After the soundcheck at the ICA Paul and I went for a walk to get some air as it was quite mild for October. We hadn't gone far when we came upon something lying by the kerb. It was a roll of pornographic film screens that someone had obviously dumped. Paul, ever the artist, thought he might do something with them back at Rehearsals. We were making our way back to the ICA when a cop car pulled up beside us. The cops must have clocked us and seen Paul stooping to pick up the screens. I remember thinking, 'Oh fucking hell, no, we've got a gig to do and they're gonna nick my bass player.' I didn't even stop to consider I'd have probably ended up in the cells with him.

"The cops eventually let us go but I'd borrowed a friend's car for the night and Paul had left the screens in the car. The next day my friend rings up to say his wife had found the screens and, of course, he'd no idea where the fuck they'd come from. This was the night Paul ended up with Patti Smith. We had a show coming up at Barbarella's in Birmingham, and as Patti was playing up there the following night he went with them. When I saw him about to take a swing at her for jumping onstage I thought well, this'll make going over to New York a bit more interesting."

It was at the ICA show that Stephen 'Roadent' Connelly entered The Clash's domain; his having recently arrived in London from his native Coventry following his release from Winson Green Prison. "I only had a few quid left so I wasn't about to go wasting money on a ticket for the show," says Roadent. "I hung about the stage doors till the band arrived and then approached Joe to see if they needed a hand with the gear. I also didn't have anywhere to live and when Joe heard about it he offered me a mattress at Rehearsals."

Roadent duly moved into the upstairs space at Rehearsals, sharing the basic amenities with Simonon, who was already living there. The two were soon thick as thieves owing to their having the same mischievous nature. Indeed, it was Simonon who would confer Roadent his enduring nickname. He would also receive a new pair of socks courtesy of The Clash kitty. He would also gel with Strummer owing to their shared passion for history and politics. For Jones, however, the ice was never to thaw. "The only one I found it hard to get on within the Clash was Mick . . . But then, didn't everyone?"

A fortnight on from the ICA, The Clash staged their own "Night of Treason" at the Royal College of Art in Kensington Gore on November 5. Instead of fireworks, bottles and glasses were soon flying owing to a section of the crowd proving hostile towards The Clash throughout. When the bully-boy hecklers began taking their grievances towards the band out on the fans, Jones says it was touch and go whether they should abandon the show, or even just retreat to the dressing room until order was restored. However, seeing Sid Vicious come charging in from the wings compelled Strummer and Simonon to down their guitars and dive in to help even up the numbers. Since his release from Ashford Remand Centre, the future Sex Pistol was temporarily bedding down at Rehearsals with Paul and Roadent. On returning to the stage they both angrily demanded to know why Jones as to why he hadn't jumped in with them. "Well, someone's gotta keep in tune . . ." came the reply.

All the leading music weeklies had been keeping tabs on The Clash, of course, but as yet only *Melody Maker* had published an in-depth interview with the band – although by now, Caroline Coon's interest in The Clash was no longer strictly professional owing to her now seeing Paul Simonon. Following the ICA and Royal College of Art shows, the *NME*'s Barry Miles arrived at Rehearsals tape-recorder in hand. Terry Chimes didn't participate in the interview and wasn't even at Rehearsals. Indeed, by the time said interview went to press, The Clash would be on the lookout for another drummer. "I just thought I'm not happy and what's the point of being here if I'm not happy," says Chimes. "I thought Bernie would be happy with my leaving, but surprisingly, he wasn't. He said to me, 'Look, you're the foil. Whenever they (Strummer, Jones and Simonon) come up with something, you say what the man in the street or the press would say. You immediately confront them with the rational argument against what they're saying. If they can get past you, they can get past the world without being shot down in the first minute.'"

Chimes was already tiring of Rhodes' politicking so remained unmoved by his argument. He would, however, agree to honour The Clash's up-and-coming commitments, which included a demo session for Polydor Records at a recording studio in Marble Arch. Having lost out on the Pistols, Chris Parry had realigned his sights accordingly.

Rhodes's choice of producer for the session was none other than Guy Stevens, who would, of course, be at the production console – nominally, at least – for The Clash's breakthrough third album, *London Calling*. (Rhodes was acquainted with Stevens from the latter's running the weekly "R&B Disc Night" at the Scene Club in Ham Yard, Soho, during the early sixties.) For Mick Jones, however, Stevens's appointment was a double-edged sword. On the one hand, Stevens had been pivotal in the Clash guitarist's favourite band Mott the Hoople's formation – not least his bringing in Ian Hunter as frontman. He also came up with their name, having read the Willard Manus novel whilst serving a short term in prison. But the mercurial Stevens had also been instrumental in getting Jones sacked from his first band, Little Queenie.

"Polydor set us up to do some demo recordings and Bernie suggested we try working with Guy," the guitarist revealed. "We went in and banged out four or five numbers which were the first in our live set. I think Guy went to the pub or something and didn't come back, so I don't know how they got finished. I was really excited about going into the studio and it was probably overwhelming. I didn't notice anything that was going on in too much detail because I was just getting carried away with it all."

The five songs in question were 'White Riot', 'London's Burning", 'Career Opportunities', 'Janie Jones' and '1977'. Stevens's going AWOL meant Polydor's in-house engineer had little option but to take over. He'd no real understanding as to who or what The Clash were, and his insistence that Strummer enunciate every syllable left the band somewhat jaded with the results.

'Anarchy In The UK' b/w 'I Wanna Be Me' was released in the UK on November 26, 1976. Though picture sleeves would become synonymous with punk, the first 2,000 copies of the Pistols' debut were issued in a simple shiny black bag accompanied by one of Jamie Reid's now-iconic torn Anarchy flag posters. EMI had signed the Pistols, but their intention was to release the single on their subsidiary Harvest label (established in 1969 to cater for bands in the emerging progressive rock genre such as Pink Floyd). McLaren refused to countenance the idea. The Pistols were an EMI act and it was going to have EMI on the label. The label's marketing department was now expected to comply with McLaren's demand to do away with

The single that started it all: Anarchy in the UK on the original EMI record label

what he considered the usual clichéd promotional packaging. When questioned as to how anybody was supposed to find a single hidden away in a nondescript black bag, McLaren retorted that he didn't want "anybody" to find the record; he only wanted the "somebodies" to go into their local record store and ask for the single by name.

"What we had to do was find a way of focusing our anger to make a definitive statement of what the Sex Pistols were about," says Steve Jones in *Lonely Boy: Tales From a Sex Pistol*. "Signing to EMI – the most old-fashioned and best established of all British record labels – and releasing 'Anarchy in the UK' as a single would be back-of-the-fucking-net as far as that was concerned."

While one can understand Caroline Coon's need to give the London scene an identity, by categorizing what was happening as "punk" she unwittingly diminished its potency. Whereas record shops would have been stumped as to what to do with the Pistols' single, they could now lump the record in with 'New Rose', 'Blitzkrieg Bop', 'Little Johnny Jewel', 'Hey Joe' and 'I'm Stranded'. Having one of their acquisitions wilfully defacing of the Union Jack flag would have undoubtedly ruffled the well-heeled feathers up in the rarified air of EMI's corporate boardroom. It's highly doubtful the company's new chairman, Sir John Read, and its board of directors – which included Conservative Shadow Chancellor of the Exchequer Geoffrey Howe and former Attorney General Lord Shawcross, who'd served as Britain's chief prosecutor at the Nuremberg military tribunal - would have looked favourably on those of its staff within EMI Records that were party to the poster. After all, the wreaths commemorating the country's dead in both world wars were still on display at the Whitehall Cenotaph. Those EMI staffers who were complicit in the poster idea thought they could disassociate themselves by claiming ignorance. Yet a version of Reid's poster did feature EMI circular logo and the record's catalogue number.

Unsurprisingly, Caroline Coon declared "Anarchy in the UK" Melody Maker's 'Single of the Week'. *Sounds'* Alan Lewis was equally fulsome in his praise yet felt honour-bound to point out that 'Anarchy' was the "same old rock 'n' roll . . . only younger and more intense then we've heard it for a long while." The NME's Cliff White, who might normally be found reviewing the R&B and soul releases, dismissed the Pistols' debut as "lousy". He was also astute enough to recognise that by releasing a single, the Pistols had been assimilated into the system.

The tried-and-tested means of promoting a new single or album was to send the act in question out on a national tour. McLaren started plotting the Anarchy in the UK Tour while the Pistols were at Lansdowne Studios. This was to be no commonplace run-of-the-mill tour, however, because the Pistols were the leaders of what the music press, at least, were hailing as the most exciting scene to come out of London since the sixties' pendulum stopped swinging. McLaren hadn't had much involvement with the Pistols' touring itinerary since handing the day-to-day reins to Nils Stevenson back in late-February, he was astute enough to recognise that while the Pistols enjoyed sizeable followings in London, Manchester and Birmingham they were still relative unknowns elsewhere in the country. Though Stevenson had quit in a fit of pique the day of the EMI signing over McLaren's reneging on his supposed promise of a co-management arrangement and was now managing Siouxsie and the Banshees, he'd agreed to a brief return to duties on the impending tour.

Tipping his hat to his impresario hero, Larry Parnes, McLaren had elected to put a punk package tour together akin to those made popular in the late fifties and early sixties. The problem facing McLaren, of course, was finding the bands to constitute a bill worthy of filling venues outside of the major cities. Hitting on the idea of a Sex Pistols/Ramones co-headline tour, he invited Talking Heads to shore up the bill alongside The Vibrators (reportedly with Chris Spedding). By the time Sounds' leader hit the newsstands, however, all three bands had withdrawn from the tour. The two New York acts would, rather disingenuously it has to be said, subsequently inform the *NME* their decision to pull out of the tour stemmed from their being "allowed sufficient time to arrange promotion". Danny Fields went so far as to say The Ramones were considering their own headline tour that would be "better organised".

"To be honest, I can no longer remember why we pulled out of the Anarchy tour," says John Ellis. "It might well have been that we were trying to establish ourselves as independent of the punk scene, which we saw as having a very restrictive view of music-making. We might also have been acting on the advice of our management."

Since playing the two London dates in July, The Ramones had played a string of West Coast dates and were slowly but surely establishing themselves betwixt the US seaboards. Around the time of McLaren's co-headline proposition, they were set to play a four-night residency at Atlanta's Electric Ballroom. According to Sharon

Powell, who was one of the managers at the Great SouthEast Music Hall where the Pistols would open their ill-fated January 1978 tour, says the Electric Ballroom had a capacity of around 800. "The Electric Ballroom was located within the Grand Ballroom of the Georgian Terrace Hotel on Peachtree Street. It was hugely important to the Atlanta scene at the time because it was where you played after you outgrew the [Great SouthEast Music] Hall, but before you made it to the larger venues as an artist."

McLaren was still keen to add a dash of Lower East Side allure to the tour, however, and after several late-night transatlantic calls, The Heartbreakers were slotted onto the bill. Thunders and Nolan were still basking in their ex-New York Doll *cause célebre* status, but Sire and the other US-based labels were keeping The Heartbreakers at arm's length because of their offstage proclivities. Indeed, the band themselves playfully hinted at their self-destructive nature by posting the gig flyer: The Heartbreakers: Catch them while they're still alive. "I never went into managing the Heartbreakers thinking I was ever going to get them to change their ways," their put-upon manager, Leee Black Childers, told the author back in 2011. "I lost count of the times I would have to put a bucket by Johnny's amp so that he could throw up between songs. Johnny always said that he could rock out just as good when he wasn't high. That was true, of course, but in the early days, it was most definitely the exception rather than the rule.

"Malcolm called me from London and asked, 'Do you want to tour England with my group the Sex Pistols?' At the time I'd never heard of the Sex Pistols, but I said I would call him back after speaking with Johnny. I asked Johnny if he wanted to go on tour in England with the Sex Pistols. Johnny had never heard of them either, but, of course, he remembered Malcolm. He said something like, 'He was the weird guy who looked after the Dolls for a couple of months and made us dress like Commies. But then he thought about things for a minute and said, 'It could be fun. And it's a trip to England. Let's go.' So we did. We arrived on the night of the Bill Grundy show. Nils and Sophie met us at the airport. Nils was in one of those big, fluffy Vivienne Westwood sweaters and he had a cute pixie haircut. I thought he was Sophie, so I said, 'Hello, you must be Sophie.' That went down really well with Nils, I can tell you."

McLaren still needed a 'named' act with the bona fide punk

credentials to ensure putting enough bums on seats to ensure the tour at least broke even. EMI's contract didn't cover tour expenses and any losses the tour incurred would come out of the Pistols' £20,000 advance. There was, of course, only one band that met the criteria – The Damned. It wasn't that McLaren had anything against the band. After all, he'd put his hand in his pocket to pay for the nascent Damned to rehearse with Chrissie Hynde. His antipathy was aimed at Jake Riviera who was now also managing The Damned. McLaren viewed Riviera as little more than an irksome irritation, while Riviera was openly dismissing McLaren as a "second-rate haberdasher". The warring parties would, however, agree to a temporary cessation of hostilities for the greater good.

What's surprising, given McLaren had re-established a working relationship of sorts with Bernard Rhodes, is his overlooking The Clash in favour of inviting The Vibrators onto The Ramones co-headline tour. The Clash were now forging their own furrow, of course, but they had nonetheless agreed to support the Pistols at Coventry's Lanchester Polytechnic on November 29. McLaren still couldn't resist having a dig at Rhodes by having The Clash billed as "Special Guests" yet placing them bottom of the bill on the tour's revised itinerary.

"Malcolm couldn't stand the fact that I'd put another group together," says Rhodes. "Forget what you've read elsewhere, because that was the real reason why he put the Clash at the bottom of the bill on the Anarchy Tour. And while everyone might have been talking about punk following the Bill Grundy thing, we still had to open the shows on that tour – and opening a show is difficult enough without the world watching you."

"Ironically, my first gig working for the Clash came at the 'Lanch' in my hometown of Coventry when they supported the Pistols," says Roadent. "It was a good gig, with both bands putting in good, solid performances. After the show, however, the polytechnic's Student Union held an emergency meeting where they decided to refuse payment to either group because they thought 'White Riot' and 'God Save the Queen' – or 'No Future' as it was called at the time – were both fascist songs."

The finalized tour itinerary consisted of 19 dates, commencing with Norwich's University of East Anglia on December 3, and taking in major cities such as Newcastle, Leeds, Manchester, Liverpool,

Sheffield, Glasgow as well as off-the-beaten-track venues such as the Bournemouth Village Bowl and Torquay's 400 Ballroom, culminating in a triumphant homecoming show at the Roxy Theatre in Harlesden on Boxing Day.

Another means of garnering more interest at some of the larger venues, of course, would have been to invite local punk-enthused acts onto the bill: Buzzcocks (Manchester), Suburban Studs (Birmingham), Penetration (Newcastle), The Jam (Guildford), The Jolt (Glasgow) etc.

McLaren was back at the flat dotting the i's and crossing the t's on the tour itinerary when EMI plugger, Eric "Monster" Hall, called to say he'd secured the Pistols a slot on that evening's edition of Thames TV's weekday news magazine show, Today. Hall had just come off the phone with Today's producer, Michael Housego. It seemed the promo video to Queen's latest single, "Somebody to Love", hadn't been cleared for broadcast by the Musicians' Union and therefore couldn't be screened on the show as intended. Upon being told that it would prove difficult to line up another EMI act at such short notice, Housego enquired about the Pistols. Another version of events has it that Queen were supposed to appear on Today in person but had had to withdraw at the eleventh hour owing to singer Freddie Mercury either suffering from toothache or was actually at the dentist. Fate, it seemed, was again determining the Pistols' path. If whoever was responsible for getting the clearance for the Queen video - or had Mercury's toothache held off another day - the Pistols would have undertaken the tour and continued to remain an EMI act – most likely seeing out the original two-year contract. For regardless of McLaren's or Rotten's future protestations, there was little likelihood of EMI sanctioning the release of "God Save the Queen" in the Queen's Silver Jubilee year – or indeed any other year.

The Pistols were busy rehearsing for the tour alongside The Clash and The Damned at the Roxy Theatre in Harlesden, and McLaren was initially reluctant to interrupt for what was just another regional TV appearance. The Pistols had featured in LWT's London Weekend Show, which had aired the previous Sunday lunchtime. The show's host, Janet Street-Porter, had interviewed the band at Denmark Street and she and her crew had also filmed a recent gig at the Notre Dame Hall, a Catholic-run basement venue on Leicester Place, just off Leicester Square, for inclusion in Street-Porter's 'punk special'. Earlier in the month, the Pistols had mimed along to "Anarchy in the UK" on *Nationwide*, BBC's long-running current affairs show.

Hall launched into his spiel about how the Pistols could plug the tour alongside a 30-second clip of Mike Mansfield's 'Anarchy' promo video. Sensing McLaren wasn't about to waver, Hall played his trump card by saying how EMI held a 50 per cent share in Thames Television. McLaren finally acquiesced, but only on the proviso that EMI provided a company limo to ferry the Pistols to Thames Studios on Marylebone Road and return them to Harlesden afterwards. There was always an ulterior motive with McLaren, of course. Once the Pistols had been dropped off at the studios, the limo could then head over to Heathrow to pick up The Heartbreakers and their entourage and deliver them to the Roxy Theatre.

On being escorted through to Thames' Green Room, the Pistols were bemused to find Siouxsie Sioux Ballion, Steve Severin and their fellow Bromley Contingent regulars, Simon Barker and Simone Thomas. Before setting off to the studio Malcolm had called the shop and cajoled into rounding up whoever might be available to serve as a human backdrop while the Pistols were on air. "Simon got a call from Malcolm who said he'd pay our train fares if we went along to hang out and stand in the background," Siouxsie later reflected. "We were shown into the Green Room where everything is free, so we started drinking immediately. Everyone, the group and us, were all getting completely pissed. Bill Grundy came in to see us and even then I was winding him up. He kept on leering at me."

Matlock says that by the time the Pistols arrived Siouxsie and her friends had all but laid waste to the complimentary fare. He remembers getting his hands on a lukewarm can of lager. John and Paul were equally shortchanged, but Steve managed to grab himself a bottle of Blue Nun wine.

Michael Housego had been forewarned by Hall that EMI's latest acquisitions were courting publicity to promote their debut single by any means necessary and that Grundy should, therefore, be extra careful in handling the Pistols. Housego took Hall's warning onboard but believed an old pro such as Grundy would know how to handle a rock band. And what could possibly go wrong in three minutes?

Today was in its eighth year and was broadcast Monday – to Friday between 6 – 6:30 p.m. Even if any of the band were aware of *Today*, there was no way they could have possibly known the show went out live. The 52-year-old Grundy had spent most of the afternoon enjoying an extended liquid lunch with his pals from *Punch* magazine so was in his cups come showtime. He was known to be antagonistic on occasion, but he was in a particularly foul mood that day as he felt it beneath him having to interview a band he'd never heard of.

"If you were to ask me about Mozart or Beethoven or Haydn, I think you might get an intelligent answer," Grundy said in *The Wicked ways of Malcolm McLaren*. "I didn't know anything about pop music and when I saw 'Bill and the Sex Pistols' (listed on that day's running order) that was the first: I didn't know what the Sex Pistols was, is or were. I thought that all I was going to do was introduce yet another ghastly pop group and – end of programme."

As a result of Grundy's truculence, the battle lines were drawn more or less from the moment the autocue sprang into life – especially as Jones began playfully reading out Grundy's lines in an attempt to throw him off-kilter. Grundy simply ignored Jones and launched into his pre-prepared spiel about "punk rock being the latest craze" before informing the viewing audience the Pistols were as 'drunk' as himself. The screen then cut to Mike Mansfield's 'Anarchy' promo. Once the camera was back on Grundy he looked to score points by suggesting the £40,000 EMI advance should have been contrary to the Pistols' supposedly anti-materialistic view of life. The question was aimed at the band as a whole, but Matlock was the only one showing much interest at this stage. His chirpy "no, the more the merrier" retort merely antagonised Grundy all the more. And it was while Grundy was pressing Matlock about the advance that Jones blurted out "We've fuckin' spent it, ain't we?".

This should have been the cue for Housego to step in and have Grundy apologise to the viewers and warn the band the show was being broadcast live. Instead, the interview continued unabated. Grundy was either so full of himself or too pissed to care but he purposely had Rotten repeat the word "shit". Had he the presence of mind, Grundy might have realised he'd gained the upper hand as Rotten visibly reddened on camera. Instead of acknowledging his victory with a knowing smile and steering the subject back onto the forthcoming tour, Grundy turned his lecherous eye towards Siouxsie who coyly responded by saying how she'd always wanted to meet him. Siouxsie's comment was meant tongue-in-cheek given that she was a svelte 21-year-old and Grundy was overweight and the wrong side of 50, but it nonetheless provided the latter with another gilt-edged opportunity. All he'd have needed to do was make a suggestive face to the camera and bring the interview to a close. Instead, he embarrassingly suggested he and Siouxsie should meet up after the show. With the Blue Nun having kicked in by this point, Jones called it as he saw it and let rip by calling Grundy a "dirty old sod" and a "dirty old man". It's also worth pointing out that Jones was wearing a SEX Tits T-shirt throughout the interview. Jordan's swastika armband had proved too much for the *So it Goes* production crew, but a T-shirt bearing a pair of breasts was deemed by Thames as being acceptable for prime-time family viewing.

Grundy, who died in February 1993, must have surely spent the remainder of his life ruminating over what possessed him to utter those fateful 16 words that made the Sex Pistols a household name overnight whilst sending his career into a tailspin from which it would never recover: "Well, keep going chief, keep going. Go on, you've got another five seconds. Say something outrageous."

Grundy's actions were both irresponsible and reprehensible, and unfortunately for him, he'd said them to the one Sex Pistol who was indeed as drunk as himself. Hearing Jones call Grundy a "dirty bastard" should have had Housego reaching for the plug, and yet Grundy was allowed to push the envelope further. Jones duly obliged by calling Grundy a "dirty fucker" and a "fucking rotter". (The term "Rotter" – a beastly, despicable character' - had long-since disappeared from the English vernacular but had recently resurfaced in a TV ad campaign for Cadbury's Schweppes tonic water which carried the tagline "You can always tell a rotter by his Schweppes.")

It was surely a measure of Grundy's conceited arrogance that he turned to the camera to tell the viewers he'd "be seeing them soon", but inwardly he must have known he'd overstepped the mark. Indeed, he can be seen mouthing the words "oh shit" as the credits roll. For his "willful goading" of the Pistols, he received a two-week suspension.

This wasn't the first instance where someone had said 'fuck' on live TV. That dubious honour went to McLaren's friend, the controversial film and theatre critic, Kenneth Tynan, who'd dared to utter the dreaded "F-word" during a live debate on the subject of censorship on the late-night weekend satirical show BBC-3 in 1965.

Steve's tossing it into the usually sedate domain of tea-time telly with such carefree abandon had the Thames switchboard lighting up like the Oxford Street Christmas lights. 47-year-old lorry driver, James Holmes, was so incensed that he put his boot through his TV set.

"We knew we'd been a bit naughty, but we hadn't fully twigged that it had gone out live until we went back and all the phones started ringing in the Green Room," Jones recalled in *Lonely Boy*. "All these angry members of the public were calling in to say how outraged they were. Me and Siouxsie were answering the phones and telling them all to piss off, which didn't do anything to calm them down."

Thames issued an immediate on-air apology – and continued doing so for the remainder of the evening – expressing its regret over the interview and to apologise for the foul language. Though Thames suspended Grundy with immediate effect, the damage to *Today*'s esteem was to prove irreparable and the show was cancelled early into 1977. In a 2008 poll conducted by Fremantle Media (Thames TV's parent company), the Pistols' *Today* interview was voted the most requested TV clip ever.

McLaren would subsequently wax lyrical about how the Pistols' appearance on *Today* had been "history in the making". This was long after the event, however. At the time he was gripped with panic and feared it was the end of the band. In hindsight, of course, McLaren's fears proved somewhat prescient for the Grundy debacle did indeed bring about the end of the Sex Pistols as a creative musical force. "Malcolm totally shit himself in the studio," Lydon revealed in *Anger is an Energy*. "He said, 'I overheard they're going to call the police. Quick, everybody run!' I've always known Malcolm to be a back-down coward; he'd never meet that final hurdle. And maybe that's because his ambitions were different."

There would be mixed reactions at Manchester Square. EMI's marketing head, Mark Rye, was said to be doing cartwheels around the office. To his mind, there was no such thing as bad publicity, and if handled correctly sales of 'Anarchy' would go through the roof. EMI Records Group Repertoire Division's general manager, Paul Watts, saw things very differently, however. EMI Records might have contributed the lion's share of EMI's profits, but it was nonetheless housed within a huge corporate machine and

the sale of a few thousand extra copies of a pop record paled into insignificance against safeguarding the corporation's reputation.

Mike Thorne hadn't seen the *Today* interview so was blithely unaware of the headache awaiting him when he arrived for work the following morning. "Everything was going smoothly and I'd arranged with the Pistols to meet one morning to discuss the next single. I'd already booked the following Saturday afternoon to work with them on demos of candidates for the next single at Manchester Square. There were always a few star-spotters hanging around outside, but I was dimly aware of having to sidestep more wide-eyed humanity than usual that morning. I'd barely had time to make a cup of tea when faces appeared in the door of my poky little office. 'Did you see what happened on TV last night? 'No.' 'Have you seen today's papers? 'No.'

As far as Fleet Street was concerned Christmas had come around early. Instead of worrying about coming up with new angles to lambaste James Callaghan's beleaguered government, tabloids and broadsheets alike declared open season on the Pistols. The *Evening Standard* declared the Pistols "Foul-Mouthed Yobs", while the *Daily Express* posed: "Punk? Call It Filthy Lucre". The *Daily Mail* threw its hat into the ring with "Four-Letter Punk Group in TV Storm", but by far and away the most eye-catching – and ultimately, most enduring – couplet was the *Daily Mirror*'s "The Filth and the Fury". EMI Records managing director, Leslie Hill, would also find himself in Fleet Street's crosshairs. Despite his having had no personal involvement in EMI's procurement of the Pistols, he suffered the indignation of having the *Daily Mail* descend on his home in Gerrard's Cross and canvass his neighbours.

Reflecting on the incident that instantly elevated the Pistols from the music weeklies to the front pages, Jones said how the Pistols had been on the "normal progression" one might expect of an upwardly mobile band. "We'd just made a great record, people were showing up to see us and getting converted, there was a real scene. Getting recognised for what we did by the music press was fun and it was something we could cope with. But then overnight we were on everyone's fucking breakfast table and the *Sun* and the *News of the World* were door-stepping us in Denmark Street."

The repercussions were far-reaching. The workers (predominantly female) at EMI's pressing plant in Hayes, Middlesex, had gone out on strike and were refusing to handle the Pistols' single. The publicity surrounding the incident was enough to propel 'Anarchy in the UK' into the UK Top 40 (#38). However, with Woolworth's, WH Smiths and Boots had long-since gone public in their denouncement of the Pistols by refusing to stock the single, the strike at the Hayes pressing plant delayed stock reaching the independent record stores still willing to sell the single, which in effect stymied any hope of the single advancing any higher on the chart.

London's Capital Radio, Manchester's Piccadilly Radio, Birmingham's BRMB and Sheffield's Radio Hallam all pulled single from their play-list, Indeed, Radio One's John Peel was a rare voice in the wilderness in his support of the Pistols: "I was frankly appalled because if you took any four or five lads off the street, made them feel important, filled them with beer, put them on television and said, 'Say something outrageous', they'd say something outrageous. I rather suspect that – as a middle-class individual of 38 – if they did the same to me, I'd do the same. So for those people then to wring their hands in horror and say 'This is outrageous', is just bare-faced hypocrisy."

Tony Prince's bosses at Radio Luxembourg admonished him with a one-night suspension for having dared to offer the Pistols an on-air invitation to perform live on his show.

The Anarchy in the UK Tour

Dec 3 . . . . .Norwich East Anglia University . . . . . Cancelled
Dec 4 . . . . . Derby Kings Hall . . . . Cancelled
Dec 5 . . . . . Newcastle City Hall . . . . Cancelled
Dec 6 . . . . .Leeds Polytechnic . . . . Played
Dec 7 . . . . .Bournemouth Village Bowl . . . . Cancelled
Dec 9 . . . . Manchester Electric Circus . . . . Played
Dec 10 . . . . Lancaster University . . . . Cancelled
Dec 11 . . . . Liverpool Stadium . . . . Cancelled
Dec 13 . . . . Bristol Colston Hall . . . . Cancelled
Dec 14 . . . . Cardiff Top Rank . . . . Cancelled
Dec 15 . . . . Glasgow Apollo . . . . Cancelled
Dec 16 . . . . Dundee Caird Hall . . . . Cancelled
Dec 17 . . . . Sheffield City Hall . . . . Cancelled
Dec 18 . . . . Southend Kursaal . . . . Cancelled
Dec 19 . . . . Guildford Civic Hall . . . . Cancelled
Dec 20 . . . . Birmingham Town Hall . . . . Cancelled
Dec 21 . . . .Plymouth Woods Centre . . . . Played
Dec 22 . . . . Torquay 400 Ballroom . . . . Cancelled
Dec 26 . . . . London Roxy Theatre . . . . Cancelled

ANARCHY IN THE U.K. TOUR

SEX PISTOLS

FIRST MAJOR U.K. TOUR WITH SPECIAL GUESTS THE DAMNED

JOHNNY THUNDER'S HEARTBREAKERS

(Ex New York Dolls from USA)

THE CLASH

TOUR DATES

Tickets From

Date	Venue	Tickets From
FRI 3 DEC	NORWICH University	Students Union, U.E.A.
SAT 4 DEC	DERBY Kings Hall	Kings Hall, Derby
		R.E. Cords, Derby, Burton
		Nottingham Record Centre
SUN 5 DEC	NEWCASTLE City Hall	City Hall
MON 6 DEC	LEEDS Polytechnic	Village Bowl
TUE 7 DEC	BOURNEMOUTH Village Bowl	Students Union, Leeds P
		Hime & Adamson, Manc
THU 9 DEC	MANCHESTER Electric Circus	Virgin Records, Manchester
FRI 10 DEC	LANCASTER University	Students Union, Lancas
SAT 11 DEC	LIVERPOOL Stadium	Virgin Records
MON 13 DEC	BRISTOL Colston Hall	Top Rank, Cardiff
TUE 14 DEC	CARDIFF Top Rank	Buffalo Records
		Colston Hall
WED 15 DEC	GLASGOW Apollo	Apollo, Glasgow
THU 16 DEC	DUNDEE Caird Hall	Caird Hall
		Students Union, Techno
FRI 17 DEC	SHEFFIELD City Hall	City Hall — Wilson Pec
SAT 18 DEC	SOUTHEND Kursaal	Usual Agents
SUN 19 DEC	GUILDFORD Civic Hall	Usual Agents
MON 20 DEC	BIRMINGHAM Town Hall	Town Hall
TUE 21 DEC	PLYMOUTH Woods Centre	Virgin Records
		Woods Centre
WED 22 DEC	TORQUAY 400 Ballroom	400 Club
SUN 26 DEC	LONDON Roxy Theatre Harlesden	Roxy Theatre

SINGLES AVAILABLE

THE DAMNED. NEW ROSE HELP (BUY 6)
Available from even your dumbest dealer

SEX PISTOLS. ANARCHY IN THE U.K. (EMI 2566)
Available from your cleverest!

TOUR PRESENTED BY
ENDALE ASSOCIATES
IN ARRANGEMENT WITH
MALCOLM MACLAREN

—We're On A Road To Nowhere

"It was totally surreal. Before I went down for breakfast each morning I'd pull out my tour poster and cross out the name of whichever venue had cancelled and write in the substitute venue. But by lunch, I'd have scribbled that one out and replaced it with another. And then we'd hang around in the hotel waiting to see what happened next"

Roadent

G iven that only three of the original dates would proceed as scheduled, the Anarchy Tour of December 1976 surely ranks as the rock 'n' roll tour that never was. It's only in hindsight that the tour has come to attain such significance, of course, as at the time the Pistols, Clash and Heartbreakers – and for a time, The Damned – found traversing the country hoping they'd be allowed to play anything but momentous. Not since the days of Larry Parnes' early-to-mid-sixties roster roustabouts had a touring line-up been bursting with so much emerging talent, but the knee-jerk reaction to the Pistols' appearance on *Today* ruined any hopes McLaren may have been harbouring to emulate his Tin Pan Alley hero. The Pistols and The Damned were now both signed acts and had released their respective debut singles, but before the bruhaha surrounding Steve Jones's going toe-to-toe with Bill Grundy punk rock was viewed by the mainstream media as being little more than an insular fancy dress fraternity with accredited affiliations in Manchester and Birmingham. Now, however, it was a flourishing youth movement. As with the seat-slashing Teddy boys of the late-fifties, and the beach-brawling mods and rockers of the mid-sixties, punk had its own music and mode of dress. McLaren had positioned himself so that he'd cash in on the chaos by outfitting the latest teenage craze, but with venues cancelling on a near-daily basis he would be the one left out of pocket – if only because both The Clash and The Heartbreakers were being funded from the Pistols' EMI advance.

The Damned would be travelling separately from the other bands as McLaren had insisted Stiff cover their act's on-the-road costs. "Being signed to Stiff," Captain Sensible bemoaned, "meant that if the latest Elvis Costello record didn't sell, then the next Ian Dury record didn't get made. It was very cramped in the back of that tour van and it constantly smelled of sweat and stale farts. And there was very little in the way of luxuries."

The opening tour date in Norwich was one of the first to fall so the Pistols tour party headed straight for Derby. They arrived at their hotel (Derby Crest) to find the lobby teeming with journalists. McLaren was in no mood to pander to the press, however and ordered everyone to their rooms. It initially appeared that the show at derby's Kings Hall would go ahead but sometime on Friday afternoon, the local Leisure Committee insisted on the proviso that the Pistols first consented to perform a private matinee show in front of the committee to determine whether the band's stage act was suitable. McLaren initially complied with the request only to have a change of heart after securing a promise from Manchester Square that EMI would pick up the tab for two nights stay at the Derby Crest. He even went as far instructing Goodman to arrange for the Pistols' equipment to be set up on the Kings Hall stage.

"I have vivid memories of Derby," says Mike Thorne. "It was an unseasonably warm Saturday afternoon and the Kings Hall was empty except for the local promoter, Dave Cork, who was watching his business disintegrating around him. Then, back the hotel, I was huddled in a tiny room with Malcolm and the Pistols with the press banging on the door and the phone ringing off the hook. Increasingly large cash offers were being made but Malcolm refused each one in turn."

The Clash and The Heartbreakers closed ranks behind the Pistols, but The Damned, of course, were holed up in a b&b and therefore unable to keep pace with the unfolding developments. They were still under the impression the Pistols would be performing for the Leisure Committee. When asked by the local media for his thoughts, the band's tour manager, Rick Rogers, issued a statement saying there was nothing offensive about The Damned' stage act and they'd be happy to play the Kings Hall.

With Sunday night's show at Newcastle's City Hall having also fallen by the wayside, the tour party headed for Leeds. Once again, they arrived at their hotel (The Dragonara) to be met by another Fleet Street welcoming committee. Having stuck two fingers up at Derby Council's attempt at censorship, McLaren held an impromptu press conference in the hotel's foyer where he gleefully informed the gathering the highlight of the following night's show would be the Pistols' 'No Future' with its opening couplet "God bless the Queen and her fascist regime".

McLaren had again confined the tour party to their rooms, but Jones and Cook willfully disregarded his instructions by sneaking down to the bar. A hack from the *Daily Mirror* cajoled the pair to throw a few potted plants around – having first handed the manager £25 to turn a blind eye. The *Mirror*'s Monday morning edition screamed: "Punk Rock Group Wreck Hotel", but banner headlines about uprooted plants and soiled carpets were the least of McLaren's worries, as more and more dates tumbled.

The Leeds Polytechnic show was set to proceed as scheduled, however, and before heading over to the venue McLaren gave an interview to a Yorkshire Television news crew while the band sat looking suitably bored in the background. Upon being asked about the Pistols being regarded the "most revolting band in the country", McLaren launched into an oratory about how the Pistols were creating a generation gap in Britain for the first time in a generation.

Three days later than scripted, The Clash got the Anarchy Tour underway but the adverse publicity surrounding the Pistols meant they were on a hiding to nothing. The Heartbreakers would at least get the antagonistic crowd rocking with their Lower East Side shuffle, but The Damned would be largely met with indifference. While they were out onstage, Rick Rogers was pleading his charges' case over the confusion arising in Derby. His petitions fell on deaf ears, however, as McLaren had been angling for an excuse to expunge The Damned from the tour before leaving London.

The Pistols were never going to live up to the hype that was now enveloping them. When dedicating 'Anarchy in the UK' to "the Leeds council, Bill Grundy and The Queen" failed to ignite the crowd, the Pistols settled into playing by rote. "Although permission had been debated at length in the mayoral chambers, the Leeds gig was given the go-ahead and was to prove a resounding success," says Mike Thorne. "I vaguely remember the Pistols' performance, but, ironically, it was the Damned who were the standouts on the night. The day before the show I called EMI's general manager, Paul Watts, to bring him up-to-speed on the situation. I also suggested it would be good for morale - and a thoughtful gesture by the company - if we picked up the tab for a nice relaxing dinner at the Dragonara.

"There had been an incident earlier where Steve and Paul had naively consented to smash a plant-pot for a gentleman of the press, but we succeeded in avoiding the flashpoint that would give the hacks another shock/horror opportunity. As luck would have it, several guys were sitting at another table that happened to be local councillors. The mood around the table was upbeat and positive to start with. Malcolm and I were called upon to implore everyone to hold it down occasionally - especially when the odd bread roll was lobbed towards the councillors as the press were still there in force, of course. The bill came to something like £300, which was a lot of money at the time, but it was money well spent nonetheless."

EMI were set to hold their Annual General Meeting (AGM) the day after the Leeds Polytechnic show. While the corporation's corporate arm may have been looking to distance themselves from the Sex Pistols, its Music Division was still very much behind the band. At the AGM Leslie Hill gave his brief, which outlined plans for the Pistols to go into the studio at the earliest opportunity with Mike Thorne to record their follow-up single which was scheduled for release in either late-January or early February 1977, with an album to follow in March or April. He also attached sales figures for "Anarchy in the UK" - the single having sold some 9,000 copies to date - in the hope the figures might help sway any decision on EMI's future relationship with the band.

To his credit, Sir John Read began his address by saying he wasn't looking to lead a witch hunt against the Sex Pistols, but as chairman, he believed it was his role to safeguard EMI's interests as well as protect its share price on the financial market. In other words, he wasn't about to allow the antics of what he saw as a smutty pop group besmirch the corporation's reputation. EMI would do everything within its power to restrain the Pistols' public behaviour but Read readily admitted this was an area in which the corporation had no real control. Though he made no mention of terminating the Pistols' two-month-old contract, neither did he confirm the label would be standing by the band. For those who knew how to read between the lines, however, Read's ambiguous comment as to whether EMI would release any more Sex Pistols records left little doubt the band's days at EMI were numbered.

Mike Thorne, however, says he hadn't stopped to consider whether Emi would drop the Pistols and once he'd returned to Manchester Square after the Leeds show he'd continued working on marketing "Pretty Vacant" as the Pistols' follow-up single. He also remains convinced that EMI would have released "God Save the Queen" in the run-up to the Silver Jubilee celebrations.

"If I didn't believe there was any chance of releasing 'God Save the Queen', or 'No Future' as it was still at the time, I wouldn't have bothered recording a demo of the song when we brought the band into Manchester Square during one of the forced breaks in the (Anarchy) tour."

This was the December 11 recording session where Thorne made his surreptitious approach to Matlock to let him know that while everyone within EMI Records was hoping he and Rotten could sort out their differences, should this prove insurmountable then EMI would be happy to listen to whatever solo plans he might be fostering. "I didn't see anything untoward in what I did and I wouldn't have cared if John, Malcolm or anyone else found out about it," he explained. "After all, Glen was the real talent in the Pistols and everyone at EMI liked him as a person. I maintained a good personal relationship with Glen throughout the whole contract termination fiasco and after he left the Pistols. As he'd recently bought a car I accompanied him up to Glasgow to sound out Midge Ure about joining the Rich Kids."

The Pistols arrived in Manchester the day before their date at the Electric Circus to learn that, despite repeated assurances from Leslie Hill, EMI was withdrawing tour support. McLaren seriously considered cutting his losses and returning to London but underwent a rethink upon being informed by Sophie Richmond that a royalties cheque from EMI Publishing had arrived at Dryden Chambers that very morning.

The 2000-capacity Electric Circus in Collyhurst, northeast Manchester had once been a thriving picture palace bringing the stars of the silver-screen to lighten the gas-lit gloom, before being transformed into a bingo hall to tempt the housewives from the surrounding high-rise council estates. By December 1976, the Electric Circus was predominantly catering to Manchester's heavy metal scene. McLaren thought to add local flavour by inviting Buzzcocks to stand in for The Damned.

The Pistols had come to regard Manchester as something of a home from home, but their return to the city wasn't entirely without incident. Come the day of the show the Midland's management informed McLaren that owing to reports of more late-night revelry, his booking was being rescinded forthwith. McLaren managed to make alternative arrangements with a hotel in nearby Withington. The show itself would be marred by violence both inside and outside the venue – the culprits being a gang of local football hooligans who pelted anyone entering the Electric Circus with bricks, bottles and anything else that came to hand.

Thunders and Nolan were well-versed on hostile crowds but they must have wondered what they'd let themselves in for as mounted police charged hither and thither to keep the thugs at bay whilst the venue's beleaguered security staff attempted to get everyone inside. "Some loonies were going around the hall asking people whether or not they were punks." Dave Goodman later recalled. "And if the answer was yes, they would punch them!"

The following four original dates in Lancaster, Liverpool, Bristol and Cardiff had all fallen through, but McLaren had at least managed to secure a booking in Caerphilly to replace the latter date. Rather than run up unnecessary hotel bills in the interim, however, it was decided to return to London. Upon his return to the capital, McLaren visited

Manchester Square to see for himself just who was still fighting the Pistols' corner. To his bemusement, he found everyone within EMI Records from Leslie Hill down was suddenly unavailable. EMI's press office was no longer fielding calls relating to the Pistols, while the band's supposedly loyal A&R man, John Bagnall, had dispensed with his safety-pins and was back to wearing flares.

The show at Caerphilly's all-seater Castle Cinema was notable for the local council mounting a Christmas Carol protest in a car park directly opposite the cinema. Rhymney Valley District Council had petitioned the high court without success to have the show cancelled.

"The tour staggered through a few more gigs, not good for business on the road but terrific for record sales," says Mike Thorne. "The outrage over what happened on *Today* had long-since started to percolate throughout Manchester Square and eventually reached the Chairman's office. EMI was a pillar of the establishment at that time, and Sir John Read and the directors could reasonably expect an eventual mention in the New Year Honors list and the attendant letters they could tag on the end of their name. But here were these noisy children causing outrage and singing sarcastic songs about our nice Queen in the year before her lovely Silver Jubilee. This would simply not do. Rumours started circulating that top management would unilaterally drop the Pistols from the label – over the vociferous protests of the A&R and Marketing departments.

"The last time I saw the tour was in Cleethorpes, a blue-collar seaside resort in Lincolnshire, on the east coast of middle England. I remember an express train from King's Cross and then shivering through the change to a local on a bare platform with snow slanting sideways. It was appropriate they played the Winter Gardens because the rain and sleet were even more robust when roaring in off the North Sea as I walked from the bed and breakfast after a solid seaside dinner in the company of just one other misfit, a lonely travelling salesman. Although I was handling the company's most newsworthy group, I still hadn't been granted a company car. That night, the Pistols were anxious, but the Clash were outstanding. I had no reassurances to offer on behalf of Sir John. The hall was about half full but cheerful and involved. The group were unsettled and apprehensive, even John. Something was brewing back at Manchester Square, but I couldn't read the tea leaves.

"I was working at Manor Studios in Oxfordshire when Nick called to give me the news that the Pistols were being dropped. He wanted me to hear it from him directly rather than elsewhere. Nick was then summoned to an evening meeting with Sir John Read. Nick wore his dark blue suit and a quiet tie, but there was no controlling his hair. It wasn't so much a meeting as Nick wasn't allowed the opportunity to ask any questions. Nick and I both seriously thought of resigning, but we didn't because we knew it wouldn't have made the slightest difference."

The same night the Pistols were in Caerphilly, Billy Idol and Tony James's new band, Generation X, were making their debut at The Roxy, a new punk rock-friendly venue located at 41 - 43 Neal Street in London's Covent Garden. The Neal Street lease had been taken up by Andy Czezowski and Susan Carrington, together with their friend Barry Jones, the latter reportedly pawning his guitar so they could stock the bar and hire stage lighting on opening night. "Gene October had booked a Chelsea show at the club through his gay contacts," says Czezowski. "It was still called Chaguaramas when Gene went there but was undergoing a name change to the Roxy. It made no real difference to our plans, but what none of us realised was that the club had gone into receivership and the change of name was an attempt at some kind of legal way to stave off bankruptcy and stay open.

"By the time I went to see the owners Billy and Tony had quit Chelsea to form Generation X, they even took Gene's drummer [John Towe] with them. Bill was still playing the guitar at that point but he wasn't that great. When they found Derwood (Andrews), who could really play, Bill gave up the guitar and focused on his singing. They already had management but they weren't happy and asked me to manage them as I'd briefly looked after the Damned. That was the reason for my going to Neal Street to see about the possibility of switching the show from Chelsea to Generation X. "The club looked worn and tired, like the owners; one-handed gay barrister, Rene Albert, and his boyfriend. They agreed that we could still use the club on December 14, so I signed the contract with Rene. The first thing we did was clean the place up. There was a stench of failure about the place."

Czezowski had approached McLaren to see about the Pistols headlining The Roxy's official New Year's Day opening, only to have his overtures rebuffed. "We'd signed a deal to take on the Roxy for

Generation X featuring Billy Idol and Tony James

three months starting on New Year's Day 1977," says Czezowski needed a band to play the official opening night and thought, 'Let's ask Malcolm.' Like I say, we didn't socialize with Malcolm or Vivienne; it was just that I did Vivienne's books at the shop. It was most likely Donovan (Letts) that introduced us to Vivienne because he used to visit her at the shop as he was running Acme Attractions for John Krevine. We also knew John's business partner, Stephen Raynor. They were treading on Malcolm and Vivienne's patch by importing zoot suits and Forties and Fifties clothes from America much the same as Malcolm and Vivienne were. They were also importing jukeboxes, but I don't know whether the one at 430 King's Road came from them.

"In hindsight, there were two reasons why Malcolm wouldn't let us have the Pistols: one was that he wanted to keep the myth about the Pistols not being allowed to play anywhere, while the second reason was that he didn't want anyone else taking his limelight.

It was a shame because the band were really up for doing it. They were there most nights. John loved being at the Roxy as it allowed him to hide away from the pressures surrounding the Pistols at that time. Malcolm let himself down and he let the Pistols down. When Joe said the Clash would love to play the opening we went to see Bernie at his Citroen repair workshop in Camden Town. Bernie was initially reluctant but eventually said 'okay' so long as we only advertised the show by word of mouth. I told him that the club only held around 150 people, and with the crowds we'd pulled for Generation X and the Heartbreakers the following night there was no need to print up any flyers. What did Bernie do? He went and printed up some flyers."

Rhodes' horse-trading with Czezowski and Carrington concluded with The Clash agreeing to 50 per cent of the door against a £100 guarantee. "Having the Clash endorse the Roxy put us on the map," says Susan Carrington. "It was an amazing night. We squeezed in wave after wave of people. There were probably about 400 kids packed into a venue with a capacity of 100. After that night, our lives became a travelling circus, even though we stayed in one place."

A chance meeting with McLaren and Leee Black Childers at The Ship pub on Wardour Street in the run-up to the Generation X show resulted in The Heartbreakers playing The Roxy on December 15. "I often get asked what the Clash were like on the night but I was too busy running around making sure everything was running smoothly that I didn't see them. It was the same with Generation X and the Heartbreakers, all I cared about was making enough money to pay the bills and keep the club going. It was a constant machine, booking the bands and printing up the flyers etc."

Despite McLaren's endeavours, the second half the original tour itinerary now lay in waste. However, a return to Manchester's Electric Circus in place of the long-since cancelled Guildford date and a second replacement date the following evening at Cleethorpes' Winter Gardens brought about an upturn in fortunes – despite the latter outing necessitating an all-night drive to Plymouth for what was to prove the third and last of the original tour dates to escape local council interference. In an attempt to end the tour on a high, McLaren booked a second date at Plymouth's Woods Centre for December 23. When the following night's replacement show at

Penelope's Ballroom in Paignton went the same way as its Torquay predecessor, McLaren thought to save any unnecessary expenditure by instructing the local promoter to bring the second Plymouth date forward. Having somehow got wind that the disgruntled road crew were plotting their revenge for his and Rhodes's high-handed management style, McLaren caught the last train to London. The crew reportedly exacted their roadie rage on the unsuspecting Rhodes by defecating in his bed.

The Anarchy Tour collective would come together again on Christmas Day. Caroline Coon and Jonh Ingham were looking after a friend's house in Cambridge Gardens, west London. "It was an 'open invite' because the majority of the people that came had nowhere else to go," says Ingham. "Steve was there from the Pistols, Paul was there from the Clash, I think he came with Roadent. Captain Sensible was there as was Sid, Soo Catwoman, Ray Stevenson, all the Heartbreakers and Leee Black Childers. Walter and Billy were totally out of it and poor Leee had his hands full. Johnny kept trying to call New York collect to speak with his girlfriend so it was my job to keep an eye on him. Mick and Sheila Rock lived close-by so they swung by. Mike Heron (Scottish singer, songwriter, best known for his work in the Incredible String Band) was also there for a time. He was having a full-on conversation with Captain Sensible. When I asked Mike what they were chatting about, he told me that Sensible had confessed to loving the String Band.

"Things got a little out-of-hand later in the evening because Steve Jones nicked a fur coat that belonged to a friend of Marc Zermati's. I knew Steve had nicked his coat and there was little likelihood of the guy getting it back. I was trying to placate him in my schoolboy French when he pulled a knife from somewhere and flung it at the door. It made one of those cartoon 'boing' noises as the blade embedded itself in the wood. That sobered a few people up. The situation was resolved by Jerry Nolan, I think."

While McLaren was preoccupied in keeping the Anarchy Tour and the Sex Pistols in the headlines, Westwood was busy cementing the foundations for her own future fashion house empire overseeing the latest refurbishments at 430 King's Road. Rather than carry out the renovations themselves, as they had done previously, they enlisted the help of Ben Kelly (who would later design the interior of the Haçienda) and his draughtsman associate, David Conners, to oversee the work. The provocative pink plastic letters and Rousseau's telling aphorism that had stopped many a Londoner dead in the tracks gave way to hi-tech opaque white-flashed opal glass. A small brass plaque affixed to one of the plates gave away the only indication to the shop's latest guise - Seditionaries: clothes for heroes. The glass panels would soon prove too tempting a target for football hooligans. Having to replace the expensive panes became too much of a bugbear; so much so, McLaren and Westwood installed protective wire-mesh screens over the plates.

The shop's radical new exterior was totally at odds with the tried-and-tested rules of retail in that passers-by couldn't see inside. This, however, was merely an extension of McLaren and Westwood's mantra – as with McLaren's insistence that "Anarchy in the UK" be housed in a plain black bag so that only those purposely seeking the record might find it, he and Westwood didn't want just anybody coming in off the street to purvey their wares; as far as they were concerned, the curiosity-seeking window-lickers could hang around outside John Krevine's Acme Attractions a little ways further down the King's Road.

Seditionaries' interior was equally minimalistic and hi-tech. The surgical bed and jukebox were consigned to history. The gymnasium wall bars survived the cull but were polished and moved into the centre of the shop to serve as clothing racks. The walls themselves were covered with floor-to-ceiling black and white shots of Dresden following the allied blanket-bombing campaign of February 14, 1944 when some 800 RAF Lancaster Bombers and another 400 American B-17 bombers deluged the baroque city with tonnes of incendiaries reducing it to a smoking ruin and left some 130,000 Germans dead or dying amid the rubble.

In contrast, the wall directly behind the new kidney-shaped counter was covered with an upside-down full-colour print of Piccadilly Circus; the print having first been spliced into sections to allow access to the cupboards behind it. In keeping with the bombed theme, McLaren smashed holes into the suspended ceiling through which two searing spotlights protruded. Tacky sixties-style nuclear chairs draped in fluorescent-orange nylon provided the seating, while the floor was covered in rugged industrial grey carpeting. Conners' pièce de résistance was a cage mounted on a table within which a rat paced up and down. "We did Seditionaries for £2,000, and that £2,000 changed the world." Conners would later tell Westwood's unofficial biographer, Jane Mulvagh. "It was all ideas. Money had almost nothing to do with it. Intimidation, that was it."

The music industry grapevine was awash with rumours that EMI were set to drop the Sex Pistols after the Christmas Holidays. With everyone of any import at EMI proving impervious to their advances, the music weeklies were reliant on McLaren to keep them abreast with what was occurring. Speaking with the *NME*, McLaren scoffed at the rumours, saying EMI were already lining up 'Pretty Vacant' as the follow-up to 'Anarchy in the UK'. Conversely, he then played devil's advocate hinting that should EMI go ahead and terminate the Pistols' contract then there were several other interested parties waiting in the wings to snap them up. Or as he succinctly put it during a 2007 interview: "If you didn't take from this guy, then you took from that guy; there was always another whore further along the street."

On January 4, 1977, with EMI still dithering as to their intentions in regard to the Pistols' recording contract, the band flew out to Holland on a mini three-date promotional tour (two shows in Amsterdam and a third in Rotterdam), as well as make an appearance on the Dutch TV show, *Disco Circus*. The promo trip was arranged by Hilary Walker, the second-in-command at EMI International. On being informed about the proposed trip before the Christmas break, McLaren had sought assurances from Walker that the trip was confirmation the Sex Pistols were to remain an EMI act. Walker responded by saying she preferred to concentrate on her job of promoting the Pistols in EMI's overseas territories rather than allow herself to be influenced by the in-house rumour mill. This wasn't without its difficulties because the heads of EMI's overseas offices were all aware of the furore surrounding the Pistols and were therefore wary of inviting the band to their respective territories. Walker was, of course, aware that a decision was in the offing, but as EMI Holland had proved amenable to the idea of a promo visit, she'd set the ball rolling for what she saw as the first stop on a full European promotional campaign.

Overseas promotion tours were part and parcel of EMI's strategy, but with the Pistols' reputation preceding them, Graham Fletcher from EMI International accompanied the band as their official liaison. Fletcher had accompanied Mike Thorne to the 100 Club Punk Festival and had been championing the Pistols ever since. Fletcher insists nothing whatsoever untoward occurred at Heathrow while the Pistols awaited their early-morning flight as he'd seen to the checking-in and never let the band out of his sight. Imagine his astonishment when Leslie Hill called him at the Pistols' hotel in Amsterdam later in the day demanding an explanation for *The Evening News'* banner headline: "These Revolting VIPs! Sex Pistols in Rumpus at Airport"

The accompanying report told of how the Pistols had supposedly caused uproar at Heathrow "spitting" and "vomiting" their way onto the KLM flight to Amsterdam. Fletcher was understandably mystified as to where the "story" could have come from as the closest any of the band had come to throwing up was Rotten's messing about disgorging chewed-up orange peel into a complimentary sick-bag.

Fletcher's version of events at Heathrow was buttering few parsnips at Manchester Square, however, as Sir John Reid had taken it upon himself to call a high-ranking acquaintance at KLM who'd confirmed the story was true. Leslie Hill, Bob Mercer and Nick Mobbs all conducted their enquiries into the incident and found the story utterly spurious. Hill would go so far as to petition Read in person because of the adverse effect he feared EMI's terminating the Pistols contract would have on his staff. From that moment on, however, the dye was cast. Knowing the Pistols' fate was sealed, Hill called Fletcher and gave him instructions to have McLaren waiting by the phone at nine o'clock the following morning. Having given McLaren the news that the Pistols were no longer an EMI act, Hill then flew out to Amsterdam to speak with him in person. By the time Hill was airborne EMI's Group Press Relations issued the following press release:

EMI AND THE SEX PISTOLS
EMI and the Sex Pistols group have mutually agreed to terminate their recording contract.

EMI feels it is unable to promote this group's records internationally because of the adverse publicity which has been generated over the last two months, although recent press reports of the behaviour of the Sex Pistols appear to have been exaggerated.

The termination of this contract with the Sex Pistols does not in any way affect EMI's intention to remain active in all areas of the music business.

"I was in the snowy Oxfordshire countryside producing my first major-label album at Manor Studios," says Mike Thorne. "Manor Studios were owned by Virgin Records, or Richard Branson to be precise. One day, in a jolly piece of courtesy, we had Richard delivering the afternoon tea. Shortly afterwards, Nick called to forewarn me that the announcement was about to go out on the wire that EMI was set to drop the Pistols. Those establishment decorations and old boy connections would be safe, and EMI's loss would be Richard's gain."

McLaren, however, was telling anyone willing to listen that as far as he was concerned the Sex Pistols were still an EMI act because he'd yet to see a single piece of paper relating to the band's termination. Away from the microphones he knew the game was up, however, as he'd instructed Steven Fisher to book a seat on the available flight to Amsterdam. McLaren and Fisher then spent much of the day holed up with Hill discussing how best to dress up the contractual corpse; the end result being Glitterbest receiving the outstanding £20,000 from the Emi contract and a further £10,000 from EMI Publishing.

On January 17, while the Pistols were at Gooseberry Studios with Dave Goodman recording a demo version of a new song called "EMI", the label issued a final press release officially severing all links with the band: "In accordance with the previously stated wishes of both parties and the verbal telephone agreement made on Thursday, January 6, 1977, the documents terminating the contract between EMI and the Sex Pistols have now been signed. EMI Records wish the Sex Pistols every success with their next recording contract."

This wasn't the end of the Pistols/EMI relationship, of course, as following Thorn EMI's corporate acquisition of Virgin Music Group in 1992 (for a reported £560 million), the Pistols' back catalogue came under its dominion.

The Sex Pistols were now free agents, yet despite his having tabled a near facsimile of the EMI contract back in October, Polydor's Chris Parry chose to focus his energies on securing The Clash's signatures. Just as he had with the Pistols, Parry had jumped the gun by

Johnny Thunders with Johnny Rotten in the background, 1976. Photo Ray Stevenson

arranging for The Clash to record a set of demos at Polydor's studios. He did so believing the fates wouldn't prove so cruel as to pull the rug out from under his feet a second time, but unbeknown to him Rhodes was busy negotiating a six-figure deal with CBS.

"Chris Parry had tabled an offer for £40,000 but I wasn't gonna turn down £100,000 from CBS, was I?" says Rhodes. "Obie [Maurice Oberstein, CBS' London CEO] wasn't all that interested in punk, except for the dollars he could add to the balance sheet. I was on my way to CBS' offices in Soho Square when I bumped into Malcolm. I knew he was desperate to secure the Pistols another label so that he could get 'God Save the Queen' out in time for the Silver Jubilee so I invited him to come along. Obie was excited at the prospect of getting the Clash and the Pistols. He said he'd give us £100,000 there and then to set up our own label and CBS would distribute the records. Malcolm said he was interested but wanted to have a word with me in private before giving his answer.

"As soon as we got outside Malcolm changed his tune and said he wasn't going to be held to ransom by CBS. He then asked me if he could borrow a fiver for a cab back to the King's Road. I thought, 'How can you turn down £100,000 and then ask me for a fiver?' But that was Malcolm. I gave him the fiver and watched him walk off before rushing back inside to explain what had just happened to Obie. Obie just shrugged his shoulders and said I could have the whole £100,000 for the Clash."

Parry is said to have actually broke down and sobbed on learning he'd lost out on the Pistols to EMI. CBS' offering The Clash £100,000 no doubt had him again reaching for the Kleenex. They do say, however, that he who laughs last laughs longest and the adage was certainly true in Parry's case as he would sign The Jam to Polydor in February 1977 for just £6,000 (though the deal would be renegotiated in The Jam's favour).

—When The Two Sevens Clash

"I've heard it said often enough that The Clash were ripped off by CBS, but you have to remember the times we were living in. The country was going to shit and who was to say what might happen? EMI had only offered Malcolm £40,000 for the Pistols and they were supposed to be the leading punk group. What was I supposed to do? Tell Maurice Oberstein to keep his £100,000 and give me £40,000 instead?"

Bernard Rhodes

Rastafarian founder, Marcus Garvey, had prophesied 1977 as the year of great political upheaval; the year the Rastafarians would return to Ethiopia, the spiritual homeland where their ancestors had lived before being dragged off to a life of slavery in the colonies. It's ironic therefore that the year of the two sevens clashing would see The Clash sign a recording contract enslaving the band to CBS. The contract was woefully one-sided. Aside from having to cover their recording costs, The Clash would also have to pay their way whilst out on the road. "It's the deal later used as a classic example of the kind of contract that no group should ever sign, says Roadent. "They had to pay for their

Opposite: Bernie Rhodes (left) masterminded The Clash as their manager

tours, recordings, remixes, artwork, expenses, you name it. And of course, Bernie creamed his 20 per cent off the top tax-free."

"Signing that contract did bother me a lot," Strummer would subsequently lament to Caroline Coon later that same year. "I've been turning it over in my mind, but now I've come to terms with it. I've realised that all it boils down to is perhaps two-year's security. Before, all I could think about was my stomach . . . Now I feel free to think - and free to write down what I'm thinking about. And look, I've been fucked about for so long I'm not going to suddenly turn into Rod Stewart just because I get £25.00 a week. I'm much too far gone for that, I tell you."

The Clash had been forced to call upon a University of Sussex acquaintance of Billy Idol's called Rob Harper for the Anarchy Tour, but Harper had since refused all of Rhodes' entreaties to join the band full-time. Terry Chimes had allowed himself to be coaxed back into The Clash fold for the New Year's Day Roxy opening, and with CBS keen to start recouping their six-figure outlay as soon as possible, the amiable Chimes agreed to accompany The Clash into CBS' (long-since demolished) No. 3 Studio on Whitfield Street, just off Oxford Street to record their debut album. The album would be recorded and mixed over three consecutive long weekends, commencing on February 10, 1977.

No 3 Studio was chosen simply because it offered a reduced weekend rate. However, with the recording costs coming out of The Clash's advance, speed was of the essence. To ensure the needle stayed in the red during the marathon sessions, speed of an altogether different nature was thrown into the mix as Mick Jones subsequently revealed to Caroline Coon: "Two years ago we did the band's first interview on Janet Street-Porter's *London Weekend Programme*. And me, being all naïve, I blamed bands taking too many drugs for the great mid-seventies drought in rock. I recall saying it really well and a year or so later I found myself doing just as many drugs as them! I was so into speed, I mean, I don't even recall making the first album!"

The first-weekend session was taken up laying down the basic tracks of the thirteen songs slated for the album. One of The Clash's enduring endearments is their determination to give the fans full value for money. On discovering the album's running time came in at less than 30 minutes, it was decided to include their version of Junior

Murvin's "Police and Thieves", which, at 6:05 minutes, was some three times longer than the majority of the bands own compositions.

Murvin's lament about gang war and police brutality in his native Kingston – co-written and produced by Lee 'Scratch' Perry – had proved a hit in Jamaica the previous year. The Clash believed its subject matter would strike a similar chord with their audiences. According to Mick's recollections, Perry initially struggled to grasp what The Clash were attempting: "Lee had been telling Bob Marley about it, and he was saying, 'Well, I'm not sure about what these punks are about,' Marley was one of the guys who said, 'No, you should see, it's good.' He kind of responded by writing that song, 'Punky Reggae Party'. He was asking questions and finding out if we were rebels, too."

Rather than kid himself that he could emulate Murvin's falsetto range, Strummer sang the vocal in his customary gruff style leaving Jones to harmonise the higher notes. Prior to releasing the album, CBS issued "White Riot" as the lead single on March 18. There was little chance of the song feature on Radio One's daytime play-lists, but the band's burgeoning fanbase the single would scrape into the UK Top 40 (#38).

The eponymous parent album was released on April 8; the front sleeve bearing Kate Simon's shot of Strummer, Jones and Simonon striking a suitably moody pose on the cobbled access ramp of the old Tack Room opposite the entrance to Rehearsals. The photo serves as an introductory statement of intent for the album's no-nonsense onslaught. From the staccato drumbeat intro to "Janie Jones" to the lilting melancholic refrain of "Garageland", the listener is carried along on a ride of relentless rhythms, accentuated with primitive yet proficient rock 'n' roll rebellion. The first pressing of *The Clash* carried a red sticker on the sleeve, which, in accompaniment with a coupon in that week's *NME*, allowed fans to send away for the now highly-collectable four-track *Capital Radio* EP. Aside from the title track, which remained a set favourite throughout The Clash's career, the EP featured a 27-second snippet of "Listen" and a band interview conducted with the *NME*'s Tony Parsons whilst riding about on the Circle Line.

'Capital Radio' was a rant against the popular London radio station of the same name – particularly their then Head of Music, Aiden Day, who is namechecked in the lyric. "They're even worse because they had the chance, coming right into the heart of London and sitting in that tower right on top of everything," Strummer told Caroline Coon in a 1977 interview. "But they've completely blown it. I'd like to throttle Aiden Day. He thinks he's the self-appointed Minister of Public Enlightenment. They say, 'Capital Radio in tune with London'. Yeah, yeah, yeah! They're in tune with Hampstead. They're not in tune with us at all. I hate them. What they could have done compared to what they have done is abhorrent. They could have made the whole capital buzz. Instead, Capital Radio has just turned their back on the whole youth of the city."

The Ramones had begun recording the follow-up album to their eponymous debut, *Leave Home*, back in October at Sundragon Studios on 21st Street and Fifth Avenue. Producing the album was Tony Bongiovi, who along with his business partner, Bob Walters, was in the process of renovating the defunct Avatar Studios on West 53rd Street into the Power Station. At this juncture, Bongiovi had produced three Gloria Gaynor albums, a couple of Jimi Hendrix posthumous releases, and was working with Talking Heads on the trio's eponymous debut album. The Ramones were known to him, however, as he'd once employed Tommy at the Record Plant. Tommy would again receive a co-production credit on the album.

Assisting Bongiovi on both the Talking Heads album and The Ramones' follow-up was Ed Stasium, who would go on to produce several future Ramones albums. "I'd never heard [the] Ramones before although I'd heard of them via Lisa Robinson's *Rock Scene* magazine, Stasium reflected in 2002. "I got in, and I was like, 'What the heck is this?' After an hour, I got it. I thought it was great. It's what every kid wants to do. It wasn't about virtuosity but the feel, and the lyrics were so ridiculous. It gave me that good smack in the face that everyone could use every ten years. The simplicity, the power and the comedy [was] why I latched onto them – and their personalities. They're very likeable people. The songs have extremely memorable melodies, too."

The Ramones' approach to recording was just as minimalistic as on their debut, the songs recorded live and laid down within two takes. "It was straight in, straight out, no messing," Stasium continued. "It was very professional. No one wanted to waste time or money. Joey was a workhorse. He knew exactly what he was going to do – his

The Ramones' *Leave Home* charted 37 places lower than their first album

songs were embedded in his mind and soul. When Joey double-tracked his vocals, all the nuances were the same.

Leave Home was released on January 10, 1977. Despite receiving largely favourable reviews in the US, the album peaked some 37 places lower than *Ramones* on the Billboard 200. It would, however, chart in the UK, debuting at #45. As with *Ramones*, the 14-track album's running time came in at under 30 minutes but owing to Sire having set the budget at $10,000 more emphasis was given to the mixing and engineering. The opening track, 'Glad to See You Go', related to Dee Dee's recently departed girlfriend Connie, who was something of a familiar face on the New York scene from her having once dated Dolls bassist, Arthur Kane. Connie was said to be so possessive of Kane that she'd once cut his thumb to stop him flying out to LA. Indeed, she'd injured Dee Dee on several occasions, including slicing his buttocks with a broken beer bottle.

The Ramones were touring *Leave Home* – primarily in New

York and California with a few stadium dates opening for Blue Öyster Cult - when Sire announced they were having to remove the fifth track, 'Carbona not Glue' – which some would argue was the catchiest song on the album - from the track-listing as Carbona was a household cleaning fluid and the label was anxious to avoid a lawsuit. "Danny Fields played Legs and I an advance copy of the album at his apartment," says John Holmstrom. "It's pretty laughable when you stop to think about it now but Danny was worried that we would think the album was too polished or something. Obviously, we loved the album from start to finish, but Danny wanted to know which song stood out the most – which song was the obvious single. "So we say, 'Carbona not Glue' is easily the best song. Danny pulled a face and said he was afraid we'd choose 'Carbona' because that was the one song they couldn't release as a single."

McNeil was in complete agreement: "I was shocked. It was such a great song, so radio-friendly - like a song the Beatles or the Stones would have written if they were just starting out in 1976, with great harmonies and catchy lyrics."

After the initial pressing of Leave Home, Sire replaced 'Carbona not Glue' in the US with 'Sheena Is a Punk Rocker' and 'Babysitter' in the UK. "Something like 'Carbona not Glue' has to be tongue-in-cheek," Tommy reflected in *Hey Ho Let's Go: the Story of The Ramones*. "It's absurd, like saying you should try something *more* poisonous [than glue]. I have a feeling Dee Dee was talking about his childhood, how he thought it was a release when he was a kid. I thought of it as parody. Maybe it wasn't."

"I still feel that if the Ramones had had a hit single early in their career then things would have maybe been different for them," says Roberta Bayley. "They wrote great bubblegum pop songs with catchy melodies and hilarious yet intelligent lyrics. They could have been the new Bay City Rollers if they'd have scored that early hit. It was the same with Blondie. While they were having hit after hit in England and elsewhere, no one in America was interested in them. I wouldn't think to denigrate Blondie's talent as a band – because they were another great band – but the industry people only really persevered with Blondie early on because of Debbie's looks."

One of the few industry people to persevere with Blondie because he recognised their potential was Marty Thau. Thau was still technically the manager of the now-defunct New York Dolls but had set up Instant Records with Craig Leon and Sire Records co-founder, Richard Gottehrer. Gottehrer had started out as a songwriter, working out of the Brill Building, and had scored several hits - including a US #1 in the summer of 1963 with 'My Boyfriend's Back' by The Angels – before going into partnership with Stein.

Most evenings, Thau, Leon and Gottehrer could be found at CBGBs casting their inquisitive eye over the bands onstage. Thau believed Blondie was the diamond in the ruff, and that with a little buffing they could progress to the next stage. "Marty was always a champion of Blondie," Leon reflected. "Quite honestly both Ritchie and I thought he was out of his mind. The band's playing was really slovenly and they were ramshackle looking. Nobody really took them seriously, but Marty said they were going to be the only band that really makes it out of CBGBs. He said they were going to be the biggest thing ever. He had the same vision about the New York Dolls. He wasn't so right about the Dolls, except that they became very influential, but he was quite right about Blondie."

Gottehrer was initially hesitant but having watched Blondie run through their stage set at a band rehearsal he came away grinning from ear to ear. He recognised that the band were reaching beyond their grasp in terms of musicality.

Gottehrer and Leon accompanied Blondie into Plaza Sound Studios where the latter had recorded Ramones to record two songs with the view to releasing them as a single: 'X Offender' (Originally titled 'Sex Offender') and 'In the Sun'. However, rather than issue the single via their own Instant imprint, Thau, Gottehrer and Leon began sounding out their respective contacts within the industry in the hope of securing a deal for Blondie. After countless rebuttals, an old friend of Gottehrer's called Larry Uttal took the plunge offering the band a two-single deal. Uttal had built up Bell Records before selling the label to a conglomerate fronted by Clive Davis that became Arista Records. He'd recently got back in the game with his newly incorporated Private Stock label.

The deal Thau and Gottehrer orchestrated with Private Stock was that they would release 'X Offender' while guaranteeing an album within 30 days of the release or Blondie would be freed from their contract. 'X Offender' was released in June 1976. It was never likely to trouble the charts, but the buzz surrounding the single was enough to force Private Stock's hand in picking up the album option. The contract weighed heavily in the label's favour, of course, and Blondie would come to realise the mistake of allowing their exuberance in landing an album deal to forego the sagacity of first seeking independent legal counsel.

Having given The Ramones, Blondie and the other CBGB bands their break, Hilly Kristal hit upon the idea of capturing the zeitgeist by staging a festival at the club and recording each of the acts for a *Live at CBGBs* album/documentary. He intended to hire a portable recording studio and invited Craig Leon to engineer and produce the album. The festival went ahead and the album was indeed recorded, with The Ramones, Blondie, Television, The Patti Smith Group and Talking Heads all participating. Unfortunately for Kristal, the backbiting amongst the rising Bowery bands was already in evidence. The Ramones were already signed to Sire, of course, but with Private Stock picking up the Blondie album option and Talking Heads and the other leading lights all in varying stages of contractual negotiations, by the time the CBGBs album was completed they all gave back word and refused to sign off on their songs. As a result, the album featured the bands that soon fell by the wayside: The Shirts, Tuff Darts, The Miamis, The Laughing Dogs et al. Indeed, the only act of any prominence to appear on the *Live at CBGBs* album were Mink Deville.

McLaren was in the midst of advanced negotiations with LA-based A&M Records when Matlock dropped the bombshell that he was leaving the band. He'd been unhappy with his lot in the Pistols for several weeks, and with Rotten's ego swelling by the day owing to the media's ongoing fixation with the "King of the Punks", he'd reached the conclusion it was better to cut his losses. Over the coming weeks, McLaren held several meetings with Matlock in the hope of bringing about a change of heart in his bassist – to cajole him into trying to get along with John for the greater good. These were usually one-on-one though Steve and Paul were present on at least one occasion. "I knew there were two ways of going about it," Matlock reflected. "I could have said, 'John's not so bad, I can work with him', or what I felt inside. So I said what I was feeling – that I couldn't stand the bloke. Well, that's not strictly true because I actually didn't mind him in some ways, I just knew I couldn't continue being in a band with him. Malcolm saw the wisdom in what I was saying – he was having

John Lydon with Malcolm MacLaren after the former had appeared in court on drugs charges in 1977. Rotten later sued MacLaren. Photo: Evening Standard/Getty

his own problems with John by this stage – but he couldn't help himself in playing this whole divide and conquer thing. Instead of discouraging Steve and Paul from getting on my case all the time – at least since we came off the [Anarchy] Tour – he actively encouraged them to say stuff that he knew would get back to me."

Speaking with Julien Temple in *The Filth and the Fury*, by which time, of course, the four founding Pistols had come together for their money-grabbing Filthy Lucre tour, John Lydon lays the blame for

the breakdown in his and Matlock's relationship at McLaren's door -
that their erstwhile manager had purposely gone out of his way to set
one against the other. The Machiavellian mischief-making McLaren
unquestionably played his part, but Lydon must also shoulder some
of the blame for creating the schism that effectively killed the Pistols
as a creative force.

When Lydon joined the Pistols in August 1975, he'd quickly
surmised that he would have little luck trying to argue against Jones
and Cook in regards to band policy as the guitarist and drummer
were like Siamese twins and that any decision they made would
come in the form of a block vote. However, he'd been wrong to
assume Matlock would side with Cook and Jones simply because
he'd been with the band two years or so and was working at the shop
while he was the outsider. Had he not proved such an inverted snob
in attacking Matlock over his perceived middle-class roots and his
audacious acknowledgement of The Beatles' musical legacy, then it
might have been they – as the Pistols' songwriting duo – that dictated
band policy. The singer, of course, always garners more attention
than the musicians in the band, so when Rotten began making noises
about getting rid of Matlock, Jones and Cook were savvy enough
to recognise that the Johnny Rotten's of this world were a rare
commodity while bassists were two a penny.

What no one within either the Pistols or their inner circle was
aware of, however, was EMI's interest in whatever career path
Matlock chose should he ever leave the Pistols. Back in December,
Mike Thorne had taken advantage of one of the unforeseen hiatuses
during the Anarchy Tour to get the Pistols into EMI's in-house
studio at Manchester Square to record some demos. While Rotten,
Jones and Cook were taking a breather in a local pub, Thorne had
let Matlock know that he had a future at EMI away from the Pistols
should he ever consider such a move.

Matlock was indeed contemplating such a move because as far as
he could see the Pistols were in danger of becoming an anglicised
version of The Monkees. He considered himself a serious musician
and saw little point in remaining with a band that were being
banned from playing at every turn. He was also astute enough to
recognise McLaren's ongoing obsession with having the retitled
'God Save the Queen' as the Pistols follow-up single recorded and
released in time to coincide with the forthcoming Silver Jubilee

celebrations could only result in more banning orders.

Having taken Thorne up on his offer and received his £3,000 Glitterbest golden handshake from for services rendered, Matlock formed Rich Kids with Midge Ure and Steve New – both of whom had ties, albeit tenuous, to the Pistols' saga. The Rich Kids would score a UK Top 30 hit in February 1978 with their eponymous power-pop debut single.

Matlock's replacement in the Sex Pistols was, of course, Sid Vicious. Matlock harboured no feelings of ill will towards his former bandmates and even went so far as to offer to teach Vicious how to play the Pistols' repertoire. His easy-going nature was to prove his undoing, however. Instead of rushing off and informing Caroline Coon or Jonh Ingham of his decision to quit the Pistols he agreed to keep quiet until McLaren returned from a series of meetings in LA with A&M Records co-founders, Herb Albert and Jerry Moss, at their Burbank offices. In doing so, he unwittingly allowed McLaren the upper hand as within days of his departure the latter sent a telegram to the *NME* insisting Matlock had been sacked for liking The Beatles.

Speaking on the *Never Mind the Bollocks* edition of the *Classic Album* documentary series, Steve Jones belatedly acknowledges his mistake in allowing Lydon to undermine Matlock's position in the Pistols and ultimately replace him with Vicious. It shouldn't have mattered that Matlock was always polite, forever washing his feet, or had a preference for "wanky Beatles chords". He was the only Sex Pistol able to formulate their ideas into a structured tune.

Legend has it that McLaren and Rhodes colluded to exchange bass players between their respective acts around the time of the Anarchy Tour. Matlock even hints at such in *I Was a Teenage Sex Pistol*. Mick Jones, however, stringently denies any such arrangement was contemplated. Matlock may have been more musically gifted than Paul Simonon, but there was only ever going to be one bassist for The Clash.

Sid was born Simon John Ritchie in May 1957 to John and Anne Ritchie. Anne was a vivacious, straight-talking twenty-five-year-old who'd already been married and divorced by the time she hooked up with Ritchie. The handsome, yet doleful Ritchie was coming to the end of his two-year stint of national service in the Royal Guard at the time of his son's birth. On his return to Civvy Street, he found work as a publisher's rep in London. The couple soon fell into debt, however, and Ritchie suggested they seek a fresh start in Ibiza. Anne and three-year-old Simon were to go out while Ritchie supposedly sorted out his affairs. Neither Anne nor Simon would ever see him again. They would remain in Ibiza for some eighteen months before reluctantly returning to London.

When Anne subsequently became romantically involved with Christopher Beverley, she and seven-year-old Simon relocated to Tunbridge Wells in Kent. The couple were married in February 1965. Anne would later describe meeting Chris Beverley as akin to "winning the football pools" but within weeks of their tying the knot, Beverley was diagnosed with cancer and died soon thereafter. Anne and Simon carried on living in Tunbridge Wells for another three years before returning to London in the summer of 1971, setting up home in Stoke Newington. On leaving school in 1972, Simon started as a trainee cutter at Simpson's – a local factory of some repute owing to its production of Daks trousers. His apprenticeship would prove short-lived, however, and the following year saw him enrol at Hackney Technical College where he encountered John Lydon.

Prior to his joining the Pistols, Vicious was fronting the Flowers of Romance, which featured Keith Levene and future Slits drummer and guitarist, Paloma 'Palmolive' Romera and Viv Albertine. Vicious had penned several songs, such as 'Brains on Vacation', 'Piece of Garbage', and 'Belsen Was a Gas', which would be incorporated into the Pistols set in late-1977.

Within weeks of coming together, Vicious threw Palmolive out of the band following a disagreement over his supposed racist views and fascination with Nazi imagery. It was while Flowers were seeking a new drummer that Vicious had volunteered himself for the Banshees' debut at the 100 Club Punk Festival.

The Matlock/Vicious saga was still ongoing when McLaren flew out to LA to meet Herb Albert and Jerry Moss. The meeting had been set up by McLaren's friend, Rory Johnston who'd relocated to the US the previous summer and was now living in LA. Johnston was enrolled at the Hammersmith College of Art when he'd first encountered McLaren and the fledgling Sex Pistols. "To pay the rent I worked nights as a barman both at Dingwalls in Camden Town, and The Portobello Hotel, which was situated close to Basing Street

Studios, Johnston explained. "Attending Hammersmith at the same period was Mick Jones, who would of course later form the Clash. I became friendly with Mick based on common interests in music. I was living in Ladbroke Grove, and as he only lived a couple of stops further along the Hammersmith Tube line we'd run into each other all the time. Mick was very influential in getting me interested in the emerging pre-punk scene. Incidentally, Joe Strummer was working a few hours a week at the Portobello as a dishwasher the same time I was working there.

"Owing to the UK licensing laws at the time pubs would close at 11 p.m., whereas hotel bars could remain open at the discretion of the management. This was for guests only, but Malcolm would occasionally bring the band along for some after-hours drinking as Alan Jones, who worked at SEX, was the Portobello's night receptionist. The Portobello was a magnet for musicians, artists, fashion designers, TV and film industry types etc. It had a very casual 'the lunatics are running the asylum' atmosphere where sometimes you couldn't tell the staff from the guests. It was Alan who introduced me to Malcolm and also took me to one of the Pistols' early shows. I can't remember which one it was now, but if memory serves it was most likely the first 100 Club date (Tuesday, March 31, 1976). I honestly didn't expect them to be all that good, but I was hooked after two songs. I was completely floored at their energy and the tension in the music. The atmosphere was both electric and dangerous. I remember thinking, finally, here's a band to blow away the cobwebs and expose the raw nerve that had been missing from rock 'n' roll for years!"

On relocating to New York Johnston landed a job working for The Wartoke Concern. Wartoke was a management and publicity company," Johnston continues. It was run by a lady called Jane Friedman who managed Patti Smith and John Cale amongst others. I knew Jane from working at the Portobello. I stayed with Jane during my time in New York before heading over to LA a few months later. Punk was beginning to explode back home by the time I arrived in LA, but this of course was light years before email or faxes, so communications were terrible. International calls were very expensive, and as the US music press viewed punk as being a bunch of snotty-nosed kids that couldn't play their instruments, news from London was hard to come by.

"I was aware of the Pistols' signing with EMI and their subsequent firing, of course. On a whim, I called Malcolm and offered my services as an 'experienced' music person based on my experiences with Wartoke. Amazingly, he agreed. He said he needed help planning a trip to LA with Steven Fisher, and asked me to set up some meetings with labels and publishers? I remember thinking, 'Shit! What the fuck do I do now?' While I was working from my office in LA - actually a payphone on Hollywood Blvd - the Pistols were hurtling towards another label deal in the uproar following the ejection from EMI. Malcolm and Vivienne were living in a small flat in Clapham or Wandsworth as I remember. Most of the time when I called he'd be in bed. I'd keep the calls as short as possible to save money. I was generally making it up as I went along, based on what I could glean from the calls and whatever press I could find. Anyway, a few weeks later I picked up Malcolm and Steven at LAX in my very banged up '63 Ford Thunderbird. I'd started to reach out to some of the bigger labels including MCA, Epic, Casablanca, and Warner Brothers. Capitol was off the list because of their relationship to EMI.

"The first visit was hysterical. Malcolm arrived in full bondage gear with his trousers tied together at the back of the knees. Steven was dressed in full English lawyer uniform: black jacket, grey pinstripe trousers, starched shirt, and a black tie with a Windsor knot. They looked absolutely bizarre! It was meant to be a 'welcome to LA' meeting at A&M. I think Gerry Moss wanted to vet Malcolm himself after Derek Green had shown interest in signing the Pistols. Derek ran the London office. When we arrived at the A&M offices people just stopped and stared open-mouthed at them. The deal was done very quickly, however, and I started working out of the A&M offices. My job was to be overseer of the operation to make sure A&M kept the Pistols' message pure, which was basically, 'Go fuck yourself!'"

The A&M contract, which excluded publishing rights, was a two-year, eighteen track deal. Glitterbest received £75,000 on signing, with a further "75,000 to be paid in March 1978. Derek Green had been so enthralled by the energy of the Dave Goodman's demos that McLaren played him that he'd practically begged Albert and Moss to outbid CBS and Warner Bros. in procuring the Sex Pistols. He purposely chose to avoid meeting the Pistols in person, however, for fear their behaviour might put him off. It was a decision that was to prove very costly for A&M.

The Pistols signed with A&M Records on March 9, 1977, but with "God Save the Queen" intended as the first single, a publicity stunt signing was conducted on the Queen Victoria Memorial opposite Buckingham Palace. In *The Filth and the Fury* John claims Vicious' dad had been on duty at Buckingham Palace whilst his estranged son was putting his name to the mock A&M contract. This was pure hyperbole, of course. With an inquisitive bobby beginning to show an interest, the Pistols posed for the cameras before scurrying back into an awaiting Daimler and speeding off into the early morning London traffic for a press conference at the Regent Palace Hotel in Piccadilly.

The press conference was the first occasion where Derek Green came face-to-face with A&M's latest acquisition, and so was completely at a loss on being informed by McLaren that Matlock, the Pistols' sole recognisable tunesmith was no longer in the band. Managing to regain his composure, Green told the press gathering how the Pistols presented A&M with a unique business opportunity to be linked with a new force in rock music.

Following on from the press conference the Pistols- were whisked off to Wessex Studios where Chris Thomas was mixing "God Save the Queen" before then traversing London to A&M's offices on New King's Road to choose the B-side for the new single.

During the 30-minute car ride, Vicious started taunting Cook, calling him a cross between an albino gorilla and Rick Wakeman. The taunting soon escalated into a drunken free-for-all with Cook suffering a black eye before Jones settled the issue by throwing one of Vicious' shoes out of the window.

Green was using the occasion as a chance for the Pistols to meet the people who would be working on promoting 'God Save the Queen' following its scheduled release date, Friday, May 25. It was a day none of Green's staff was likely to forget. On getting out of the Daimler Vicious dropped the vodka bottle he'd been nursing and cut his foot on the broken the glass. With blood gushing from the wound, he hobbled into the Promotion Office and passed out in a chair. On regaining consciousness he staggered into the Gents and somehow managed to break the toilet bowl while cleaning his injured foot. Wandering out into secretarial pool he thrust his bloodied foot at one of the secretaries demanding that she fetch him a sticking plaster.

Vicious' boorish antics paled against Jones lecherous behaviour, however. Having mistakenly wandered into the ladies' toilets the amorous guitarist grabbed the girl as she rushed for the door. Rather than risk a mass walkout, Green hurriedly selected "No Feeling" for the B-side before sending the Pistols and McLaren on their way.

The following day saw Rotten go before the bench at Marlborough Street Magistrates Court on a charge of possession of amphetamine sulphate following his arrest back in January. He pleaded guilty and was duly fined £40. That same evening, Rotten, Vicious and Jah Wobble went to The Speakeasy to meet up with Jones and Cook. At some point, Wobble got into an altercation with 'Whispering' Bob Harris, who was with his engineer friend George Nicholson. Wobble took exception to *The Old Grey Whistle Test* having thus far ignored the Sex Pistols. When Harris told Wobble that the Pistols wouldn't appear on the show as long as he was in charge, the latter reportedly struck him while smashed a bottle and hit Nicholson over the head, leaving the hapless engineer with a head wound requiring fourteen stitches.

When reviewing Alan G. Parker's *No One Is Innocent* in June 2007, Wobble denied anything untoward happening at the Speakeasy that night - despite Harris's having gone into detail over the sordid incident in both his memoir, *Bob Harris – the Whispering Years*, as well as on the 2007 BBC series, *Seven Ages of Rock*. "We showed up separately but the minute I saw [Sid] there I thought, 'Oh shit, this is a nightmare', Jones reflected. The guy's nickname was 'Whispering' Bob Harris, for fuck's sake – he wasn't an East End gangster. He didn't need a fucking glass pushing right up in his sound engineer's face or one of Rotten's mates threatening to kill him. Anywhere you went that Sid turned up, you knew there was going to be trouble."

Harris came away from The Speakeasy unscathed, but the unprovoked attack left him deeply disturbed. The next morning he called his American manager, Philip Roberge, into action. Having spoken with Roberge on Saturday morning, Green spent the rest of the weekend contemplating his options. It wasn't so much his reputation that he was worried about, but rather what might occur next should he choose to bury his head in the sand and ignore the Pistols' seemingly willful predilection for violence.

The first McLaren heard of the incident was when a letter from Roberge arrived at Dryden Chambers on Monday morning. When Green called him at Dryden Chambers later that same day, McLaren

GOD SAVE THE QUEEN
(Cook/Matlock/Rotten/Jones)

Original sound
recording made by
A & M Records Ltd.

Time: 3.10

**AMS
7284**

AMS 7284A*
Ⓟ1977 A & M
Records Ltd.

SIDE 1
45 RPM

Copyright
Control

SEX PISTOLS
Produced by Chris Thomas

UNAUTHORISED PUBLIC PERFORMANCE BROADCASTING AND COPYING OF THIS RECORD PROHIBITED

said he'd do all he could to bring the band into line. Green, however, remained unmoved for Harris was a close personal friend. With his mind in utter turmoil, instead of going into the office the following morning he stopped off to collect a friend before driving to Brighton, spending the afternoon hurling pebbles into the surf while using his colleague as a sounding board. Knowing A&M stood to make a lot of money from the Pistols, Green arrived at the only viable solution available. Allowing for the eight-hour time difference between London and LA, Green called Jerry Moss and tended his resignation. To his surprise, however, Moss refused to accept his resignation and instead told Green that there was no way A&M would choose the

Pistols over their trusted lieutenant.

On Wednesday, March 16, Green met with McLaren and Fisher at his office to "discuss a most important contractual point". McLaren assumed they were there to iron out some problem with the promotional campaign for "'God Save the Queen'. A&M's artwork department had initially worked up a rough cover showing the Pistols posing outside Buckingham Palace with the sentries on duty unimaginatively clutching UB40 signing-on cards. McLaren had rejected the idea out of hand and instead pressed for a plethora of promotional material - handbills, posters, stickers etc. - that Jamie Reid had designed around Cecil Beaton's official Silver Jubilee portrait of the queen. A&M reportedly had no truck with Reid sticking a safety-pin through the queen's mouth but shied away from Reid's idea to have swastikas over her eyes.

McLaren and Fisher were therefore understandably thunderstruck when Green handed them a handwritten note – that was about to be released to the music press – stating that A&M was terminating the Pistols' recording contract with immediate effect. The initial 25,000 copies of the "God Save the Queen" single that had already been pressed were to be destroyed along with the mater plates. The only aspect Green was willing to discuss was how much it was going to cost the label to get rid of the Pistols.

In a fit of hubris, McLaren told reporters that the Pistols' sacking had been orchestrated by Rick Wakeman and several other A&M artists who'd threatened to leave the label if the Pistols remained on the label. He claimed to have espied a telegram from Wakeman lying atop Derek Green's desk in which the keyboardist wizard supposedly told Green to start dishing out safety-pins to the label's other acts. Had McLaren bothered to peruse the date on the telegram he would have seen that Wakeman had sent the telegram several days before the Speakeasy incident and that Wakeman's comment was nothing more than a light-hearted joke.

Seeing as he'd played a significant role in getting the Pistols signed to A&M, Rory Johnston had naturally expected to be kept in the loop as to what was happening. When a week passed without any word from London he decided he could wait no longer. "The day before I was due to move into A&M's offices I called Malcolm to ask if everything was all right. As usual, it was one of those calls where he was half asleep. He said, 'Oh hi, Rory, didn't you hear? We got kicked

Press advertisement for The Damned's *Music for Pleasure* album

off the label again.' Of course, I hadn't heard a thing because there was no way to communicate easily. I was stunned as I had start label hunting all over again."

McLaren would subsequently later make light of the episode saying that should anyone ask him what he did whilst managing the Pistols he'd tell them that he just walked in and out of offices being handed cheques. However, at the time of the A&M sacking the Silver Jubilee was less than three months way.

—Trying To Forget Your Generation

"I'd gone to Torquay Polytechnic at the end of summer 1974, straight out of school, to take a year-long Art Foundation course. I'd met a new girlfriend in the art department and not only did she have the same Iggy and New York Dolls records in her collection as I did, but she'd also shown an interest in learning bass guitar and wanted me to teach her. Within a year we'd moved to London together and started rehearsing a new band, she'd changed her name to Gaye Advert . . . and the rest is history."

TV Smith

The Roxy is often viewed as something of an incongruous setting for what quickly became the epicentre of the London punk scene because the stage and bar areas were on different levels. There was, however, a small bar – little more than a plank of wood resting on two beer barrels – situated to the rear of the downstairs stage area. Located within a spit and bondage-stride from the Covent Garden Opera House, the former fruit

Opposite: The Adverts outside London's Burlington Arcade

and veg warehouse had opened as Chaguaramas at the turn of the Seventies. "It was a right old dump, says Czezowski. "There was no stage, chewing gum on the floor, smelly carpets, ripped leatherette seating, a single, sad broken disco mirror-ball and an empty champagne bucket. The toilets were disgusting too. The funny thing was, I thought 'Wow, this is fantastic.' You could just sense and feel the club at its peak, oozing with ghosts from crazy club nights and parties in the past. I felt such a sense of excitement to think we could bring this sad old place back to life again.

"Barry (Jones) was in a band at the time and felt this would be a great outlet for them, having somewhere to play and rehearse. Fortunately, he knew every young band and musician on the scene, which was a great boost to the club when we started booking and promoting. We really had to pull all the stops out to make this happen as we only had seven days before Generation X's first date. None of us had done anything like it before, so we were learning on the fly."

With a couple of bands booked, the stage built, and the bar fully stocked, the only thing missing was a DJ. Czezowski and Carrington headed out to Forest Hills in South London to speak with Don Letts, whom they knew from his working at Acme Attractions. Czezowski says Letts was initially sceptical as he didn't think punk crowds would like dub reggae. "There were two decks at the Roxy and people would come up to me with requests," says Letts. "I'd tell them to fuck off; why listen to something that you've already heard? I played reggae and, from the first night, it turned out that the punks liked it. If I tried to play something else, they'd be like, 'Put the reggae back on.'"

While having no musical ambitions of his own (though he would, of course, join Mick Jones' post-Clash outfit, Big Audio Dynamite on keyboards), 21-year-old Letts was savvy enough to recognise what was happening about him at The Roxy was worthy of documenting for posterity. On being gifted a Super 8 camera by fashion editor, Caroline Baker, Letts emerged from his DJ booth to film the acts onstage – reportedly selling most of his possessions to procure rolls of film for his camera. Filmed during the 100 days of Czezowski and Carrington's stewardship of The Roxy, Letts' *Punk Rock Movie* features live footage of The Clash, Generation X, The Heartbreakers, Siouxsie and the Banshees, Wayne County & the Electric Chairs,

Slaughter and the Dogs, The Slits, Eater, Subway Sect, X-Ray Spex and Mark Perry's Alternative TV. The film also includes footage of the Pistols' April 3, 1977 show at the Screen on the Green. A preliminary, 60-minute version of the *Punk Rock Movie* was shown in autumn of 1977 at the Institute of Contemporary Arts in London.

"Donovan didn't ask permission to film the bands or anything like that," says Czezowski. "He wouldn't have needed to as things were very fluid. He invited us out to his place in Forest Hill (in south-east London) to see the daily rushes on the two-minute reels he was using. Jeannette [Lee] was also there. She was Donovan's girlfriend at the time and also worked at Acme with him."

Aside from the likes of The Clash, Generation X, Siouxsie and the Banshees, Buzzcocks and The Jam, The Roxy would play host to a gamut of punk-related acts hailing from every corner of the UK – more often than not with Czezowski agreeing to a booking without first hearing them play. Many of these bands would secure recording contracts on the mere basis of their punk affiliation, but only a handful – Penetration, Wire, Slaughter & The Dogs, Squeeze, The Only Ones, X-Ray Spex and The Adverts would go on to enjoy chart success.

The Vibrators were also regulars but were never truly considered part of the Roxy scene. "We were a working band and not in the country long enough to part of the so-called 'Roxy scene'," says John Ellis. "We were probably a bit too old for it anyway. The Roxy was small and very grungy, like many famous venues. I think our not being regarded as part of the Roxy scene was why we were ignored by the cool media."

It's at The Roxy that "gobbing" – the so-called punk tribute – took root. John Lydon has said the vile practice came about owing to the more moronic elements of the Pistols' audiences picking up on his having to clear his sinuses while onstage. The real culprit, however, according to Rat Scabies, was Lydon's fellow Sex Pistol, Steve Jones.

During an interview on the BBC's three-part *Punk Britannia* series (first broadcast in June 2012), Scabies said that Jones had mischievously spat at him from the stage when the two bands had played together at the 100 Club in early July 1976. Scabies had retaliated in kind, and this, in turn, spread into the more boisterous elements in the audience.

When punk "broke" in the wake of the Pistols' ill-feted, expletive-

laden appearance on *Today*, the tabloids willful sensationalizing of
the more unsavoury aspects of the "new teenage cult", resulted in
gobbing became widespread almost overnight. Headline acts could
afford to bring proceedings to a halt and threaten to walk off if the
gobbing persisted, whereas the bands making up the support bill had
little option but to suffer in silence.

X-Ray Spex's effervescent singer, Poly Styrene (born Marianne Joan
Elliott-Said) had already recorded a reggae/rocksteady-style single,
'Silly Billy', for GTO Records (under the stage name Mari Elliott)
when she saw the Sex Pistols play Hastings Pier Pavilion in early July
1976. She was accompanied on the night by her friend, and future
X-Ray Spex manager, Falcon Stuart. It was her nineteenth birthday
and by the end of the evening, she'd decided to form a band. "It was
the summer of '76 at the end of [the] Pier and the senior citizens were
ballroom surfing in the tearooms on the first floor," she reflected.
"But something strange was happening downstairs in the disco
space. The Sex Pistols had landed. They were pounding through
their set in front of a small exclusive London audience on an awayday
excursion to the seaside. After three minutes you knew they were
going to make it: the new order was on its way."

   Born in Bromley, Kent, to a dispossessed Somali aristocrat father
and a legal secretary of Scots/Irish descent, young Marianne was
raised by her mother in Brixton following her parents' divorce. As
a mixed-race child, she often found herself a target for racist abuse.
"It's always worse when you're a kid and I used to get it from both
sides," Poly said in a November 1977 interview with the *NME*. "I got
it most from black kids, especially when I was 14 and really felt black,
wearing me hair in dreadlocks an' that, wanting to be black . . . but the
black kids just took the piss out of me."

   Adopting the name of the fashion label she'd chosen to sell her
homespun autographed couture from a stall on Beaufort Market in
the Kings Road, Poly's singing voice was made all the more distinct
owing to her wearing braces on her teeth. Indeed, her discordant
style has since been described as being "powerful enough to drill
holes through sheet metal". Another factor that served to distinguish
X-Ray Spex from the plethora of bands trying their luck at The Roxy
was their utilising a saxophone in their sound.

   "I took a few saxophone lessons then practised a lot on my own

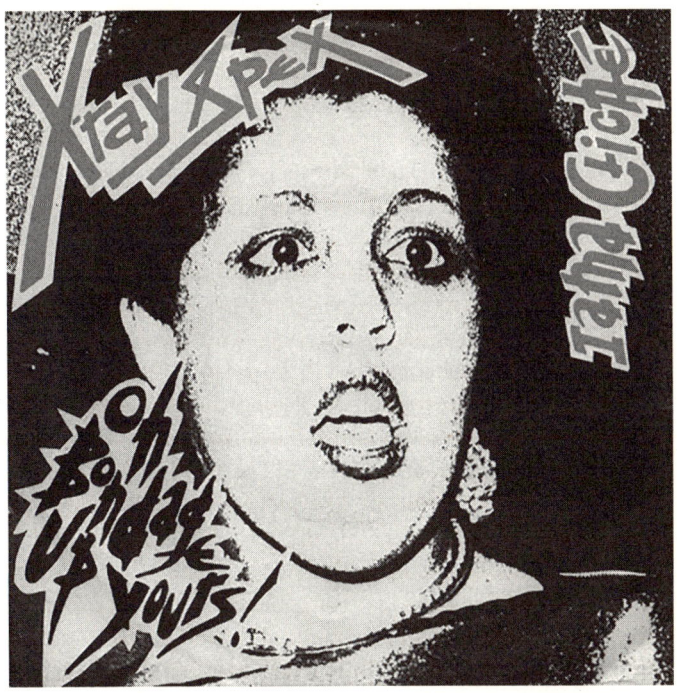

Poly Styrene fronted X-Ray Specs and was one of the women to make it in punk

and busked a bit," says Susan Whitby, who was 15 at the time of her joining X-Ray Spex (adopting the stage name Lora Logic). "I joined a folk band for a few weeks but didn't really like that. I was really rebellious and I wanted to do something different with my life and get into another world. Around autumn '76, I saw an ad in *Melody Maker* looking for 'punk' musicians. I didn't even know what punk was but I just showed up. The manager for X-Ray Spex liked the idea of having another woman in the band with Poly so I made it. We got on so well, really hit it off and rehearsed a lot. It was like a dream." Lora's tenure with the band was to prove short-lived, however, owing to her age.

After just six rehearsals, X-Ray Spex made their debut at The Roxy on March 11, 1977, sharing the bill with The Drones and Chelsea. The Slits' Viv Albertine remembers it being at The Roxy that she first encountered Poly: "She (Poly) was a bit scary because she had this incredible confidence. Also, unlike most of us, she seemed to have proper talent and to really know what she was doing. She seemed a bit above everything else that was going on there. Her voice was a cut above everyone else, as was her songwriting. She was the real thing. She was very pure of thought. She didn't indulge in bad feelings. She was rather innocent, certainly very trusting."

The song that would ultimately come to be regarded as X-Ray Spex's anthem, 'Oh Bondage Up Yours!' features on *Live at the Roxy WC2*, which was released via Harvest Records in July 1977. "I suggested we look at maybe recording the bands because Barry (Jones) had a four-track studio," says Czezowski. "Barry was initially reluctant as he thought we were 'exploiting' the bands but he soon came around to the idea. Through a friend of a friend of Barry's, we were put in touch with Mike Thorne at EMI. Mike was young and very keen and got us a £10,000 advance to record the album. The money went very quickly. Something like £5,000 went towards hiring the Manor Mobile Studio. I was also keen to sign the publishing but Barry put his foot down on that one. I'd honestly no idea there was a CBGBs live album in the making at the same time. In fact, it was purely coincidental because I hadn't even heard of CBGBs."

'Oh Bondage Up Yours' was also chosen as X-Ray Spex's debut single following the band's signing with Virgin Records. The single surprisingly failed to chart, but they would have better luck with the follow-up singles, 'The Day the World Turned Dayglo' (#23) and 'Identity' (#24) in April and July 1978 respectively.

Another new band proving a popular draw at The Roxy were The Adverts. Tim Smith and Gaye Advert had located to London from their native Devon in late-1976. Having recruited guitarist, Howard Pickup (born Howard Boak), and drummer Laurie Driver (born Laurie Muscat), the quartet threw themselves into rehearsals determined to catch the punk wave. The Adverts made their Roxy debut in mid-January 1977 supporting Generation X.

"We went through quite a lot of phases," says Smith. "First of all, I practised alone with Gaye in our West London bedsit, teaching her the songs on bass while I played along on guitar. As Gaye and I had moved up from Devon we didn't really know anyone in the London scene, which made it quite difficult to recruit members for the band."

Contrary to general perception, Gaye's taking up the bass wasn't because of Suzi Quatro. "I saw Suzi on *Top of the Pops* and she was really amazing, of course, but I loved the sound the bass coming through the speakers at the gigs I went to as an art student in Devon. To me, the bass had the most impact. The rhythms were much more interesting than flowery guitar solos. I'd probably been playing for nine months or so by the time Tim and I moved to London."

"Initially I went down the route of putting small ads in the music papers to find a guitarist, but everyone who answered was completely unsuitable," Smith continues. "Most of them seemed unable to grasp the complexity of the songs I was asking them to play and were expecting to play standard blues or rock formats. Then there were others who were more interested in showing off and playing long self-indulgent guitar solos. That was the last thing I wanted. Then when Howard joined, first of all, I taught him the songs at his flat, both of us playing the guitar. Then the three of us went into the rehearsal studio and practised there. At that point, I stopped playing guitar because Howard immediately seemed the right man for the job. He'd been in bands and really knew how to play, but he didn't have the cliché pose of the typical rock guitarist and really applied himself to learning the songs. Even better, he lived just a couple of streets away, so I could walk down and practice with him. Better still, he worked at a rehearsal complex called Cabin so we were able to hire a practice room there at a discounted rate.

"I'm pretty sure Cabin was in Fulham," says Gaye. "I know it was only a short walk from the bedsit Tim and I were renting in Hammersmith. Moving to London was so exciting. We were 19 or 20, but we were so desperate to get away from Devon and London was where everything was happening. I don't remember how we came up with the name 'The Adverts' as I wasn't usually part of the discussions. We were originally going to call ourselves 'One Chord Wonders' because that's what everyone was saying about punk, that the bands couldn't play. And 'One Chord Wonders' was one of the first songs Tim wrote."

"We rehearsed like that for quite a long time, unable to find a drummer. A mate of Howard's called John Towe, who was working at the rehearsal rooms, was interested in joining, but he was already committed to playing with Generation X. John recommended someone he knew who'd expressed an interest in playing drums - and that's how Laurie, who'd never actually played drums in his life before, arrived in the band in late 1976 and we were able to rehearse as a four-piece."

Gaye remembers Towe joining after Laurie Driver's departure in 1978, however. "I'm not saying John wasn't in line to join the band before Laurie, it's just that I don't remember it that way. We struggled for time getting a replacement for Laurie. When we played on The Old Grey Whistle Test we had one of the road crew playing drums. It is true that Laurie hadn't played drums before joining. It was something he fancied doing and he picked it up very quickly."

Smith says the music media didn't initially question The Adverts having a girl on bass. " It didn't make much difference, apart from the fact they concentrated more on Gaye's looks than her ability, in the usual sexist way. Nearly all punk bands were scorned for being amateurish by the old school music press, no matter what gender you were. Later on, some of the new journalists who'd made their name with the punk scene made a few derogatory comments to the effect that people were only interested in the Adverts because of Gaye. But I think that was just revisionism. Actually, in the early punk scene, there wasn't any discrimination.

"I hated that whole 'first punk pin-up' thing," says Gaye. "It certainly wasn't something I was seeking. It actually ended up causing some friction in the band but what can you do? And being a so-called 'punk pin-up' didn't save me from being gobbed at gigs. Funnily enough, it wasn't so much the gob landing on you but rather it landing on the strings. That was just awful because you obviously had to keep playing, running your fingers along the strings."

"The Roxy was small and shabby with a ramshackle low stage and carried its seedy origins as a gay nightclub with it," says Smith. "But it had a special quality. You could feel the love that had gone into making the place happen. Even in the seventies, it was difficult to create a club for a niche music market in the centre of London. These days it would be impossible. I remember the excitement of playing there the first time, getting to play in front of people after months of being stuck in the rehearsal room. We were supporting Slaughter and The Dogs and it was in the very early days of the Roxy opening, so it hadn't quite reached the iconic status it would achieve. It wasn't even all that full. But there was a buzz in the air about the up-and-coming punk scene and the whole evening was a thrill.

Once The Adverts made their Roxy debut things quickly started gathering apace. They acquired a manager on the strength of their inaugural Roxy performance, while one of the songs, the anthemic "Bored Teenagers", deservingly made the track-listing on *The Roxy London WC2* album.

When The Adverts supported The Damned on February 14, 1977, Brian James was so impressed with what he heard that he brought them to Stiff's notice. Jake Riviera and Dave Robinson were equally captivated and offered The Adverts a single's deal. "We were all very excited about signing with Stiff," says Smith. "It felt like exactly the right thing to be happening to us. Two months earlier we hadn't even played a gig. Then to be taken on by what at the time was probably the most important cult label in the UK seemed a massive step forward. Gaye and I were from Torquay, and Torquay in the mid-to-late-seventies was not the easiest place and time to have a band - particularly a band that performed all its own material. The only group that anyone knew who'd ever made it out of the tourist backwater that is the Southwest of England to any kind of international success was a rock band called Wishbone Ash. But now it was our turn."

"It really was exciting," adds Gaye. "We were young and totally inexperienced. We'd only played a couple of gigs and we were signed to a record label. Brian was a lovely guy and really supportive of the Adverts from the beginning. We'd no idea that he'd spoken about us with Jake Riviera, but the next thing we knew Jake showed up at one of our shows with a contract."

The self-deprecating 'One Chord Wonders' would be released via Stiff at the end of April 1977. The single failed to trouble the chart yet would be hailed as a "headlong rush of energy" by both *Melody Maker* and *Sounds*. Stiff Records also signed The Adverts onto The Damned's forthcoming UK tour; the tour poster tongue-in-cheekily reading: "The Adverts know one chord, the Damned know three. See all four at ..."

"We went out on the road with the Damned at an extraordinary time in music history, right in the first wave of an epoch changing movement," Smith continued. "And we were both giving it everything we had to audiences who were as excited about it as we were. To me, that double bill and the gigs we played were what punk rock was all about."

The Damned's much-anticipated debut album, *Damned Damned*

Damned, was released in mid-February 1977. "We recorded it in under 30 hours and that included the mixing," Captain Sensible would boast to the *Record Mirror*'s self-proclaimed "punk correspondent, Barry Cain around the time of the release. "The album was taken live and we had some real fun doing it. We were slightly apprehensive about it at first but the record gave us a chance to really listen to our work. We realised that some of the things we play onstage were all wrong. The album has certainly tightened up our whole approach. Robert Plant checked us out at the Roxy the other night. He's a good geezer – well, I'd buy him a pint. His long hair and the different culture didn't matter."

"Everything happens in a seven-year cycle," Rat Scabies added. "Music progresses but attitudes remain the same. There was Liszt, then this geezer Wagner bowls up with something a lot heavier and he gets slagged off. I just hope we can do something constructive for the kids years from now. I'd like to open a club and put on the kind of music that won't be acceptable then like punk is now. That's something bands like the Stones and the Who have never done with all their millions. I like to think we give people their money's worth. The fans know they can come and see us and do what they like. It's a party."

Cain would also interview The Damned at Stiff's Bayswater offices. The interview would go so well that the band would invite Cain to accompany them out to New York in April where they are set to play a clutch of CBGBs dates before flying onto LA.

Cain was also the last journalist to interview Johnny Rotten before the Pistols' appearance on *Today*. He was also the sole music journalist allowed to bear witness to Sid Vicious' unveiling as a Sex Pistol at the Notre Dame Hall on March 21, 1977. Cain had been working at *Record Mirror* for several weeks by the time of the interview. He was already aware of the Pistols but like many of his peers had assumed they would prove to be more hype than substance. It took but a solitary hearing of the promo copy of the 'Anarchy In The UK' single that EMI had delivered to the paper's north London offices to bring about a rethink, however. "When I heard 'Anarchy' my heart just went 'boom'! Then, when I discovered that John was an Islington boy like me, I thought it would be interesting to interview him. So when the opportunity did arise, I grabbed it. The interview was early in the evening at EMI's offices in Manchester Square. I think he was a tad relieved when he found out that I'd also grown up in a shit bit of Islington and had ducked and dived as much as he had. It was a great interview, and John was, and still is, a wonderful interviewee."

When subsequently writing up the interview, Cain would declare the Pistols as "subtle as a sawn-off shotgun." Yet did he know that late-November evening that an unsuspecting world was about to get both barrels.

The Adverts were traversing the UK with The Damned on the latter band's debut UK headline tour in support of *Damned Damned Damned* when The Clash embarked on their own 25-date headline White Riot Tour, commencing with a show at Guildford Civic Hall. Accompanying The Clash on the punk-package tour were The Jam, Buzzcocks, Subway Sect and The Slits (Birmingham-based, The Prefects, would also appear on the bill at several shows). By this juncture, Buzzcocks had sent a seismic shockwave through the music industry by self-releasing their four-track EP, *Spiral Scratch*, on their own New Hormones label. The band recorded the four tracks in late-December 1976 with Martin Hannett (credited on the label as "Martin Zero"), who would go on to serve as a partner/director with Tony Wilson's Factory Records, at Manchester's Indigo Sound Studios. Howard Devoto later recalled the whole process taking just five hours – "Three hours to record the tracks, with another two for mixing."

Having espied an ad in the local paper about Indigo's offer to record and press a single for £500, Pete Shelley galvanised the rest of the band to beg, steal or borrow the cash from their respective families and friends. The initial 1,000 run soon sold out. Owing to Buzzcocks' burgeoning popularity the EP would go on to sell 16,000 copies, either by mail order or through Virgin Records' Manchester outlet. The manager there is said to have cajoled his counterparts at other Virgin stores to promote the EP.

Within a month of their groundbreaking release, Buzzcocks had also parted company with Howard Devoto. Citing a dissatisfaction at the direction punk was taking for his quitting the band, Devoto turned his back on music in favour of finishing his Humanities degree. Before the year was out, however, Devoto would form Magazine with guitarist and new songwriting partner, John McGeoch. Having signed to Virgin Records, Magazine made their live debut at

Manchester's Rafters at the end of October 1977. Following Devoto's departure, rather than recruit from without, Shelley took over on vocals, Diggle switched from bass to his preferred guitar, and Garth Smith rejoined on bass.

As with Buzzcocks, both Subway Sect and the all-girl Slits were as yet unsigned and were therefore on the tour at The Clash's largesse. "Number One for me at the moment are the Subway Sect," Joe Strummer told Caroline Coon for *Melody Maker* around the time of the tour. "They've got some good ideas. The Slits are good, too. Palmolive on drums! She's the female Jerry Nolan. But like everyone, they need to do thirty gigs in thirty days and they would be a different group. Then they'd be great. The same with us."

The Slits have been deemed in some quarters as being post-punk despite their forming in 1976. Having been thrown out of Flowers of Romance by Sid Vicious for having the gall to stand up to him, Palmolive (who was going out with Joe Strummer and living with him at 101 Walterton Road at the time) decided to form her own all-girl band. This was hardly a novel idea as The Runaways had achieved a modicum of success in the US. It was certainly groundbreaking in England at the time, however. Siouxsie and Poly Styrene were fronting the Banshees and X-Ray Spex respectively, but the idea of girls playing drums, guitar or bass was unheard of on the UK music scene – at least until The Adverts came along.

Aside from Palmolive, the inaugural Slits line-up featured Kate Korus on guitar, Suzy Gutzy on bass and 14-year-old Ari Up (born Ariane Forster) on vocals, although Gutzy would soon be replaced by Tessa Pollitt. In March 177, Viv Albertine went to the Coliseum in Harlesden to see The Slits open for The Clash. The Slits had approached her to play bass as Pollitt was new to the instrument. Albertine, however, was determined to stick with the guitar, despite her playing being rudimentary at best. She wasn't overly keen on joining an all-girl outfit. Within five minutes of The Slits coming onstage, however, Albertine has had a rethink – she now desperately wanted in. She called Nora Forster's house in Shepherd's Bush and asked to speak with Ari. A meeting was set up at the band's dingy Daventry Street rehearsal space. Kate Korus was tellingly absent. "I'm not very good and I've no idea how to jam," Albertine told them. "Neither can we and it's fine," the others chimed back. The Slits asked the displaced Korus to be their manager, but she refused.

Audiences on the forthcoming tour will initially struggle with The Slits' amateurish and discordant fusion of punk, dub and reggae, but they will get better.

The Clash hadn't yet played 30 dates but were raring to go as they'd finally found a replacement for Terry Chimes in the happy-go-lucky 21-year-old Nickie 'Topper' Headon. (He would soon be rechristened 'Topper' by Paul Simonon on account of his supposedly baring a resemblance to Mickey the Monkey from the *Topper comic*). Strummer would subsequently claim The Clash auditioned every jobbing drummer in London following Terry Chimes' departure. Topper already knew Mick Jones from his having auditioned for London SS, and their paths had crossed again at a recent Kinks show at the Rainbow Theatre in Finsbury Park. "I'd never seen them [The Clash] play but I was really excited as soon as I did," Topper told the *Melody Maker* soon after his arrival. "They are incredible. I really wanted to join. They are by far the best band in the country."

Born and raised in Bromley, Topper moved to Dover whilst at secondary school following his schoolteacher parents' relocation to the Kent coastal town. Whilst at school he'd taught himself piano before switching to drums. He would acquire three O Level passes, but left school without bothering to sit his A levels. He went to work as a shipping clerk at a firm where on the docks – where, coincidentally, his boss was the father-in-law of soon-to-be Clash road manager, Johnny Green. After twelve months of diligently processing outgoing shipments, Topper's mind was beginning to wander – and it would wander all the way to London. The first thing he did upon arrival in the capital was to marry his childhood sweetheart, Wendy. With the nuptials taken care of he then set about perusing the Musicians Wanted section in the *Melody Maker* classifieds. Bernard Rhodes would churlishly dismiss Topper as a "provincial tosser" but there is no truer adage in rock 'n' roll than that of a band only being as good as its drummer. With Topper able to play a variety of styles, The Clash's engine room was now stoked to the max.

For the past nine months or so The Clash had been singing about wanting a riot of their own in "White Riot". With the punk rock genie now well and truly out of its bottle, they were about to get their wish. On Monday, May 9, The tour rolled back into London for a sell-out show at the aforementioned Rainbow Theatre. The 3000-capacity all-seater Rainbow was by far the biggest venue The Clash had played to date. In its former guise as the Astoria Theatre, the cinema had staged numerous one-off music events during the Sixties – most notably the night Jimi Hendrix first set light to his guitar in March 1967. The audience's overexuberance on the night resulted in some 200 stall seats being trashed. As anticipated, the following day's tabloids screamed about the "Punk Rock Shock Horror!", but the hyperbole was wholly unwarranted as an agreement had been reached beforehand whereby The Clash would cover the cost of any damages incurred during the performance.

The Jam were initially content to show punk solidarity, but it wasn't long before their management – namely Paul Weller's dad, John – started voicing his displeasure at what his charges were getting in return for the alleged four-figure sum they'd handed over to play the opening ten dates on the tour. As a result, the Woking three-piece, whose own incendiary debut album, In the City, was holding its own on the UK album chart, left the tour immediately after the Rainbow date.

It wasn't only rival acts that The Clash would find themselves at loggerheads during the tour, however. CBS's decision to ride roughshod over the group's supposed "artistic control" by releasing "Remote Control" as the follow-up to "White Riot" left the band fuming – especially as they'd already informed *Melody Maker* that their follow-up single would be 'Janie Jones'. On the plus side, of course, the band's displeasure over the 'Remote Control' debacle was that it incited them to pen 'Complete Control', which many fans consider one of the best songs within the Clash canon.

Getting thrown off A&M would provide McLaren with an endless stream of anecdotes in later years, and had the Pistols not written 'God Save the Queen' he may well have bided his time in selecting his next victim. A&M's terminating the Pistols' contract before the ink had barely dried left the band somewhat deflated. So much so that McLaren hit upon the idea of sending the band on a short getaway break to Jersey with Jamie Reid acting as chaperone. Jersey was, and is, a respectable holiday destination for both the British and French alike and the island's indignant dignitaries had no intention of allowing the vile and disgusting Sex Pistols to defile its splendour. They were summarily prohibited from checking into their hotel by the local police and given 24-four hours to vacate the island. Reid

The Clash wrote 'Complete Control' after CBS released
'Remote Control' as a single without the band's permission

succeeded in securing bookings at another hotel whose manager
had no objection in taking the Pistols' shilling, but he and the band
were kept under close surveillance until it was time for them to head
for the airport. The Pistols had no sooner returned to London when
McLaren's new *aide-de-camp*, John 'Boogie' Tiberi, suggested an
alternate excursion to West Berlin.

The 26-year-old Anglo-Italian Tiberi had been a face on London's
Soho scene since the late sixties. He'd been working as a photographer
at an advertising studio when he'd happened upon The 101ers playing
one of their residency shows at The Elgin pub in Ladbroke Grove.
Having been captivated by the charismatic Strummer, Tiberi took
on the role of the band's unofficial photographer before agreeing to
become their manager. Indeed, it was he who was responsible for
booking the then unsigned and relatively unknown Sex Pistols as

support for The 101ers at the Nashville Rooms the previous April.

Tiberi was so captivated by the exciting new scene surrounding the Pistols that he readily followed Strummer when the latter quit The 101ers. He admits to his being initially impressed with Rhodes' vision for The Clash but soon tired of his "left-of-centre" rhetoric.

"Bernard was a very interesting character, with some very interesting ideas, but I quickly sensed that it wasn't going to work," says Tiberi. "I'd been the one running the show with the 101ers, and Bernard wanted 'complete control' of what Joe, Mick and Paul were doing.

"I can't say I actually worked for the Clash but when I left I took a month out before deciding I'd better do something positive with my life. I was vaguely aware that Nils Stevenson was no longer involved with the Pistols, so I went to see Malcolm at the shop. It was around the time of Glen's leaving. He told me to come back the next day as he might have something for me. I went back the next day, and that's when he offered me the job as road manager. Malcolm said that he'd need to get a reference from Bernard. I'm still not sure that he was joking."

Upon their arrival in Berlin, Tiberi hired a Volkswagen to ferry them around the separated city's sights such as the Reichstag Building, and the Berlin Wall. Tiberi had even thought to bring his Super-8 camera along and shot footage of the Pistols goofing around at Checkpoint Charlie. They would have crossed through the most notorious of the Berlin Wall's eight official border crossing points to peruse East Berlin's "cheap essential scenery" had Sid not left his passport back at the hotel.

Soon after their return to London the Pistols played a free show at the Screen on the Green in Islington with The Slits in support – said support slot most likely coming at the behest of Rotten who was now romantically linked with Ari Up's mother, Nora. Jon Savage, who was reviewing the show for the *NME*, believed the Pistols to have improved since their first appearance at the cinema back in November - even if the majority of the songs making up the set-list was "beginning to sound all too familiar".

There'd been no shortage of takers following the Pistols' being dropped by EMI, but a second sacking in as many months had made them something of pariahs within the music industry. The only label willing to table an offer was Virgin Records. McLaren was loath to break bread with Richard Branson, but he was desperate to get "God Save the Queen" into the shops in time for the Silver Jubilee. Branson claims to have contacted Leslie Hill the morning after the Pistols' appearance on *Today* offering to take the band off EMI's hands. Hill has since gone public to say he has no recollection of receiving such a call, however. Regardless of whether Branson made the call, he was about to get his wish.

By the advent of the twenty-first century, the Virgin logo was near-omnipresent, but Branson's first step on the entrepreneurial ladder came with the launch of *Student* magazine in 1968. By seriously undercutting the competition in advertising the hit records of the day in *Student*, Branson became something of an overnight success. When the taxman started looking into his selling records that had been declared export stock, Branson was forced to repay all unpaid VAT, as well as receiving a hefty £70,000 fine. Branson's parents are said to have remortgaged their home so that Branson could repay the outstanding VAT. Branson's fortunes would quite literally take an upturn, however, following the phenomenal success of Mike Oldfield's *Tubular Bells*, which has sold in excess of 16 million copies worldwide.

Much to McLaren's chagrin the Sex Pistols signed with Virgin on May 12, 1977, for a one-album deal worth an initial £15,000, with a further £50,000 going into the Glitterbest coffers in return for Virgin having the right to release Sex Pistols product in all world territories.

'God Save the Queen' b/w 'Did You No Wrong' was released on Friday, May 27, 1977. For McLaren, it was a case of déjà vu when the workers at CBS' pressing plant in Aylesbury (CBS served as Virgin's distributors in the UK), imitated their counterparts at EMI's Hayes plant in threatening strike action if they were forced to handle the controversial Pistols platter. Unsurprisingly, all four major music weeklies made "God Save the Queen" their respective 'Single of the Week' with *Melody Maker*, *NME* and *Record Mirror* all placing the Pistols on the front cover. Equally unsurprisingly, Boots, W.H. Smiths and Woolworths refused to stock the single. Indeed, Woolworth's would refuse to even list 'God Save the Queen' on its instore Singles chart, little realising the kudos they gifted the Pistols in doing so. Jamie Reid's cross-media campaign also fell foul of the censors, with both Thames and LWT rejecting the proposed 'God Save the

Queen' TV advert out of hand. The promotional video to 'God Save the Queen', shot by Julian Temple at the Marquee in the run-up to the single's release, was shelved indefinitely and wouldn't resurface until being included in *The Great Rock 'N' Roll Swindle*.

Capital Radio and every other commercial radio station across the country refused to air the single or broadcast the radio adverts. (The IBA (Independent Broadcasting Authority) instructed all commercial radio and TV stations not to broadcast the Pistols single as it contravened Section 4 (10) (A) of the IBA act.) The BBC banned the single on the grounds that it was in "gross bad taste", but Radio One begrudgingly allowed John Peel to air the song twice during the first week of June. Despite such unprecedented draconian measures, during the first week of its release 'God Save the Queen' sold upwards of 150,000 copies and slammed onto the UK chart at #11. The following week – Silver Jubilee week - the single shoot up to #2, only being denied the coveted top spot by Rod Stewart's version of Crazy Horse's "I Don't Want to Talk About It".

History may have recorded that Rod Stewart topped the chart during the week of the Silver Jubilee, but there is compelling evidence to suggest shadowy governmental figures purposely kept "God Save the Queen" off the top spot to spare Her Majesty's blushes. CBS, who distributed both singles, and have always acknowledged that the Pistols outsold Rod Stewart by at least two-to-one the week prior to Silver Jubilee week. Branson has always maintained the BPI (British Phonographic Institute) placed pressure on the BRMB (British Market Research Bureau) to drop all the chart-return shops connected with Virgin Records from that particular week's census. His argument is given credence by the fact that the BPI's then head, John Fruin - who was also Managing Director of WEA Records at the time - subsequently lost his job in 1981 owing to irregularities over chart placings of several WEA acts.

Two days prior to the Queen's Royal Progress trip down the River Thames from Greenwich to Lambeth in a re-enactment of the famous progresses taken by Queen Elizabeth I, McLaren and Virgin collaborated on a special Jubilee Boat Party – aboard the Queen Elizabeth, appropriately enough - to celebrate the release of "God Save the Queen". In the absence of a stage, the Pistols set up at the boat's stern. As the boat sailed past the Houses of Parliament the band is said to have launched into "Anarchy in the UK". While a piratical jaunt along the Thames looked a jolly jape on paper, no one seemed to have spared any thought for the acoustics. As such, the Pistols' short set was marred by feedback throughout. "[It was] another of Malcolm's ideas," Paul Cook reflected. "Let's go down [the river] in the boat and play 'Anarchy' outside the Houses of Parliament. Brilliant! It doesn't get much better than that. Apparently, you're not allowed to do that on the Thames – but no, you are actually. It's just because it was us. They knew the Pistols was on the boat and that was it, the police turned up."

Two police riverboats had come alongside the Queen Elizabeth, but with everyone aboard seemingly behaving themselves they were powerless to intrude. Indeed, the evening may well have passed without incident had Jah Wobble not punched a French photographer. The beleaguered captain was still smarting at his being duped into believing Virgin had hired the boat to promote one of their German electronic acts. Having put out an SOS call to the river police, he cut the power and turned the boat around. By the time the Queen Elizabeth arrived back at Charing Cross Pier scuffles broke out as police officers boarded the boat and set about manhandling the revellers down the gangplank. "Once the police got onto the boat they turned the electricity off," says Jordan. "The only person who could carry on playing was Paul. I was sitting on a table just to the left of him, banging the top of it. It went from me to Paul, me to Paul, this little protest. We stayed there while everyone else was hauled down the gangplank and into the waiting meat wagons – Malcolm, Vivienne and Branson first."

McLaren, Westwood, Sophie Richmond, Ben Kelly and Rotten's younger brother, Jimmy Lydon, were taken to Bow Street Police Station. McLaren had raised his fist at the waiting officers, calling them "fucking fascist bastards". When his case was eventually heard the following February he was duly fined £100. Westwood was found guilty of obstructing a police officer and fined £15 with £15 costs.

There had been plenty of arrests but the individual band members managed to slip away undetected. The *Daily Mirror*, having been the only national newspaper to report the boat party arrests, therefore took it upon itself to launch a moral crusade against the Pistols; the paper's June 12 banner headline declaring "Punish the Punks". Jamie Reid was the first to suffer the backlash. He was set upon by four men near his flat the day following the *Mirror*'s dictum, suffering a broken nose and a fractured right tibia. The following Saturday, June 18, Rotten, Chris Thomas, and Wessex Studio's in-house engineer, Bill Price, were set upon by a gang of knife-wielding thugs in a pub car park. Thomas came away with a slight cut to his face, while Price received a nasty cut along his left arm from trying to fend off their assailants. Rotten, being the obvious target, suffered cuts to his face and left hand, severing two tendons. As he scrambled into the back of Thomas' car one of the thugs slashed him on the thigh with a machete and would surely have been left with a permanent limp had he not been wearing thick leather trousers. He would suffer a second attack whilst attending a Pirates' show at Dingwalls the following week.

Two days on from the attack on Rotten, Thomas and Price, Paul Cook was assaulted by five Teddy Boys armed with a crowbar on the Goldhawk Road, close to Shepherd's Bush Tube station. This attack was more sartorial than sectarian, however, as the Teds supposedly took offence to a Sex Pistol wearing Beetle crushers.

The Pistols were gearing up to whatever backlash awaited them once 'God Save the Queen' was out in the shops when 999 finally settled upon their enduring name. The nucleus of the band were brothers, Keith and Guy Lucas. Singer/guitarist Keith was already established on London's live circuit having co-founded Kilburn and the High Roads with Ian Dury. Dury had been his tutor at Canterbury College of Art, and the two would often get together at the student house where Keith was living to jam or listen to Gene Vincent and Eddie Cochrane records. Guy Lucas also had affiliations with the Kilburns, his having played guitar on several of the band's demo sessions. Dr. Feelgood's management would approach Keith following Wilko Johnson's departure from the band, but the Lucas brothers had already seen for themselves that punk was in the ascendancy. Rather than trade off Keith's former glory with the Kilburns, the brothers gave themselves a punk makeover. Keith became 'Nick Cash', while Guy opted for 'Guy Days'.

Cash and Days placed an ad in *Mélody Maker* seeking a drummer and bassist. Auditions were held at Manos Studios on the King's Road. Tony James, Jon Moss, Chrissie Hynde and future Spear of Destiny and Stiff Little Fingers' drummer Dolphin Taylor would all be passed over in favour of Jon Watson and Joe Strummer's old art school friend Pablo Labritain, who'd sat in on early Clash rehearsals. Labritain's connection with Strummer would bring Bernard Rhodes to their door, but the latter's overtures were soon rebuffed. Billed as "The Dials", the quartet made their debut at Northampton Cricket Club towards the end of January 1977. Further name-changes ensued but having tired of Gene Carson's Fanatics and 48 Hrs. By May 1977 they'd settled on 999. Unsurprisingly, one of the band's first original numbers was called 'Emergency'. 999's now-iconic logo – a cheap raffle ticket bearing the serial no. AS8502 and thumbprint - was designed by George Snow, who would go on to design the sleeves for their early singles.

Taking their lead from Buzzcocks, 999 released their July 1977 debut single, 'I'm Alive' b/w 'Quite Disappointing' on their own Labritain label. *Sounds* lauded 999 as "One of the best pop groups to emerge in years [that] might, conceivably, be bigger still than the Sex Pistols," and made 'I'm Alive'their 'Single of the Week'. Owing to their having built up a steady following with residencies at both the Hope & Anchor and the Marquee they soon sold out the initial 10,000 pressing. Again, as with Buzzcocks, this was enough to tempt United Artists into signing the band. Their first single for UA, 'Nasty Nasty' (b/w 'No Pity') surprisingly failed to chart but has since been proclaimed a seminal punk classic.

Speaking with Phil Singleton from the *God Save Sex Pistols* website, Cash said that 1978 was the band's most visible year in terms of gigging and releasing product. During that year 999 would release two albums and four singles. Yet despite their growing popularity, their eponymous debut album stalled at #53, while the follow-up, Separates, disappeared without a trace. And of the four singles, only the latter, 'Homicide', only just troubled the Top 40.

Still smarting at his being squeezed out of The Roxy by the club's unscrupulous landlords jacking up the rent in the hope of milking the punk cash cow, Andy Czezowski entered into negotiations with Terry Draper who ran Crackers discothèque at 203 Wardour Street about staging weekly punk nights there. Crackers was significantly larger than The Roxy, with a 650 capacity. With the deal all but finalized, Czezowski began booking bands and printing up flyers. He also informed the music press of his intentions. "BZZZZ, BZZZZ, BZZZZ: There is nothing like a rumour, nothing in the world," *Sounds* trumpeted in its June 2, 1975 issue. "In this case, the rumour

is a POSSIBLE new club, POSSIBLY run by Andy Czezowski of Roxy
founder fame, POSSIBLY in Berwick Street, Soho, with a POSSIBLE
opening night early next week . . . Remember where you read it first.
Possibly . . . *Sounds*, 25.6.77."

Since vacating The Roxy, Czezowski had overseen the release
of the *Live at the Roxy WC2* album and was working alongside the
manager of Slaughter & The Dogs, Ray Rossi (brother of the band's
guitarist, Mick), with the view to staging ten or so gigs up and down
the UK featuring those acts that featured on the album. The first
of these was booked for July 9 at Manchester's Belle Vue Arena
featuring Slaughter and The Dogs, Johnny Moped, Eater and X-Ray
Spex.

Speaking with *Sounds* about the Crackers proposal, Czezowski
said how he'd already come up with a couple of names for his new
club: "One was the 'Void' and the other the 'Vortex', not realising it
was the name of a group of artists from the 1920s and '30s. There was
also a Noël Coward play of the same name from that period. "Barry
and Susan and I had gone our separate ways by this time but I was
still keen to find another venue. I was out and about one day when I
bumped into an acquaintance called John King, and it was John that
told me about Crackers. We went to see the place and it was more
than adequate for our purposes

"I got it all going and it was looking good and then I find out he
(Draper) got rid of me. I turned up one day and two thugs on the
door asked what did I want? I said, 'I'm putting the club on. Don't
you remember me? I set this all up. We got a deal to rent it off you.'
'No I've never seen you before' they replied. That was the end of that
and I was out before I was in!"

Unbeknown to Czezowski the duplicitous Draper had hooked
up with a guy called John Miller (aka John McKillop). Miller, an
ex-Irish Guard, has since given an alternate account as to how The
Vortex got its name. He'd recently come out of the Irish Guards and
was looking at setting up a business whereby he'd supply security to
the clubs operating in London's West End. By chance, he'd swung
by Crackers to speak with Draper just as a gang of drunken Scottish
football hooligans began making a nuisance of themselves. Having
helped diffuse the situation, Miller and Draper fell into conversation,
by the end of which the former offered to take over the Crackers on
Monday nights when the club was closed. Rather than charge Miller

a nightly rent, Draper opted for the bar takings. Miller supposedly then came up with 'Vortex' for his club. (Tuesdays were also soon given over to punk nights)

The Vortex opened on Monday, 4 July with Buzzcocks headlining and their fellow Mancunians, The Fall and John Cooper Clarke in support. Rumour has it The Heartbreakers gatecrashed the party by jumping up onstage and running through a couple of songs after Buzzcocks had finished their set.

Further gigs were quickly arranged with Siouxsie and The Banshees, The Adverts and Generation X all headlining. The Vortex would soon become notorious for attracting violent crowds. So much so, that Paul Weller would be inspired to pen The Jam's "'A' Bomb in Wardour Street', name-checking the venue within the lyric.

"The bouncers were real heavy types – leftovers from the Sixties," says Czezowski. "They exploited the fighting and even insisted on strip-searching the girls. It was despicable. I went down there on opening night and they said I couldn't come in. They were prepared to stop me physically as well. After all the aggro we had with the Roxy I thought, 'I'm not doing this again.' I did, of course, but the [Brixton] Fridge was different because things had moved on by then."

— Observation, We Want Action

"The spring of 1977 turned out to be a huge turning point in the Hollywood scene; the punk-rock storm clouds that'd been gathering and building steadily turned into a killer tornado. Word spread quickly on the street that the Damned, the first UK punk band to visit America, were playing a two-night, four-show run at the Starwood. Anticipation ran high because since their first album had come out in February, the Damned had usurped The Clash as our favourite English band."

Pleasant Gehman

July 1977 saw the opening of LA's foremost punk-orientated club, The Masque; a subterranean concrete enclave nestled beneath the Pussycat porn theatre on Hollywood Boulevard in West Hollywood. The Masque was the brainchild of Scottish-born rock promoter, Brendan Mullen, an entrepreneurial amateur musician who'd relocated to LA in 1973. The original club would remain open for a little over six months before being closed down in January 1978 by the city's Fire Marshals owing to Mullen's

Opposite: The Damned outside Stiff Records' office in Alexander Street

failure to procure the requisite city permit to stage live music.

The Masque's coming into being was pure happenstance as Mullen had initially rented the warren of dingy, airless rooms as somewhere where he and his friends could play raucous rock 'n' roll free from the risk of police intervention. An opportunity soon presented itself, however, when the landlord offered Mullen the 10,000-square-foot basement for just $850 a month. All Mullen need do was rent out the other rooms to local bands and he could live there for free. "I was tooling off Hollywood Boulevard searching for a cheap space when I spotted an open doorway in a grimy alley," Mullen wrote in his 2007 opus *Live at the Masque: Nightmare in Punk Alley*. "[I] went down a flight of greasy stone stairs, and, just like Theseus stalking the Minotaur, dragged string and some old hose pipe behind me, fearful of not being able to find the way back out from this pitch-black, seemingly endless labyrinth of doors, corridors, passageways, stairwells, tunnels, and musty odd-shaped rooms."

The basement was part of the Hollywood Center Building, the five-storey structure at 1655 North Cherokee Avenue that movie mogul, Cecil B. DeMille, had built to serve as his Hollywood HQ. By Mullen's reckoning, he was the building's first occupant since the Don Martin School of Radio and Broadcasting vacated the premises some 30 years earlier. "I advertised cheap band rehearsal facilities in the *Recycler*, and the Berlin Brats, Backstage Pass, and the Motels were my first customers," Mullen reflected. "Punk rock, British, American, or otherwise, was not the main agenda. I filed the dba ("doing business as") paperwork and the bank account under New Era Productions but rechristened the space the Masque. I was compiling a list of insane names that people were coming up with . . . like the 'Pit and the Pendulum', the 'Toilet', 'Wankers Disco', the 'Hellhole', 'Slime-O-Rama', the 'Puke Bowl', and God knows what else."

The "Masque" had also featured on the list, but Mullen initially didn't think any more of it than he had the other names. Indeed, it was only due to his business associate, Al Hansen, constantly bemoaning how the "Masque" sounded like some antiquated private homosexual club that Mullen's inbuilt "contrarian reaction to authority" kicked in. "The more he (Hansen) bad-rapped the name, the more contrarian I'd react. I said the dictionary definition of masque was a form of 'cheap, amateur, histrionic medieval entertainment.' Finally, Al stormed out in disgust, saying, 'Where the fuck is the punk meaning in that?' so the 'Masque' it was, literally because an older man (Hansen was in his early 50s at the time) seemed to be telling me what to do, and as fate would have it, I never saw Al the Jewish art leprechaun again."

Al Hansen's being inadvertently responsible for the Masque getting its name wouldn't be his sole contribution to LA's embryonic punk scene, however, as his daughter, Bibbe, explained: "While dad was there with Brendan the Controllers came and rented a room. I think they were one of the first people in, and that's how dad ended up managing them."

Mullen, who was to suffer a fatal heart attack in October 2009, said that he was still looking to utilize his subterranean acquisition as a rehearsal space and then hopefully expand into a recording studio. "The Controllers were one of the first, so one day I asked them, 'Where do you play?' And they're like, 'Well, nowhere . . . but we're hoping to get a gig at the Orpheum.' I'm bored out of my mind and so I said, 'Would you consider playing a party this weekend for friends?' Somebody sprayed the graffiti: 'Do something or go home,' and that was it."

"The Controllers needed a place to play loud," their frontman, Johnny Stingray, revealed. "Brendan was impressed enough by our tenacity and cash flow to rent us a tiny room on a monthly basis. [He charged us] $2 an hour provided we didn't mind practising in the middle of the night. We didn't."

Mullen subsequently invited The Controllers to help provide the entertainment for another of his parties, but it wasn't until he begrudgingly acquiesced to another of his tenants' petitions to stage a showcase for *Slash* magazine that the LA scene first began taking root.

"By the fall of '77, Brendan was hosting regular shows," Stingray continued. "We were trying our best to be the house band by weaselling our way onto as many shows as we could."

X vocalist/bassist, John Doe (born John Nommensen Duchac), agrees that it was Mullen's turning the Masque over to live music that served as the real turning point. "At first there were only fifty people there. Then there were seventy-five, then a hundred. By the end of '77, when the Whisky had ten people at their club and there were two hundred people at the Masque, our bands started getting booked at the Whisky. Then the *LA Times* got behind it."

Theresa Kereakes, the co-founder of *Lobotomy: the Brainless Magazine*, says she became aware of The Masque almost the minute it opened, but questions the ownership of the lease.

"The Masque began as a rehearsal space. The shows came later. A girl called Jenny Body, a.k.a Jenny Schorr, was in a band called Backstage Pass. It was Jenny that found the place, together with her bandmate, Marina Del Rey. They leased the Masque. Brendan managed it. I don't think he could lease it on his own because he was from Scotland. Jenny and Marina were locals and from prominent families. I don't know the business details, but this is what I remember. I am currently housemates with Spock (born Joanna Dean) from Backstage Pass and have known her for 40 years, so she knows these details first-hand. I'm not sure if the details are well-known, but it's how the Masque got started."

The Masque's graffiti-laden interior was squalid beyond description, but during its short life, every LA punk band of note - The Dickies, Avengers, X, The Weirdos, The Dils, The Bags, The Screamers and The Germs - would all grace the one-foot riser that served as a makeshift stage. "It was very dark down there," says Kereakes. "There was a steep stairway going down into the place. It's been almost 40 years since I was in there, but I still remember those stairs . . . There were a few little rooms, and then a bigger - but by no means large - open music room with lots of spray-painted graffiti on the walls. It was like our secret world. It had to be. Can you imagine telling your folks you were going to a porn theatre to watch a punk rock band?"

The Masque certainly lived up to its dictionary definition, becoming something of a continuous alternative masquerade ball where the regulars – especially the girls – could leave their humdrum lives at the top of the stair and be their true selves for a few hours. "The Masque was like heaven and hell all rolled into one, "says Hellin Killer (a.k.a Helena Roessler) who would subsequently go on to become Sid Vicious' temporary squeeze during the Sex Pistols ill-fated January '78 US Tour "It was the greatest thing since sliced bread. You could always go there . . . it was like a clubhouse. It was like a bomb shelter, a basement, all these weird rooms, stairways going up to a cement ceiling . . . it was so amazing, such a dive, but it was our dive."

Those hip Los Angelians tuning into Rodney Bingenheimer's KROQ radio show had been receiving a nightly education on what was happening on the London and New York punk scenes since the station had gone back on the air in August 1976. Bingenheimer was a well-known face on the LA music scene from his Rodney Bingenheimer's English Disco, which catered to visiting British rock royalty of the day. The New York Dolls and The Stooges had both performed live at the club, and Elvis was known to swing by on occasion for a pint or two of Watney's Red (Watney's was the brewery Paul Cook was serving his electrician apprenticeship before committing himself to the Sex Pistols, of course). "Gary [Bookasta, KROQ's owner] wanted me to play glam rock but as soon as I went on the air, from the first show on, I went right onto punk," Bingenheimer explained to Brendan Mullen and Marc Spitz in 2001. "The first thing I played was the Ramones. I could play whatever I wanted. As far as LA the bands, I played the Berlin Brats, who had one foot in glam, the Dils and the Motels, who were more new wave. By early '77 bands were handing me demos, and sometimes I'd play those, too."

The Germs wouldn't release their only album until October 1979, yet the four-piece fronted by Darby Crash (born Jan Paul Beahm) were one of the first bona fide LA punk bands. Crash and his ever-present sidekick, Pat Smear (born Georg Albert Ruthenberg), had settled on "The Germs" when putting a band together on their being kicked out of high school. The duo had initially hit upon the idea of calling the band "Sophistifuck and the Revlon Spam Queens", and only gave it up on realising the difficulties they would face trying to fit the name on a T-shirt.

Theresa Kereakes' fellow *Lobotomy* co-founder, Pleasant Gehman had only recently relocated to LA aged just 16 when she first encountered the future Crash and Smear at a Queen show at LA's Santa Monica Civic Auditorium at the end of March 1975. Having devoured *Creem*, *Rock Scene* and *Andy Warhol's Interview* from the age of 12, Gehman was hopelessly enamoured with rock 'n' roll and had arrived in LA with dreams of hanging out backstage at the Whisky and the Rainbow drinking champagne with rock and movie stars. To assist in making her fantasy a reality she scored a part-time job working the box office at the Whisky. She'd been sharing a spliff with one-time Hollywood heartthrob Tony Curtis at the Queen show when Crash and Smear had caught her eye. "They both looked amazing," she reflected. "The taller one (Smear) was bare-chested and bare-footed, with a long black satin cape billowing out behind him as they came past. The other (Crash) was a real-life Bowie action figure, dressed head-to-toe in white, a fluorescent red rat-tail mullet framing his ice-blue eyes and powdered cheeks, with a perfectly rendered lightning bolt crisscrossing his face. My prayers had been answered!

"They took their seats a few rows in front of me. Never one to ignore an omen, I decided to take fate into my own hands. I grabbed a matchbook from my purse, borrowed a pen from Tony Curtis – can you believe that! – and scrawled 'Aladdin Sane, You Cosmic Orgasm – Call Me! (Along with my phone number, of course) and tossed the matchbook with pitcher precision. The next day they called me, and my life was changed forever. Our affinity was immediate. We quickly became an inseparable trio. They were living at the beach, so I'd cut school and we'd go hang out at Santa Monica's Lifeguard Station #26, which was known as the 'Juvenile Delinquent Beach'. Of course, I had major crushes on both of them. In fact, I couldn't decide which one I liked the best until the decision was made for me when Georg – or 'Bobby Pyn' as he was calling himself then – made his move. I was his first official girlfriend."

It was at a subsequent Queen LA show at The Forum in early March 1977 – in support of their *Day at the Races* album - that The Germs first began to take shape. Crash and Smear were loitering with obvious intent outside Freddie Mercury's suite at the Beverly Hilton in the hope of gaining an audience with the singer when two teenage female Queen obsessives called Terri Ryan and Belinda Carlisle arrived with the same intention. Despite their repeated knockings, Mercury was either otherwise engaged or simply not in his room. The quartet eventually tired of holding their vigil, and instead hunkered down on the carpet further along the corridor to trade information about the other couple's lives. With Crash and Smear already looking to put a band together, the conversation inevitably turned to music. By the end of the evening, Crash and Smear asked their new friends if they'd like to get involved.

The four would get together in Smear's parents' garage. To call these gatherings "rehearsals" would be stretching credibility as Smear was the only one with any understanding of a musical instrument - and his capability on the guitar was rudimentary at best. This mattered little of course, as punk rock eschewed all musical proficiency. With Crash already having nominated himself as singer, Carlisle and Ryan were left to fight amongst themselves as to which role they would take in the fledgling band's rhythm section. Whichever way they decided, Carlisle ended up on drums. The girls also underwent a punk name change: Ryan settling on 'Lorna Doom' while Carlisle opted for 'Dottie Danger'.

The Damned's two-day, four-show run at the Starwood in West Hollywood followed on from the band's CBGBs run that *Record Mirror*'s roving reporter, Barry Cain, had reported on. "The Damned were in town to play a couple of shows at the Starwood," Gehman continued. "They were set to make an in-store appearance at Bomp Records in Burbank the same day that a local band called the Weirdos were playing a show at the Orpheum Theatre. We were drinking cold duck and we were pretty much gone. Bobby and Pat were telling anyone that would listen that they had a band, and someone said, 'Well if you're a band why don't you play with the Weirdos tonight? They had only rehearsed like four times or something and didn't really have any songs as such; they more or less did it as a dare."

"Bobby Pyn and Pat were at the Damned in-store when Bobby came up to us," Weirdos' frontman, John Denney remembered. "[He] said in quite a timid 'small boy's voice, 'We have a band. Can we play?' we thought it was the perfect setup for us – a band of young kids who could barely play at all wouldn't threaten us because we'd been gigging without a drummer."

Flyers for The Germs' upcoming debut at the Orpheum were hastily printed and posted around West Hollywood. Disaster struck, however, when Carlisle suddenly fell ill. The diagnosis was mononucleosis, a highly-infectious disease more commonly known as "mono" or glandular fever. Carlisle was forced to move back in with her parents while she recuperated. Infinitely more devastating, however, was having to bow out of The Germs' debut outing. She still attended the Orpheum date, heartily cheering on her last-minute replacement, Becky Barton. In keeping with The Germs' stage-name theme, Barton, whom Carlisle knew from her Newbury High art class days, playfully called herself 'Donna Rhia'.

Since opening its doors in February 1926, the Orpheum Theatre had played host to some of the most venerable names in show business – including a young Judy Garland (billed under her real name Francis Gumm), Jack Benny, Lena Horne, Ella Fitzgerald, Duke Ellington, Aretha Franklin and Stevie Wonder. Little Richard had also Wop-bop-a-loo-mop alop-bom-bomped the Orpheum's boards, but the theatre had surely seen nothing quite like The Germs.

The Germs' debut would last for all of five minutes before someone pulled the plug. As musicianship was hardly the order of the day, it's most likely someone associated with The Weirdos took umbrage to Crash's plunging one of the headline act's microphones into a jar of peanut butter and smearing it over his naked torso. The Germs came away from the Orpheum fully vindicated, however; caring little about their brusque removal from the stage or that they'd come close to outnumbering their audience. "We made noise," Smear reflected. "Darby stuck the mic in a jar of peanut butter. It was a dare; we had no songs or anything! Lorna wore her pants inside out, and Darby covered himself in red liquorice. . . we made noise for five minutes until they threw us off."

"When the Germs went on it was obvious very fast [that] they had no music at all," Denney continued. "They were just kids literally playing feedback and banging around smearing mayonnaise and peanut butter all over themselves and the PA. It was very amusing and really entertaining, but the gag wore out fast . . . it became tedious and unfunny after about ten or fifteen minutes."

Lorna Doom would remain with The Germs until their original split in 1980. Belinda Carlisle would, of course, go on to achieve worldwide fame with The Go-Go's

'God Save the Queen' was still treading water in the UK Top 20 when Virgin released 'Pretty Vacant' in early July. Somewhat amazingly, given Rotten's deliberate emphasis on "Va-*cunt*!", the single escaped censure and provided the Pistols with their second Top Ten hit (peaking at #6). Equally surprising, was Rotten's guest appearance on Tommy Vance's Capital Radio show – billed as "The Punk and His Music" – during which the singer talked of the recent attacks whilst picking some of his favourite music. The decidedly un-punk tracks chosen included Tim Buckley's 'Sweet Surrender', Augustus Pablo's 'King Tubby Meets the Rockers Uptown', Bowie's 'Rebel Rebe', Dr Alimantado & The Rebels' 'Born for a Purpose', Bobby

Byrd's 'Back From the Dead', Lou Reed's 'Men of Good Fortune', Can's 'Halleluhwah' and Gary Glitter's 'Doing Alright with the Boys'.

The Tommy Vance interview was broadcast on Saturday, July 16, by which time the Pistols were in Sweden as part of a 13-date Scandinavian tour. Ironically, given that he didn't suffer any vigilante retribution personally, the tour came about owing to an irate Sid calling McLaren during the middle of the night threatening to do him physical harm unless he got the band out of the country.

The Pistols were playing the second of two opening tour dates at Daddy's Dance Hall in Copenhagen when Mike Mansfield's promo video for 'Pretty Vacant' was aired on *Top of the Pops*. McLaren would openly chastise Rotten for his being lethargic in front of Mansfield's cameras, but his sluggishness is largely due to the video being shot at some ridiculously early hour. Vicious remained motionless throughout the shoot. At first glance, his vapid, ashen expression could be seen as adoptive surliness. In hindsight, however, we know it was most likely his suffering the effects of heroin withdrawal. The Heartbreakers are credited with bringing heroin onto the London punk scene. Indeed, both Rotten and Steve Jones have since admitted to experimenting with heroin in the American band's company. Rotten would try heroin just the once before returning to his preferred daily cocktail of speed and weed. Jones would admit to trying the drug several times during his time in the Pistols before becoming a full-blown addict in the early-to-mid-Eighties.

While it's undoubtedly true The Heartbreakers smuggled a small stash of heroin in their equipment when travelling over to London to participate in the Anarchy Tour, the drug was readily available in London for those with the cash and right connections. Nancy had acquired a habit whilst slavishly hang around the New York Dolls; naively thinking she was Jerry Nolan's girlfriend. She'd introduced the gullible Vicious to heroin as soon as the opportunity presented itself.

With 'Pretty Vacant' hurtling up the charts Virgin were desperate to get the Pistols on *Top of the Pops*. With McLaren in LA looking to raise finance for what would become *The Great Rock 'N' Roll Swindle* and meeting soft porn flick director, Russ Meyer, Virgin's head of press, John Varnum, invited Rotten out to a Greek Restaurant in Soho before the Pistols flying out to Denmark. "We put this thing up of, 'It's going to be right next to Cilla Black and Des O'Connor: it's

The Ramones on stage at the whiskey A Go Go in Hollywood Photo: David Arnoff

going to be fantastic," Varnum told Jon Savage. "So he said, 'I never thought of that, right, OK', which was fine. I was doing Virgin's press and promotion and arguing their case: it had to be argued."

McLaren is said to have flown into a rage on discovering the promo video was set to screened on *Top of the Pops* and called Rotten ordering him to retract his consent. There wasn't much Rotten could do as the Virgin promotion wheel was already turning. McLaren made subsequent calls to Branson, only to be told that it was too late in the day to retrieve the video. It was the first powerplay McLaren had lost, and from that point on the battlelines with Branson were drawn. The "Vacant" promo video saga could be construed as revenge on Branson's part over McLaren's willfully conspired with Barclay Records' Eddie Barclay to flood the UK market with import copies of "Anarchy in the UK", which was in direct contradiction to the terms of the Virgin contract.

Following on from the second of the Danish Daddy's Dance Hall dates, the Pistols crossed over into Sweden. The normally reserved Swedes took the Pistols to their hearts. Vicious' own childlike innocence and naivety proving especially popular amongst the local kids. The show at Stockholm's Student Karen, Happy House would be marred with a local Hells Angels-type gang known as "The Ragarre" attacking fans as they made their way out of the venue. The "Rags" were intent on getting at the Pistols so the local police were forced to provide the band with an escort back to their hotel with the fanatical bikers giving chase.

The Stranglers would also find themselves the focus of the Ragarre's attentions when they visited Sweden later in the year. "We were battle-hardened but that was quite heavy!" says Jean Jacques Burnel. "The Raggare were kind of American Grafitti-ists, they looked like fifties rock 'n' rollers with greased hair and college jackets. They drove these huge old American cars and they didn't like the whole punk thing, which we represented apparently. Since we were the only band going out there on tour, they came after us.

"The venue was a large wooden chalet in the middle of the forest and about sixty of these cars turned up and broke through the perimeter fencing. They broke into the hall, beat up our crew and destroyed our equipment. The promoter locked us in the basement but we broke out and Molotov Cocktailed one of their cars! When the police finally turned up, they immediately escorted us to the ferry from Helsingborg to Copenhagen. We were meant to play Stockholm the next night but it was pulled. End of tour . . ."

The Pistols were in Sweden when Vicious flew back to London to face the music over his being caught in possession of a flick-knife at the second night of the 100 Club Punk Festival. Anne Beverley arrived at Wells Street Magistrates' Court to offer her son moral support on her brand-new 250cc motorbike. Mick Jones, Paul Simonon, Caroline Coon and Jonh Ingham all gave evidence in Sid's defence. "I was so sure that Sid was set up over the glass-throwing incident at the 100 Club that I put up my house as collateral for his bail," says Ingham. "Sid was a smart guy hiding behind a mask that he presented in public to hide his true emotions. This was partly due to his having a horrendous childhood. He was such a nice guy, though; he really was. And up for anything. I remember Caroline telling me how she took Sid along to a party that *Vogue* were throwing at some really flash hotel. They had a grand piano in there. Sid took one look at the piano and rushed across. Luckily, Caroline spotted him out the corner of her eye and screamed, 'Sid! No!'

"I was standing outside the court when he arrived in a cab. He was in the Pistols now, of course, and so I wasn't sure how he would act. He came running over, literally dragging Nancy by the wrist saying, 'Nancy, Nancy, this is Jonh. He put up my bail.' It took me all of thirty seconds to sense that Nancy was trouble with a capital 'T'.

"Sid's solicitor made an impassioned speech about how a custodial sentence might jeopardise his client's future career. The prosecution went into their shtick about how Sid was this violent character, but they only had one police officer giving evidence so it was obviously a put-up job."

The judge agreed with Ingham's assessment and swiftly brought the proceedings to a conclusion with a £125 fine.

In early August 1977, The Clash, The Damned, The Jam, The Boys, The Police, Eddie and the Hot Rods and Dr. Feelgood all travelled over to southwestern France to play the Second European Punk Festival at the Arenes de Plumaçon bullring in Mont-de-Marsan alongside local punk acts Strychnine, Marie et les Garçons and Asphalt Jungle in front of an estimated 4,000-strong crowd. The Jam, however, would withdraw owing to the promoters' insistence that they go on after the Hot Rods and the Feelgoods – circa 3 am

Sunday morning – when they'd been contracted to go on before both the other bands.

Since the release of their third single, "Stretcher Case Baby", The Damned had become a quintet following the arrival of Lu Edmunds on second guitar. *Record Mirror*'s Barry Cain remembers the first three-quarters of their set being beset with sound problems: "It was awful. I think I said something about Dave Vanian being left stranded like a dying goldfish in my piece. They were playing several new songs such as 'Problem Child', 'You Take My Money' and 'Politics' – which Brian cheekily dedicated to the Clash – but you couldn't hear them. Lu was brought in to shoulder some of the donkey work from Brian, but, again, you couldn't judge whether it was working or not. There was much niggling between the Damned and the Clash that day. Sensible ended up being forcibly removed from the stage when the Clash were on for letting off some stink bombs."

The Boys were also beginning to garner mentions in the UK music press. Their singer/guitarist, Matt Dangerfield, and keyboardist Casino Steel had both featured in varying London SS line-ups; both having accompanied Bernard Rhodes, Mick Jones and Tony James to Denmark Street to meet the Sex Pistols. Dangerfield's art college friend, "Honest John" Plain, was brought in on guitar with two of the latter's workmates at the T-shirt printing company he was working – bassist, Duncan 'Kid' Reid and drummer Jack Black – joining soon thereafter. Mick Jones and Tony James were both in the audience when The Boys made their live debut at the Hope and Anchor in Islington in mid-October 1976.

The quintet signed with the London-based NEMS label (Alternatively known as NEMS Records & Tapes) in January 1977 and released their debut single, 'I Don't Care'. A second single, which was also set to appear on their eponymous debut album, "First Time" and "Turning Grey"), had just been released with *Sounds* making it their "Single of the Week". The 1978 follow-up album, *Alternative Chartbusters*, features the Spector-esque 'Brickfield Nights', a paean to the lost innocence of youth set to a transcendent power-pop melody.

The Clash also introduced several new songs in their set at Mont-de-Marsan: 'Complete Control', 'Clash City Rockers', 'The Prisoner' and '(White Man) in Hammersmith Palais'.

With its lilting ska rhythm, '(White Man)' was by far and away

The Clash's boldest move yet in terms of songwriting. Slowing down the tempo was considered heresy as it went against the punk grain but The Clash were keen to show their versatility. Aside from recording Junior Murvin's 'Police and Thieves' for their debut album, The Clash had also worked up an arrangement of The Maytals 'Pressure Drop' for the White Riot Tour.

Strummer had penned the lyrics to "White Man" after attending a reggae all-nighter at the Hammersmith Palais with Don Letts and Roadent at the beginning of June. "There was me and about twenty other white faces and it was really packed," he revealed. "The whole thing felt a bit weird. I got the impression the crowd wanted gutsy roots music to respond to, but band after band came on looking and sounding just like the Jackson Five. They were totally out of touch with their audience. Hence 'White Man'."

When asked by the *NME* at the time of the single's release in June 1978 to specify whether the unnamed groups wearing Burton suits and turning rebellion into money jibe within the lyric was aimed at The Jam, Strummer said he was targeting the power-pop fad that was being hyped by certain music journalists as being the next big thing. No one was buying that particular line, however.

The Clash were said to be nervous about recording such an overtly reggae-influenced song as at the time it was a massive step into the unknown. Including Junior Murvin's "Police and Thieves" on *The Clash* was one thing, but "'(White Man)' was their attempt at penning a reggae song. "We were a big fat riff group, like rock-solid beats," Strummer subsequently reflected. "We weren't supposed to do something like that."

It was a gamble but one that paid dividends. "White Man" would stall at a disappointing #38 on the UK chart following its June '78 release, and yet it became a firm staple in The Clash's set throughout their career. It was to prove Strummer's favourite out of all the songs he ever wrote and was played at his funeral in December 2002.

The world was still coming to terms with Elvis's death from a heart attack when the Sex Pistols got their cloak-and-daggeresque SPOTS Tour (Sex Pistols On Tour Secretly) at Wolverhampton's Lafayette Club on August 19. needless to say, the boys had little sympathy upon hearing of the King's passing. "Elvis was dead long before he died," Rotten opined when asked to comment on the King's demise.

"His gut was so big that it cast a shadow over rock 'n' roll. But our music's what's important now."

Contrary to McLaren's subsequent hype in *The Great Rock 'N' Roll Swindle*, the Sex Pistols weren't "banned on the land" at any time during 1977. Indeed, many venues were desperate to have the Pistols play, but by booking the band into venues under a variety of throwaway names such as 'Tax Exiles', "'Special Guest', "'Acne Rabble', 'The Hamsters'" and 'A Mystery Band of International Repute', while relying on word of mouth ensuring each venue was packed to the rafters, nonetheless made for excellent copy.

"I was at Sid's Notre Dame debut and saw the Pistols' opening US dates in Atlanta and Memphis but the SPOTs show at the Lafayette club was something else," says Barry Cain. "Despite it pouring with rain there was a crowd queuing around the block. The Pistols arrived and tried pushing their way through to the front entrance. Somebody shouted out, 'We want Rotten', little realising his spiky-haired hero was standing right beside him."

"They really were great fun those five or six shows," says Roadent. "I'm not even sure which I enjoyed the most, the shows themselves, or the thrill of trying to keep each date under wraps as we descended on places like Middlesbrough, Scarborough etc. I felt like a Nazi spy, or an agent provocateur, sneaking around making coded telephone calls to venue owners to see if we were still on or whether the local council had got wind of the evil coming to their town. That's what happened in Blackburn. Blackburn King George's Hall was one of the confirmed dates, but it fell through at the eleventh hour owing to pressure from the local council.

"It was like playing hide and seek and if we got tumbled, which happened on occasion – especially once the bloody music press picked up on what we were doing - I'd have to call Malcolm and get him to try and book an alternative show somewhere in the vicinity. Otherwise poor old Barbara" [Harwood, the band's homoeopathic medicine student driver], "would have to drive us back to London as we couldn't risk booking into a hotel for the night in case the manager alerted the police. I think the band really enjoyed those shows as well - especially Sid. What people seem to forget is that Sid had a terrific sense of humour and he really was a joy to be around. The band had just done the Scandinavian tour, and although this was before he started mutilating himself and trying to live up to his own myth, he was beginning to develop a relationship with the fans. And I think those SPOTS shows served as a watershed in that they signalled the end of John's holding the spotlight."

In August 1977, The Adverts released 'Gay Gilmore's Eyes' b/w 'Bored Teenagers' as the first single via the band's new deal with Anchor Records. The song's lyric centred around Gilmore having donated his corneas – as well as various organs – for possible transplant following his execution by firing squad at Utah State Prison in Draper, Utah, back in January. Capital punishment in the US had been suspended in 1972, but the 36-year-old Gilmore, having been convicted of two callous murders, insisted the state of Utah put him to death instead of commuting his sentence to life imprisonment.

The publicity surrounding Gilmore's fight to be put to death by firing squad catapulted the single into the UK Top 20 in September 1977 (peaking at #18) and earning The Adverts a slot on *Top of the Pops*. "In popularity terms that was the high point," Tim Smith reflected. "Suddenly everyone liked us, we were on television. The only trouble was, it then froze. That was what people wanted from us. We hadn't frozen, we'd only just started, and a band that should have developed into something extraordinary was hampered by public expectation.

"I suppose every band is defined by what it's already done, really. Which is okay if you're the Ramones and just repeating the format album after album - but not if you want to change and develop. Much as I still love 'Gary Gilmore's Eyes', it was stylistically very much a one-off, a story song, and a bit of a gimmick. The rest of what I was writing was more about real life, what it felt like to be coming out of my teens in the late seventies. I don't regret releasing it as the A-side, but in hindsight, I wish I'd saved 'Bored Teenagers' for the next single rather than putting it on the B-side. My thinking at the time was, there had already been a version released on the Live at the Roxy album, so there wouldn't be any interest in it as a stand-alone single. Then there's the fact that it was only one-and-a-half minutes long. But actually, now I don't think any of that matters. In retrospect, I think 'Bored Teenagers' is the Adverts' second hit that never happened."

Conversely, Gaye Black was delighted by the success of 'Gary

Gilmore's Eyes'. I didn't see it as a hindrance," she says. "I don't deny the pressure was on after that, but it's what you want as a band, isn't it? You want your singles to be hits because it enhances your status. And you also get to go on shows like *Top of the Pops*."

Other notable punk-related releases during the summer of 1977 included The Vibrators' debut long-player, *Pure Mania*, which just about bruised the UK Top 50 (peaking at #49). The track-listing included 'Stiff Little Fingers', which was to provide a certain band from Northern Ireland with their name.

Having signed with Stiff Records, Elvis Costello had released his debut single, 'Less Than Zero' back in March. The single failed to trouble the UK charts but Costello's debut album, *My Aim Is True*, peaked at # 14 in the UK and reached a very respectable # 32 on the *Billboard* 200 following its July release. Subsequent singles, "Alison" and '(The Angels Wanna Wear My) Red Shoes' would also fail to chart, but 'Watching the Detectives' gave Costello his first single success – and a nice Christmas Present – in reaching #15 on December 24.

The Stranglers had signed with United Artists at the start of the year. Their debut single, '(Get A) Grip (On Yourself)' stalled at #44 on the UK chart. It subsequently transpired that some of the sales had been mistakenly attributed to a different artist. Despite the anti-climax, the band remained upbeat. "We played the Penthouse Club in Scarborough (February 25, 1977) a few weeks after," Jean-Jacques Burnel explained on The Stranglers official site. "Suddenly we realised that there was a huge difference from previous times because people were aware of the single. It got played a bit on the radio. The difference was massive once we actually had a record out."

Free of chart returns mismanagement, the band's debut album *Rattus Norvegicus* scored The Stranglers a Top 5 album (#4) – jumping a massive 42 places from #46. The first 10,000 copies came with a complimentary single: 'Peasant in the Big Shitty (live)' and "Choosey Susie". To celebrate the album's launch, the band threw a party at the Water Rat, which was situated on the Kings Road close to SEX. "It was held at the Water Rat to cock a snook at our rivals and to encroach on their territory," says Burnel. "We were just after a fight and trying to be provocative..."

May and June of 1977 were taken up with a 33-date UK tour before returning to the studio to begin work on their second album,

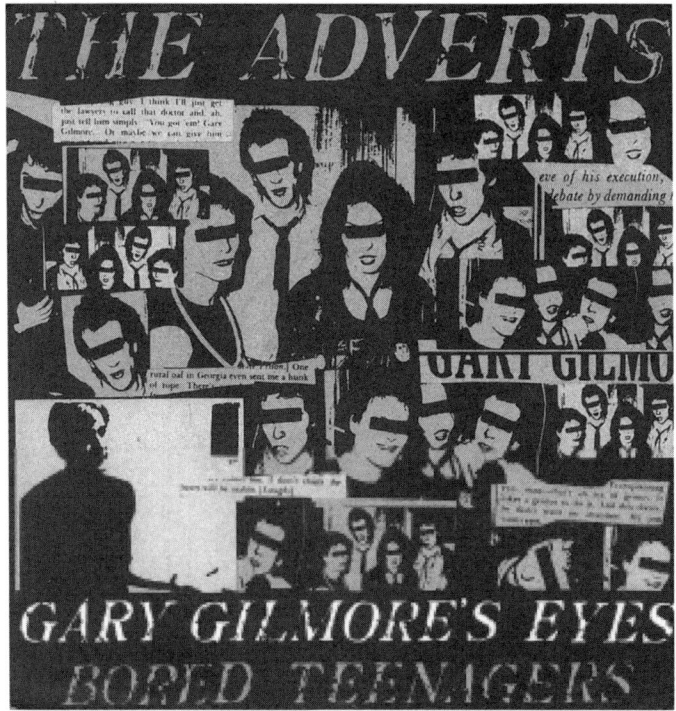

No More Heroes. The title track was released in advance of the album and emulated the success of 'Peaches' in reaching #8 on the UK chart. The album itself was only denied the top slot on the album chart by a Diana Ross and the Supremes *Golden Greats* album.

Having changed their name from The Nightlife Thugs to Boomtown Rats, the Southern Irish sextet – fronted by Bob Geldof – relocated to London and signed with Ensign Records. Their debut single, 'Lookin' After No. 1', surprisingly came within a whisker of giving the Rats a Top 10 hit at the first attempt. The eponymously-titled album would reach a respectable #18 following its September release. Their second album, *A Tonic for the Troops*, would produce three hit singles – 'She's So Modern'(12), 'Like Clockwork' (#6) and 'Rat Trap'" – which gave them the honour of scoring the first 'New Wave No. 1' in November 1978. The album itself would peak at #8.

Ian Dury, the colourful ex-Kilburn and the High Roads frontman, had released his debut solo single via Stiff Records, 'Sex & Drugs & Rock & Roll' in August 1977. The single was credited as an Ian Dury solo despite featuring future Blockheads Chaz Jankel (the A-side's co-writer), Norman Watt-Roy and Charlie Charles. The *NME* proclaimed 'Sex & Drugs & Rock & Roll' their 'Single of the Week', but the BBC's decision to ban the single because of the lead song's suggestive title. There was, of course, little chance of the single troubling the mainstream chart owing to Stiff's policy to delete singles after just two months. Sales of Dury's debut solo album, *New Boots and Panties!!*, would prove disappointingly modest, while the lead single, "Sweet Gene Vincent" emulated its predecessor in failing to chart. Despite his being 37 years old in 1977, Dury's quirky left-of-centre lyrics proved popular not only punks but also the mainstream record-buying public. 'What a Waste' and 'Make Love with Me'(The first single released as Ian Dury and the Blockheads) proved a surprise hit peaking at #9 on the UK chart during the spring of 1978, while 'Hit Me with Your Rhythm Stick' (b/w 'There Ain't Half Been Some Clever Bastards') topped the chart the following January. Dury's popularity deservedly brought about renewed interest in *New Boots and Panties!!* and saw the album climb to # 5 in February 1979, some 17 months after its release. Further singles success came with 'Reasons to be Cheerful, Part 3' hitting the UK Top 3 during the summer of 1979.

Never Mind the Bollocks here's the Sex Pistols was released with all the attendant fanfare On Friday, October 28, 1977. The album – under its original guise, *God Save Sex Pistols* - would have been ready for pressing much sooner had McLaren not purposely stalled for time whilst courting Warner Bros. for the all-important North American market; this despite Branson's offer to match whatever deal Warners tabled. Branson was desperate to get the album out in time for the Christmas market. The problem he faced was that there were at least three different versions of each available track. He was also insisting the album include all three previously-released Pistols 45s – if only because other than "Holidays in the Sun" (intended as the lead single from the album) and 'Bodies' the Pistols hadn't penned any other new songs since Matlock's departure.

Virgin had originally set the release date for November 10, but upon discovering a bootleg album entitled *Spunk* (Sex Pistols UNKnown), with a track-listing made up of Dave Goodman's Denmark Street and Gooseberry Studio demos was in circulation, Branson leapt to the fore.

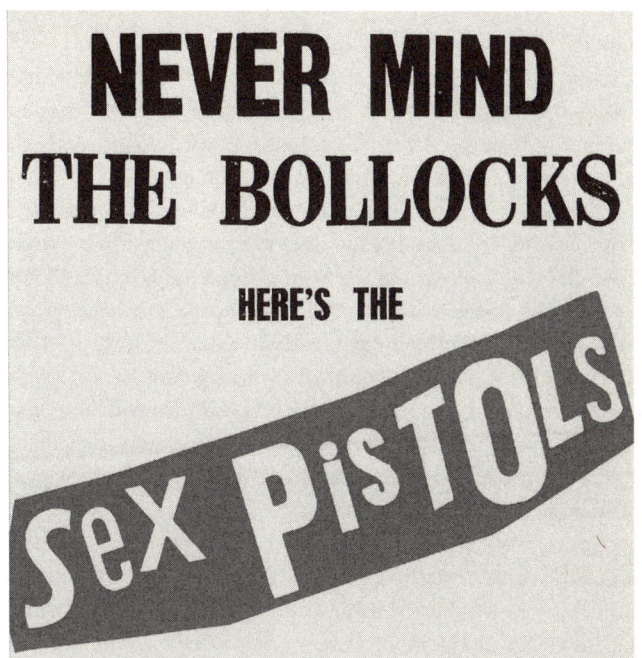

Release of the Sex Pistols' *Never Mind the Bollocks, Here's the Sex Pistols*
was held back in the the UK while MacLaren courted Warner Bros in the USA

(The bootleg's existence came courtesy of *Sounds'* October 22 issue).

Glitterbest owned the Denmark Street and Gooseberry Studio recordings but allowing Eddie Barclay to release them surreptitiously was in direct breach of the Virgin contract. McLaren, of course, cared little about the legalities as the *Spunk* album allowed him to get revenge on Branson over the "Vacant" promo being screened on *Top of the Pops*. When Branson demanded that McLaren retrieve the *Spunk* master tapes from Barclay, the latter brazenly declared that he "didn't desire to get them back".

McLaren had come to regard himself and Eddie Barclay as being cut from similar calculating cloth. When Barclay entertained McLaren and Steven Fisher at his Louis XIV-style penthouse offices on the Avenue Foch in Paris while sealing the deal that allowed his label to release Sex Pistols product in France, Switzerland, Zanzibar and Algeria, he'd served them caviar, lobster and vintage champagne. The Virgin signing, however, had been little more than a "cheese sandwich and cheap plonk affair."

'Holidays in the Sun' would come in for criticism following its October 14 release. Though *Melody Maker* and *Sounds* proclaimed 'Holidays' as their respective 'Single of the Week', both papers hinted at the overt similarities between the song's chugging D, C, Bm, Am, G and that of The Jam's 'In The City'. Despite a lack of airplay owing to the lyric referencing the notorious Nazi concentration camp, Belsen-Bergen, 'Holidays in the Sun' pierced the UK Top 10 (#8), providing the Pistols with a hat-trick of Top 10 hits. However, the single was still riding high on the chart when the Belgian Travel Service issued Glitterbest with an "Infringement of Copyright" summons on their summer holiday brochure from which Jamie Reid had lifted the artwork for single's sleeve. Virgin immediately withdrew the sleeve from circulation and issued further pressings in a plain white bag.

According to Chris Thomas, Vicious' contributions on *Never Mind the Bollocks* were restricted to 'God Save the Queen' and 'Bodies', but his playing was buried so deep in the mix that it was virtually impossible to decipher them. Indeed, Vicious' primary input during the entire recording process at Wessex came with his encountering Freddy Mercury in the conjoining corridor between the two studios: "So you're the bloke that's supposed to be bringing ballet to the masses?" Vicious sneeringly enquired. "Ah, Mr Ferocious!" Mercury playfully reposted. "Well, we're trying our best!"

Virgin had initially intended releasing *Never Mind the Bollocks* – a phrase Steve Jones had picked up from one of the band's early followers – as an eleven-track album with "Submission" included as a free one-sided single (replete with a full-colour poster designed by Jamie Reid). Such was McLaren's determination to undermine Virgin's scheduling, however, that he insisted "Submission" be included on the album – regardless that the "finished" masters had already gone to press. The delay would have proved disastrous for Virgin as copies of *Spunk* were already beginning to appear in many of London's music retail outlets. In a last ditched attempt to gain the upper hand, Branson ordered the album rush-released - with or without 'Submission'.

The ongoing hype surrounding the Pistols pretty much ensured the album would prove a massive hit. Advance orders in excess of 125,000 would see *Bollocks* slam onto the UK chart at #1; the icing on

'Holidays in the Sun' single bag became collectable as it was withdrawn after the Belgian Travel Service sued claiming Jamie Reid's artwork infringed their copyright

the cake surely coming with the album dislodging EMI stalwart, Cliff Richard, in the process. The album was still sitting pretty at the top of the chart when a female police constable warned the manager at Virgin's Nottingham store that having the lurid pink/yellow *Bollocks* sleeve on open display in his shop window was contrary to the Indecent Advertising Act of 1899. The bemused manager, Christopher Searle, dismissed the WPC's warning as so much bluster. When officers returned to the shop later that same week to find the album sleeve still on display, however, Searle was arrested and charged under the archaic act for having blatantly refused on four separate occasions to adhere to the police's instruction and remove the poster displays from his store window.

When Searle subsequently appeared at Nottingham Magistrates Court on November 24, Branson hired John Mortimer QC (he of *Rumple of the Bailey* fame) to defend Virgin's interests. The prosecution's case rested largely on the term "bollocks" being deemed offensive – regardless of it having appeared in the writings of such literary luminaries as Shakespeare, Dylan Thomas and James Joyce. The wily Mortimer had prepared for such an eventually and called upon Professor James Kingsley, the head of English Literature at Nottingham University. Kingsley also happened to be an Anglican vicar and took the stand dressed in his ecclesiastical robes. He proceeded to inform the court that the word "bollocks" appeared in records dating back to the middle-ages when it was used as a slang term for the clergymen of the day. He then went on to add that while "bollocks" was indeed colloquial slang for testicles, it was also used in everyday vernacular to signify when someone was talking nonsense. In his opinion, he, therefore, took the album's title to mean: Never Mind the 'Nonsense', here's the Sex Pistols.

Having recently returned from a mini-European jaunt, The Clash flew over to Belfast to kickstart the 21-date Get Out Of Control Tour at the troubled city's Ulster Hall Polytechnic with Richard Hell and the Voidoids in support. Their attempt to be the first punk-affiliated act to play Belfast would ultimately be thwarted by timid insurance brokers who withdrew the Ulster Hall's policy owing to The Clash supposedly having several outstanding insurance claims against them back on the mainland. When the assembled throng outside the Ulster Hall – which included the then-unknown Stiff Little Fingers' frontman Jake Burns – heard the show had been cancelled, they marched en masse to the Europa Hotel where The Clash were rumoured to be staying. To their credit, the band came out onto the street and tried assuaging the crowd by announcing their intentions to re-stage the show at the nearby Queens University. When some disgruntled fans lay down in the road in protest, however, officers from the Royal Ulster Constabulary moved in and pandemonium ensued. "The most horrible thing was the way the kids were treated – the way they were pushed around," Mick Jones reflected a few days later. "They didn't have a chance to understand what was happening so they were disappointed in us. Obviously, it wasn't our fault, but you can't explain that to eight hundred people personally."

On the afternoon of the doomed Ulster Hall show, Jones and Strummer paid a visit to a local radio station, Downtown Radio, to give an interview. As they were both wearing zip-infested popstar fatigues courtesy of the band's in-house designer, Alex Michon –

they'd no sooner alighted from the car when they were pounced upon by security officers suspecting them of belonging to the loyalist paramilitary organisation. The Clash would incur the music press's collective consternation by posing on the barricades. Strutting about Camden Town in their urban guerrilla chic was all well and good but doing so on the Bogside where people were being either maimed or murdered on a near-daily basis was utter folly – regardless of the band's intentions.

The Clash would have surely heaped further ridicule on themselves had the Ulster Hall show gone ahead as planned as the stage backdrop on the tour was a blow-up of a Belfast street scene, replete with Saracen armoured cars and cowering civilians. One could argue The Clash were simply expanding on the Rocco Macauley shot adorning their debut album's rear cover, but the people of Belfast lived with the everyday threat of violence. Jones, for one, was harbouring reservations about using the backdrop. "I didn't think we should put it up here, because they aren't going to particularly want to be reminded of it," the guitarist told Chris Salewicz later into the tour. "In Bournemouth, it's great because everyone is fucking asleep and it's really heavy because everyone is confronted by this stuff. But in Belfast, they don't need to be reminded."

On a more positive note, and much to the band's obvious delight, renowned American writer Lester Bangs was chronicling the tour for the *NME*. Yet while Bangs – or "Mo-lester" as Paul Simonon had playfully rechristened him - would become hopelessly enamoured with The Clash, Roadent had finally grown weary of Mick Jones's highhanded attitude. "It was in Edinburgh as I recall," says Roadent. "It was obviously my job to see that everyone had what they needed for that night's show – strings, skins, plectrums etc. When I got back at the venue (Clouds) Mick, being his usual self, came through the door shouting, 'Where've you been? Have you got my stuff?' He didn't even give me chance to respond before saying something about how I'd asked Richard Hell's people if they needed anything before asking him. And that's when I uttered the immortal line, 'Fuck off, Mick; you need a valet, not a roadie.' I got my train fare back to London off of Bernie, and the next day I went to the King's Road to see Malcolm and landed a job with the Pistols."

GOD Save THE QUEEN

Sex PistOls

—The Kids Are All Hopped-Up With Nowhere To go

"I walked into Media Sound on the first day [of recording Rocket to Russia and Jonny [Ramone] had the Pistols'
'God Save the Queen' record and he said, 'These guys ripped us off and I want to sound better than this.' And we put it on and said, 'No problem...."

Ed Stasium

Johnny Thunders would often point an accusatory finger at Steve Jones for "borrowing" his trademark Dolls' riffs and licks, but to suggest the Pistols ripped off The Ramones' sound for 'God Save the Queen' borders on the ridiculous. Indeed, The Ramones would go as far as laying the blame for poor sales of their third album, *Rocket to Russia*, at the Pistols' door saying how they'd "changed the punk image for the worse". Joey would assert that interest in The Ramones' latest vinyl offering stymied following a feature about the Pistols' impending January '78 visit to the US on the popular news magazine show, *60 Minutes*: "Everyone flipped out and then things changed radically. It really kind of screwed things up for ourselves."

Legs McNeil would, unsurprisingly, given his fixation with

Opposite: Sex Pistols, God Save The Queen artwork became an iconic image

The Ramones, side with Johnny and Joey: "Safety pins, razor blades, chopped haircuts, snarling, vomiting - everything that had nothing to do with the Ramones was suddenly in vogue and it killed any chance Rocket to Russia had of getting any airplay."

With Sire allocating upwards of $30,000 for the new album, The Ramones entered Media Sound Studios, a converted Episcopalian church funded by the people that had financed the Woodstock festival. Tony Bongiovi and Ed Stasium were again at the production helm though Tommy Ramone would receive another co-production credit. (*Rocket to Russia* was to prove the last Ramones album before Tommy stepped down to be replaced by Marky Ramone – born Marc Bell.) "[Media Sound] had a Neve 8078 recording desk, a wide selection of old microphones and great acoustics," Stasium reflected. "It also had one of the biggest drum sounds around – not that you can tell from '*Russia*' because Tommy once more kept the drums down in the mix.

As with *Ramones* and *Leave Home*, "brevity" was the byword during the recording process. "It doesn't matter if you spend $100,000 or $30,000 it's best to do it quickly," Johnny Ramone explained to Everett True in 2002. "If the engineer said a take was good, we'd go on to the next one. You don't wanna sit there and bullshit: it's your money they're spending."

As soon as the guitar and bass parts were completed Johnny and Dee Dee would head for the nearest bar. Joey, ever the perfectionist when it came to laying down his vocals, stayed long into the evening. This, of course, could simply have been one of the OCD behaviours that plagued the singer throughout his life.

Rocket to Russia features several iconic Ramones songs – 'Teenage Lobotomy', 'Sheena is a Punk Rocker', 'Cretin Hop' and'Rockaway Beach'. It was also the first Ramones album to include a ballad in 'Here Today Gone Tomorrow'. Despite The Ramones' grumblings about the Pistols' supposedly stealing their thunder, their giving the album a more commercial sound helped propel *Rocket to Russia* up to #49 on the *Billboard* 200. The album as a whole has a Beach Boys-esque surf feel and includes a souped-up cover of The Trashmen's 1963 hit "Surfin' Bird", while Dee Dee's unerring ability to find beauty in the unlikeliest of settings is splendidly encapsulated in the lead single, 'Rockaway Beach'. ('Sheena is a Punk Rocker' had been released as a single back in May.) To the uninitiated, 'Rockaway Beach' conjures up images of 1950s Americana: perfectly-formed suntanned teenage boys and girls lounging on sun-kissed sand against a backdrop of vintage rock 'n' roll. The real Rockaway Beach – an Irish-American enclave located on the Rockaway Peninsula in Queens – is a far cry from Dee Dee's poetic musings. "The place is a sewer," Legs McNeil opines in the sleeve-notes to the 2001 CD reissue of *Rocket to Russia*. "Crowds of vicious girls in bikinis and high heels, drinking tallboys of beer out of little brown bags, waiting to get into the next fight. Everyone [is] stoned on Quaaludes and Tuinals . . . to romanticize such a toilet was akin to writing about finding true love at Spahn Ranch."

Sire had recently struck a distribution deal with Warner Bros. But with Warners well into negotiations with McLaren to secure the North American rights to *Never Mind the Bollocks*, *Rocket to Russia* was largely left to fend for itself. "Warners were all geared up to break the Ramones," Seymour Stein reflected. "When that didn't happen, unfortunately, they got tarnished with an image of being a cult band. Just one big hit and they could have sold a million albums. That's all it would have taken."

Warners' lack of interest in The Ramones saw the band having to promote *Rocket to Russia* opening for Tom Petty and The Heartbreakers (not to be confused with the New York-based Heartbreakers) and Iggy Pop. Whilst out with Iggy, The Ramones' truck housing all their equipment was stolen – including Johnny's prized blue Mosrite guitar. "We lost almost $30,000 worth of equipment," Dee Dee said during a band interview with *ZigZag* magazine. They then proceeded to bemoan the financial plight that came with being in The Ramones – how they were each living on a salary of $100 a week. "That's about £55," said Johnny. "Touring costs us $750 a day, and sometimes we only get paid as little as $250. In San Francisco (where "Rockaway Beach" reached No. One on the radio station charts), we'll probably play at Winterland to 4,000 for just $750."

The Ramones were headlining a string of US dates in support of *Rocket to Russia* when disaster struck backstage at the Capitol Theatre in Passaic, New Jersey on November 19, when Joey suffered second and third-degree burns to his throat and chest whilst running through his vocal exercises. Joey was rushed to hospital but returned to the theatre to do the show. "It was something his voice teacher had told him to do, says Jane Schacht, who served as The Ramones' PR, "breathe steam to clear the sinuses. You're meant to do it over an open pot, not a teapot. Someone had put plastic over its nozzle and it exploded in his face. At the hospital they put cream on Joey's face – that's the worst thing you can do to a burn, it should be ice. So he went back and did the entire show without missing a beat – the salve melting on his face, like a clown, white, white, white. I'm standing next to Linda Stein who has no idea how badly burnt he is. I wanted to kill her – why was he on stage?

Joey was admitted to the New York Hospital Burn Centre where he remained for three weeks, his throat and vocal chodes a teeming mass of blisters. The remainder of the US tour dates had to be cancelled to give him time to recuperate in readiness for a tour of the UK. Joey would, however, put a gloss on his suffering in penning the lyrics to "I Wanna Be Sedated" whilst backstage at the Cambridge Corn Exchange during the UK tour.

The climax of the UK tour came on New Year's Eve with a sell-out show at the Rainbow Theatre with Generation X and zany Scottish punksters The Rezillos in support. The Ramones were simply phenomenal on the night as is evidenced on the *It's Alive* album, returning to the stage for three encores. The New York-based writer, Victor Bockris, was friends with the band and at the Rainbow that night. "They were very innocent, fresh and sexy," he reflected. It was very pleasing to see because people who've been on the road so long normally get toasted. I walked in the dressing room after they came offstage and Sid Vicious was sitting on a stool with Nancy kneeling in front of him, her head buried in his crotch. He looked very beautiful, vibrant and alive. Johnny Rotten was also there, surrounded by his entourage, maintaining a stony silence."

"We recorded *It's Alive* on the Island Studios mobile," says Ed Stasium. "I remember there was a lot of Swedish porno magazines on the bus. Other than that, it was very calm. The album is a terrific representation of the band in 1977. The Ramones always played faster in a live situation than on record. That came from Johnny's philosophy of 'Get in, get out, see how many songs you can fit into thirty minutes.' Occasionally, Joey would have to stop singing because he ran out of breath or skip words because they were going too fast."

1977 was proving a momentous year for Blondie. Their manager, the colourful and controversial Peter Leeds, had raised the necessary

$500,000 to buy the band out of the Private Stock contact – with $100,000 going to Richard Gottehrer for his share in the band – and they were now signed with the London-based label, Chrysalis Records. Blondie's first UK release under their new English aegis was "Rip Her to Shreds"; the single being coupled with previous Private Stock releases "X Offender" and "In the Flesh". The single failed to chart despite Chrysalis' blatant exploitation of Debbie Harry while promoting the single with the tagline "Wouldn't you like to rip her to shreds?"

The band were understandably furious, none more so than Harry herself. "That's the problem of art and commerce," she told Kris Needs. "We came from the New York City underground. We were trying hard to be artists. We didn't have any idea about merchandising or marketing. The whole thing was a complete, gigantic shock and smack in the face. Everything was horrible – we're losing our identity."

Blondie were already proving popular in Australia, but their profile Down Under received an unexpected boost when the ABC network TV show *Countdown* mistakenly aired the promo video to 'In the Flesh' instead of the one to 'X-Offender', which had recently been released there. Chris Stein has since suggested the show's host, Ian "Molly" Meldrum, was responsible for the switch. "'X-Offender' was too crazy and aggressive while 'In the Flesh' wasn't representative of any punk sensibility. Over the years, I've thought they probably played both things but liked one better."

Whilst touring the UK in support of *Rip Her to Shreds*, Blondie would be supported by the then-unknown XTC. The Swindon-based quartet had formed back in 1972 and had gone through several guises before hitting on "XTC". They'd rarely ventured beyond the confines of Wiltshire, but the advent of punk had allowed them an inroad to the London club scene – despite their disinterest in being associated with the new teenage musical trend. "I really didn't like the phrase 'punk'," the band's singer/guitarist, Andy Partridge explained. "It just seemed kind of demeaning. I didn't like 'new wave' either because that was already the phrase used for French cinema of a certain period. Our music was blatantly just pop music. We were a new pop group. That's all."

Partridge says he was left feeling "underwhelmed" on first hearing 'Anarchy in the UK', and says that it was thinking the Pistols being "rather average" that had spurred him on. XTC got their break courtesy of John Peel's inviting the band to record a session for his show after catching them performing at Upstairs at Ronnie Scott's in Soho. The Peel Session proved instrumental in their subsequently securing a recording contract. "[John] was responsible for us getting a recording contract. As soon as we recorded that session for the BBC, suddenly three or four record labels wanted to sign us up."

Having passed on CBS, Harvest and Island Records, XTC signed with Virgin; their three-track EP being released in early October 1977.

By the tail-end of 1977, the LA punk scene had cranked up several gears. The Germs were still creating chaos at every turn; Derby Crash often taking to the stage near-incoherent from a cornucopia of drugs and taunting the audience between songs whilst nevertheless delivering intensely theatrical and increasingly musical performances as they slowly but surely honed their craft. They recorded their debut single, "Forming" on a Sony 2-track reel-to-reel recorder in Smear's parents' family garage. On sending their efforts off to a local pressing plant, however, they were left fuming on finding someone at the plant had printed the note: "Warning: this record causes ear cancer". (The single was released in July 1977 on the independent What? label.)

The Damned would inadvertently prove the inspiration for The Dickies coming into being after their guitarist, Stan Lee and bassist Billy Club (born William Remar) attended the London band's LA meet-and-greet at Bomp Records in April 1977. "One day Stan suddenly decided that he wanted to play guitar," says The Quick's Steven Hufsteter. "I was giving him lessons. He wanted to have a band like Bad Company. He wanted to be like Ritchie Blackmore from Deep Purple. I told him, 'Stan, you can't play that stuff. You gotta be punk rock. You're not good enough . . . it'll take too long for you to be that good. Why don't you just play punk rock?' He was real sceptical. At first, he thought I was insulting him, but then he listened to the Ramones and that's when he decided to form a punk band. The Dickies never really thought of themselves as punk even though they were completely embraced by that scene." Punk rock or no, The Dickies would be the first band from the LA scene to secure a recording contract with a major label in signing with A&M Records. Their debut album, *The Incredible Shrinking Dickies*, would reach #45 on the UK chart in July 1979.

Another of the bands rising to prominence on the rapidly-burgeoning West Hollywood scene were The Screamers. The band's founders, Tomata du Plenty (born David Xavier Harrigan) and Tommy Gear, had first come together in Seattle in 1975, where they'd formed The Tupperwares (with Gear going by the name "Melba Toast"). "The Tupperwares were like a bubblegum band," du Plenty reflected. "Once we became the Screamers, Tommy said, 'Let's go to LA and see how far we can take this.' You know, so we took it somewhere . . . I knew this girl in England who kept sending me fanzines about the Sex Pistols," du Plenty explained. "Before that, I had a bowl haircut. I looked like Peter Noone from Herman's Hermits."

Owing to legal threats from Tupperware's legal department, the band elected on a change of name to the Screamers. Gear and du Plenty decamped to LA where they were soon joined by the rather more mundane-sounding David Brown and Keith "KK" Barrett on keyboards and drums respectively. Brown would leave soon thereafter to set up the seminal punk label, Dangerhouse Records, however, and would be replaced by Paul Roessler. "When the Screamers came to LA from Seattle the punk thing was happening in England," Gear added. "We decided in a conscientious way to have a sense of solidarity with it." It's said The Screamers created a visual presence with studio photos of the band appearing in various local magazines even before they'd played a single show.

X's Baltimore-born bassist/vocalist, John Doe (born John Nommensen Duchac), had relocated to LA in 1976. Inspired by Patti Smith's Horses album, he'd set about forming X from the moment he arrived in the city. Having encountered guitarist, Billy Zoom (born Ty Kindell), courtesy of a newspaper ad, the two started jamming together regularly. Zoom, a gifted guitarist who'd once played with Gene Vincent, was another who'd had his head turned by The Ramones. Doe was dating a girl he'd met at a poetry workshop called Exene Cervenka (born Christine Cervenkova). The 21-year-old Cervenka had only recently arrived in LA from her native Florida. When Doe asked her if he and Zoom might restructure one of her poems to use as a song, Cervenka brazenly told him she'd prefer to sing it herself. "I'd never even sung before except around the house," she subsequently revealed. "Billy and John had been in so many bands [between them] and were so well versed in music. They knew big band, country, jazz and rockabilly . . . they'd seen Jimi Hendrix play, and I was just a little bratty poet. I didn't know anything."

The trio had soon settled on the name "X", but finding a drummer was to prove rather taxing - K.K. Barrett and Nicky Beat of The Weirdos sitting in with them on occasion. When Doe caught D.J. Bonebrake playing with The Eyes at The Masque, he knew their search was at an end. "I was playing with the Eyes and John saw us play," says Bonebrake. "They were looking for a replacement drummer. This must have been near the end of '77. John said, 'You wanna try out for my band?' I played in five bands at the same time 'cause I get bored, so I said, 'Oh, yeah, I'll do this.' I did a rehearsal with them and I liked the music. So I was playing with the Eyes and playing in X – sometimes at the same show – until John said, 'You need to be in our band exclusively. You need to commit.' They pressured me to do that, and I agreed."

Though The Dead Boys have long been associated with the CBGBs/New York scene they did hail from Ohio. The band evolved out of a Cleveland-based band called Rocket From The Tombs that took their cues from Iggy, MC5, Lou Reed and Alice Cooper. RFTT had established themselves on the Cleveland circuit, but guitarist Cheetah Chrome and drummer Johnny Blitz (born Eugene O'Conner and John Madansky respectively) were attuned to what was happening on New York's Lower East Side. The Iggy worshipping Stiv Bators (born Steven Bator) had auditioned for RFTT as singer only to be rejected. Chrome and Blitz had had the prescience to keep his number, however. Recruiting Jimmy Zero (born William Wilden) as second guitarist and bassist Jeff Magnum (born Jeff Halmagy) the five-piece adopted the name Dead Boys from the RFTT song, 'Down In Flames', and played a handful of shows before relocating to New York in the summer of 1976 – reportedly at Joey Ramones' behest. (Other members of RFTT would go on to form the art-punk outfit, Pere Ubu)

The Dead Boys quickly established themselves as a CBGBs favourite – predominantly owing to Bators' Iggy-esque stage antics which included slashing his chest with a mic stand. They signed with Sire Records and released their debut album, *Young, Loud and Snotty*, in October 1977.

Soon after signing with Warner Bros. the Sex Pistols embarked on a

Although associated with New York's CBGBs The Dead Boys came from Ohio

nine-date Dutch tour, commencing with a show at Rotterdam's Eksit Club on December 5. Finding themselves free from the restraints that were plaguing them at every turn in the UK, the Pistols were incendiary on the night. Vicious, who was already on a high from the band having reworked 'Belsen was a Gas' and incorporated it into their set, would cite the Eksit Club show as being the best the Pistols had ever played. However, he was also still smarting from McLaren's botched attempt to abduct Nancy and bundle her on the first available flight to New York.

Said kidnapping attempt had taken place several days before the band's flying out to Holland while the unsuspecting bassist was visiting the dentist. McLaren concocted a plan that saw Sophie Richmond lure Nancy away from the Maida Vale mews flat where she and Vicious were living under the guise of a shopping trip in nearby Paddington. When Nancy realised what was afoot she became hysterical and Richmond was forced to call Glitterbest's new offices on Shaftesbury Avenue for reinforcements. McLaren, Boogie and Roadent had arrived soon thereafter. "I can honestly say that I'd no idea what Malcolm was planning," says Roadent. "Me and Boogie were at the new office on Shaftesbury Avenue going over the itinerary for the up-and-coming Holland tour when Sophie called demanding to speak with Malcolm. One minute Malcolm's sitting by the window perusing the music press' speculative reports on the *Swindle* film project and what have you. The next thing I knew we were hurtling along Oxford Street in Boogie's car heading for Paddington. I stayed with the car as I could see it was all going to end in tears – and not necessarily Nancy's.

"What Malcolm failed to understand is that Nancy – for all her faults – was Sid's first love. I know it sounds slushy and non-punk, but you only had to spend ten minutes in their company to see that they really did love each other. Another thing people fail to realise is that when the Pistols played at the Notre Dame Hall and the Screen on the Green earlier in the year, Sid was still John Simon Beverley at heart. But by the time of the SPOTS Tour, Sid Vicious had fully emerged from his shell and was vying with John for centre stage. After all, Sid had known John from their Hackney Tech days, and knew 'Johnny Rotten' was merely the public face his mate presented as a Sex Pistol, and that he could get his share of the headlines by living up to his punk persona."

Vicious was not best pleased upon his return from the dentist and learned of McLaren's skullduggery and threatened to kill those involved in the kidnapping if they should attempt any other stunts that interfered with his private life.

Immediately upon their return from Holland, the Pistols undertook the seven-date 'Never Mind The Bans' UK tour. The opening date was at Brunel University in Uxbridge on December 16. This was the Pistols' first London outing since the Screen on the Green in early April. In the audience that night was Jim Walker. The future PiL drummer had recently arrived in London from Boston – where he'd been enrolled at Berklee College - believing it was his destiny to play in a band with Rotten. What should have proved a triumphal return to the capital, however, ended in disaster owing to McLaren having hired a woefully inadequate PA. The Ramones were touring the UK at the time and were in attendance that night. "It was a fiasco," Lydon would lament while speaking about the show in *England's Dreaming*. "We were in that big hall, which was jam-packed, nobody really knew why anybody was there, least of all us. I was very confused by the sheer popularity of it. I thought, 'This is horrible, it shouldn't be like this'. I'd seen us as a small clubby band. We were way ahead of ourselves. We didn't know how to get past the first twenty rows."

The pitiful PA at Brunel reduced Rotten's voice to little more than a whisper for the following night's show in Coventry and brought about the rescheduling of the next show at Wolverhampton's Club Lafayette. Following on from the rescheduled Wolverhampton show, the Pistols played the Stowaway Club in Newport on December 23 and the Links Pavilion in Cromer on Christmas Eve before heading up to West Yorkshire for a Christmas Day bash at Ivanhoe's in Huddersfield where they were set to perform a benefit matinee show for the children of local striking firemen and those belonging to the laid-off workers at a local factory. The Pistols would bring their haphazard 1977 touring schedule to a festive finale with a normal show later in the evening.

Aside from providing funds for a banquet replete with a giant cream-filled cake, Glitterbest also provided a variety of Sex Pistols-related sundries including 'Anarchy in the UK' handkerchiefs and see-through *Never Mind the Bollocks* T-shirts. Three special coaches were also laid on to ferry the youngsters to and from the venue. Throughout the matinee, the band were in a relaxed mood. Rotten, playfully sporting a "Never Mind the Rich Kids we're the Sex Pistols" T-shirt, launched himself into the cake and engaged the gleeful audience in a free-for-all food fight before returning to the stage covered in cream and sponge. "It was great to do it for them because they were all broke and nobody gave a damn about them," says Lydon. "These people weren't going to have a proper Christmas, so we laid it all on, flooded the place with cake and presents for the kids. Here we were, the alleged most toughest band in the world, and at the kids' matinee show we'd have to play to seven-year-olds. There's an awful lot you have to leave at the door to do that."

After the later show, Sid and Nancy approached Boogie offering to have sex atop a *Never Mind the Bollocks* poster in return for some cash to score heroin. Boogie agreed to their proposal, but Sid reportedly failed to rise to the occasion. "Nancy wasn't allowed to travel anywhere with the band," says Tiberi. "And it wasn't a case of it being a question that Sid couldn't ask. He didn't want Nancy there, either. She was only at the Christmas day Huddersfield show because she connived her way up there by ordering a cab on the Pistols' account. You can imagine how that went down with Malcolm.

"Sid was Nancy's meal-ticket ... if you know what I mean," he continued. "She didn't have anyone else in London so with Sid out on the road she didn't have any money. I never went near that place (Pindock Mews) if I could help it. I hated it there ... everyone did. She got her revenge though because when Sid out on the road he didn't have easy access to smack. At that time Sid only had a minor habit ... what we called 'clucking'. Another thing most people fail to understand - and I'm not imagining this - is that Sid was on probation the whole time he was in the Pistols. When I came on board - which was the day after Sid joined the band - the Pistols were already a tight, professional band and Sid was either going to fit in or he wouldn't - especially with Paul, as he was the driving force onstage, setting the tempo for the songs. Steve and John had built up a symbiotic relationship from the 100 Club Punk Festival onwards. I was really impressed with their work ethic. I must have seen them sixty times in all and not counting the US shows - they put in maybe two lacklustre performances.

"Sid's probation wasn't, you know, 'set in stone.' There wasn't a pantomime trapdoor beneath his feet, but he knew the ground rules and followed them ... at least until we got to America. But, of course, and again I'm not imagining this, there was a real chance that Sid would have been let go had the US tour been delayed ... a 'for his own good' kinda thing. When Glen left, the Pistols were a three-piece with a bass player. John, Steve, and Paul were the core. They were the ones that recorded the album."

Julian Temple filmed the Ivanhoe's show for punk posterity, but the majority of the footage remained locked away in the director's vaults until BBC4's 2013 screening of the *Never Mind the Baubles – Christmas '77 with the Sex Pistols* documentary.

As was perhaps to be expected, both the *NME* and *Sounds'* 1977 end-of-year readers' polls were weighted with punk or punk-related acts. Indeed, the Pistols, Clash, Ramones, Iggy Pop, Stranglers, Elvis Costello and Ian Dury all featured in the *NME*'s Top 30 Albums, while Tom Petty and the Heartbreakers' eponymous 1976 debut was the only non-punk-related album in the Top 10 of *Sounds'* corresponding list. It was a similar tale with the Top 30 Singles; the Pistols' "Pretty Vacant" and "God Save the Queen" both making in the *NME's* Top 5. Radio Stars' debut single "Dirty Pictures" appeared in the lower reaches of the chart whereas their follow-up *Stop It* EP – despite the band performing the catchy "No Russians in Russia" on Marc Bolan's ITV show, *Marc* – was strangely absent. The band's vocalist, Andy Ellison, knew Bolan from their having been in John's Children together. Radio Stars were signed to Chiswick Records. Their third single of 1977, 'Nervous Wreck', scraped into the UK Top 40 following its late-October release and secured the band a slot on *Top of the Pops*.

The Jam appeared on the same August 24, 1977 episode of *Marc* as Radio Stars, performing 'All Around the World'. Both the 'In the City' single and album of the same name featured in the end-of-year polls. The Jam had established themselves as one of the most invigorating bands to take to a stage, yet while Paul Weller would go on to be acknowledged as one of the finest songwriters to emerge from the punk or indeed any other music scene, he was very much still learning his craft by the end of 1977. So much so, that when Polydor pressed the band for a follow-up album within six months of the debut, there was little new material in the locker. As a result, *This Is the Modern World*, would receive something of a mauling at the hands of the critics – even if the band's appeal proved sufficient to lift the album to a respectable #22 on the UK chart.

The Damned released four singles during 1977 yet surprisingly none would trouble either the *NME* or *Sounds* end-of-year polls. Nor would they trouble the UK Singles Chart. The fourth single, 'Don't Cry Wolf', was to prove the last seven-inch offering before Brian James quit the band.

Penetration's debut single, 'Don't Dictate' is another glaring omission on the *NME* poll, despite it since being proclaimed a punk classic. Pauline Murray had formed Penetration in her native County Durham after catching the Pistols play in neighbouring Northallerton and Scarborough. They soon attracted a following, while their energetic thrashing and bashing brought them to the attention of Virgin. None of the band's five singles would trouble the charts but their debut album, *Moving Targets*, reached a respectable

Steve Severin and Siouxsie Soux of Siouxsie and the Banshees at the Rainbow Thatre
support Johnny Thunders on November 20, 1977. Photo: Gus Stewart/Redferns

#22 following its October 1978 release.

Another band absent from the polls were Siouxsie and the Banshees, but this omission stemmed from their having as yet failed to secure a recording contract. They were the only band from punk's so-called "first wave" yet to do so – despite *Sounds* putting them on its front cover that December. In *England's Dreaming*, Jon Savage puts this down to the Banshees' collective "intense excitement of ambition outstripping ability."

"We weren't musicians," Siouxsie was honest enough to admit. "Talking about breaking down walls and actually doing it are quite different things. In our naivety, we started making this noise that was ours." The Banshees would eventually sign with Polydor in June 1978 and enjoy immediate chart success with 'Hong Kong Garden' reaching #7 on the UK chart. Their debut album, *The Scream*, was released later that same year, narrowly missing out on the UK Top 10.

The Heartbreakers' released their only studio album, *L.A.M.F.* (New York street-gang slang for Like a Mother Fucker", in October 1977. Thunders and Co. had decided to go for broke in the UK rather than return to New York and almost certain destitution. "The boys needed food and they needed drugs," Lee Black Childers explained in a 2012 interview with the author. "There was little point in going home as no record company interest in the states because everybody was expecting Johnny or Jerry to die at any moment. It wasn't any different in England but by playing two or three shows a week we managed to get by. When we eventually got a deal with Track Records, they put us in a nice little studio in Soho – not too far from their offices on Carnaby Street with a sweet engineer called Speedy Keen. I warned Chris Stamp, who was the owner of Track, that it was imperative they didn't give anything to Johnny – no booze, no pot, no cocaine, and certainly not to give him any heroin! But of course they did and that kinda put paid to things where the album was concerned. That album could and should have been a classic.

"There were other problems with Track of course. I ended up having had to break into their offices to retrieve the master tapes. Well, not me personally, you understand. We hired a kid to scramble up the front and slide through a window. There were lots of Who recordings in that office that were most likely very valuable, but I told the kid that he should only think about the Heartbreakers' masters. We were breaking the law after all."

The Heartbreakers' brand of punk rock 'n' roll should have given them a hit album but owing to poor mixing the album sounded muddy. Jerry Nolan was so incensed by the results that he would quit The Heartbreakers soon after the album's release.

The Emerald Isle is synonymous with all types of music and yet punk was slow in taking root in Northern Ireland; if only because except for The Clash's thwarted attempt to play the Ulster Hall, every other mainland punk act made no effort to traverse the Irish Sea. The band that has since become synonymous with the Northern Irish punk scene, of course, is Stiff Little Fingers. Jake Burns (vocals/guitar), Henry Cluney (guitar), Gordon Blair (bass) and Brian Faloon (drums) started as Highway Star, fumbling their way through rock standards of the day – interspersed with Rory Gallagher numbers - in the local pubs and clubs. Jake and I met around 1971 but really became friends in '74," says Cluney. " I started going over to his house during school lunches. He had a guitar and the thing just fascinated me. I just had to get myself one. We formed a few bands that didn't play anywhere. Highway Star was our first semi-serious attempt."

"Basically, it was all just playing for fun," Burns explained during a 2003 interview. "It was for the fun of getting together and making a big dumb noise – that was the point of it. But then we realised we weren't that bad. I mean, we were never very good, but we certainly weren't awful.

"There were three places {in Belfast] you could play. The university was the pinnacle, supporting someone proper, or there was a club called the Pound Club which was down by the old Oxford Street bus station. The third place was a bar on Corn Market called Mooney's. those were the three venues that might allow some scruffy-arsed kids in to play."

Their first 'proper' gig at Mooney's went so well that the club's owner/manager offered to manage them. There was a caveat, however. the guy in question didn't like Cluney and his offer only held if they sacked their friend. The others soon realised their mistake and invited Cluney back into the fold. The temporary sacking was to prove a blessing in disguise.

"Henry [had] discovered the whole punk thing," Burns continued. "I'd heard it as well on John Peel. I wasn't as convinced as Henry was – he was an overnight convert. I thought the Damned were funny and I thought the Pistols were exciting. There was something about them that was exciting, but nothing actually latched into my brain as, 'This is important,' I thought, 'It's fun, I certainly like it and we can certainly do it,' but I didn't see it as a complete life-changing experience that Henry had."

"It's true their sacking me changed everything," says Cluney. "It's also true that Jake didn't like punk at first. It was only me badgering him to listen to the early stuff like the Pistols, Damned and Clash etc that brought him round. When I came back into the band there was really only one direction we were going in."

Burns says it was hearing *The Clash* for the first time that gave him a tantalising glimpse of the future. "That's when I realised, 'No, this is what I want to do.' Up to that point, I'd been singing other people's songs about bowling down Californian highways when I'd never been further west than Galway in my life. That was when we decided what we were going to do. So everything changed. It was go get your hair cut . . . go and do everything."

Blair didn't share the rest of the band's passion for punk, however, and was replaced on bass by Ali McMordie. A band name more in keeping with punk was required. They originally settled on "The Fast" and got as far as booking a gig under that name before discovering there was already a band called The Fast playing out of CBGBs. Cluney called the manager of the pub where they were set to play telling him not to advertise them as The Fast. "I was on the phone to the guy that was promoting the show," says Cluney. "We couldn't call ourselves the Fast because the New York band had beaten us to it. When the guy asked what we gonna call ourselves I didn't have a clue what to say. He kept saying, 'I need a name or I can't book you.' We'd been playing punk records all day and so Jake grabbed up the nearest sleeve. It was the Vibrators' *Pure Mania* album. He looked at the song titles on the back of the sleeve and shouted out, 'Stiff Little Fingers. Tell him were called Stiff Little Fingers.' Ali, Brian and I were going, 'What?' Jake said, 'Don't worry, we can always fucking change it after the first gig.'"

Thanks to Belfast-based journalist called Colin McClelland, Burns was put in touch with Gordon Ogilvie who worked for the *Daily Express*. Upon discovering the band had penned a song about the ongoing "Troubles" in Northern Ireland called "State of Emergency", Ogilvie handed Burns a type-written sheet containing the lyrics to "Suspect Device". This was soon followed by a second type-written sheet containing the lyrics to 'Wasted Life'. The band quickly worked up tunes for the two sets of lyrics. Ogilvie was impressed with what he heard and he and McClelland became their management.

"Gordon showed up at an early SLF gig with Colin," says Cluney. "He got talking to us and basically said that we should be more than a cover band. There was no argument from us when Gordon suggested

Audience members at The Vortex in 1977. Photo Ray Stevenson

we start writing about the 'Troubles' as that shite was literally going on around us on a daily basis. And it's not as though we hadn't been talking about it prior to Gordon's suggestion as we already had a song or two that were going in that direction. I think we had 'Suspect Device' and 'Italian Lobster' might have been in the same group of songs. At the time it was all just really optimistic."

'Suspect Device' and 'Wasted Life' were subsequently recorded at a local radio jingles studio and released under the band's own Rigid Digits label. The single was packaged in the form of a cassette with a cover depicting a cassette bomb. What was considered a clever marketing ploy in the band's rehearsal room didn't go down so well in London, however, as record company execs proved loath to open packages bearing a Belfast postmark owing to the IRA's recent letter-bomb campaign on the British mainland. Indeed, one record company phoned the band requesting a second copy as they'd pitched the first in a bucket of water for fear it was a genuine suspect device. Cluney, however, remains sceptical as to whether this really happened. "I remember our being told about record companies being scared off by the Belfast postmark but I think it was a bit over-exaggerated. It was probably just an excuse as to why they passed on us. But it was good publicity anyway."

Thankfully, John Peel had no such reservations about which part of the British Isles his mail arrived from. He would play both songs repeatedly over the coming weeks. This soon led to a distribution deal through Rough Trade and would go on to sell in excess of 30,000 copies.

—To Many Problems

*"The whole US tour was a travesty.
In hindsight, the Pistols shouldn't have
gone to America. We should have taken
some time off, and then focused our
energies on the forthcoming European
tour. The Atlanta show was okay in terms
of an opening show, and the shows in
Memphis and Tulsa were passable.
But none of those shows were what you
would call good. John certainly didn't
enjoy them, and neither did Paul. I kept
saying to them, 'We'll do better tomorrow,'
but it didn't get any better . . ."*

John 'Boogie' Tiberi

No one at Warner Bros. was expecting *Never Mind the Bollocks* to emulate its UK success on the *Billboard* chart, but the positive feedback – particularly from the label's own WEA (Warner/Elektra/Atlantic) stores – was indicative that America was ready to embrace the Sex Pistols. Bob Regehr, head of Warners' Artist Relations Department, would be overseeing the tour. Once he'd received confirmation from McLaren that a window would be kept free for the first two weeks in January 1978, Regehr set the tour ball in motion by contacting Premier

Opposite: Sid was aware he was on probation with The Pistols

Talent Agency in New York. His next step came in flying Rory Johnston to New York to meet with Premier Talent's Executive Vice-President, Barbara Skydel. "I was dealing with all the American label activities from a management perspective," says Johnston. "Premier Talent was the hottest rock agency in America at that time and Warners were keen for me - or Malcolm - to meet with Barbara and Frank.

"Malcolm either didn't want to or couldn't make the trip but was satisfied that I could decide which agency we'd go with. I knew Premier would be the best bet when Barbara didn't throw me out of her office when I told her we only wanted to do a tour of Texas. Although the Pistols signed with Warners in November '77, negotiations had started earlier in the year. I definitely made two trips to New York to speak with Premier."

Bob Regehr was desperate for the Pistols to play New York and mooted the idea of the band playing Madison Square Garden at $1 per head. McLaren, however, wasn't for budging, but would begrudgingly consent to the Pistols performing on NBC's prime-time show, *Saturday Night Live*.

The US tour was set to commence at the Leona Theatre in Homestead, Pennsylvania, on December 28, 1977, with two other northern "rust-belt" dates booked at Chicago's Ivanhoe Theatre and Cleveland's Agora Ballroom on December 31 and January 1 respectively. Pere Ubu were booked as support for the northern dates. Following a show in Virginia at the Alexandria Roller Rink on January 3, 1978, the tour would then head for Georgia's state capital, Atlanta, before swinging through the Deep South that had so captivated McLaren during his on-the-road adventures with the Dolls. Indeed, the final tour date at Winterland in San Francisco on January 14 only came about owing to Rory Johnston's digging his heels in. "Winterland was down to me telling Malcolm that we had to do something to pacify Warners. He'd gotten his way with not playing LA, but I told him that we had to play California and that we ran the risk of Warners pulling tour support if we didn't. I'm not sure Warners would have pulled the support, but the threat worked."

McLaren had one last caveat up his sleeve, however. As the Pistols would be playing predominately to working-class audiences, he insisted that the ticket prices for all the dates should be pegged at $2.

This didn't sit too well with the promoters and a compromise was reached whereby ticket prices - except for Winterland where tickets would retail at $5 - were raised to $3.50 with Warners agreeing to cover any shortfalls.

With the Never Mind the Bans Tour climaxing at Ivanhoe's on Christmas Day, the leg-weary Pistols would have been left with just a two-day break before flying out to America. What no one had anticipated, however, was McLaren's choosing to leave it until the last minute before applying for the visas that would allow the Pistols into America. He might not have been expected to know all the ins and outs of the US State Department's policy regarding the all-important visas, but he surely knew the Pistols' collective criminal past was going to prove problematic. Jones had the most convictions but these were petty offences ranging from breaking and entering, drunk and disorderly and use of a motor vehicle without insurance. Cook had two convictions for theft against his name whilst Vicious could boast two charges of assault, and his being caught in possession of a flick-knife. By far and away the most serious conviction as far as the US Embassy officials were concerned, however, was Rotten's drugs conviction from the previous March.

Rory Johnston says he was half-expecting the visa applications to be denied first time around. "The unwritten rule concerning drugs offences is that your first visa application will always be turned down. Malcolm knew that as well as I did - the Stones being a classic example! The second application would have been approved but leaving it so late in applying for the visas royally fucked things up! Those northern shows that were cancelled would have been great for the Pistols."

Rather than test the veracity of Johnston's "unwritten rule" theory, Warners sent its top legal eagle, Ted Jaffe, into battle. Jaffe had first made a name for himself serving as John F. Kennedy's commissioner of foreign claims, had joined Warners from Atlantic Records following Warners' purchase of Atlantic in 1968. He'd secured the Stones' entry into the US in November 1969 when their visas were denied owing to varying drug offences and was therefore confident of achieving similar success with the Pistols. Jaffe proved successful and the US State Department issued the Pistols with two-week visas. There was one non-negotiable proviso, however. Warners would have to post a $1million surety to guarantee the band's behaviour during the tour.

Bob Regehr was anxious to break the Pistols in America but was equally keen to protect the label's seven-figure surety. Though he'd been happy to deal with Rory Johnston during the negotiations for the album rights, he decided to bring in someone he could rely on to oversee the tour. With his shoulder-length hair and dead slug moustache, Noel Monk wouldn't have looked out of place in The Eagles. He'd cut his rock teeth working as the stage-manager at the Fillmore East in New York and had spent the last ten years overseeing tours by the likes of Johnny Cash, the Moody Blues and the Rolling Stones.

The general misconception surrounding the Pistols' '78 tour is that the US Embassy's initial stance in refusing to issue the visas also resulted in the cancellation of the band's appearance on *Saturday Night Live*. The *SNL* slot was scheduled for Saturday, December 17, 1977 – eleven days before the original US tour date in Homestead. McLaren's dilly-dallying over the visas, however, resulted in Elvis Costello standing in for the Pistols on *Saturday Night Live*.

The Pistols arrived at JFK late on January 3, 1978, to find the Pan Am terminal teeming with reporters. Pandering to the press wasn't part of Monk's remit, however. Pausing long enough to allow the *New York Post* to grab a shot of the band for its morning edition, he and his security team bundled the jet-lagged Pistols aboard a bus to ferry them to the Delta Airlines terminal and a connecting flight to Atlanta. Tiberi was aware of the reception committee that awaited them in New York as McLaren had briefed him on the surety Warners had put up to get the Pistols into America. "Somebody at Warners had briefed Malcolm about the need to protect their surety and to make him understand the reasoning behind Monk's hiring his own security," Tiberi explained. "When we got off the plane at JFK, Monk was waiting for us on the other side of the barrier. He motioned us through, saying everything had been taken care of. I don't even remember us having to show our passports. A CBS film crew was there to film our arrival. It made the evening news and what you see is the band climbing into what was effectively a minibus. You can see the footage in the *Swindle* where Steve is gurning through the window. It made the evening news. Malcolm must have somehow caught CBS' clip because when we arrived at the hotel in Atlanta there was a telex waiting for me that said, 'Too much press!'"

The Great SouthEast Music Hall Emporium may seem something of an incongruous setting for a Sex Pistols show seeing as it was housed above a bowling alley within the long-since demolished Broadway Plaza shopping mall. However, the GSEMH's then General Manager, Sharon Powell, says Atlanta was regarded as a "musical Mecca" at that time of the Pistols' visit. "The Great SouthEast Music Hall was one of the premier clubs in the US Whenever a record company sent one of its new acts out on a promotional tour, Atlanta was a popular stop."

Powell is also keen to stress that Atlanta was far from the Southern ideal that McLaren had imagined: "Atlanta has always been sort of a separate entity from the rest of the South. Malcolm thought that by having the Sex Pistols doing shows in the South they were really gonna hit us with shock and awe. What he didn't understand was that punk had been a serious part of our music for years. The Great SouthEast Music Hall was patterned after the Bottom of the Barrel in Union City (New Jersey), and so we were initially influenced by the New York punk scene: the Dolls, Iggy, the Ramones etc. We also loved the Clash, but we were listening to the Pistols very early on. I was carrying my firstborn son at the time of the show, and *Never Mind the Bollocks* was about all he heard in the womb. Atlanta also had its fair share of punk-orientated bands such as the Restraints and Angelust. The Fans had self-released their EP the previous year, and Phillip "Fly" Stone from the Nasty Bucks often dressed in trash bags onstage."

The irony surely wasn't lost on the Pistols upon discovering their first stateside interview was to be aired on NBC's *Today*, which at the time was America's highest-rated early morning "infotainment" show. With Monk and his team anxious to keep the band's location away from the media, Warners' Director of Publicity, Bob Merlis, had booked a suite at the Westin Peachtree Plaza Hotel in downtown Atlanta where the band would face questions from NBC News anchorman Jack Perkins.

Merlis was enjoying his second stint with Warners having rejoined the label in 1974. He'd been in his current role of Director of Publicity for the last 18 months or so. As such, he'd been designated to meet the Pistols' upon their arrival in the U.S. He'd been at LAX awaiting a flight to Pittsburgh when a call to the office alerted him to the Pistols' visa applications having been denied. Though he was privy to the inter-office gossip surrounding Warners' signing of the Pistols, he was meeting the band in person for the first time. "Oh there was a great deal scepticism in the office," says Merlis. "The Sex Pistols were regarded by some of my colleagues as being 'barbarians that should be kept at arm's length,' but we were already moving with the times and the 'punk rock revolution.' Our 'punk baptism', as it were, came in working with Sire and the Ramones, so it was a case of 'bring on the Sex Pistols.' My boss, Bob Regehr, was something of a risk-taker. His approach was, 'Let's see what happens.' I was unfamiliar with the Sex Pistols' music as I hadn't heard the album at that time. But of course, I knew all about the band from the adverse publicity they were generating in England. Like Bob, I fully believed we could turn the Sex Pistols into a successful act in the US I don't think they would've gotten as big as say, Led Zeppelin or the Who, because they were so anti-establishment. But they would have recorded more albums -pretty much as the Clash did. Johnny Rotten was extremely charismatic, Cook and Jones were already very accomplished musicians, and Sid would have gotten better on the bass ... maybe."

NBC's report, which was aired the morning after the Pistols' show, began with footage of NYPD Port of Authority officers awaiting the band's arrival at JFK while a female voiceover said how the authorities had been warned the Pistols might attack their fellow passengers before switching to Perkins standing in front of the stage at the GSEMH after the band had departed the stage. Perkins also bemoaned the Pistols' supposed insistence on being paid $10 to give a "bleep, bleep interview."

"Jack Perkins was the wrong guy for the interview - totally the wrong guy for the job!" says Merlis. "I booked a nice room at a downtown hotel. The band showed up, only he didn't really want to talk to them. They picked up on that and started doing things like demanding payment to do the interview. They would have done it for free if he hadn't been such a jerk!"

Whenever the Pistols needed to hit the ground running they more often than not they tripped over their shoelaces. And so it was to prove in Atlanta. They couldn't even cite ring-rustiness for their putting in a below-par performance, as they'd played 17 shows in December – their busiest month in terms of live shows. *Billboard* magazine chose to call it as they saw it, declaring: "Sex Pistols Shoot Blank on First Atlanta U.S. Gig."

Barry Cain was of the same opinion but believes there were mitigating circumstances for the band's poor showing. "Atlanta was a totally different vibe to a UK punk gig. In the UK, the aggression was honest and aimed at the sky, whereas in the US the aggression was perfidious and aimed at the Pistols. A pure lack of understanding. Punk in a place like Atlanta, back then at least, could only ever be a fashion statement. I mean, what the fuck did 'God Save The Queen' or 'Anarchy in the UK' mean to your average American?"

"Alf Martin, who was the editor at *Record Mirror*, asked me to go over and cover the two opening shows in Atlanta and Memphis. It was one of the last jobs I ever did as a staff writer. If I could get an interview, fine, but it wasn't important. The paper sorted the flights and hotels and even gave me some spending money. I was good to go, and hot to trot. A fucking adventure!"

With Virgin having insisted that any UK-based reporters pay their way, Cain hadn't anticipated any favours from anyone attached to the Warners' press office. "I seem to recall no British journalists were allowed access to the Pistols. The only interviews were with American media. But this suited me down to the ground, 'cos 'I'm a lazy sod,' ha-ha."

Safe in the knowledge that gaining an interview with the Pistols wasn't a prerequisite, Cain nonetheless thought it only polite to pop backstage and say hello to the band seeing as he'd interviewed them several times. Finding his way through to the dressing room barred by Glenn Allison, a Stetson-wearing, 6ft 5" 280 lb. bearded behemoth who worked at the GSEMH but had been co-opted onto the tour by Noel Monk. "I walked up to the guy and said something like, Please tell the band Barry Cain from *Record Mirror* says, 'Hello.'" Allison duly obliged and returned a couple of heartbeats later to inform Cain – with deadpan delivery: "the Sex Pistols say 'hello' back."

Cain would, however, inadvertently end up conversing with a Sex Pistol whilst awaiting his flight to Memphis. "I think I'd heard Sid had gone missing in Atlanta, but it was still a surprise when he turned up out of the blue with Glenn Allison. Sid came and sat next to me in the airport waiting lounge, his arm swathed in bandages after he'd slashed it with a broken bottle or something. Good looking guy up close. McLaren had ideas of Sid headlining in Vegas after the split. Might even have done it, too."

Vicious did indeed go AWOL after the GSEMH show in search of a fix. With Monk determined to keep to his schedule the rest of the band flew onto Memphis, Johnston says he and McLaren – and possibly Boogie Tiberi -- stayed behind in Atlanta in the hope of locating the errant bassist. Realising the unlikelihood of two Londoners and an ex-pat trying to find Vicious in a city the size of Atlanta, Monk delegated Glenn Allison to assist them in their search.

Vicious' "Mr Fixer" was Freddi Griffin, a local drummer and one of the more flamboyant characters on Atlanta's alternative music scene. "Sid showed up at the apartment wanting some heroin but we didn't have anything like that," says Griffin. "We gave him Angel Dust and he shot up. I know doing PCP when you're dope-sick sounds horrible, but Sid seemed to dig it. He kept saying, 'I want another whoosh, Joey!' He was a huge Ramones fan apparently and decided that I resembled Joey Ramone. He said something like, 'I don't want to call you "Freddi"; you're Joey.' I think it was his way of getting closer to me, he felt that we were getting to be mates or something.

According to Griffin, sometime the following morning McLaren and Allison arrived at his door. "I'm still not sure how they tracked him down. Poor Sid didn't want to leave, but of course, he didn't have any say in the matter. Malcolm wasn't going to take no for an answer; he was rattling Sid's breakfast meds in front of him. More Valium, I suppose. Apparently, Malcolm had made the rounds of the local musicians and groupies until he found someone who knew who Sid had been with. So Sid rejoined the tour unwillingly, but he actually wanted to stay with me - at least as long as he could keep playing my records and doing drugs.

Tom Forçade was bankrolling *Punk* magazine on occasion but John Holmstrom says he was still stunned on being handed a ringside seat on the Pistols' tour. "Tom called me on the afternoon of the Memphis concert and from out of nowhere invited me to join the tour," he explained. "He'd already bought me a plane ticket to Memphis and promised me a ticket on the door at the Taliesyn Ballroom. I frantically picked up the ticket, but the banks were closed by then. ATMs didn't exist yet so there was no way for me to get any money. The few dollars I was able to scrape together would enable me to get a cab to JFK, and then from Memphis airport to the venue. After that, I would be left with a couple of penny rolls, but I wasn't worried as Tom had told me that we would meet up after the show."

The Memphis show had been oversold owing to the local Fire Marshalls restricting the attendance and Holmstrom arrived at the Taliesyn fearing he was going to be left out in the cold. "When I got to the venue there were dozens of cop cars outside. It was surreal. I quickly discovered that a riot had just taken place because of bootleg ticket sales and that there was no ticket left for me at the door. More importantly, as far as I was concerned, there was no sign of Tom Forçade. I asked to see someone connected with Warners, and just seconds before security kicked me out of the lobby Warners' rep Gary Kenton – God bless him! -appeared and let me into the venue. Ironically, it was only because of Sid going missing, and because of the bootleg ticket riot that led to the show being further delayed that I was able to catch the show."

Having failed to link up with Forçade, Holmstrom had been hitch-hiking his way back to Memphis airport when he says he was picked up by what he describes as "three pimps driving a Fifties Cadillac". "These pimps tried to sell drugs to me," he continued. "When I said I was dead broke they attacked me. I threw my suitcase at them, blocking their attempt to stab me with a switchblade knife, opened the car door and ran for my life. I wandered around a weird suburban ghetto area until, as if by magic, the airport appeared next to the road.

"I could not wait to get back to New York but I'd lost my plane ticket during my near-mugging. I called the airline to see what they could so but the next thing I know Tom Forçade rolls up in a stretch limousine and proceeds to reveal his plan about documenting the Sex Pistols tour (Lech Kowalski's *D.O.A.: A Right of Passage* was released in 1981), while explaining that I would produce a book and a *Punk* magazine cover story. To me, this made perfect sense seeing as the Sex Pistols had become the biggest entertainment story in the US at the time."

Holmstrom was going to need photos for *Punk*'s cover feature on the tour so Forçade arranged for Roberta Bayley to join up with the tour. "I was at home one night when someone called me from *High Times* magazine and told me I had a ticket to San Antonio in the morning and to pack my bags," says Bayley. "They wouldn't give me any details, but Holmstrom, who was already out on the tour, said to just do it. The Ramones were playing that night at the Palladium. There was an 'after-party' at Julian's Billiards next door to the Palladium. I was freaking out because I was leaving first thing in the morning and I had no cash so David Johansen lent me fifty bucks."

From Memphis, the tour rolled on to Texas for a show at Randy's Rodeo, a large Texas-style ballroom that proudly boasted being "the finest western dance hall and night club in San Antonio."

At the time of the Pistols' visit to San Antonio future Go-Go's bassist, Kathy Valentine had only recently returned to her native Austin after a lengthy sojourn living in London where she'd joined the fledgling Girlschool after responding to the all-girl band's add in *Melody Maker*. "This was when I figured out that punk was what was happening," she says. "I saw Eddie and the Hot Rods, the Vibrators, Boomtown Rats, and Buzzcocks. I was back in Austin by October '77 and started a band called the Violators. I was so excited to see the Pistols. I didn't care where they were playing; I just couldn't believe they were coming anywhere near us! There was some talk of the Violators opening for the Pistols but I didn't think we were anywhere near ready. I don't remember paying any attention to the opening bands because we were either outside hovering around the tour bus hoping to meet the Pistols, or socialising with people we knew from the scene. In fact, I met a cute punk that night and brought him back to Austin to be my boyfriend. I was maybe 10 - 15 feet from the front but I wasn't afraid. It was all very exciting and a big adventure. They were the Sex Pistols! It was about being there and being part of the spectacle. I knew all the songs by heart. The Violators were playing 'Pretty Vacant' in our set."

The Pistols had played to hostile audiences in the past, but they'd never experienced anything quite like the reception that greeted them at Randy's Rodeo. Kathy Valentine's fellow Violator, Jesse Sublett, would describe the storm of beer, bottles, food, spit etc. as being a "punk baptism of Texas" as the Pistols launched into "God Save The Queen."

"The Pistols hit the stage blasting like a pack of howling coyotes loose in a chicken pen: blowtorch guitar, machine-gun drums, snarling vocals, sneering faces, bass rumble, says Sublett. "They were half rock 'n' roll messiahs, half sideshow freaks. Johnny Rotten fomented chaos and rebellion; Steve Jones and Paul Cook anchored it with napalm-drenched Eddie Cochran riffs and a backbeat crackling like a nail gun. Sid Vicious spewed venom."

Rory Johnston says he sensed the rapidly-darkening mood at Randy's. "So much stuff was being hurled at the stage that I ended up hiding behind the PA. I could see this sheriff standing a few feet from me get hit smack on the side of the head with a bottle. He was only a little guy, and the force of the bottle caused him to stagger back. He was in total shock and started reaching for his gun. I thought, 'He's going for his gun and he's looking at me!' When I saw him draw his gun, I dashed out over to the sound booth to warn Malcolm that someone was going to get killed. The booth was empty! I found Malcolm hiding outside. It was utter chaos, but I still think San Antonio the best rock 'n' roll show I've ever seen."

"Randy's was the most hostile crowd I have ever been around," says Holmstrom. "Roberta and I stood several rows back from the insanity - away from the front of the stage because it was so violent. It wasn't like a mosh pit; it was more like a team of gangsters intent on killing their enemy. It was scary! Period! I was kind of happy to hear later that Sid missed hitting his stupid tormentor with the guitar, and that he hit Ted Cohen, the Warners' executive, instead. It seemed like poetic justice. But then the lights went out, and the crowd began to murmur. I think that if the lights had stayed off for any length of time, there would have been a riot. Fortunately, the lights soon came back on, and the Pistols delivered the most desperate, crazed performance I have ever seen."

After the show McLaren was said to be ecstatic, playfully asking which of the photographers had captured Vicious in mid-swing as such a snap would surely be adorning the front cover of newspapers around the globe. "Malcolm never approached me," says Bayley. "Maybe Joe (Stevens) or Bob (Gruen), I don't know. Supposedly, Joe got the shot and Malcolm just said something like, '£10,000 shot, that one!' From where I was standing, it just seemed like a moment of confusion. As far as I know, Joe's photo was never published -if it even exists. Ironically, many years later, I realised that I got the shot, albeit from the back.

Following on from an uneventful sojourn to Baton Rouge, the Pistols returned to Texas for a show at the Longhorn Ballroom in Dallas. The tour bus arrived at the Longhorn Ballroom some time mid-afternoon after yet another gruelling all-night drive; the "John Wayne scenery" that had captivated Rotten and Vicious having now lost much of its allure. The tour was now entering its second week and the onboard relationships were proving as barbed as the prickly pear cacti dotting the lunar-esque landscape; the early ambience having all but disintegrated. So much so, that Jones and Cook had cajoled McLaren into letting them fly to Dallas with him, Sophie Richmond, Boogie Tiberi, and Rory Johnston.

Virgin were preparing to release "Belsen Was a Gas," as the Pistols' fifth UK single, but Rotten was intent on attacking the ultimate sacred totem - religion. Unbeknown to the rest of the Pistols or McLaren, he'd been furtively working up a lyric for a new song he'd tentatively titled "Sod In Heaven." ("Sod In Heaven" – re-titled "Religion" – would subsequently feature on PiL's debut album, *Public Image: First Issue*)

Rotten had revealed the new lyric to the rest of the band whilst en route to San Antonio, but the response hadn't been what he'd been expecting. "I wrote 'Religion' during the [US] tour and Malcolm said, 'Ooh no, that's bad for the image, can't do things like that. I wanted to get them away from three-chord rock 'n' roll into something more spicy. But they wanted to do what Malcolm wanted them to do. He would give this, 'Waay, we're all mates and he's the odd one.'"

Vicious had no sooner stepped inside the Longhorn Ballroom when he was besieged by a gaggle of LA punkettes that had driven from California to see the Pistols. One of these was Gabi Berlin. "I was 20 years old and studying photojournalism in college," she explained. "I was into Iggy Pop, Brian Eno, Roxy Music, and Bowie, of course. I first heard the Sex Pistols on Rodney Bingenheimer's radio show. I'm pretty sure 'Holidays in the Sun' was the song he was playing. I remember I had to pull over the car and start screaming and dancing.

"Our favourite hangout was the Masque in central Hollywood, which was situated beneath a porno theatre on Santa Monica Blvd. We were there one night, and Hellin (Killer, a.k.a Helena Roessler) had heard about the Sex Pistols' tour and was tearing around the place trying to get people together to go to Dallas. I was used to doing road trips and was one of the few people in our group that had a car: a little blue super VW beetle."

"Yes, it was my idea to go to Dallas," says Killer. "I was not one to take 'no,' or even 'it's impossible' for an answer! So when I realised the Pistols weren't coming to LA, I started asking everyone we knew that had a car. Gabi had a VW bug, and thankfully she said 'Yes!'

"I rushed home, begged gas money from a friend, and went back to the Masque," Berlin continued. "Hellin, Trudie (Arguelles), and a couple of other of our girlfriends were ready to go. I remember we waited for 'Dad.' That's Terry Graham, or 'Terry Baghdad' as he was calling himself. Terry was later in Gun Club. There was another girl named Lamar who I think was from San Francisco. I feel foolish now but then it was total hero-worship when the Pistols came through the door at the Longhorn Ballroom. Sid walked up all skinny and cute like a puppy dog. He asked if we'd bought tickets, and when we said we had he became outraged. There was a little old lady in the ticket booth, and he stalked over and demanded she refund our money. She was terrified! I clearly remember her cowering in her booth. She didn't say a word, just gave us our money back. Then Sid put us all on the guestlist for the rest of the tour."

The Longhorn Ballroom, of course, is where Vicious ended up with a bloodied nose onstage. "I've either heard or read all the varying theories as to how Sid came by his bloody nose that night," says Killer. "After pushing my way to the front of the stage right in front of Sid, I placed myself firmly in the edge of the stage hanging into the corral fence that was in front of the stage. It made for a great place for a short person like me to hang on to. I can't tell you how excited I was. Back then smoking was allowed everywhere. I had a cigarette in my hand and was jumping up onto the stage to share it with Sid. Holding it for him so he could lean over to get a drag every few bars!

"Well, this was great and felt special. There I was sharing my smoke with Sid Vicious, and him smiling down at me. I'm sure you've seen the footage of that show. It was packed, and I was crushed up front there. We were having the time of our lives . . . at least, I know I was! As I said, I had been hanging onto that fence rail so I could kinda sit on the front of the stage and reach up to Sid. I got knocked off at some point, so I grabbed the rail to pull myself back up just as Sid leaned over to say something to me. And as fate would have it, I head-butted him square on the nose with the top of my head! Bob (Gruen) got a good record of what happened after that on film. I looked up and blood was pouring down Sid's face, and he, of course, loved that! Couldn't have planned something like that if you tried! After that, Sid leaned over and kissed me on the mouth and we were both covered in his blood. I was in love! I mean, really, how romantic is that? It was sealed that we would be friends . . . and lovers. Although at the time, I guess I didn't know any of that. We were just a couple of punk kids having a great time in our lives."

"It was kinda hairy in Dallas," says Roberta Bayley. "I know I've been quoted elsewhere as saying that I was worried for my personal safety. I didn't mean that I was worried for my life! I just meant that I didn't want to be pushed around, manhandled, or have somebody rip the sleeve off my cashmere sweater as some asshole bouncer did the first time I saw the Clash. I've been in the trenches and seen many a crazed out of control concert - the Beatles three times, and the Stooges, for instance - so I can honestly say I didn't sense any real threat of violence at the Pistols, shows just a fear of drunken assholes or overly enthusiastic security guards. I was a slight young woman of 27 and did not enjoy being shoved around."

The tour's penultimate show at Cain's Ballroom would have passed without incident had it not been for a local Christian pastor staging a protest outside the venue in shades of what occurred in Caerphilly during the Anarchy Tour some 13 months earlier. Bob Regehr and his team were viewing the final tour date at San Francisco's 5,400-capacity Winterland Ballroom as the acid test that would prove whether the Pistols were capable of making the necessary leap from clubs to arenas. Such concerns were salved when all the tickets sold out within 24 hours of going on sale.

The Pistols were set to go onstage at midnight, with the performance being broadcast live via a local radio station KSAN-FM. According to John Holmstrom, McLaren had wanted an open stage from 5 p.m. onwards so that "any kid with a guitar could come along and plug in and play." He even went so far as to secure radio time to announce his "come one, come all" intentions. "Malcolm thought by inviting any kid with a guitar to come to the show he'd find a band that might blow the Pistols off the stage. He thought it would be fantastic!"

On Friday, McLaren met with legendary Bay Area promoter Bill Graham to sort out any last-minute arrangements for the Winterland show as well as discuss promotional ideas such as having the Pistols pay a visit to Alcatraz and pose for publicity photos. McLaren and Johnston accompanied Jones and Cook on a sight-seeing jaunt, but, as events would ultimately prove, the three-day gap betwixt the Cain's Ballroom and Winterland dates left him with too much time on his idle hands when the news came through that the next show at the Helsinki Worker's Hall in Finland on January 18 had fallen through owing to the Finnish authorities having revoked the Pistols' work permits.

The revocation of the permits was due to mounting pressure in the Finnish press, which had begun in earnest the same day the Pistols had arrived in America. The country's leading newspaper, the *Helsingin Sanomat,* had published a hostile editorial in which it fancifully cited the Pistols' most important instrument was "a mechanical distorter which produced a sound like spitting." The Helsinki cancellation provided more headlines but it also presented an unanticipated five-day lay-off before a show in Stockholm on January 20.

The sensible option would have been to return to London - if only to allow the leg-weary Pistols a couple of days rest before then flying out to the Swedish capital. In *England's Dreaming,* Jon Savage says the idea for the Rio jaunt came about because Tiberi had mentioned his having a friend who worked at the *Daily Express* having a contact number for the fugitive Great Train Robber Ronnie Biggs. "It was actually Malcolm that had the contact number for Biggs," says Tiberi. "I think he had a hotline to the *Daily Express.* It was me that came up with the idea to go to Rio, though. But it was while we were in London and it looked like we wouldn't be going to America. The Rio thing came about while the visa thing was still up in the air. I got out my atlas and said to Malcolm, 'Well if we can't go to America, let's go to Brazil?'"

Legs McNeil had begrudgingly joined up with John Holmstrom and Roberta Bayley in San Francisco. "Legs was in LA on assignment for *High Times,* hoping to interview Hugh Hefner at the Playboy Mansion. That was never going to happen so Tom had him travel up to San Francisco. Boy was he pissed that he didn't get to interview Hefner! The last thing Legs wanted to do was interview Johnny Rotten as he hated the Sex Pistols with some weird passion. Roberta gave Legs her backstage pass to get us a story - which he refused to do! He wrote a bullshit story that was more about Legs McNeil than the Sex Pistols.

"What is most disappointing to me, however, is that Legs did a taped interview with Malcolm right after the break-up. In fact, he might have been the first person to learn about the Pistols' break-up. Now, if Legs was a 'co-founder' of *Punk* as he claims, he would have given us the scoop, right? But no, Legs had no loyalty to the magazine. If not for Tom Forçade, we would have run the four photos Michael McKenzie took in Tulsa which appear in Punk #14. That would have been all we had! I am so glad we were the first US magazine to introduce the Pistols to America. I always had great respect for the Pistols. And Roberta and I both feel that going on that tour - thanks to Tom Forçade, the world's most misunderstood genius -was the experience of a lifetime." (In November 1978, the "world's most misunderstood genius" would put a gun to his head at his Greenwich Village apartment. He was 33 years old)

The Pistols would ultimately prove a disappointment at Winterland, but John Holmstrom has a theory as to why the "craziest rock 'n' roll tour" he's ever experienced ended in something of a damp squib. "Compared to the shows in San Antonio and Dallas, Winterland was definitely a let-down. But you have to remember that this was the Pistols' first show in a big auditorium, so the sound was uneven. And you have to take into account everything that was happening offstage by the time we got to San Francisco. Everyone was feeling the strain. I only spoke with Boogie and Rory Johnston a couple of times, but I sensed they were encountering a lot of frustration with the Warners' thugs during the tour - as all of us did. It started off bad and got worse and worse as the tour went on. I remember seeing Boogie getting physically manhandled out of Winterland. 'But I'm the fucking sound man!' he yelled."

Holmstrom says McNeil was still pissed at his being dragged away from LA, and that his mood didn't improve any on being told that he'd been delegated to go backstage after the show to speak with Vicious. "Roberta slipped Legs the pass that Paul Cook had given her because she or I would have been recognised by Monk's goons and kicked out," says Holmstrom. "No one associated with the Sex Pistols even knew who Legs was. Giving Legs the pass was a total waste of time, however, since he never understood the Pistols. And he was jealous of Sid for pulling all the girls."

While McNeil was watching Vicious with green-eyed envy, Annie Liebowitz came bursting backstage. She was there to get a photo to accompany Charles M. Young's tour feature for *Rolling Stone*. Bill

Sex Pistol's Sid and Steve talked to *Record Mirror* for a front page splash

Graham had arranged for a local artist to paint a Sex Pistols mural on one of the walls in the dressing room. In the mural, the band is standing in line waiting to be knighted by the Queen. Bob Gruen had snapped a photo of the Pistols huddled together on sofas beneath the freshly-painted mural before their going onstage. They appear relaxed in the photo, smiling for the camera even. Despite her repeated attempts to get the Pistols to again pose beneath the mural, Liebowitz's pleas fell on deaf ears.

Rory Johnston still maintains the Pistols could have been pulled back from the brink if McLaren had shown the slightest interest in saving the band. "Rotten was seething about the proposed Rio trip, but his hissy fit before going onstage at Winterland had pretty much gone ignored," says Johnston. "He was angry because he only found out about the Rio trip from one of the guys from Warners, but he would probably have gone along with the Brazil idea - if only to poke fun at Ronnie Biggs!"

When Rotten called Joe Stevens the following day he'd given no indication that he wouldn't be at the airport at the designated hour. But at some point that Sunday he'd decided that things couldn't carry on as they were. The only money he had to his name was the cash he'd grabbed up from the Winterland stage, but it was enough to cover the cab fare to the Miyako. "John arrived at the hotel sometime early Sunday evening," says Johnston. "I remember this because I'd fallen asleep and I obviously hadn't heard him knocking. The next thing I knew, he was coming through the open window. He'd climbed over the balcony from Steve and Paul's room next door. He was looking for his bag and thought I might have it. All I can assume is that Noel Monk dumped everything at the Miyako before heading off home. As I say, there was a room booked in John's name, but he wouldn't have been able to check in as the management was still on the lookout for the Pistols – even though they already had half of the band under their roof."

Johnston says he is unaware of any flights being booked for the following morning, but Joe Stevens' photo of a despondent-looking Cook and Jones sat beneath the departures board at San Francisco International is evidentiary proof. As the *NME* were happy to continue paying his expenses, Stevens had accompanied Cook and Jones to the airport for the 07:00 Pan Am flight 515 to Rio de Janeiro. Like McLaren, Stevens knew a snap of the Sex Pistols lounging about with Ronnie Biggs would be syndicated around the world. With Rotten and Vicious failing to put in an appearance, Stevens - realising he might have a far more important scoop for the *NME* - returned to the Miyako with Cook and Jones sensing "something deadly was going to happen."

Hellin Killer can no longer remember what time they arrived at Mark Mothersbaugh's house with Vicious, but the party was in full swing. "There was a whole entourage of people there, it was packed with people! There was plenty of drinking obviously, but I spent most of the time keeping an eye on Sid, constantly trying to keep him from scoring. At some point, we left to go to Lamar's place as we were staying there. I think some of the people who were at Mark's came as well."

Like all addicts in need of a hit, Vicious had only one thing on his mind. "Sid wanted to cop some dope and I suppose I knew where we could get some," St. John explained. "I hadn't seen much of the Pistols before the show but afterwards I used my pass to get backstage and hung out with Hellin and Sid. By this point, the security guy charged with babysitting Sid had pretty much given up. Vickie and I had planned an after-show party at the apartment. I knew the party would be in full swing by now, so we took a cab to a house where I knew Sid could score some dope. I wasn't doing heroin then, and as I recall, Hellin didn't do it either. I don't think she even smoked weed! I'm pretty sure we got him some.

"Everybody who was anybody was at the party. Sid was the only one there from the Pistols, though. Hellin hung onto Sid and just pampered him. I gave him the bottle of Mescal I'd bought in Juarez and told him not to eat the worm. He was already high, and now he was drinking 'crazy water.' Hellin and Sid were sequestered in my bedroom - such as it was. People forgot Sid was there because he was so out of it. The party wound eventually down, people left, and I slept in the closet."

"There is one thing from that day I feel I have to clarify," says Killer. "Later that morning, when there was hardly anyone left a friend of Lamar's showed up. Maybe he wasn't really a friend, but she definitely knew him. Anyways, he knocked at the door and asked for Sid. I remember his face like it was yesterday. He'd brought heroin with him. Damn it, I was so mad because Sid had been pretty much clean the whole tour! I told the guy not to do it, but hey, people wanna be your friend so they give you what you want, right? Well, the guy gave Sid some dope thinking he was fuckin' cool. When he took Sid into the bathroom I went in there too. I wasn't going to leave his side because I wasn't dumb! I'd seen people OD before.

"Anyway, the guy gave the heroin to Sid and I couldn't stop him from doing it. I was sitting on the side of the tub with Sid and when he shot up, he fell over backwards right into the tub. I knew something was wrong right away and turned the cold shower on him. The dope guy was already gone out the door, so I shouted for someone to call an ambulance. Sid had OD'd! I was just trying to keep him breathing. I didn't know about Lamar rushing down to the clinic, only that a doctor from the clinic showed up. The doctor shot him up with what I now know was 'Narcan'. The Narcan soon brought Sid round. I then called the Miyako and spoke with Malcolm. Malcolm said he would come round straight away."

St. John is still convinced that McLaren arrived at the apartment with Rory Johnston. And Vicious, of course, had said as much in an April 1978 *Record Mirror* interview? Johnston, however, is equally adamant that while McLaren could well have taken St. John's call at the Miyako, it was himself and Tiberi that drove over to Haight Ashbury.

St. John's version of events has a further twist as she insists that when Malcolm and Johnston arrived they went and sat in her kitchen while Vicious was in the bathroom getting high. "I'll never understand why Rory and Malcolm didn't intervene. They just sat there and watched it all go down. All I could think was, 'Why aren't you taking Sid outta here?' The two of them sat at the kitchen table, saying very little. It was very weird that they didn't stop the whole thing before it started."

Johnston is willing to concede that McLaren might have gone over there later but is adamant that they weren't ever in that apartment at the same time. "It was me, Boogie, and Paul that went over there! Funny, the girl didn't mention Paul? It was very chaotic just finding that place. We were just trying to find Sid and get him out of Haight Ashbury and back to the Miyako. And while we weren't initially sure we were in the right apartment, I can tell you that we certainly weren't sitting around!"

Johnson says he doesn't know anything about a doctor or a Narcan shot. "We must have got there just after Sid had shot up because he was laid out on a mattress in the corner. I'm no expert, but it was obvious he was OD'ing! We managed to bring him round by walking about the room. I remember thinking, 'Boy, what the fuck is going on here?' He nearly died! I called Bill Graham, and he put us in touch with a doctor in Marin County. The guy was on a retainer from Graham. He was one of those 'hippy rock 'n' roll' types that just also happened to be an acupuncturist. Malcolm wanted Sid back at the Miyako, but the doctor said he was keeping Sid in overnight for observation. He didn't get any argument from me."

"I definitely went over there with Paul," says Tiberi. "I can't remember now if it was Rory that drove us there or if we took a cab and he met us there. But, you know, who was with me really is of no importance here. The only thing worth mentioning is what a truly horrible and frightening moment it was. If whoever it was hadn't made the call to the Miyako, Sid could have died."

Having bunked down with Sophie Richmond at the Miyako, Rotten awoke sometime Monday morning determined to have a showdown with McLaren. With Joe Stevens in tow, he first went to state his position to Jones and Cook. He told them that while he was prepared to continue the Sex Pistols – either with Vicious or a new bassist – he could no longer work with McLaren. Jones, however, had also reached the end of the road: "I was getting more and more where I wanted out of the [Pistols]. And that's when I said, 'I don't want to do it no more." Cook was equally disillusioned, but he and Jones - at Joe Stevens' behest - agreed to accompany Rotten back to McLaren's room. Stevens ordered beers from room service, but Rotten was in no mood to sup with the devil that was making his life a misery. According to Johnston's recollections, Rotten accused McLaren of constantly trying to stitch him up, and that the Rio trip was just the latest in a long line of stitch-ups at his expense. Malcolm had then retaliated in kind by telling Rotten he was "turning into Rod Stewart." Realising he was wasting his breath, Rotten stormed out of the room and out of the Sex Pistols.

Johnston had purposely kept out of the way during the showdown as he felt that it was a situation that should be sorted out between McLaren and the band without external interference. "I had so many other things to deal with so I left them to it. I've no idea how or why Joe Stevens got to sit in on the meeting - even if he was rooming with

Malcolm. But Malcolm always did like to have people around him in awkward situations. I'm not going to say I sensed a split in the air, but by San Francisco, I knew we'd reached the point where something had to give. It was nothing specific, but there was definitely something hanging in the air. There was a darkness surrounding the Pistols. Warners were really pissed off with us, so that kind of matched the mood. In hindsight, I should have done more to help, but I simply didn't have the experience. It was a tragic waste as we'll never know what the Pistols might have gone on to achieve had they carried on. I still see Paul regularly. He makes light of the Pistols' legacy saying 'But we only made one album.' 'Yes,' I tell him, 'but what an album!'"

Tiberi says he'd long-since come to recognise that a parting of the ways was inevitable. "I know I'm viewing these events with hindsight here, but John and Malcolm's interpersonal relationship was none existent by the time we got to America. Malcolm had stopped speaking to John from May 1977 onwards and the denouement came in San Francisco. I would have regular discussions with John - at least once a week where I'd explain what was happening regarding certain situations, and he'd say, 'Yeah, but Malcolm's got to run it by me, hasn't he?' I'd go and tell Malcolm that he needed to speak with John, but Malcolm simply wouldn't do it.

"I saw John in the lobby when I arrived back at the Miyako after dropping Sid off with the acupuncturist. I guess I kind of knew why he was there. Rory and I had driven over to San Jose to speak with John at the Cavalier Motel the previous evening, but Monk - even though it was him that had given me the name and address of the motel - wouldn't let us see John. It seemed to me there was a lot of mind games going on. I was getting mixed signals from both John and Malcolm. I knew John had gone up to see Malcolm with Steve and Paul, but it wasn't my place to get involved. The only other person that had the right to be in there was Sid, but that couldn't be helped because of what had happened. I was outside in the corridor when John, Steve, and Paul went into Malcolm's room. Steve and Paul came out first but didn't really say much. It was when Malcolm and John were alone that Malcolm told John about going to Rio. When John left I went in to see Malcolm and that's when he told me it was all over."

The following morning Rotten accompanied Joe Stevens to New York, while Johnston drove McLaren, Richmond, Jones, and Cook to LA. The task of collecting a still fragile Vicious from Bill Graham's "Dr. Feelgood" fell to Tiberi. "I've since read that Sophie picked Sid up from Graham's doctor, but I'm pretty sure it was Boogie," says Johnston. "I can't imagine why Sophie would volunteer, and Malcolm certainly wouldn't have told her to do it. I remember Boogie turning up at the Tropicana in LA saying he'd managed to get Sid enough methadone to get him through the flight back to London. I drove them to the airport and accompanied them onto the concourse – as you could back then. We made small talk the whole way to the plane and it was really good. For the first time since I'd met the band in Atlanta, I felt that I was talking with John Beverley rather than Sid Vicious."

What Vicious failed to mention to either Johnston or Tiberi, was that he had a stash of valium capsules. As soon as the plane was airborne he popped a couple of the valium, promptly overdosed again, and slipped into a coma. Vicious was still unconscious when the plane touched down at JFK, and such was his condition that a doctor ordered him to be rushed to the nearby Jamaica Hospital in Queens. That night a raging blizzard descended upon New York, and with Tiberi holed up in a nearby hotel when Vicious regained consciousness the following morning he had no idea where he was or how he'd got there.

Johnston says McLaren, Jones, and Cook hung out at the Tropicana for at least a week before flying down to Rio. "I stayed behind in LA dealing with Rene Daalder as he was still working on the *Swindle* script. Russ Mayer had walked away by this point, but Malcolm still wanted Rene involved in the project. I had a place in LA, of course, but I ended up staying at Rene's place up in the Hollywood Hills. While Malcolm was in LA, I had Warners leaning on me to rearrange the cancelled northern shows - they still fully expected Malcolm and John would work things out. Bob Regehr was holding out for the shows and was constantly on the phone to me. What could I do at that point? I tried the whole time we were in San Francisco to convince Malcolm to re-book the cancelled dates, but he just wasn't interested. 'No, we're going to Brazil!' he'd shout. And there was nothing Warners could do as they had nothing in writing.

"I've never understood why Malcolm found going to Rio to meet Ronnie Biggs so appealing. I kept thinking, 'Why are they going to Brazil? What's the point?' One of the things I did while Malcolm was in LA was finding an actor that looked as if he might have worked in a Nazi concentration camp to play the part of Martin Bormann in the film. His name, if I remember rightly, was Jim Jeter. (At the time, the Texas-born Jeter was best known for appearing in *The Sand Pebbles* opposite Steve McQueen)

Holmstrom says he and Roberta Bayley were in their room at the Miyako when Tom Forçade arrived with an offer neither could refuse. "We were packing our stuff, and all we could talk about was how much we wanted to get home after being on the road. Then Tom showed up and asked us if we wanted to go to Rio. Suddenly, the idea of going home wasn't so important. He gave us the tickets for the red-eye back to New York, and I'm pretty sure they were first class. We hadn't been home long when we started hearing the stories: that Rotten was in NYC staying with Joe Stevens, of Sid passing out on the plane and ending up in a hospital bed at Jamaica Hospital. I bumped into Rotten at CBGBs when I went to watch Ulli Lommel filming, *The Blank Generation* starring Richard Hell. Rotten is in the tracking shot when Hell performs 'Blank Generation.' He's standing next to Cheetah Chrome of the Dead Boys, wearing the blue tartan suit from the tour. It was the perfect ending to the craziest tour in rock 'n' roll history."

It's doubtful Rotten was aware of Vicious' hospitalisation, but even if he had its unlikely to have made any difference. Legend has it that with the blizzard having brought New York to a standstill, Vicious' only contact with the outside world during his overnight stay in hospital came courtesy of a telephone conversation/interview with Roberta Bayley. Tiberi disputes this, however. "I spoke with Sid on the phone several times. And when the hospital called me the next day to say Sid was being released, I rebooked the flights to London before going over to pick him up. While Sid was in hospital he received a telegram from the 'HA crowd' 'HA' as in 'Haight Ashbury.' I still have it. It says something like, 'Hi Sid, we've burnt our leather jackets, ha-ha.'"

When the news about the Pistols' split broke in Britain, Glitterbest issued the following press release: "The management is bored with managing a successful rock 'n' roll band. The group is bored with being a successful rock 'n' roll band. Burning venues and destroying record companies is more creative than making it." The release duly appeared in the following morning's edition of *The Guardian*, but it

SireRecords press advertisement from the USA. Interesting to note they rated Radio Birdman higher than Dead Boys and The Flamin' Groovie

soon transpired that the statement had been penned by mischievous Glitterbest employees rather than McLaren and was promptly withdrawn.

The music papers had already gone to press when the news of the split broke, so it wasn't until the following week that the music weeklies were able to offer their respective takes on the split. Speaking with the *Record Mirror*, Virgin's press officer Al Clark said that there wasn't much anyone could say about the Pistols' immediate future – at least until the label could get everyone concerned in the same room - other than the band were all still under contract to Virgin.

—What Am I going To Do Now

"I used to get on with Simon Draper, who was second-in-command to Richard Branson at Virgin. He was an ex-South African army fella, but he really cared, he was genuine. He knew when the Pistols fell apart that I could end up in all kinds of problems, so he gave me something to do – go to Kingston, indulge in the latest sounds emanating from there, and help sign acts for Virgin's new reggae subsidiary label, Front Line."

John Lydon

John Rotten arrived back in London in late-January 1978 to be met by his father and brothers and a coterie of reporters. McLaren had confirmed the mounting rumours of a split via the Sun several days earlier, but Rotten mischievously declared The *Sun's* "Sex Pistols sensation: punk band splits up as Rotten walks out" exclusive as just another of their manager's publicity stunts. However, with the Pistols' January 20 show in Stockholm, and every other scheduled date of the band's proposed "world tour" having been cancelled indefinitely, the newshounds weren't for chewing that particular bone and continued to press him as to

Opposite: John Lydon with something to do...

what his next move might be. Would he be forming a new band? Would he go solo? Or maybe even replace the frontman in an already successful punk or new wave act?

The first thing he did was announce he was resorting back to his real name: John Lydon. And soon after doing so, he was en route to Jamaica where he would cast his eye – or perhaps that should be "ear" over the as yet undiscovered musical talent for Richard Branson's new sub-label, Front Line. The general misconception surrounding Lydon's Jamaica jaunt is that Branson arranged the trip with the singer in mind. Branson's original intention had been to sound out potential new acts himself in the company of celebrated sixties photographer, David Bailey. At the time, however, Jamaica was a hotbed of political unrest. When Bailey demanded extra recompense to make the trip at the eleventh-hour, Branson instead turned to Dennis Morris.

Morris had already carried out several photographic assignments for Virgin – most notably the Pistols' promo video for "God Save the Queen" at the Marquee. According to Morris, it was he who suggested to Branson that the reggae-loving Lydon was perhaps better suited to unearthing the island's as yet unsigned talents. Though Morris and Lydon were mates by this juncture, the latter insisted on bringing Don Letts along for the ride – going so far as to have Virgin take care of his flight and accommodation. Letts had introduced Lydon to dub reggae at all-night clubs such as The Four Aces in Dalston. While Letts had relatives in Jamaica, the closest he'd yet come to the island of his forebears came with his watching *The Harder They Come* at the cinema.

Upon their arrival in Jamaica, the trio booked into the Kingston Sheraton which was set to be immortalised in song in The Clash's "Safe European Home" (The opening track on the band's second album, *Give 'Em Enough Rope*). They were soon joined by *Sounds'* features editor, Vivien Goldman, who was working in Jamaica doing PR for Bob Marley. Goldman would be in attendance at Lee 'Scratch' Perry's Black Ark Studios when Lydon recorded "Dub-inspired" versions of Pistols' tracks "Submission" and "Problems". The recordings didn't pan out as everyone had hoped, owing to various "distractions" in the studio, but Lydon's ad hoc A&R trip ultimately paid dividends for Branson as Big Youth, The Mighty Diamonds, Prince Far I, and Johnny Clark would all end up signing to Front Line.

Lydon's disdain for "whitey-does-reggae" punk/new wave bands such as The Clash and The Police was well-known, of course. Yet whilst he was fundamentally in Jamaica to check out the local unsigned talent, seeing Kate Simon's photos of him hanging out with the likes of Tapper Zukie, Sly & Robbie, and U-Roy in Goldman's *Sounds* features resulted in mounting speculation as to whether the ex-Sex Pistol was contemplating a volte-face by recruiting reggae musicians for his new musical venture? This didn't prove the case, but Dennis Morris believes Public Image Limited's early sound was formulated whilst Lydon was in Jamaica: "If you listen to Public Image, [the] debut album, it was basically dub with snatches of vocals every now and then, like a Tubby mix. While we were [there] we went to quite a few dances, and these helped [John] realise that this sound could work, but in a rock way."

One sound Lydon most definitely decided wasn't for him was that of Devo – the quirky, Ohio-based synth rockers best known for their sporting garish yellow boiler suits. Devo were signed to Virgin at the time and reflecting on the Jamaican trip in *Anger is an Energy*, Lydon says that Branson – though never broaching the subject with him directly – was contemplating the idea of having Lydon front join the American band.

Mark Mothersbaugh says Branson flew him and Devo's rhythm guitarist, Bob Casale, out to Jamaica. Having gotten the pair stoned, Branson proceeded to tell them how Lydon supposedly wanted to be their new singer. And that if they agreed with the proposal, he had press from England (most likely Viv Goldman and Kate Simon) ready to get the media ball rolling: "He (Branson) said, 'Johnny Rotten is down here at the hotel. He's in the next room and there are reporters downstairs. I'd like to go down to the beach right now if you're into this because Johnny Rotten wants to join your band . . . and I want to announce to them that Johnny Rotten is the new lead singer for Devo.' And I'm going, 'Oh my God, I'm really high right now.' Regrettably, I didn't just go, 'Yeah, sounds great. Send him to Akron. He can do it for a week or two, just for the hell of it.'" For his part, Lydon says his only contact with the Devo duo came in him and Morris catching one of them spying on them through the curtains of his hotel room.

Branson wasn't the only one harbouring ulterior motives where Lydon was concerned, however. Warners had suspended the

£200,000 they had invested into the ongoing *Swindle* project, and McLaren's only hope in getting his hands on the cash was in resolving his differences with Lydon. Upon hearing Lydon was in Jamaica, McLaren handed Tiberi a cache of blank sheets of paper bearing his signature before packing him off to Heathrow. The signed sheets of paper were to be used to make various promises to Lydon should he agree to a truce and cooperate on the film. Lydon, of course, knew McLaren well enough to know that whatever promises Tiberi was making weren't worth the paper they were written on.

"My impression was that Malcolm was lost for thinking that he could bribe John into returning to the Pistols," says Tiberi. "I was happy to go out to Jamaica, but there were things that I didn't know. For instance, I didn't know Don Letts was there. And Don made it his mission - his agenda, if you like – to keep me from getting close to John. There was little love lost between Malcolm and Don Letts. All the talk about Boy, or Acme as it was before that, being competition to SEX is nonsense. Absolute nonsense! It was nothing more than a blatant rip-off!

"Branson was also there, of course. And that man is daft with a capital 'D'. Branson was all about self-promotion and feeding into the Pistols' notoriety. Virgin were talking about setting up a reggae subsidiary at the time they signed the Pistols. They had like fifty people sitting around the office all day, so they had to think of something to merit their worth. Virgin wasn't a record label in the true sense, like EMI or CBS. They were just a bunch of hippies. The Pistols' contract was so drawn out. It seemed to go on for ages. Branson had arrived in Jamaica with a suitcase filled with money, which John then handed out to any acts he thought good enough. That's not to say John wasn't a good choice. His interest in reggae wasn't ephemeral of anything, but that whole thing was nothing more than a glorified A&R trip.

And while it's true that I was thrown into the swimming pool, the tale that I was found hiding in the bushes with a tape recorder was utter fabrication; as was the tale about Malcolm instructing me to get a photo of John lounging by the pool smoking a spliff to ruin his 'punk credibility' in Britain. These were cooked up by Vivienne Goldman for her *Sounds* feature.

"What actually happened was I'd given up on trying getting John on his own. I mean, I was in regular contact with Malcolm by phone, and once I'd explained about the influence Letts and Branson were having on John, Malcolm understood the situation. So I'd given up chasing John and was sitting by the pool reading a book when John and Don ran across and dumped me, the chair, and my book in the pool. They were just larking about."

Whilst in Jamaica John gave Goldman a *Sounds* exclusive; his first proper interview since walking out on the Pistols. In the interview Lydon scotched the rumours about his supposedly poaching local musicians for his own reggae outfit, saying that although he liked reggae, he had no intention of "tampering with it". Lydon also revealed how he'd been badgering Branson to sign up some reggae acts from the first day the Pistols had signed to the label the previous May. Although Virgin was still smarting from having had its fingers burnt after investing heavily in several reggae acts that all failed to live up to expectations, Branson had already acted on Lydon's advice in signing Dr. Alimantado and releasing "Slavery Let I Go" as a 12" single in the UK.

Goldman tried coaxing Lydon into revealing what music he did intend on making upon his return to London, but as yet he was content with keeping his own counsel: "I don't care what people want to know. No one's got that kind of right. I do what I do and when I decide to release it, that's a different story. But till then, I prefer to keep quiet about it . . ."

However, when pressed by Goldman as to there being any musicians he might like to collaborate with, Lydon admitted to his being in something of a serious predicament. "There practically no musicians with my musical tastes," he said. "This means oh, cruel savage world if there's any oafs going round out there who dare to consider themselves acceptable, let me know! And I don't mean mugs and prats and tits and liggers and wankers and madmen with pea-brained ideas about changing the musical course of history, because we all know that that's impossible . . ."

Towards the end of February 1978, McLaren was forced to interrupt his filming schedule on the *Swindle* in Brazil and return to London to deal with the legal proceedings Russ Meyer had instigated over his unpaid director's fees. Upon discovering McLaren was back in London, Bob Regehr wasted little time in summoning him and Lydon to LA for a reconciliatory meeting between the protagonists to see if a compromise might at least be reached on the film. With the Sex Pistols existing now only on paper Regehr knew getting the *Swindle* film completed was the only realistic means open to recoup some of Warners' six-figure investment. Regehr was so keen to get the warring parties around the table that he wired the funds for Lydon to bring his mum out to LA with him. (Eileen Lydon had already been diagnosed with the stomach cancer that would ultimately claim her life. Following on from the meeting, Lydon flew onto Toronto to enable his mum to see her sister for the first time in many years)

Lydon had the greatest respect for Regehr but reiterated his stance regarding the Pistols and suggested that Warners' money would be better put to use financing his new musical ventures whatever they might be. Though happy to listen to Lydon's overtures, Regehr's immediate priority lay in cajoling him to giving his consent to the film. Lydon hadn't set eyes on McLaren since their acrimonious meeting at the Miyako in San Francisco. When the two came face-to-face the following morning at the Continental Hyatt House Hotel, Lydon took great delight in imposing several non-negotiable content stipulations to which he knew McLaren could never possibly comply. McLaren still had a couple of cards up his sleeve, however, and Lydon was in Toronto with his mum when he discovered McLaren was insisting the stage name "Johnny Rotten" was the property of Glitterbest. McLaren was also asking for 25 per cent of all moneys Lydon had earned as a Sex Pistol per the Glitterbest contract.

Rotten wanted nothing more than to put the Pistols behind him and move on with his life and career, but McLaren's pettiness left him seething. He decided to fight fire with fire. On his return to London, he hired Brian Carr, a no-nonsense litigation solicitor who specialised in the music business. Carr's first act in the Lydon v Glitterbest court battle, that was to endure for the next eight years, was to send a letter to McLaren asking him to supply Sex Pistols accounts – as per the band's Glitterbest contract – from the two quarters up to September 30, 1977

While Lydon was locking horns with McLaren, Jones, Cook, and Vicious shared a stage one last time performing the title track for *The Great Rock'N'Roll Swindle*. McLaren had hired the Hope & Anchor in Islington, to stage mock auditions for a stand-in singer to replace Lydon. Jones says he doesn't remember much about the session as he was mostly "drunk off his arse" at the time: "I suppose that was

Malcolm's Way of showing Johnny that the band didn't need him, but what it actually showed was the opposite."

Jones and Cook had already recorded two songs with Ronnie Biggs (whom the UK press would playfully dub "Ronnie Rotten") whilst in Rio de Janeiro. The first of these was a reworking of "Belsen Was A Gas" with alternate verses penned by Biggs. "No One Is Innocent" was a new song featuring a lyric in which Biggs blithely exonerates the crimes of Moors Murderers, Ian Brady and Myra Hindley, and Ugandan despot, Idi Amin. Later in the year, the duo worked as hired hands on Johnny Thunders' debut solo album, *So Alone*. They would also make several appearances with Thunders' ad hoc outfit "Johnny Thunders' Allstars" at The Speakeasy. Thin Lizzy frontman, Phil Lynott, had also guested on Thunders' solo album. This, in turn, would lead to another collaboration which saw Jones and Cook teaming up with Lynott and his fellow Lizzies Scott Gorham, Brian Downey and Gary Moore as "The Greedy Bastards."

Despite a total lack of airplay 'No One Is Innocent' (coupled with Sid's rendition of 'My Way') would reach #7 on the UK chart – outselling all four previous Sex Pistols singles into the bargain.

Vicious had been the first Sex Pistol to arrive back in London (January 21), but the media hadn't deemed the bassist's return of any import. Reunited with his beloved Nancy, Vicious rarely ventured from their Maida Vale drug lair other than to collect his weekly stipend from the Glitterbest offices. Lech Kowalski arrived at Pindock Mews in late-January 1978 with a film crew and *NME* scribe Chris Salewicz. The idea being that Salewicz would interview Vicious about the Pistols' break-up for *D.O.A.: A Right of passage*. Despite Salewicz's valiant efforts, however, Nancy ended up doing most of the talking as Sid was so out of it that he kept nodding off mid-sentence. "What was so striking about that visit to Pindock Mews was how tragic it all seemed,' says Salewicz today. "Sid was not at all well. He'd collapsed on a plane-flight in America, I believe and been hospitalised with pneumonia. The room that housed the bed on which he and Nancy lay was surrounded by empty prescription cough medicine bottles, including – unsurprisingly – the morphine-based Collis Browne. It seemed pretty clear that Sid had done some of those bad drugs he shouldn't have gone near before we arrived. But he was also pretty ill, in shockingly bad shape."

A lifeline of sorts appeared out of the blue in February when

Johnny Thunders invited Vicious to play bass in "The Living Dead," another of the ex-Doll's impromptu Speakeasy ensembles. Vicious had naively thought of himself and Thunders as kindred spirits of sorts, but his return to the spotlight was to end in ignominious failure. One of the songs Vicious was required to learn for the All Stars set was "Steppin' Stone", which, of course, had been a staple of the Pistols' set before Vicious' joining the band. The song's simple E/G/A/C riff proved too much for Vicious, however. Only Ones' frontman, Peter Perritt, who also appears on *So Alone* and was guesting as an All Star, told Vicious to just play the "E" note and was bemused to find the ex-Pistol didn't know where to find the "E" note on his bass.

Speaking with Nina Antonia for her 2015 book, *The One & Only: Peter Perritt, Homme Fatale*, Perritt revealed that Thunders had wanted to give Vicious the elbow and that it was only his pleadings for clemency that saw Thunders relent. Thunders had one proviso, however: that Vicious' amp be switched off during the performance. "It was Johnny's pre-condition for allowing Sid to play," says Perritt. "It became pretty clear at the soundcheck that even learning one song would be difficult for Sid. I persuaded Johnny to let Sid play as he had the enthusiasm of an innocent, and I didn't have the heart to disappoint him. Living Dead gigs had a certain amount of chaos surrounding them anyway, so Sid's silent appearance didn't seem incongruous. After three songs, Sid noticed the absence of bass sound and started haranguing the roadies to fix it. At this point, Johnny thanked him for his contribution and he was replaced by Henri-Paul (Tortosa of The Maniacs)."

Thunders had also insisted that Spungen go up on stage topless to introduce the Allstars. Perritt says Thunders hadn't intended to humiliate Nancy, and probably didn't notice the hurt in Vicious' eyes. It's been suggested that it was their ejection from Junkie Johnny's court that set Sid and Nancy on their tragic tailspin, but Perritt offers a different perspective. "Sid worshipped Johnny and enjoyed himself immensely while he was on stage . . . even if Nancy's topless introduction of the band wasn't perhaps to his liking."

Vicious would be reunited with Steve Jones in Paris for the recording of 'My Way'. McLaren had initially wanted Vicious to record 'Non, Je Ne Regrette Rien,' the French standard made famous by Edith Piaf, for inclusion on the *Swindle* soundtrack. Vicious, however, had insisted on 'My Way.' An arrangement was duly worked out which saw Vicious mock-crooning the opening verse of the Paul Anka classic before speeding things up with Jones's telltale chugging riffs giving the song a Sex Pistols feel. (The accompanying promo video was shot at the Paris Olympia music hall on the Boulevard des Capucines.)

John Tiberi, however, says the intention behind the Paris trip had nothing to do with any recording. "Malcolm and I flew to Paris to meet with Eddie Barclay from Barclay Records. Warners had stopped the money they had put into the film the moment John walked out of the band, and Malcolm was desperate to get fresh funding. We brought Sid along to film him walking through the Jewish Quarter with Nancy, but the idea to put him in front of a microphone probably came about at the hotel bar. It was Malcolm's way of saying, 'Fuck you!' – at a distance – to John. But there was never any serious intention of establishing Sid as John's replacement in the Pistols. That would never have worked. I mean, 'My Way's great and everything, but Sid and Nancy were beyond redemption by that point - literally beyond redemption."

Soon after his return from Paris Vicious was reunited with Hellin Killer. Killer had been in London several weeks when she inadvertently happened upon Sid and Nancy on the King's Road. She was unsure as to whether Vicious would remember her but her fears were instantly allayed when he came bounding towards her, hugging her. Nancy knew all about what had transpired between Sid and Hellin in Dallas and San Francisco yet welcomed her fellow American with open arms and insisted she move into Pindock Mews. "Yes, I ran into Sid and Nancy soon after I got to London. I'd booked a one-way ticket on Laker airlines from New York. I was always going off on my own, but wherever I went I had friends or acquaintances there. It was on the King's Road and I was with a couple of friends that were putting me up. I'd told them about what had happened on the tour but it was obvious they didn't believe me. When they spotted Sid and Nancy in Boy they challenged me to go inside. I was worried because he was with Nancy and I'd heard all these horrible things about her. I'd only just got inside the store when Sid turned and saw me. His face lit up and he came running over and threw his arms around me. I was so happy but I could see Nancy coming towards us. I thought, 'Oh-oh', but she was really nice and insisted I move in with them. She was a real friend to me.

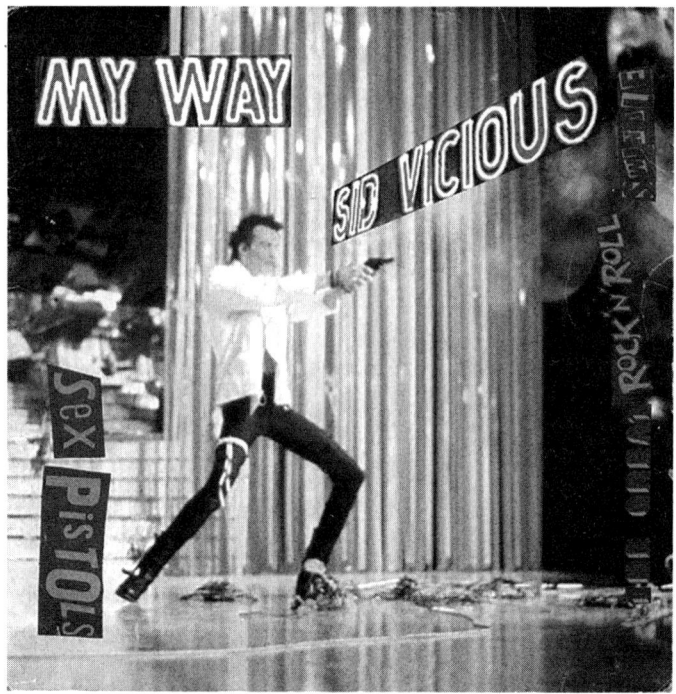

'My Way' outsold all four previous Sex Pistols singles

"While I was living at Pindock Mews we just did ordinary stuff - went out to gigs, or the local pub, or buy fish and chips. Roadent came round a few times. Steve English would also come round. What a guy! He was a bouncer who looked after Sid. He used to kinda look out for me while I was in London too. In fact, he was the one who told me my family was there looking for me! Looking back, I feel like I was fated to meet Sid, then Nancy, live with them, and look after them for a while. Sid was a huge deal to me."

Vicious was now a free agent as he'd forced McLaren to relinquish all managerial rights while they were in Paris. Seeing her beloved Sid onstage miming to 'My Way' at the Olympia in Paris was enough to convince Nancy that her beau could be a star in New York. Vicious wasn't due to receive any royalties from the sales of 'My Way' until sometime later in the year, so the couple had no viable means of raising the cash to fund their stateside venture. Help, however, was close to hand.

In a strange quirk of fate, Vicious lived around the corner from Glen Matlock, and the two would occasionally meet up for a drink in one of the local pubs. Matlock, who was still in the Rich Kids at the time, remembers it was during one of these get-togethers that the idea to do a gig together to raise enough cash for Sid to go to New York had materialised. Having recruited Matlock's fellow Rich Kid, Steve New, on guitar and ex-Damned drummer Rat Scabies, the 'Vicious White Kids' – as they would be calling themselves for the one-off show – set a mid–August date at the Electric Circus in Camden Town and knuckled down to rehearsals. (The repertoire consisting of 'My Way,' 'Something Else,' 'C'mon Everybody,' 'Belsen Was A Gas', along with punk rock standards such as The Stooges' 'I Wanna Be Your Dog' and 'Search and Destroy'.

In the run-up to the Electric Ballroom show, Vicious and Spungen received a shocking wake-up call when their occasional drug buddy – 19-year-old studio assistant, John Shepcote – overdosed on a "speedball" (street slang for a cocktail of cocaine and heroin). Shepcote's untimely demise not only brought unwarranted attention from the police but also galvanized Vicious and Spungen to seeking help for their crippling addiction in entering a Methadone program at a private hospital in Harrow-on-the-Hill, north-west London. Their attempt at rehabilitation was to prove short-lived, however, as the week following the Camden show they left London bound for New York. Hellin Killer elected to remain in London. Sid's parting gift to her was the tuxedo he'd worn in the 'My Way' promo video.

The music media was still second-guessing whether the Sex Pistols would reform when The Damned announced they were calling it a day. Poor sales of *Music For Pleasure* led to Stiff dropping the band. Rat Scabies had already walked out in disgust with the finished album. Scabies was replaced by Jon Moss, who would go on to find fame with Culture Club. This now left The Clash as the last of punk's so-called "unholy trinity". Bands were still forming, of course, but with punk having become regimented, the majority of these acts were imbued with style rather than substance.

The auguries appeared promising with the release of The Clash's fourth single, 'Clash City Rockers' in February 1978. It's ironic that The Clash had prophesied 1977 as being "ground zero" in terms of a musical changing of the guard, and yet they knowingly lifted the tell-tale riff to The Who's 1964 hit 'I Can't Explain' for their latest offering. Strummer had wanted "(White Man) in Hammersmith Palais" to be the next single, but CBS again rode roughshod over the band's objections. Strummer's objections couldn't have been too vociferous, however, owing to his having contracted Hepatitis after swallowing a lump of gob at a Clash show. "I reckon I caught it at a gig in Newcastle," he explained. "The kids in the audience were gobbing at us like mad. I mean, all of us were covered; the equipment, the lot. This bloke must've been a really good aim 'cos he got me right in the mouth. And, by accident, I swallowed it."

Mick Jones was said to be particularly pleased with "Clash City Rockers", but his euphoria was to prove short-lived. Unbeknown to him, and indeed the rest of the band, the song's final mix had been vari-speeded by the band's in-house engineer, Micky Foote. Foote had raised the question of the song's original tempo with Bernard Rhodes, proposing the band return to the studio to re-record the song. Some four months had passed since the release of "Complete Control", however, and Rhodes was anxious to avoid incurring CBS's wrath should The Clash fail to deliver a new single as per the contract and gave Foote the go-ahead to remix the recording.

CBS were also making noises about a new Clash album, but the majority of their standard set having been used up on *The Clash* – coupled with the band's determination to maintain their value-for-money policy in keeping songs released as singles off the albums – there was nothing of note in the can. Strummer playfully suggested he and Jones fly out to Kingston to get their creative juices flowing again – much to the consternation of Simonon. To everyone's amazement, Rhodes consented to the proposal. Strummer and Jones didn't as yet have John Lydon's kudos in Kingston. Indeed, the two would be mistaken for off-duty sailors by the locals. Fearful of leaving their hotel, The Clash duo returned to London ten days later with only two new songs: 'Safe European Home' and 'Drug Stabbing Time'.

The paucity of new material wasn't Rhodes's only headache concerning the new Clash album, however. Epic was still refusing to release *The Clash* in the US on the grounds the album wasn't sufficiently "radio-friendly" – this despite the album having sold upwards of 100,000 import copies in the US in the twelve-month period April 1977 – April 1978). To make The Clash's "Westway

Sound" more AOR friendly, Epic handed Rhodes a short-list of potential producers. "There was some suggestion at the time that our second album was being geared for the American market, which is why we got an American producer, Jones explained. "But it was Bernie who introduced Sandy [Pearlman] to the situation."

The 34-year-old Pearlman had forged a reputation as the powerhouse behind Blue Öyster Cult's worldwide success. Despite Mark P. deeming the Long Island rockers worthy of featuring in the first issue of *Sniffin' Glue*, the news that Pearlman was set to produce The Clash's new album was greeted with dismay and derision in equal measure. The band's relationship with Pearlman got off to the worst of starts owing to Mick Jones's old school mucker, Robin Crocker, giving the American a bloody nose when he tried pushing his way into the band's dressing room at the Lanchester Polytechnic in late-January to introduce himself. One of those who witnessed the backstage barney was The Clash's new road manager, Johnny Green. Whilst studying Arabic languages at Lancaster University, Green had been instrumental in booking The Clash as part of the Anarchy Tour package. The show didn't proceed, but only because the more militant females making up the university's Student Union revoked the invitation because punk music was sexist. Green would be denied seeing The Clash on two further occasions before finally getting his wish when they played Dublin's Trinity College on the Get Out of Control Tour in October 1977.

Green managed to secure a ringside seat that night after being coopted by the lighting crew to train a spotlight on Strummer as he moved about the stage. He performed the task so well that the crew asked if he wanted to tag along for the remainder of the tour. Much to his dismay, when he turned up at the Kinema in Dunfermline three days later the crew had to confess they'd given the job to someone else as they hadn't expected him to show. Green's journey north of the border wasn't to be in vain; however, because Richard Hell's crew had happened to be a man down. This happenstance, of course, meant Green was perfectly placed for when Roadent took his official leave of absence from The Clash in Edinburgh two days later.

In March 1978, The Clash performed "Clash City Rockers alongside another new Strummer/Jones up-tempo rocker, "Tommy Gun", live in the studio on BBC2's new "yoof" show *Something Else*. 'Tommy Gun' was The Clash's first attempt at penning a song that focused on what was going on in the wider world. Strummer says he got the idea for the lyrics while thinking about how probably enjoyed reading about their killings as much as movie stars like seeing a good review of their latest films. Released in late November as the lead single from *Give 'Em Enough Rope*, 'Tommy Gun', gave The Clash their first UK Top 20 hit peaking at #19.

The Hersham-based Sham 69 had released their debut single, 'I Don't Wanna', on Miles Copeland's independent Step Forward Records label in October 1977. The single didn't trouble the official UK Chart but its performance on the independent chart proved sufficient for Polydor to take the plunge. Fronted by the brass-necked 23-year-old Jimmy Pursey, a band of sorts had been in existence since 1975. Pursey is reportedly understood to have opted for Sham 69 over Jimmy and the Ferrets on espying the term graffitied on a wall. (It's generally accepted the original graffiti read Walton and Hersham '69, in reference to Walton & Hersham F.C. securing the Athenian League title back in 1969.)

Julie Burchill would name-check Sham 69 (about their being at the rehearsal stage) in the November 1976 issue of *NME*, but by the time the band headed into Pathway Studios in August 1977, founding guitarists Johnny Good-for-nothing and Neil Harris had been replaced by Dave Parsons, while Mark Cain had replaced Billy Bostik on drums. Bassist, Albie Maskell, would survive long enough to appear on the band's debut single before being replaced by Dave Tregunna.

Sham 69's first single for Polydor, the rabble-rousing 'Borstal Breakout', surprisingly failed to chart following its January 1978 release – despite the band having accrued a dedicated following. However, their brash debut album, *Tell Us The Truth*, was released the following month and surpassed all expectations in climbing to #25 on the UK chart.

February 1978 also saw the release of The Adverts' woefully underrated debut album, *Crossing the Red Sea with The Adverts*. By this juncture, The Adverts were signed to Bright Records. "Gary Gilmore's Eyes" had scored the band a Top 20 hit, but when the follow-up single, 'Safety in Numbers', failed to chart, Anchor released them from their contract. 'No Time to Be 21' saw The Adverts return to winning ways in breaking into the Top 40 (#36) following its

Sham '69 were fronted by the charismatic Jimmy Pursey

January 1978 release, but the album would stall at a derisory #38. "Being put into Abbey Road studios to record *Red Sea* was more than just a joke," says TV Smith. "A ramshackle, amateurish punk band in the Beatles studio! It actually worked, however. We were very motivated to make a good record, and the people and equipment we had access to by being there led to that being able to happen. The recording process went by in a kind of a blur, as the songs that had just been in my head and notebooks a year earlier came into actual being. I particularly treasure going back into the studio a few weeks after the recording and spending late nights alone with producer John Leckie in the mixing process. All the raw material was down on tape at that point and we could calmly go about bringing it all together and creating the sound of the record.

"I know John received some criticism that *Red Sea* didn't sound like the band did onstage, but I think that's not the point. When you make a record, you want it to sound the way you 'think' the band sounds onstage, you try and capture the essence of the band. I love John's production on that record and watching him polish and finesse it was really one of my favourite times ever."

The Adverts would come in for criticism from certain sections of the music press for having the audacity for daring to experiment with their sound on their October 1979 follow-up album, *Cast of Thousands*. "I still don't really understand why *Cast of Thousands* was so despised," says TV Smith. " I assume it was because the critics had decided punk was going to go in one direction but the Adverts doggedly pushed it in a different one. I was trying to create an epic boundary-changing album, the kind of thing that had been done by the prog-rock bands before but played by a bunch of punk kids so it still had a connection to real life and real people. Without me really even noticing it, punk by that period had become more and more dumbed down and conservative - to the point where it couldn't accept anything that didn't fit into its self-created standards. The original idea that 'punk' meant expressing yourself, being creative and not caring about the rules was sadly gone.

"Laurie (Driver) was also sadly gone by the time we came to record the album. Rod Latter was in a band called The Rings with Alan Lee Shaw. We found him through the usual small ads/audition process after Laurie was out of the band. We liked Rod's enthusiasm and loose playing after the stiffness of Laurie's drum parts - particularly as the band was entering a new phase anyway."

Generation X's eponymous debut album cracked the UK Top 30 (#29) during the spring of 1978. Having taken over the band's managerial reins from Andy Czezowski in early 1977, Jonh Ingham set about securing them a recording contract, finally striking a deal with Chrysalis Records in July. John Towe was no longer in the band by the time of the signing, his having been replaced by Subway Sect's Mark Laff. Ingham, however, was no longer their manager by the time of the album's March 1978 release.

Billy Idol and Tony James had both been at the forefront of the UK punk scene; Idol as one of the Sex Pistols' early followers and James as a member of London SS. Idol's pop star looks always ensured Generation X a sizeable number of gaggle-eyed females whenever they played The Roxy, but from the summer of 1977 onwards the band began edging towards a more pop-oriented sound. Idol and

Wayne County in Dingwalls Dance Hall,
Camden Town, London in 1977. Photo Ray Stevenson

James also strived to extend the band's identity by designing and manufacturing a series of op-art and pop-art T-shirts for use in photoshoots and live performances. Their debut single, "Your Generation", would score them a Top 40 hit at the first time of asking (#36) in September 1977 and secured them an appearance on *Top of the Pops* – the first punk-affiliated act to appear on the show. They would also perform their follow-up single, 'Ready Steady Go' on *TOTP* despite its failure to crack the Top 40.

'Your Generation' would also be performed on *Marc*, with Derwood Andrews using Bolan's Les Paul. James and Towe were playing with instruments borrowed from Granada TV's studios. Laff's preferring the studio's drum kit over his own would result in Granada issuing Generation X with a ten-year ban.

Buzzcocks' November 1977 debut single as a United Artists act, 'Orgasm Addict' b/w 'Whatever Happened To . . .', failed to secure any daytime airplay for obvious reasons. The band's seminal debut album, *Another Music in a Different Kitchen*, however, has quite rightly since been hailed a classic. It also served to emphasise Pete Shelley's seemingly effortless ability to craft the perfect pop song. The album's title was inspired by a collage created by the band's friend, Linder Sterling; "Howard said, 'Another housewife stews in her own juice in a different kitchen," Shelley subsequently revealed. "We shuffled it around a bit and it came out like that."

The non-album single, 'What Do I Get?' broke into the UK Top 40, peaking at #37, yet the infinitely superior double A-sided "I Don't Mind" / "Autonomy" failed to trouble the Top 50 – though this could be due both tracks appearing on *Kitchen*. 'Love You More' saw Buzzcocks return to the Top 40 (#34), while 'Ever Fallen in Love (With Someone You Shouldn't Have)' would have surely been a number one had it been released by a mainstream act.

On Sunday, April 30 The Clash performed alongside X-Ray Spex, Steel Pulse, Patrik Fitzgerald and the Tom Robinson Band at Victoria Park in Hackney in front of an estimated 80,000-strong crowd. The festival was organised by the Anti-Nazi League (ANL) in co-ordination with Rock Against Racism, Hackney Campaign Against Racism, Hackney Community Relations Commission and the Tower Hamlets Movement Against Racism and Fascism. The organisers had erected an eight-foot-high stage had hired a 10,000 watt sound system to ensure all the attendees could hear and see what was going on and yet The Clash's 12-song set was marred throughout. In the run-up to the festival, *Melody Maker* said The Clash had approached the ANL and asked to be added to the bill and did so because they were "one of the most overtly political of Britain's new wave bands". Speaking to the paper, however, Mick said they were playing because it was a "free concert". Bernard Rhodes would prove rather more succinct, saying: "Swastikas are not in this year".

Strummer was sporting a T-shirt promoting the Italian terrorist organisation, Brigade Rosse (Red Brigade). A few weeks earlier (March 16), the car belonging to Aldo Moro, Italy's former prime minister and then president of the Christian Democracy party, was fired upon the Red Brigade. Moro's bodyguards and three policemen following in a second car were killed in the exchange. Moro was being held prisoner by Brigade Rosse at the time of the carnival. When subsequently questioned by *Record Mirror* as to his motive for wearing the T-shirt towards the end of June – by which time Moro's body had been found in the trunk of a Renault 4, his having been submitted to a political trial by a "people's court" set up by Brigade Rosse - Strummer said he did so because he didn't think they were getting the press coverage they deserved. "Personally I think what they're doing is good because although it's vicious and they're murdering people – you know, they go around killing businessmen and the people they see as screwing Italy up – well, I think what they're doing because it's a brutal system anyway." It wouldn't be the last time Strummer would shoot himself in the foot over his political opinions.

By the time the *Record Mirror* interview went to press The Clash were set to hit the road on the Out on Parole Tour. The tour's tongue-in-cheek title was in response to Simonon and Headon's recent incarceration at HMP Brixton following the pigeon shooting incident at Rehearsal Rehearsals that was subsequently mythologised in the song 'Guns on the Roof'. Listening to the song - with its telling couplet of "torturing of all the women and children" and "putting the men to the gun" – one could be forgiven for thinking The Clash had witnessed a siege. In reality, Simonon and Headon had fallen foul of the anti-terrorist squad after mischievously shooting several pigeons from the roof of their rehearsal space with an air-rifle. Unbeknown to the pair, the pigeons in question were prized racing pigeons. While taking potshots at the birds, Headon had accidentally put a pellet through the window of a passing train. Unable to get hold of Bernard, Mick Jones called Caroline Coon, who was, of course, well seasoned in dealing with the machinations of the British penal system through her involvement with Release. She was also still dating Simonon.

When Simonon and Headon went before the bench at Clerkenwell Magistrates Court they duly pleaded guilty and were each fined £30 and ordered to recompense the owner of the pigeons £700. (The band's arrival at court would be immortalised in *Rude Boy*).

Strummer and Simonon's arrest when the tour stopped off in Glasgow – Strummer was arrested for having the audacity to try and stop the Apollo's notoriously heavy-handed bouncers from beating up a fan, while Simonon was nicked for going to his singer's aid – would give the tour title an even more prophetic tone. In Blackburn (a last-minute replacement to the original Liverpool Empire date) their hotel was raided by police searching for illicit substances. Steve Jones had joined The Clash onstage at King George's Hall earlier in the evening. The ex-Pistol had turned up – supposedly "out-of-the-blue" – in Birmingham the previous night. Mick Jones hadn't thought anything was amiss but when his namesake showed up in Bury St Edmunds the following night he realised something was afoot. He confronted Steve and was bemused when the latter confessed that he was under the impression he was auditioning for The Clash.

According to Sandy Pearlman, Steve Jones was rehearsing with Strummer, Simonon and Headon at the 100 Club when he dropped by during his flash visit to London at the beginning of the year. Just why The Clash would be rehearsing at the 100 Club instead of Rehearsals has never been revealed, but Pearlman says when he enquired about the strange situation he was informed that the rest of the band were angry with Mick for some reason and had sacked him. When asked what the reason might have been, Pearlman suggested that it could have been Mick's wanting The Clash to "be like Mott The Hoople". Johnny Green, however, insists that the reports of Mick's temporary sacking – as with Mark Twain's demise – have been greatly exaggerated.

If the rumours are true about the Matlock/Simonon exchange,

HMV name-checking punk and new wave acts in their press advertising

then this was the second time Bernard Rhodes had been intent on bringing a Sex Pistol into The Clash fold. Whatever Simonon's feelings were about the rumours surrounding his trading places with Matlock, Jones had no intention of letting their manager's underhand conniving go unpunished. From that point on, Rhodes's card was marked.

—Teenage Dreams So Hard To Beat

"What people don't understand is when punk started it was so innocent and not aware of being looked at or being a phenomenon and that's what everyone gets wrong. You can't consciously create something that's important, it's a combination of chemistry, conditions, the environment, everything."

Siouxsie Sioux

The art school crowd that had given the nascent London punk scene gravitas – consciously or otherwise – had long-since melted away. Indeed, while many of the Blitz Club's fashionistas that would rise to prominence on the New Romantic scene of the early-Eighties had championed the Pistols, Damned and Clash et al, they'd uniformly eschewed The Roxy in favour of Billy's nightclub even before the release of *Never Mind the Bollocks*. By the summer of 1978, punk had morphed into "new wave" with bandwagon-jumping novelty songs such as 'Going Steady' (Jilted John), 'Ça Plane Pour Moi' (Plastic Bertrand) and "'The Winker's Song (Misprint)' (Ivor Biggun and the Red Nosed Burglars) enjoying chart success in the UK. There were still several bands of note keeping the flame alive so to speak; Dunfermline's Skids being a prime example.

Opposite: Siouxsie was a punk from the early days of the scene

Skids had formed during the summer of 1977. 19-year-old Stuart Adamson and Bill Simpson had played together in a covers band called Tattoo whilst still at school. When the band fell apart the two had relocated to Amsterdam in search of adventure. Within a couple of weeks, however, the boys were back in Dunfermline. "Stuart spent most of his money in the casino on the ferry across from Hull and lasted about a fortnight before his money ran out," says Simpson on the Skids official site. "He wanted to come home, he was homesick, but even at that time, I think he'd been writing some songs. There's a few in his lyrics book that he kept, noted 'Amsterdam '76'.

"When we came back from Amsterdam punk rock was exploding and it was the perfect outlet for us," Simpson continued. "We loved the music, attitude, the bands - the Stranglers, the Clash, the Damned - we started trying to look the part, get some relevant attire from thrift shops etc. It was just an amazing time for us with all that great early music and the natural progression was to try and write our own songs. I don't think we were looking too far ahead to forming a band or anything like that, it was just having fun jamming in Stuarts bedroom - that's where 'Sick Club', 'Victims of the Weekend' (the earliest Skids songs, later recorded for the band's first demo) all started and it kind of evolved quickly from there."

Richard Jobson was only 17 when he joined forces with Adamson and Simpson but was already standing out from the crowd in his black trench coat and black and white streaked hair according to Simpson: "He just had a look and a presence about him. I never spoke to him but what happened next was we were talking about putting a band together and thought we'd audition for a singer. Stuart must've bumped into Richard somewhere and invited him along to audition. As soon as we heard he could carry a tune, the confidence and presence he had, the overall look and the fact he was of the same mindset, that was it, we'd found our singer.

The trio placed a "Drummer required" ad in the local paper, adding a caveat that "no hairies" need apply. Of the three shorthaired auditionees, 23-year-old Thomas "'Tam' Kellichan not only had the edge but also unlimited access to his uncle's van. With the line-up complete the four put their heads together to think of the all-important band name. "Marcus Zen Stars Tom Bomb" and the "Martyrs of Deal" were just two of the abstract names that were mulled over before they settled on the snappier-sounding "Skids". "I remember when we were starting off we had all these stupid names just for a laugh, Skid Marks and the Brown Jobbies and all that sort of crap," says Simpson. "I think it's just a myth really, somebody just said it for fun. You know 'Morton Sobothnik and the Silver apples' – that probably came from Richard, coming up with some daft names. Sounds good but it was never a serious thing."

Having made their live debut supporting Matt Vinyl & the Decorators and with a local Hells Angel, Mike "Pano" Douglas, now acting as their manager, Skids played a flurry of local shows while looking to broaden their horizons by hijacking a forthcoming Rezillos show at Rafters in Manchester. When the band arrived at Rafters they were politely informed by the promoter that he'd already booked a support band. Pano Douglas refused to take no for an answer, however and got his act on the bill.

Skids recorded the three songs that would make up the *Charles* EP – 'Charles', 'Reasons' and 'Test-Tube Babies' – at REL Studio in Edinburgh in October 1977. The EP was released the following February via a local record store owner's own No Bad label and would go on to sell over 20,000 copies. The EP also brought Skids to the attention of John Peel, which in turn led to their signing with Virgin Records. Their debut single, 'Sweet Suburbia' b/w 'Open Sound' spluttered to an ignominious halt at #78 on the UK chart despite their getting national exposure supporting The Stranglers. Their second release of 1978, the four-track *Wide Open* EP, would climb 30 places higher.

"When 'Sweet Suburbia' came out [Sandy Muir] put up a poster saying, 'Skids on *Top of the Pops* this week,'" says Simpson. "We listened to the Scottish chart on the Ken Bruce show on Sunday and the record had climbed 25 places. But when the UK chart came out, it had actually dropped 35 places. Basically, there was a huge amount of plugging going on down south and 'My Sharona' by the Knack was being plugged massively.

"When *Wide Open* came out Sandy put up another sign saying it was going to be on *Top of the Pops* this week, everywhere in Edinburgh that week there were people with the red and white stripes of the record in their hands, people of all ages, everyone had them." (Muir's prediction would again prove erroneous as Skids were again omitted from the *TOTP* line-up.)

The Undertones had formed in their native Derry back in 1974 but were content playing covers in the local parish halls until having their heads turned by punk. Having established themselves on the local scene and elsewhere in the province, The Undertones had headed into the studio but their demo tape would be rejected out of hand by the record companies over in London. Fortuitously, they also sent a cassette tape to John Peel and the DJ responded by offering to pay for them to record a demo within a proper studio setting in Belfast. In June 1978, the band entered Belfast's Wizard Studios to record the *Teenage Kicks* EP, which would be released on Terri Hooley's Good Vibrations label. The Undertones would sign with Sire Records in October that same year and the highly-infectious 'Teenage Kicks' would give the band their first UK hit (#31). (John Peel would cite 'Teenage Kicks' as his all-time favourite song.)

The same month The Undertones released 'Teenage Kicks' saw Stiff Little Fingers release the anthemic 'Alternative Ulster' on their own Rigid Digits label. "The song came about because Gavin Martin, who ran the *Alternative Ulster* fanzine, had come up with the idea that he wanted to put a flexi-disc on the cover and asked if he could have 'Suspect Device'," says Burns. "We said, 'You can't have it because we've just recorded it but I tell you what I'll do, I'll write you a song.' So I went away and wrote 'Alternative Ulster' and Gordon [Ogilvie] changed one line in it, which I think was the 'Alter your native Ulster' line, which is probably the cleverest line in the song."

As previously mentioned, Peter Hook and Bernard "Barney" Sumner had set about forming a band with their mate, Terry Mason, after the trio caught the first of the Sex Pistols' Lesser Free Trade Hall shows in June 1976. Sumner had been noodling about on guitar for a couple of years so Hook borrowed £35 from his mother to buy himself a bass. This left Mason little option but to take up the drums. Ian Curtis, whom they knew from seeing at various gigs in and about Manchester, responded to an ad in Virgin Records and was hired without audition. "We knew he was all right to get on with and that's what we based the whole group on," Sumner subsequently explained. "If we liked someone, they were in."

"The audition wasn't an audition," Mason reflected. "The audition was we took him out to Ashfield Valley [in neighbouring Rochdale] and we went wandering about in all the mud and crap. Ian had come quite well dressed. We were running about in the woods, and, of course, Barney being completely prepared came in wellingtons. Ian certainly got his feet wet that day. And that was the audition."

Pete Shelley and Buzzcocks' manager, Richard Boon, have both been credited with suggesting Sumner and Co. call themselves Stiff Kittens, but the quartet instead settled on Warsaw – an homage to Bowie's "Warszawa" from the latter's 1976 *Low* album – when making their live debut at the Electric Circus, supporting Buzzcocks, Penetration and John Cooper Clarke in late-May 1977. Mason was no longer a member of the band, however; his having opted to become their manager instead. Mason's replacement, Tony Tabac, had joined just two days before the Electric Circus show. I do remember seeing Warsaw at the Electric Circus," says Steve Diggle. "It was very raw, very much a young band trying to find their way. I think it would be right to suggest that, at that point, they weren't quite sure which way they would be moving in terms of music. That's perfectly natural. They sounded a bit a rougher version of the Banshees, who were one band who were never as bad as they made out in terms of musicianship. That was often the case with bands at that point. They pretended to be more inept than they actually were. But Warsaw did seem very raw."

By the time Warsaw headed into Pennine Sound Studios in neighbouring Oldham in July to record their first demos, Tabac had himself been replaced by Steve Brotherdale. Brotherdale was also the drummer in Panik, a local punk band managed by Rob Gretton. Aside from band management, the 27-year-old Gretton was the resident DJ at Manchester's Rafters, which was to play host to many leading punk bands.

Brotherdale's tenure in Warsaw would also prove short-lived but a more staple replacement came in Stephen Morris. Having responded to an ad in a music store window, Morris made his debut with Warsaw in early October alongside headliners Buzzcocks, The Prefects, and Magazine at the Electric Circus. The Collyhurst venue was set for closure and a number of Manchester bands came together to play two farewell shows. (A selection of recordings from these shows – including Warsaw's 'At a Later Date' would be subsequently released on the *Short Circuit: Live at the Electric Circus* album in June 1978.)

December 1977 saw Warsaw return to Pennine Sound to record the four songs that would appear on the self-financed *An Ideal for*

Living EP the following June. ('Warsaw', 'No Love Lost', 'Leaders of Men' and 'Failures'.) To avoid confusion with a more-established London-based punk band called Warsaw Pakt, the band decided on a name change to Joy Division, lifting the name from the sexual slavery wing of a Nazi concentration camp mentioned in Karol Cetinsky's 1955 novel, *House of Dolls*. Though billed as Warsaw to ensure a crowd, Joy Division played their first show on January 25, 1978, at Manchester's Pip's Disco. The change in name would bring accusations of supposed Nazi sympathies within certain quarters of the music press.

Joy Division's break came after participating in the Stiff/Chiswick Challenge at Rafters on April 14, 1978. Gretton was so impressed by their performance that he volunteered himself as their manager. Tony Wilson was also in attendance on the night. When Curtis supposedly berated Wilson for not putting Joy Division on *Granada Reports*, the latter promised to showcase the band on the show at the earliest opportunity. At the beginning of May, Joy Division began recording material intended for their debut album in collaboration with Richard Searling, a local DJ who also worked for RCA and Grapevine Records' head John Anderson. Anderson's decision to include synthesisers on the album's final mix didn't sit well with the band, however. As no-one could agree on what to do about remixing, the album was destined to remain unreleased, eventually surfacing as the *Warsaw* album.

Tony Wilson was to prove as good as his word and on September 20, 1978, Joy Division performed 'Shadowplay' live on *Granada Reports*; the eerie performance further enhanced by a backdrop of bleak Manchester centre-of-the-city scenes. Joy Division would subsequently sign with Wilson's newly incorporated Factory Records.

The Fall were also on the Electric Circus final weekend bill. Mark E. Smith had formed the band with three friends – Martin Bramah (guitar), Tony Friel (bass) and Una Baines (drums) – in the wake of the Pistols' Lesser Free Trade Hall shows. Smith had initially wanted to call the band The Outsiders, but Friel's suggestion they call themselves The Fall, after Albert Camus's 1956 novel of the same name, carried the day. It's said that Baines initially utilised biscuit tins as she couldn't afford a drum kit and soon switched to keyboards.

The Fall wouldn't make their live debut until the tail-end of May

Joy Division front man Ian Curtis Photo: Kevin Cummings/Getty Images

1977 at the North West Arts basement - an office/shop/café complex and part of the Manchester Musician's Collective situated on Manchester's King Street, with Steve Ormrod on drums. The show's organisers remember it being more of an "in-house" occasion as the audience was primarily made up of Collective musicians and the guys from Buzzcocks. "It was a small room and about half the audience was the Buzzcocks," says Bramah. "Mark just let fly with such venom from day one. I remember he just sort of reached into the audience and virtually poked his finger up Howard Devoto's nose."

Owing to political differences with Smith and the others, this was to prove Ormrod's only appearance with the band. He was subsequently replaced by Karl Burns who would go on to play with Public Image Limited.

Richard Boon was impressed enough by what he was hearing to fund The Fall's first recording session at Manchester's Indigo Studios. He intended to release the four tracks – 'Psycho Mafia', 'Bingo Master', 'Repetition' and 'Frightened' – via Buzzcocks' New Hormones label. Realising it was financially unviable at the time Boon returned the masters to the band. Smith would subsequently deem 'Frightened' inferior to the other three tracks, which would eventually be released as the *Bingo-Masters Breakout* EP in August 1978.

When reviewing the Electric Circus weekend fare, the *NME* lauded The Fall as being a "potentially great group [that] relay their messages amidst semi-complex, if surprisingly catchy, structures. They are angry, committed and genuine."

Two songs from The Fall's set on the night – 'Stepping Out' and 'Last Orders' – appear on the *Short Circuit: Live at the Electric Circus* compilation album.

The Sex Pistols' San Francisco show of January 1978 would prove a major inspiration for the bands/musicians on the LA scene. The Go-Go's founding bassist, Margot Olivarria, was at the Winterland show but had already caught one of the Pistols' 100 Club residency dates during the spring of 1976. "When I was 18 or so I decided to go travelling around Europe, take in the major cities and see the sights," she explained. "I grew up listening to the Beatles, the Stones, and the other 'British Invasion' bands. As you can imagine, I was really excited when I reached London. I don't remember how I came to hear about the Sex Pistols' show at the 100 Club as there really hadn't been much press about them at that time - and certainly none back home. Punk was happening in New York, of course, but it definitely hadn't yet reached LA. I hadn't even heard of the Sex Pistols when I arrived in London, so it was most likely a 'word of mouth' kinda thing. I can only think it was because I was hanging out in Soho a lot, going to shady pubs and clubs, ha-ha.

"The 100 Club was a really cool jazz venue so I was kinda surprised that it was staging punk rock shows. Though of course, this was way before punk got its reputation for violence. The support act that night were really, really terrible. They were called East of Krakatoa or something like that. They had a girl lead singer, and they were really horrible." (The support act that night (May 11, 1976) were called simply Krakatoa and featured future Academy Award-winner Hans Zimmer on keyboards.)

Olivarria initially feared she'd got the venue wrong until the 100 Club started to fill up with colourful-looking individuals. "After a while, these really interesting looking kids started to show up - people that I would later recognise as being Soo Catwoman, Siouxsie Sioux, Billy Idol and many others from the Pistols' soon-to-be-famous 'Bromley Contingent' posse. The Sex Pistols totally rocked my world that night. It was my first experience of punk rock, but to my mind, it was just the kinda primal rock 'n' roll that the Stooges and MC5 were playing. I couldn't take my eyes off of Johnny Rotten, he was just so mesmerising. I didn't know any of the songs at the time, but the energy coming off of the stage was like wave after wave. It was impossible not to be affected by it. The following day I cut my hair, made some holes in my fuzzy red sweater, and declared myself a 'punk'

"My friends and I liked glam rock when I was in school. My first ever concert was T-Rex and Slade at the Hollywood Palladium. My father drove me and two of my friends to Hollywood in the station wagon and picked us up after the show. It was a milestone event. Another early show I saw was Suzie Quatro at the Whiskey A Go Go. Suzi was super cool playing her bass in all-black leather jumpsuits. I have always been drawn to bass and drums, so although I had never played a string instrument when punk came along and convinced me that anyone could play anything, I chose the bass."

Olivarria hadn't long returned to LA when the Pistols' US dates were announced. "There was never any doubt that I wouldn't be at Winterland in San Francisco. "I hadn't been back long. I was going to school and working as a babysitter for some rich folk out in Laurel Canyon. I'd grown up in LA but was only just getting to know people within the punk scene so I ended up flying to San Francisco by myself the day before the Winterland show. I'd gotten to know a few people there from going to shows at the Mabuhay Gardens.

"Comparing the two Pistols shows I would say the one at the 100 Club was musically tighter. Glen Matlock was the bass player at the time, not that that was necessarily the reason they were tight. It was just the energy at the 100 Club with it being such a small venue. At Winterland the band was sloppy, yet so much fun. John was at the peak of his derisiveness that night. I was just so happy to be there. The after-show party was something of an anticlimax–for reasons we now know. I headed back to the house in Height Ashbury where another party was already underway. That party was totally wild! It was there that I met Hellin Killer for the first time. She was hanging out with Sid, who of course, was the centre of attention. Sid took a piss in the closet and kept bumping into walls. I also met a sexy guy called 'Boogie' and we liked each other. I didn't realise he was the Sex Pistols' road manager until we got to the Miyako, for some wild sex. When I woke up the next day, Paul and Steve came to visit Boogie so I left. I think they had to go over to Winterland to do their soundcheck or something.

"The Avengers were my favourite SF band, but I missed them and the Nuns because I was busy hanging out in the foyer checking out who was there and meeting new people. Boogie had hooked me up with all-access passes so I had the best time backstage. There were giant yellow plastic bags full of popcorn, which we opened and mixed with beer on the floor. It made a fantastic slip 'n' slide. In those days, no one was afraid to get dirty! After the show, I went to another party at the same house in Haight Ashbury. Little did I know it would turn out to be *the* party, the one where Sid OD'd! I don't remember anything from the party. I probably drank too much. Sure, I was disappointed when the Pistols broke up a couple of days later. But they had already planted a seed that would germinate all over the world. As for myself, I was grateful for having the chance to see them twice on stage.

"A few years later when I was living in New York I had some fun times hanging out with John and PiL's then drummer, Martin Atkins, at the 'PiL loft' on 19th Street. I also played bass in Martin's side-project, Brian Brain. For some reason, John wrote 'toilet' on all the appliances in the loft. I inherited the fridge when he and Martin moved out. It's funny, but I don't remember ever getting into a conversation about the Sex Pistols with John. I did tell him that I had seen the Pistols, of course, but at the time he was excited about PiL's relocating to the US, and to his mind, the Pistols was old news. I can certainly relate to that seeing what happened with the Go-Go's, but it was seeing the Sex Pistols that inspired me to pick up a bass guitar. And the Winterland show was the spark that got the Go-Go's up and running."

Within weeks of the Pistols' Winterland show, Olivarria found herself hanging out with fellow future Go-Go's, Belinda Carlisle and Jane Wiedlin, at a party in Venice Beach. Like most parties, more people turned up than had been invited and to escape the crush the trio moved outside onto the pavement. Carlisle and Wiedlin had also been at Winterland and the conversation turned to the Pistols' show and the new and exciting LA bands that were citing the Pistols as a major influence. Carlisle says she remembers little of the journey up to San Francisco as she'd most likely been tripping on acid. "My memory of the trip kicks in right before the show when I ran into other LA punks, such as photographer Jenny Lens, Hellin Killer, Margot and Jane [who was] then known as 'Jane Drano; a cute, outgoing girl who was around the Masque and Canterbury [Apartments] from the beginning."

The Canterbury was a Twenties-style apartment complex situated at the corner of Cherokee and Yucca, one block away from the Masque and would soon become home to many of the musicians on LA's fledgling punk scene. During Hollywood's 'Tinseltown' heyday, the Canterbury had catered for the steady influx of aspiring actors and starlets that arrived from all corners of the US on a daily basis. Though woefully rundown, the building still retained glimpses of its former glory. Many of the apartments boasted walk-in wardrobes and built-in vanity cabinets. What undoubtedly drew Wiedlin to the Canterbury – aside from its convenient location – was that the vast majority of her fellow residents were into doing the same things she did: "an endless stream of boozing, barfing, dancing and fucking."

"We'd all gotten into the Pistols through the UK music press and Rodney Bingenheimer who played all the latest underground music," says Theresa Kereakes. "Rodney was the first one to play the Pistols in Los Angeles. There were about a hundred of us on the scene, and we were all 'over-the-moon-excited' on hearing the Pistols were coming to the U.S. All of us made sure we got to Winterland. I mean 'everyone!' We were also very excited when we heard Hellin, Gabi [Berlin], and Trudie [Arguelles] had gone to Dallas to see the Pistols and had actually become friends with the band!

"I'm pretty sure Belinda got backstage after the show. I definitely remember Lorna (Doom) being backstage because I remember talking to her about the Avengers and how she thought they'd played with 'conviction!' I'd driven up to SF with Pleasant and Kid Congo Powers in my car. We sneaked backstage by walking in behind Sal Maida, who had just left Roxy Music to live in LA and play with Milk & Cookies."

Wiedlin knew what was happening over in London from reading about the punk scene over there in a *Women's Wear Daily* feature, but she'd yet to discover there was a punk scene much about what was happening over in London that Wiedlin discovered there was a thriving punk scene on her doorstep. "One weekend I visited a store on the Sunset Strip called Granny Takes a Trip which had started to lean in favour of the new punk rock style," she explained. "While I was there another girl came into the shop to hawk her wares and we got talking. Her name was Pleasant (Gehman). She'd recently met some other kids who were also transitioning from glitter to punk. Pleasant informed me that punk rock was not just in London – it was in Hollywood too. Well, you could have knocked me over with a feather. I was so excited! She gave me a flyer to a new club called the Masque."

"I remember our meeting very well," says Gehman. "This was way before the Go-Go's. I was designing my own T-shirts at the time. The shirts were covered with slogans, most of which were 'risqué' – especially back then. I would take the shirts to various stores such as Pleasure Chest on Santa Monica Boulevard, and Granny Takes A Trip on Sunset Strip, which was the sister-store of the famed London store. Jane was trying to sell her own T-shirts in GTAT, I remember they had two zippers stitched down the front that, when opened, would reveal the breasts – or nipples, if worn by a guy. We hit it off straight away. And yes, I did hand her a flyer for the Masque. She started hanging out with me and my crowd straight away."

The Masque was everything Wiedlin had been looking for and more. "It was dark, filthy and smelly. I thought I'd died and gone to heaven.

Richard Hell at the music Machine, London in 1977. Photo: Ray Stevenson

The first show I saw was the Alley Cats and the Controllers. There were about forty kids there. I knew right away I'd found my home."

—I'm Not The Same As When I Began

"Because of John being signed to Virgin, it was a done deal that whatever project he put together after the Pistols would sign with Branson. Again, because the Pistols had been signed to Warner in the States, PiL were signed to the label. Not long after I'd joined, a guy called Bob Regehr – who was a pretty big cheese at Warner – flew over from LA just to watch us rehearse! When he got back to LA, he called to say if we delivered the album in time for the Christmas market they were willing to put a million bucks into an account for us. That was just for promotion. Bob had recognised our potential from that one rehearsal."

Jim Walker

Whatever royalties John Lydon was owed as per the Glitterbest contract had also been suspended but while Bob Regehr was stalling on making any commitment concerning

Opposite: Public Image Ltd was Lydon's post-Pistols project

Warner Brothers' financing John's future musical ambitions, he did acquiesce to the singer's demand for £12,000. With this cash, Lydon took his first tentative steps on the property ladder in putting down a deposit on an end-of-terrace townhouse at 45 Gunter Grove in Fulham. He then retreated behind the walls of his end-of-terrace townhouse, and other than the odd backstage appearance little was seen of him. On Sunday, 16 April, however, he appeared on LTV's *London Weekend Show*; the same show that had filmed the Sex Pistols performing at the Notre Dame Hall back in November '76, as well as interviewing the band at their Denmark Street rehearsal space. Whilst walking London's streets with Janet Street-Porter, Lydon said that whilst he was rehearsing with a variety of musicians, he was no nearer to forming a new band. Citing his ongoing legal feud with Malcolm as the primary reason for his perceived sluggishness, he predicted that it could be another six months or so before he was in a position to release new music without suffering the indignity of having to hand over a 'big fat share of the profits' to his erstwhile manager. Though no one outside of Lydon's inner-circle would have been aware of it from the interview, evidence that he was writing new songs came with his comment about the press having only been previously interested in the clothes he was wearing and the colour of his hair.

During his time with the Pistols, Lydon was viewed as being the embodiment of disenfranchised youth. It was this that led to Pete Townshend inviting him to audition for the lead role of "Jimmy Cooper" in the film adaptation of The Who's 1973 rock opera *Quadrophenia*. In *Anger is an Energy*, Lydon reveals how his and Townshend's paths had first crossed during the early days of the Sex Pistols, and that since that juncture the guitarist had 'always shown a favourable, helpful point of view' towards Lydon's career. However, whilst Townshend thought him perfect for the role of the disaffected Jimmy, The Who's manager, Bill Curbishley, thought otherwise. Curbishley, who was producing *Quadrophenia*, didn't particularly like Lydon and certainly didn't think he was up to playing the lead role. To his credit, Lydon agreed with the decision as having no acting experience whatsoever meant he would at the very least require extensive coaching. The role of Jimmy would instead eventually go to Phil Daniels.

Whilst in Toronto with his ailing mother, Lydon had consented to an ad hoc interview with a local fanzine called *Pig Paper*. During said interview, Lydon said that while he didn't have any problem with Jones, Cook and Vicious continuing as the Sex Pistols in one guise or another, he'd thought the idea a non-starter on account of their individual failings.

Vicious' failings had driven Lydon to the point of despair during the Pistols' shambolic endgame. It, therefore, came as something of a surprise when Lydon revealed in *No Irish, No Blacks, No Dogs* that he'd invited Vicious to Gunter Grove to mull over the possibility of their working together again. "I wanted to work with Sid in London after the Pistols broke up because [he] told me that he had cleaned up his act. He was sick of Malcolm and didn't have any liking for Paul and Steve anymore." He'd made it abundantly clear to Sid that he was to leave Nancy at Pindock Mews but come the appointed hour he opened the front door to find the nauseating New Yorker standing beside her man. In that same heartbeat, John knew his gesture had been a glaring miscalculation on his part; his second mistake coming with not slamming the door in their faces.

The visit would be inadvertently captured for posterity by Pierre Benain, a French photographer who'd liaised with McLaren to help the latter arrange the Pistols' foray to Paris for the Club de Chalet du Lac shows in early September 1976. He'd been commissioned by the French magazine, *Actuel*, to snap some shots of Lydon in the wake of his return from America. "I called John because I had the number [and] he said it would be alright if I could come over," Benain told the BBC World Service in January 2016. The interview had no sooner started when Sid and Nancy arrived at the door. Like the overwhelming majority of those that came into contact with Nancy, Benain found her "pretty annoying" and "very hysterical".

One of the photos Benain took that day was of Vicious holding a small pocket-knife to Nancy's throat. Benain, however, says he saw no malice behind the pose and put it down to Vicious simply playing up for the camera. The afternoon would descend into farce when Spungen blithely announced that Vicious had been the main draw in the Pistols by the time of the US tour and that he had to be the frontman in any new musical collaboration. When Lydon asked what his role might be in the venture, Spungen told him he could be the drummer. Lydon was even prepared to suffer a further insult when Nancy dismissed his songwriting as "shit", but when Vicious asked to borrow some money, Lydon's temper finally snapped and he sent the pair packing. His parting rebuke came with telling Vicious that he didn't want to see him again as long as he was with Nancy. When the pair turned up at Gunter Grove a few weeks later again requesting money they were refused admittance. Vicious didn't take kindly to this and, having vented his spleen from a nearby phone box, he returned to the house and started kicking at the front door.

What happened next varies depending on who was telling the tale. Vicious would claim to his being struck with an axe. For years afterwards Jah Wobble carried the can over the axe incident, but finally set the record straight in his 2013 autobiography, *Memoirs of a Geezer*. He says he couldn't have been the one wielding the axe as he'd been sleeping off another booze binge in one of the upstairs rooms while Vicious was making a nuisance of himself at the door. The actual culprit was Paul Young, another of Lydon's friends. Careful not to mention Young by name, Wobble proceeds to explain that Vicious' head injury was the result of his losing his balance whilst backing away from the advancing Young and catching his head on the door thresher. Whatever the cause of Vicious' injury, neither Lydon nor Wobble would see their one-time friend again.

Wobble was already set to feature in Lydon's as yet unnamed new band at the time of Vicious' visit to Gunter Grove. Aside from noodling on Vicious' bass whenever the opportunity arose at various Pistols shows, Wobble owned a bass of his own - a Music Man copy – because he was fascinated and captivated by the instrument's low frequencies. "Wobble was still one of my best mates and he'd often been picking up Sid's bass to have a go – probably more than Sid did," Lydon explained. "Wobble was very much still a novice, but that's not what matters: I wanted him in."

Jah Wobble's introduction to music came at an early age when his mum Kathleen would take him along to the weekend market outside Whitechapel train station and treating him to whichever single took his fancy. The first 45 he can remember returning home with was Jim Reeves's 'Welcome To My World', whilst another acquisition was 'Froggy Went a Courting'. His true musical edification came courtesy of his older sister's collection of *Tighten Up* reggae volumes on the Trojan label; his reggae instruction being further imbued courtesy of BBC London's Sunday lunchtime *Reggae Hour*, and later by Capital Radio's *Roots Rockers* show.

Wobble suffered from OCD (Obsessive Compulsive Disorder) from an early age, but back in the late Seventies, the condition wasn't recognised as a legitimate mental health issue. As with all OCD sufferers, he always followed the same repetitive rituals. One such ritual involved to-ing and fro-ing from his parents' home on the Clichy Estate in Whitechapel. He was now back living with his parents after months of squat-hopping. There was a small library situated within the middle of the housing estate adjacent to the Clichy, and when walking to Whitechapel Station he would always walk in a clockwise direction around the library. One particular day, however, whilst returning from the station he came around the library counterclockwise. There was neither rhyme nor reason for this diversion from the norm, but he'd no sooner walked through the front door when Lydon had called offering him the bass gig in his new musical venture. To this day, Wobble believes it was his circumnavigating the library counterclockwise that day that led to his ending up in PiL.

Wobble could hardly contain himself as he rushed round to Gunter Grove; his excitement going into overdrive on discovering Lydon had brought Keith Levene in on guitar. "John was [always] looking ahead to quite different ideas from the other guys in the Pistols,' Keith told *www.punk77.co.uk*. 'So right off, me and John understood each other. There was a hatred, a cynicism, a kind of darkness, a nihilistic energy, but also a lot of mad humour. We both wanted to see the death of rock 'n' roll and to kick the ghost of rock in the arse once and for all; give the ghost a shove as he fell into the grave."

Bernard Rhodes remembers lending a sympathetic ear to Keith's plight: "Keith wasn't musically satisfied as a member of the Clash; one particular day he wanted to talk to me privately about something really bugging him. So, we walked from my studio along Chalk Farm Road towards Marine Ices talking all the way, acknowledging the music equipment store across the road Keith stressed that his unhappiness was caused by musical restrictions imposed while working with Mick Jones.

"Marine Ices was the café where I'd take breaks away from Rehearsals. It was close to the Roundhouse. Unlike every other café in Camden, Main Ices served proper cappuccino. Whilst there

I'd plot my campaigns to outmanoeuvre our musical competition. Keith wanted to be more free and experimental adopting new technology. He was especially keen to introduce the latest form of keyboards/sequencers/drum machines etc. into the Clash's sound, but Mick and Joe wouldn't have any of it. Keith obviously had a residue commitment to prog-rock due to his past musical experiences roadying for Yes.

"I now knew Lydon and Keith had something in common. They both wanted to leave their respective groups because they felt restricted musically. Although Keith liked the guys in the Clash, Lydon thought he was with a bunch of thickos - his words - in the Pistols. He particularly didn't respect Steve Jones. So over coffee, I suggested Keith go and see Lydon to form a totally fresh group. I explained to him that now was the time to catch the concept hot. Otherwise, the opportunity would be gone. The group became known as PiL and the rest is history."

Speaking on the PiL website, *www.fodderstompf.com*, in 2003 Levene reveals how he'd called Lydon after happening upon the latter's friend Paul Young outside Great Portland Street tube station: "He gave me John's phone number . . . I went round to John's one night and that was it."

When reflecting on the early days of PiL in *Anger is an Energy*, Lydon says how Levene's playing had astounded him. 'The idea was back then that after Jimi Hendrix no one could ever play the guitar again but to my mind Mr Levene's playing absolutely proved that to be not true. I thought it was very creative and very different, kind of discordant but at the same time always resolved itself musically. I found that intensely riveting and very, very inspiring. There was room for expansion in an incredible way."

Levene's guitar style may well have proved inspiring to Lydon, but he was unsure of his talent as he suggested bringing in a friend called Mikki Toldi on second guitar. After several rehearsals, however, Levene felt confident enough to tell Toldi he was surplus to requirements. All that was needed now was to find a drummer.

The fledgling PiL were now rehearsing at Rollerball Rehearsals in Tooley Street, within the shadow of Tower Bridge. Tooley Street would be given a new lease of life in the late-Eighties as part of the then Conservative government's "Thames Corridor" urban regeneration scheme. At the time, however, it was home to a hotchpotch of low-rent pubs, rehearsal spaces and greasy spoon cafés whose exteriors still bore the scorched brickwork from the fire of over a century earlier.

Aside from picking up the tab for the rehearsal space (on the understanding these costs would be recouped from the band's advance), Virgin was also providing the road crew. Wobble believes the crew were merely posing as roadies as a means of making connections within the music business to further less legitimate activities as they didn't appear to have the first clue as to looking after a band. Wobble seems to have suffered most from the crew's ineptitude. He received a jolting electric shock from his bass during an early rehearsal. Upon inspection, the 13-amp fuse in the plug of his amplifier had been replaced with rolled-up silver foil

Wobble says he, Lydon and Levene were positively brimming with ideas for new songs, which only increased their urgency in finding a drummer. Their exigence was such that Virgin placed the following ad in the May 6 issue of *Melody Maker*: "Drummer wanted to play on/off beats for modern band with fashionable outlook and rather well-known singer."

"[We] went through weeks and weeks of rehearsing with everybody who bothered to reply to my ad in the music press,' Lydon would later reveal. "It said something like, 'Lonely musician seeks comfort in fellow trendies.' I didn't use my own name because then people who didn't know how to play would have turned up and that would have set me back another two years. But the people who did turn up were terrible. Denim clad heavy metal fans.'

Wobble says that although a handful of those that responded to the ad showed varying degrees of promise, they were fearing their search would drag on interminably until the 22-year-old Canadian-born Jim Walker arrived at Tooley Street in response to the ad. "He was just right for where we were at," says Wobble. "He was undeniably a rock drummer, but he had a slightly funky, almost African tinge to his playing."

Lydon was in complete agreement: "Jim was the only person I liked from the auditions He sounds like Can's drummer (Ginger Baker); all double beats."

Walker, or "Doughnut" as he was soon-to-be-rechristened owing to his middle name Donat, arrived in London in October 1977. Before the year was out, he would meet his future wife, Caroline, audition for The Damned following Rat Scabies' departure. He'd also caught the Pistols' show at Brunel University the previous December of course. In January 1981 Walker would mischievously inform the author backstage at the Marquee that he'd never heard of either the Sex Pistols or Johnny Rotten before his joining PiL. He'd become aware of the Pistols as early as January 1977 after catching an article about them in *Rolling Stone* whilst living in Vancouver. "There was this picture of Rotten, this nasty little face and I just thought, 'This is fantastic! I've gotta be with that guy! He looked like the kinda guy that I could relate to because I didn't relate to people. As a kid I was nuts, I mean really nuts, so I thought, 'Punk's kinda interesting'."

Not long after seeing the *Rolling Stone* article Walker relocated to Boston and enrolled at Berklee College of Music. Though his drumming style leaned towards jazz rather than rock, his interest in punk led to his being invited to join The Furies, one of the first American punk groups. "We were a good little band. We'd definitely have been signed if we'd have come over to the UK. We were kinda like a combination of the Heartbreakers and a very New Yorky sorta influenced sound 'cos our guitar player/songwriter was into the Stooges and the New York Dolls."

Whether The Furies would or wouldn't have got signed had they relocated to the UK became a moot point some six months later when they split and went their separate ways. Having spent several weeks drowning his sorrows in alcohol, Walker sobered up long enough to mull over his immediate future. With punk at the forefront of his planning, his options were limited to Los Angeles, New York, or London. Deciding a visit to LA could be put back for a later date, it was either New York or London, and assuming New York would be every bit as crime-ridden and cockroach-infested as Boston, he headed for the airport with £675, a drum kit and a return ticket. Having passed up on The Damned, Walker decided to wait until the coming year before perusing the *Melody Maker* classifieds.

Walker says that on espying Virgin's *Melody Maker* ad he'd known instantly the "well-known singer" mentioned cryptically within the text referred to John and had a mate into making the call. He'd already thrown his hat into the ring a couple of months earlier by firing off a letter to Lydon via Virgin. "I'm Canadian and a bit of a hunter," he explained, "and once I really want something I stalk it. When the Pistols broke up I thought, 'Rotten's got to be in another band soon and I'm gonna be in that band as well. So I wrote a letter to him and then posted it to Virgin." The letter did reach its intended target but Lydon had tossed it in the bin.

Walker says he arrived at Tooley Street "ready for anything" and was slightly taken aback to find none of his potential new bandmates there to welcome him. "It was just me and this other guy who looked just like an accountant or bank clerk. (Walker's rival for the PiL drum stool that day was Mark Sanders who many years later would collaborate with Jah Wobble.)

"Eventually John, Keith, and Wobble came through the door. I had to sit there like a coiled spring while the other guy was auditioning. I remember nabbing a fag from Rotten just to have something to do with my hands. We played along to 'Belsen Was a Gas' and 'EMI', I think. They didn't have any finished songs – and even if they had it would have taken me time to familiarise myself with the pattern. It went well. I was pretty explosive. I hit the drums so hard I was literally breaking them and they loved that. We played for about ten minutes and they were like, 'We want you!' Levene was shouting, 'He's the one! He's the one!'"

Speaking to *Melody Maker*'s Caroline Coon in July about how the new songs were shaping up, Lydon enthused: 'The way we write songs is so easy. Someone will bash something out and everybody will fall in and I'll babble something over it. Which is great because let's face it, there's so much to yell about - more than ever! My number one target has always been hypocrisy... I'm now writing the best words I ever have. I know now how to put things more clearly, how to attack where it hurts most."

Lydon also informed Coon that if all went according to plan the band would be in a position to start gigging in around six weeks. On the evidence of what she heard at Tooley Street that day, Coon thought six months a more realistic timeframe. Of the half dozen new songs she heard, she felts two or three could be shaped up in a recording studio right away. She also listed the band names the quartet had been toying with since Walker's inclusion – "The Carnivorous Buttuckflies", "The Future Features", "The Corny Various", "The Windsor Uplift" and "The Royal Family". In truth, Lydon had already decided on the name and their debut single, "Public Image" – which Coon cited as being a "biting punk rocker in true Sex Pistols tradition" - would serve as the perfect calling card.

"'Public Image' was very fresh sounding and energetic," says Wobble. "It had been the first song that we had worked on in [Rollerball] rehearsals. Keith spent a few days working out the guitar part; the resultant harmonically rich sound complemented my deep bass groove perfectly. Jim just needed to add a classic rock backbeat, John added his vocals and we all instantaneously knew that we had a winner."

The simple yet highly infectious rumbling bass line on the open "E" string was the first Wobble had presented to Lydon and Levene. "I liked playing in 'E' simply because it was the lowest note on the bass," he continued. "Sonically my bass amp is very simple."

'Public Image' was recorded at Advision Studios in Fitzrovia, Central London. Advision was the first studio to employ 8, 16, and 24-track recorders as well as the UK's first computer-aided mixing desk. As such, it was used to dealing with professional acts, yet whilst Lydon was familiar with studio protocol; it was unfamiliar territory for Levene, Wobble and Walker. John Leckie, the producer/engineer that would be overseeing the session, had recently left Abbey Road Studios to strike out on his own and had spent the past two weeks working on ex-Dr. Feelgood guitarist Wilco Johnson's Solid Senders album at Virgin's studio, The Manor, in Oxfordshire.

The Advision session wasn't without incident. Having spent several hours perfecting Walker's drum sound, Leckie and his assistant, Ken Thomas, popped out for a short break Upon their return, however, they discovered Wobble had been messing around with the mixing desk. What's more, he'd poured beer into the mixer. The boisterous bassist would also steal Leckie's wallet and refused to hand it back until the following day. Leckie was equally frustrated with Levene's antics in the studio. "[Keith] was mad and insisted on having his guitar amp in the control room at full volume!" Leckie subsequently told *The Independent*. "Levene took the multi-track tape home that night and came in the next day having forgotten it and accused me of stealing it!

"The track was pretty much a live take with Levene's guitar double-tracked and John did his vocal through a Space Echo dub style. I did a rough mix and went home. The next day the band never showed up and my rough mix was the record. I got no credit, but Richard Branson did give me £250! It wasn't stressful just a lot of fun!"

Public Image represented a fresh start for Lydon with his own band

'Public Image' was completed at Wessex Studios where *Never Mind the Bollocks* was recorded. The session saw Lydon reacquainted with Wessex's resident engineer, Bill Price, who'd assisted Chris Thomas on all the *Bollocks* sessions. The recording process was a whole new frontier to the wide-eyed Walker. "PiL were supposed to be recording everything with Bill Price," he says. "Had we done so then the album would have been as well made as the A-side to 'Public Image' but unfortunately for us Wobble beat the shit out of the assistant engineer (Jerry Green) while we were in a nearby pub."

Wobble has since tried dismissing the fight as being a "couple of band-aids job" but Walker says he gave Green a bit of a hiding. Wobble and Green came to blows over the cassette copies of the day's session. Wobble was anxious to get back to Stepney and asked Green if they might collect the tapes from the studio so that he could be on his way. There had been some friction between the two during the mixing and when Green made some disparaging remark Wobble let rip. "It was all very ugly and unpleasant," says Walker. "The guy was covered in blood but he gave as good as he got. The pub landlord called the police so Wobble jumped into Dennis Morris' car. Once he'd cleaned himself up a bit Wobble came back to the pub and we headed back to Wessex to grab the master tapes. We ended up grabbing the wrong masters though we didn't realise it until we got back to Gunter Grove. Dr. Feelgood were working on their new album (*Private Practice*). They called us up the next morning saying, 'You've got our tapes; we'll send a cab round.'"

Ironically, 'Public Image' b/w 'The Cowboy Song' was released on October 13, 1978; the very day that the news broke of Nancy Spungen's murder at the Hotel Chelsea and Sid Vicious' arrest. The single would deservedly crack the UK Top 10. Lydon had penned the lyrics as a means of airing his ongoing grievances at the exploitation he suffered at the hands of McLaren and the UK media. "' Public Image', despite what most of the press seemed to misinterpret it to be, is not about the fans at all," he said in a *Melody Maker* interview soon after the single's release. "It's a slagging of the group I used to be in. It's what I went through from my own group. They never bothered to listen to what I was fucking singing; they don't even know the words to my songs. They never bothered to listen, it was like, 'Here's a tune, write some words to it.' So I did. They never questioned it. I found that offensive, it meant I was literally wasting my time, 'cause if you ain't working with people that are on the same level then you ain't doing anything. The rest of the band and Malcolm never bothered to find out if I could sing, they just took me as an image. It was as basic as that; they really were as dull as that. After a year of it they were going, 'Why don't you have your hair this colour this year?' And I was going, 'Oh God, a brick wall, I'm fighting a brick wall!' They don't understand even now."

While the UK music press was waxing lyrical about Public image

Limited in the wake of the release of 'Public Image', The Clash were in New York with Sandy Pearlman adding the final touches to the new album at the Record Plant. (The album's working title was *All The Peacemakers*.) These last-minute tinkerings could have been administered at Basing Street Studios where the twelve tracks slated for the album had been recorded, but of course, the Portobello Road skyline comes in a very poor second compared to that of Manhattan. Jones and Strummer had been in America since the beginning of August; their having flown out to San Francisco to lay down vocal and guitar overdubs at the Automatt. Pearlman would subsequently boast of there being "more guitars per square inch on this record than in anything else in the rest of Western civilisation," and CBS were said to be unhappy with the results at the Automatt. There was little need of Simonon or Headon's presence at the Record Plant but Jones and Strummer had supposedly thrown their guitars out of the pram and insisted the whole band be in attendance for the final mixing.

It was during The Clash's time at the Record Plant that Jones joined Vicious' ad hoc backing group, The Idols (featuring ex-Dolls Jerry Nolan and Arthur Kane, and Steve Dior whom Jones knew from his Warrington Crescent days) during the ex-Pistol's Max's Kansas City September residency. Though no doubt pleased to see his old friend again, Jones had little interest in accepting Nancy's invitation to get up onstage. Indeed, it was only Strummer's cajoling that saw him relent. "We just about managed five songs," Jones subsequently reflected. "Five songs for five bucks. It was a nightmare between shows, it was full-on. (Vicious was required to play two shows per night during the residency)as full-on. Sid was sort of semi there. It was a serious drug thing. Me and Joe kept looking at each other 'cos we couldn't believe it. The people there were as far out of it as you can be without actually being dead."

The Max's residency dates were reasonably well attended but in all likelihood, the attendees were there to see if this would be the night the Sid Vicious train wreck finally came off the rails. Vicious completed the final Max's residency date on September 30. With no other shows lined-up until a brace of dates at a club in Nancy's home town Philadelphia a couple of weeks hence, Vicious and Spungen withdrew from public view; spending their days holed up at the Hotel Chelsea blotting out their miserable existence with a cornucopia of drugs procured with the money they'd received for the Max's shows.

Vicious' celebrity status was such amongst New York's underbelly that each night brought a steady stream of visitors to Room 100.

Once the heroin they'd smuggled into New York hidden inside a Fairy Liquid container had run out, the couple had resorted to standing in line at the Spring Street Clinic to get their daily Methadone fix. The synthetic opioid was no longer their only drug de jour, as they were soon also hooked on barbiturates such as Tuinol and Dilaudid. Vicious was recognisable to the other Spring Street junkies and therefore an easy target. After one beating too many, he began carrying a Jaguar K-11 knife for protection. During the first week of October, their survival fund received a sizable boost following a $20,000 royalty payment transfer from Virgin for "My Way". As neither of them had a US bank account, Vicious and Spungen stashed the cash in the bottom drawer of a bedside cabinet. Having $20,000 – some $100,000 in today's money – at their ready disposal meant Nancy was on the phone to every drug dealer on the Lower East Side. Vicious awoke on the morning of October 12 to find a trail of blood leading through into the tiny en-suite bathroom where Spungen – dressed in just black knickers and bra – lay slumped on the floor between the toilet and washbasin; a single stab wound to her abdomen.

No one has ever been brought to book for Spungen's murder. It's now forty years and counting and the events of 11/12 October 1978 are still shrouded in myth, mistruths and mystery. With Vicious supposedly confessing to his having done the deed to the first officers on the scene at the Chelsea, the NYPD pretty much viewed it as an open-and-shut case – this despite whatever remained of the $20,000 being missing and several of those who'd visited Room 100 that fateful night all saying Vicious had been so out of it on Tuinol that he hadn't moved off his bed the whole time they were there. There were also eye-witness reports of Spungen being seen arguing with a guy rumoured to be a leading drug dealer around the estimated time of death with Vicious still lying comatose on the bed.

Spungen's autopsy was conducted by New York's Associate Medical Examiner, Dr Geeta Natarajan. She confirmed Spungen had died from external and internal haemorrhaging as a result of the single stab wound. The wound itself, however, wasn't immediately fatal and Spungen could easily have been saved had she or a third person raised the alarm. The likelihood of Vicious

Sid with his ad hoc backing band The Idols (ex-New York Dolls) Jerry Nolan and
Arthur Kane, and Steve Dior whom he knew from his Warrington Crescent days

managing to rouse himself from his stupor and getting into an
argument with Spungen and stabbing her is remote in the extreme.
But even if that scenario came to pass, why would Spungen then
drag herself into the en-suite bathroom instead of crawling out into
the hallway and summoning help? However, if the drug dealer or
another third party had stabbed Spungen – either intentionally or
in the heat-of-the-moment - they would have prevented her from
making for the door and raising the alarm. Safe in the knowledge
that Vicious was unlikely to stir, they could have stood guard in the
bathroom doorway till Spungen lost consciousness before taking
their leave with the cash.

According to the medical report, the stab wound would have taken
some two hours to bleed out, and yet Spungen made no tangible
attempt to raise the alarm. Vera Mendelssohn, the 48-year-old
sculptor living in the room adjacent to that of Vicious and Spungen,
told police that she'd been wakened around 7.30 a.m. by strange
whimpering sounds emanating through the wall but that she'd been

too afraid to investigate. Were the strange whimpering noises heard by Mendelssohn Spungen's final death throes?

By the time The Clash's second album, *Give 'Em Enough Rope* as it was now called, was released on November 10, 1978, they and Bernard Rhodes had parted company. Jones and Strummer were still in San Francisco when Rhodes attempted to reclaim the "complete control" he's said to have demanded from the band some two years earlier by informing the music press that The Clash were to play a show at the Harlesden New Roxy on September 9 without first consulting them. The Clash had last played London at the end of July and the 1600 tickets had sold out within days of going on sale. The Clash found themselves wedged on the horns of a dilemma, not of their making. They were loath to disappoint their fans yet were keen to get the album finished. Jones viewed Rhodes's act as nothing short of an ultimatum and treated it as such. Strummer wasn't yet ready to contemplate a parting of the ways with Rhodes, yet readily sided with Jones in their staying put in San Francisco. Their refusal to come home like dutiful lapdogs would force Rhodes into postponing the Roxy date.

Instead of flying out and confronting his rebellious charges, however, Rhodes issued a statement to the music press whereby he claimed The Clash were postponing the Roxy date to Saturday, September 23, as a protest against the minimal airplay their records were being afforded. This was to shatter the last vestiges of faith Strummer and Simonon had in their manager. Indeed, the normally taciturn Simonon would contact the *NME* and openly challenge Rhodes's authority.

Simonon and Headon had ostensibly flown out to New York to hear the latest mixes of *Give 'Em Enough Rope*, but a discussion as to what they should do about their manager's high-handed actions was now high on the agenda. Rhodes flew out to New York towards the end of September for showdown talks with the band. Said talks would end in stalemate, but with the new album in the can and the European leg of the Sort It Out Tour set to commence at Belfast's Queen's Hall on October 13, The Clash returned to London. Their attempts to right Rhodes's wrongdoings in honouring the Roxy date before flying out to Belfast would be thwarted by the GLC's restricting the club's admittance to just 900 – this despite the Roxy's management having removed some 500 seats to create a dance area. By the time news of the cancellation went out on local radio, however, hundreds of fans were either outside the venue or en route.

The Clash could have simply beat a hasty retreat and left the Roxy's management to take the flak. Instead, the band dutifully hung around to explain the situation and hand out promotional "Tommy Gun" T-shirts as a conciliatory gesture. (They would also schedule two Roxy dates to accommodate all those with tickets over October 25/26.)

Rhodes could hardly be held to account over the GLC's restriction policy, but he was fundamentally to blame for the whole fiasco.

Ari Up of The Slits in 1977. Photo Ray Stevenson

Upon their return to London after the last of the European dates at the El Paradiso in Amsterdam on October 23, the band issued Rhodes with a solicitor's letter informing him his managerial contract would be rendered null and void as of December 1, 1978. Having vented his spleen in the *Melody Maker*, Rhodes had his solicitors obtain a court order whereby all Clash earnings were to be paid directly into his account.

The Clash approached the *NME*'s Clash-friendly journalist Barry Miles to sound him out about sharing managerial duties with CBS' Head of Publicity, Elle Smith. Miles would subsequently say how the figures The Clash provided for analysis proved beyond doubt that Rhodes had "ripped them off something rotten". He and Smith would ultimately pass on the offer, but only because they feared their time would have been taken up with trying to recoup the missing money. Jones was initially sceptical when the band then turned to Caroline Coon as he was anxious about letting one of their girlfriends oversee their affairs.

Give 'Em Enough Rope received less-than-complimentary reviews yet surpassed both the group and record company's expectations by reaching #2 on the UK chart. Indeed, the album may well have claimed the top spot had Britain not been in the grip of *Grease*-mania.

— Facing The Final Curtain

"There were aspects of stardom I didn't like, which were of no consequence, really, but the positive things far outweighed the negative. By the time I came to write Setting Sons, *I felt my writing was more like prose set to music."*

Paul Weller

Groundhog Day is a popular tradition celebrated throughout the US and Canada each year on February 2. Said tradition derives from the Pennsylvania Dutch superstition that should a groundhog (a.k.a. the woodchuck) emerge from its burrow on this day and see its shadow it will retreat to its den and winter will persist for six more weeks. However, if the groundhog doesn't see its shadow because of cloudiness, spring will supposedly arrive early. For Sid Vicious, alas, February 2 would be forever winter.

The previous day Vicious' lawyer, James Merberg, succeeded in presenting the presiding Judge Betty Ellerin with sufficient evidence hinting at several major inconsistencies in the prosecution's case. Vicious had spent the whole of the holiday period holed up at Rikers Island, New York City's main jail complex situated in the East River between Queens and the Bronx, following his assault on Patti Smith's brother Todd in the trendy Manhattan discothèque Hurrahs on West 62nd Street. Smith had taken offence to Vicious chatting up his girlfriend and

Opposite:Front cover image from the sleeve of The Jam's *Setting Sons* album

received a beer glass in the face for his troubles. "We got him out of there and into a taxi pretty quickly," says Peter Gravelle (a.k.a Pete Kodick), the freelance photographer who would procure Vicious' fatal stash. "But it was a pointless exercise as there were a dozen witnesses who'd all seen Sid do it. The police arrested him the next morning."

Merberg's diligence in court was to prove to be Vicious' downfall, however. The consensus was that he would be held over at Rikers until Monday, February 5. McLaren was flying out to New York on the Sunday with Steve Jones and Paul Cook. The idea being that Jones and Cook would then assist Vicious record an album of rock 'n' roll standards to raise funds for his defence at the coming trial. (Given that Vicious' posthumous releases, "Somethin' Else" and "C'Mon Everybody" – both of which were recorded in Paris during the "My Sessions" the previous June – would each reach #3 on the UK chart and outsell "God Save the Queen" in doing so suggests the mooted album would have achieved similar success.)

Swayed by Merberg's arguments, Judge Ellerin released Vicious into his mother's care.

Anne was at the courthouse with Vicious' new girlfriend, Michelle Robison (not "Robinson" as is so often stated), an aspiring actress and low-maintenance groupie with whom he was now living despite it contravening his strict bail conditions. Peter Gravelle was also outside the courthouse. "Sid emerged dressed in just his jeans and a grubby T-shirt. It's fucking freezing in February in New York and the hotel where his mother was staying was a good ten blocks away. Yet all Sid was interested in was whether Anne had got anything for him. She had, of course, but the stuff she'd got for him was total crap and he asked me to go out and get him something a little bit stronger." Gravelle said he'd see what he could do and went on his way. When he arrived at Robinson's brownstone apartment at 63 Bank Street in Greenwich Village at around 8 p.m. Vicious was climbing the walls – despite his latest Rikers Island detoxification. Also present at the "party" that fateful Thursday evening was photographer Eileen Polk, Jerry Nolan and his girlfriend Esther (Steve Dior's sister), and musicians Howie Pyro and Jerry Only. Having introduced Gravelle to all as "the guy who'll be doing my solo album cover", Vicious whisked the photographer away to the bedroom at the end of the lobby. Polk took this as her cue to leave, but as she, Pyro and Only

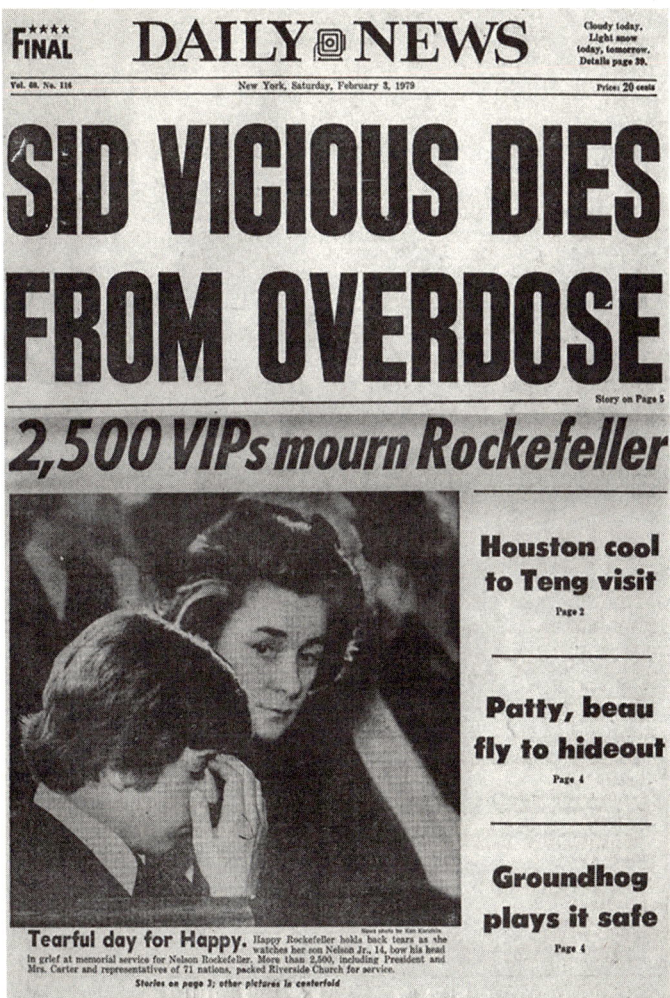

★★★★ FINAL   **DAILY ◉ NEWS**   Cloudy today, Light snow today, tomorrow. Details page 39.

Vol. 60. No. 116   New York, Saturday, February 3, 1979   Price: 20 cents

SID VICIOUS DIES
FROM OVERDOSE

Story on Page 5

2,500 VIPs mourn Rockefeller

Houston cool to Teng visit
Page 2

Patty, beau fly to hideout
Page 4

Groundhog plays it safe
Page 4

Tearful day for Happy. Happy Rockefeller holds back tears as she watches her son Nelson Jr., 14, bow his head in grief at memorial service for Nelson Rockefeller. More than 2,500, including President and Mrs. Carter and representatives of 71 nations, packed Riverside Church for service.

Stories on page 3; other pictures in centerfold

were heading for the door they heard strange noises emanating from the bedroom. Upon bursting into the bedroom they found Vicious lying prostrate on the bed.

Unbeknown to Gravelle, the heroin he'd procured was almost 100 per cent pure. Although Vicious only cooked up a small dose, his freshly detoxed body couldn't cope with the hit and he OD'd. "He was as sick as a dog," says Gravelle. "We managed to revive him by plying him with cups of tea and cigarettes and frog-marching him around the room. I stayed until around 2 a.m., and he certainly didn't do any more drugs whilst I was there because I'd given the rest to his mum."

As with Spungen's murder, it's unlikely the truth will ever emerge as to what occurred that night. The version of events that Anne Beverley subsequently gave to the NYPD has Vicious waking up at some point during the early hours of Friday morning and coming out of the bedroom in search of the remainder of the heroin. Anne, who was sleeping on the sofa in the living area, says Vicious must have found the heroin she was keeping on her person before then returning to the bedroom where he shot up the fatal dose. It's been said elsewhere that Anne wilfully gave Vicious the heroin as she feared he wouldn't beat the second-degree murder rap and most likely spend the next 20 years behind bars. Anne never actually admitted to giving Vicious the heroin but evidence of her complicity in his death was provided by New York's Chief Medical Examiner, Dr Michael Baden. Upon examining the body at the scene, Baden quickly ascertained the fatal dose had to have been administered more recently than either Anne or Michelle Robison had stated to Sergeant Richard Houseman, the first police officer at the scene.

Robison was still hysterical and sobbing uncontrollably when Baden arrived through the door, but this is understandable seeing as she'd woken to find Vicious dead in bed beside her. Conversely, Anne was strangely calm. Indeed, it was only when Baden threw doubt on their version of events that Anne's veneer cracked. According to Houseman, Anne instantly became aggressive, launching into what seemed to him to be a well-rehearsed mantra about her being the sole executive to the Sid Vicious estate. Instead of questioning Anne or Robison further, the police chose to list Vicious' death as suicide - which also rather conveniently closed the book on Spungen's murder. To this day, the general public's perception of the whole tragic saga is that Vicious killed Spungen and then killed himself because he couldn't live with the guilt. It's a neat scenario – and certainly, one that suited the NYPD. Yet no one deserves to go to their grave accused of a murder they didn't commit . . . not even a strung-out ex-Sex Pistol.

The author has read through an illicit copy of the NYPD's report into Spungen's murder, ironically enough whilst engaging on a visit to Nancy's grave at King David Cemetery in Philadelphia during the filming of Who Killed Nancy in June 2007. Though lengthy, the report is woefully inept. Despite their having lived out of Room 100 for several weeks, the report claims the investigating officers found just three fingerprints in the entire apartment. The names of potential suspects that the likes of Steve Dior and Peter Gravelle had put forward whilst being interviewed had been blacked out. Had Vicious lived to stand trial there is every likelihood that he would have been acquitted for lack of solid evidence.

Jonh Ingham, like many others that knew Vicious before his hooking up with Spungen, says he wasn't surprised when the news came through from New York. "No, I wasn't surprised when I saw on the news that he was dead. On one hand, it wasn't unexpected but it's always both a shock and a sadness to know that someone has died at such a young age.

"If anything, my overriding feeling was one of sorrow. Firstly, because Sid was in such a bad place when he died - dependent on drugs and still feeling the need to live up to being 'Sid Vicious'. Secondly, I felt sorry for him because he was way out of his depth in a place like Rikers Island. It reminded me of Sid's time at Ashford, which was just a Remand Centre, and the wake-up call that had been for him."

Vicious was still kicking his heels in one of the holding cells at Third Homicide Division's headquarters on East 51st Street when Polydor released 'Down in the Tube Station at Midnight' as the second single from The Jam's third album, *All Mod Cons*. The song narrates the tale of an unnamed third-party who is accosted by right-wing thugs whilst awaiting the tube train that would take him home to his unsuspecting wife. 'Down in the Tube Station at Midnight' was the biggest hint to date of Paul Weller's potential song-crafting prowess yet stumbled to a halt at #15 on the UK chart.

While promoting their second album, *This Is the Modern World*, The Jam had accompanied Blue Öyster Cult on one of the latter band's US tours. America had taken both The Who and The Kinks to their hearts during the sixties 'British Invasion', and yet The Jam weren't well-received on the BÖC tour. As a result, *This Is the Modern World* failed to even break into the *Billboard* 200. The trio returned to the UK knowing their future as a Polydor act hung in the balance.

The next album would have to be a hit, regardless. When the time came to return to the studio, however, Weller was suffering a severe case of writer's block. Indeed, such was his malaise that he readily admits to his having had zero interest during the writing/ recording process for what was to become *All Mod Cons*. So much so, The Jam would have to completely re-record a new set of songs for the album after Chris Parry rejected the first batch as being sub-standard.

"When I first heard the tune [to 'Tube Station'] I knew it was a good 'un but must admit to having reservations," says Dennis Munday, was working for Polydor at the time. "No matter how much I liked it, it wasn't commercial enough to give Polydor what it wanted – a Top Ten hit. The complicated wordy and kaleidoscopic violent storyline was too heavy for daytime radio. Although a top twenty single, the company wrote the song off as just another Jam single.

"It was suggested at the time that The Jam were coming back with this single, although I'm not sure from where, as every single and album had charted [in the UK], and the band were highly thought of outside of Polydor's boardroom."

Weller would take such criticisms to heart and use them to The Jam's advantage as *All Mod Cons* has been rightly acknowledged as one of the truly essential albums of the mid-to-late Seventies. Of more immediate import, it gave Polydor the Jam hit they were seeking in reaching #6 on the UK chart. "I'd found my feet," Weller reflected in a 1998 *Uncut* interview marking the album's twentieth anniversary. "After This Is the Modern World, I thought, 'Am I going to let this slide or fight against it?' My back was against the wall. It was a matter of self-pride."

In his 2006 book, *Shout to the Top*, Dennis Munday makes no mention of Chris Parry having rejected the original recordings out of hand. "The band had demoed many of the songs before going into Eden and RAK studios in July and August to record the album masters. 'David Watts', 'It's Too Bad', 'To Be Someone', 'Mr. Clean' and 'Fly' were all demoed on June 29 in Polydor's studio, and all the arrangements are close to the final recordings."

None album singles, 'Strange Town' and 'When You're Young', would give The Jam two further UK Top 20 hits following their respective releases in March and August 1979. In the October of that year, The Jam would score a Top Three hit with 'Eton Rifles',

With *Give 'Em Enough Rope* being tailored to the US market it was natural
The Clash would turn their touring attentions to conquering America

while the parent album *Setting Suns* peaking at #4 on the UK chart
would cement The Jam's standing as a mainstream act.

The Clash were in Seattle at the start of their debut US tour when
Johnny Green dropped the bombshell of Sid Vicious' untimely
demise; the news of their friend's senseless death proving an
unwelcome start to the day for Joe, Mick and Paul. With *Give
'Em Enough Rope* having been tailor-made to appeal to the US
mainstream market it was perhaps only natural The Clash began
focusing their energies on conquering America. Though still railing
against the USA in song, away from the mic Strummer and Co. were
hopelessly enamoured with America. CBS, however, were rather less
enamoured with the idea of bringing The Clash over to America as
Give 'Em Enough Rope was still treading water in the lower reaches
of the US chart. From a financial viewpoint bringing The Clash over

to promote an album that had as yet failed to crack the *Billboard* 100 could be construed as throwing good money after bad, but the US import sales of *The Clash* was evidence enough that there was a market for the band. CBS's reticence was such that the tour only went ahead because of Caroline Coon dipping into her own pocket. "The Clash were close to breaking up because of the problems with Bernard Rhodes and we faced all sorts of other difficulties," she told *Q* magazine for its May 2001 retrospective of the tour. "Our record company refused to finance an American tour. Luckily, our American label, Epic, although a little afraid of the politics, knew this band could be huge so I spent £3000 of my own money flying to New York where I arranged for Epic to give us $30,000 to fund the tour."

Coon had pulled off an impressive coup in getting CBS to capitulate, yet The Clash upped the antipathy by insisting on calling their inaugural US outing the "Pearl Harbor '79 Tour". Needless to say, the inflammatory title brought about further unrest at Soho Square. Believing The Clash would see the error of their ways, CBS instructed Epic's marketing team got on with promoting the trip as the Give 'Em Enough Rope Tour. Epic hadn't counted on the band's obduracy, however. Even as the tour logistics were being mapped out in New York, back in London the Camden-based Fifth Column T-shirt company – owned by Clash fan, Chris Townsend – was busy running up a batch of T-shirts featuring a kamikaze pilot and rising sun on the front and a foundering American battleship adorning the back.

Before embarking for the US, The Clash went into Wessex Studios to record a souped-up version of Sonny Curtis's 'I Fought the Law', and two new songs 'Gates of the West' and 'Groovy Times'. These tracks would subsequently be released as *The Cost of Living* EP alongside an extended version of 'Capital Radio'.

Kicking off with a "warm-up" show at Vancouver's Commodore Ballroom on January 31, The Clash crossed the border into the US for shows in San Francisco and Santa Monica before wending their way over to the eastern seaboard. There were plenty of raised eyebrows when the band's US promotor, Wayne Forte, suggested booking The Clash at the 3,800-capacity Palladium, but he'd already done his homework. Speaking with Bob Plotnick, owner of Bleecker Bob's in Greenwich Village, Forte discovered the store had shifted over 1,000 import copies of *The Clash*. He, therefore, estimated that while 1,000 domestic album sales would equate to a concert-going audience of around 300, 1,000 import sales meant one thousand devoted Clash fans living within the tri-state area; fans who wouldn't simply buy a ticket to see The Clash but could also be relied upon to bring a friend.

The Big Apple was abuzz about The Clash by the time the band arrived in town and the lucky 3,800 ticket-holders crammed into the former cinema on West 14th Street were in for a night they would never forget. Indeed, *Rolling Stone*'s Tom Carson would laud The Clash for "unleash[ing] one of the most staggering performances I've ever seen. It was music of heroic grandeur, epic sweep and visceral force; each song was faster and meaner than on record and had twice the impact."

The Clash had no sooner returned from the US, CBS issued 'English Civil War'. Both the single and *The Cost of Living* EP gave The Clash two more Top 30 hits. Owing to the US tour's success Epic finally got around to releasing an amended version of *The Clash* in the US. The album replaced four tracks from the original version – 'Deny', 'Cheat', 'Protex Blue' and '48 Hours' - with five non-album singles and B-sides: 'Complete Control', "Clash City Rockers', '(White Man) In Hammersmith Palais', 'I Fought the Law' and 'Jail Guitar Doors'. 'The album also featured a re-recorded version of 'White Riot'. Initial copies came with a bonus seven-inch single featuring 'Groovy Times' and 'Gates of the West'.

Another band to take the Stiff Little Fingers approach to choosing a throwaway name when making their live debut in 1977 were the Blackburn-based Stiffs. The Stiffs were more punk-pop or glam-punk; their strong sense of melody more in keeping with Rich Kids, Buzzcocks and Generation X. Frontman, Phil Hendriks and guitarist Ian "Strang" Barnes started writing songs together whilst still at Queen Elizabeth Grammar School. Having recruited drummer Tommy O'Kane and Mark 'Ossie' Young on bass, the quartet honed their repertoire of originals and covers playing local church halls and youth clubs. Young would soon be replaced by 'Big' John McVittie.

The title of The Stiffs' February 1979 debut single, 'Brookside Riot Squad' (b/w 'Standard English' and 'DC-RIP') came courtesy of a graffitied bus shelter close to Hendriks' home. It's a fantastic song and showed a true hint of Hendriks and Barnes' song-crafting capabilities. The single was released via their own Dork Records label and sold reasonably well in Blackburn and neighbouring towns. However, it would be their follow-up single, 'Inside Out'(b/w 'Kids on the Street') that brought The Stiffs to prominence with John Peel brazenly declaring it "the greatest record in the history of the universe" whilst on air. He not only played 'Inside Out' incessantly on his show but even went so far as to interrupt fellow Radio One DJ Mike Read's show to insist that he play the record. Peel would also book The Stiffs for two radio sessions. Peel's fascination with The Stiffs is understandable as one never left one of their shows without singing the words to one song or another. (Indeed, the author still remembers handing a beaming Peel a Stiffs button badge at one of their Marquee shows in early-January 1981.)

During the summer of 1980, The Stiffs signed a long term deal with EMI's subsidiary label, Zonaphone. Their initial recordings for Zonaphone – 'Innocent Bystander', 'Volume Control' and 'Best Place In Town' – were produced by Dale 'Buffin' Griffin and Pete 'Overend' Watts, but somewhat surprisingly, the ex-Mott the Hoople duo's efforts weren't to EMI's liking. Despite re-mixes, the tracks were consigned to the vaults, which left The Stiffs with no follow-up to 'Inside Out'. Further frustration came with their hitherto loyal A&R rep, Chris Briggs, suddenly departing for Phonogram Records. Although the band were busy gigging up and down the country and recording new material, with Briggs gone no-one at EMI seemed to care one way or the other. EMI finally got around to booking The Stiffs into Rockfield studios in late-1980, and, happy with what they heard, released 'Volume Control' (b/w 'Nothing Left To Lose') as the band's debut single for Zonaphone.

'Volume Control' would be afforded significant daytime Radio One airplay, with DJ Paul Burnett going so far as to proclaim The Stiffs "The Slade for the Eighties". Gary Bushell was another champion, praising 'Volume Control' as "piledriving pop-punk of the first order". Despite such plaudits, the band's intended second single for Zonaphone, 'Innocent Bystander', was inexplicably cancelled. When EMI announced they were putting any plans to release a Stiffs album on hold indefinitely, the band's management demanded the band be released from their contract. It could be mere happenstance but when The Stiffs visited Manchester Square in early January 1981 to meet with their new A&R guy while they were in town playing the Marquee, the newly-signed Duran Duran were in an adjoining office. Taking Hendricks' leopard-skin trousers and eyeliner out of the equation, there was nothing to separate the two bands in terms of their punkish appearance. Whether EMI were already attuned to what was happening at the Blitz Club, but the Duranies had undergone a serious makeover by the time 'Planet Earth' was released the following month.

With Radio One DJs and music journos such as Gary Bushell and *Melody Maker*'s Carol Clerk championing them, it was only a matter of time before another label snapped them up. Sure enough, a deal was soon struck with Stiff Records. The Stiffs would be left dumbfounded, however, when their new label masters insisted they record their high-voltage version of the Glitter Band's 1975 hit, 'Goodbye My Love' – reportedly at just 12 hours' notice – instead of an original number.

Following its February 1981 release, 'Goodbye My Love' (b/w 'Magic Roundabout') received regular airings on Radio One and spent several weeks in the National Airplay charts. Had it not been for distribution problems at Stiff, the single may well have reached the Top 40. For reasons best known to themselves, Stiff decided to send The Stiffs out on a national tour supporting the UK Subs. The tour undoubtedly raised the band's profile, but the headliners' hardcore following proved hostile towards them on more than one occasion as the author can testify. Stiff's decision not to pick up the option for a second Stiffs single left the "Slade for the Eighties" in limbo, a state from which they would never recover.

The tracks that had lain gathering dust in the EMI vaults would finally see the day on the 2001 album, *Innocent Bystanders*. When reviewing the album, *Kerrang!* lauded The Stiffs as being "one of the (punk) era's best-kept secrets that's only just been let out."

Despite their being regarded as something of a novelty act by the UK's mainstream music media, Adam and the Ants had nonetheless built up a dedicated following – "Ant people" as they'd taken to calling themselves. Adam's mantra around this time being: "You either love or hate the Ant sound. You love to hate the Ants. There can be no neutrality."

Having signed with Decca Records, Adam and the Ants had released their debut single, 'Young Parisians' in October 1978. The A-side's acoustic cabaret-style did little to enhance their standing in the music press, however. The Ants' tenure with Decca would prove short-lived – ostensibly because of the label's failure to market the band. The Ants would subsequently sign with the independent label, Do It Records, and release 'Xerox'. The single failed to trouble the charts, but rather than hit the panic button Do It allowed the Ants time to hone their distinctive sound. The label would ultimately be rewarded when the Ants' seminal debut album, *Dirk Wears White Socks*, hit #1 on the UK Independent Albums Chart.

While supporting The Clash on the Sort It Out Tour, Joe Strummer had opined how The Slits had the potential to be a great band if they could hone their rough-and-ready live sound. To the casual ear, this seemed a mighty big ask but Island's Chris Blackwell decided to take the plunge and signed The Slits to his label. "Nora phoned Island Records and set up a meeting with Chris," Viv Albertine reflected. "It [was] easy, just like we expected. We think we're good. Lots of record companies want us. Why wouldn't Island? At the meeting we tell Chris we love the label and that we want to be on it. He's amused and says yes.

"He loves reggae, which should bond him to us a bit more, but there's something old fashioned about him." At the time of the signing Blackwell was obsessing over sixties chanteuse, Marianne Faithful, who was midway through recording her Broken English album for the label. "We don't understand why he's so excited about her," Albertine continued. "We've seen her around over the past couple of years, hanging around squats, drugged up. She's the past, we're the future." The Slits' contract with Island was a one-off album deal for £45,000. The girls were insistent they be allowed full creative control. Blackwell surprisingly agrees to their non-negotiatory demand.

Island suggested Matumbi's Dennis Bovey as producer. It was to prove an inspired choice as Bovey is already something of a living legend within the reggae world. Albertine says she and the rest of the band liked Bovey from the off. In turn, Bovey revealed that he wouldn't have considered coming onto the project had he not liked the songs. With Bovey onboard, a two-week block session is booked at Ridge Farm Studios in Surrey.

By the time The Slits came to signing with Island, Palmolive was no longer in the band. "We held auditions and a load of boring rock drummers come through the door and bang away, smashing their cymbals all through the songs," says Albertine. "None of them have heard of reggae. They don't like soul. Hopeless." Help was at hand, however. While out on the road The Slits have accrued a wide and eclectic band of followers. One of these is Paul Rutherford of future Frankie Goes to Hollywood fame. Rutherford's friend, Budgie is currently playing with the Liverpool-based Big in Japan, alongside Holly Johnson (also of future FGTH fame) and Jayne Casey. "We know he'll have the right attitude, just because of the company he keeps," Albertine continued. "He comes down to London and plays with us. He's inventive, has a light touch, is rock-steady and, most important of all, has no problem whatsoever with Ari giving him extremely detailed instructions about the rhythms, the hi-hat patterns and no cymbal bashing."

The resulting album, *Cut*, would reach a highly-respectable #30 on the UK chart following its September 1979 release. In accordance with their creative control, the girls had initially intended the cover to feature a shot of all three of them naked whilst holidaying in Europe with Nora only for Albertine's mother to scotch the idea with a hapless slip of a coffee mug. Pennie Smith was brought in to shoot the girls at Ridge Farm. They were already semi-naked and getting tribal by smearing themselves in mud when a friend of their manager who'd recently returned from Africa suggested they add loincloths to their look. Two decades on, Albertine's mum would admit to deliberately ruining the holiday snaps as she was horrified at the thought of her naked daughter appearing on an album cover.

The Skids' debut album, *Scared to Dance*, was released towards the end of February 1979 and would break into the Top 20. The album's lead single, the anthemic "Into the Valley" would go one stage further in cracking the UK Top 10. "'Into the Valley' just kept going on and on and on," says Simpson. "We sold about 240,000 copies I think, which is a shame because we just missed out on a silver disc for a quarter of a million! But that's about twenty times more copies than you need for a number one these days anyway.

The Into the Valley Tour would see The Skids break every house attendance, a record only recently set by Siouxsie and the Banshees. Simpson wanted to keep the momentum going by releasing "Melancholy Soldiers" as the follow-up single, but the band's management felt there were already too many singles from the album. "'Masquerade' came out and got to number 14 and we thought, right, we're kind of a mainstream band now. So we had a look and an image, the clothes, it was just really exciting and we were young. It was the era of tapered baggy trousers, shoulder pad T-shirts etc. from PX and Johnsons in London."

Be Bop Deluxe frontman, Bill Nelson, who'd just released a solo album under the moniker Bill Nelson's Red Noise, was a huge admirer of The Skids and travelled up to Dunfermline to watch the band demoing 'Masquerade'. This was to prove a prophetic meeting of minds. Not only would Nelson agree to produce The Skids' second album (*Days in Europa*), but his doing so would see Stuart Adamson undergo a rethink about leaving the band. Much to everyone's consternation, *Days in Europa* would surprisingly fail to crack the UK Top 30. The disappointment would be compounded by the album's lead single, 'Charade', suffering a similar fate. However, 'Working for the Yankee Dollar' would buck the trend, giving The Skids another Top 20 single.

Stiff Little Fingers released their debut album, *Inflammable Material*, the same day Sid Vicious shuffled his mortal coil. The album would surpass all expectations in reaching #14 and spending some 19 weeks on the UK chart. Signing with Rough Trade was great for us," says Cluney. "We got a great deal as it gave us distribution for the first single. We also saved the [Rough Trade] shop with sales of *Inflammable Material* because of the 50/50 deal we had with them. The sales for the album were just mental! We really had no expectations for anything special happening but it was so nice to see. Rough Trade really loved the album – especially seeing as Geoff Travis owned the label and co-produced the album. He was maybe a wee bias."

SLF were already known as the 'Irish Clash' by the time of the album's release and the decision to include a reggae crossover in the form of Bob Marley's "Johnny Was" gave the band's dissenters even more ammunition. Burns, however, has never denied the influence The Clash had both himself and SLF as a whole – even if the suggestion to cover "Johnny Was" came from Gordon Ogilvie. Indeed, he would pen "Strummerville" in homage to his hero soon after Strummer's death.

"[Johnny Was'] is a fantastic song and I could see exactly how it would fit in with what we were trying to do," Burns revealed. "The trouble was, the way Bob Marley does it, it's really gentle, almost a love song to this guy, and I thought, 'That's not going to fit the style of the band.' And so I listened to the way the Clash handled 'Police and Thieves.' What they'd done was take the top line and make it the bass line, so I just did it the other way round and made the bass line the guitar line."

Perhaps the biggest surprise on *Inflammable Material* is the track, 'Barbed Wire Love', which could be considered a love song of sorts – even if the song's lyrical core is just as abrasive as every other self-penned track on the album. "We were in the middle of writing the first batch of songs," says Burns. "Obviously a lot of it was concentrating on Northern Ireland and the circumstances that we'd grown up in and we felt we were in danger of being seen as a bit dour and serious. Also, we knew that a lot of people were going to level a lot of these criticisms against us saying, 'You've no sense of humour, you're always writing about the troubles.'

"So we gathered together as many clichés as we could find or reference points to our own songs and put them all into one song and basically took the piss out of ourselves. We wrote it round at Gordon's flat and when we came up with the idea for the doo-wop middle eight, I actually fell off the sofa laughing. But it worked and it's become a real favourite over the years."

March 1979 saw Virgin release 'Silly Thing' as the third single to be lifted from *The Great Rock 'N' Roll Swindle* soundtrack. The single's reaching #6 on the UK Top 10 proving the Pistols' popularity was in no way diminishing. It also provided McLaren with some much-needed cash to keep the ongoing *Swindle* film project on track. In the wake of the single's release, Steve Jones and Paul Cook joined Sham 69 on stage at the Glasgow Apollo for a three-song encore that included 'Pretty Vacant'. This led to speculation within the music press that Pursey and Tregenna were quitting Sham 69 to collaborate with Jones and Cook in a "Sham Pistols" supergroup. The speculation proved well-founded, but while the collaboration would get as far as the recording two brand new compositions – 'Some Play Dirty' and 'Natural Born Killer' – the venture would fall foul to ego with the two ex-Pistols reportedly walking out on a recording session citing the relationship with Pursey as being "worse than working with Rotten."

Jones and Cook subsequently teamed up with Lightning Raiders' bassist, Andy Allan, who'd played on 'Silly Thing' to form The Professionals.

The Ramones made their cinematic debut in Allan Arkush's *Rock*

'N' Roll High School alongside P.J. Soles, perhaps best known for her appearance in John Carpenter's *Halloween*. The film's executive producer, Roger Corman - the so-called 'Pope of Pop Cinema' – had shot some 200 films and had a fan in Johnny Ramone: "I like his films. They got a lot of violence and action."

Whilst growing up in his native Fort Lee, New Jersey, Arkush had supposedly daydreamed in class about staging go-cart races in the school's hallways, blowing up the school and having The Yardbirds play amongst the carnage. He and future Gremlins director, Joe Dante, got as far as collaborating on a film treatment called *Heavy Metal Kids* (After the Todd Rundgren song of the same name), which was a cross between *The Girl Can't Help It* and *High School Confidential*, for possible production by Corman's New World Pictures. With Disco sweeping America in the wake of *Saturday Night Fever*, Corman instead envisioned naked cheer-leaders bouncing around in the school gym gyrating to the lilting strains of Donna Summer and the Bee Gees.

Arkush decided to press on with his vision. Though not a punk fan per se, he'd caught *Punk* magazine's Corman-inspired "Mutant Beach Party" photo-spread featuring Joey Ramone and Debbie Harry. Having retitled his treatment *Rock 'N' Roll High School*, Arkush approached Cheap Trick. However, with their multi-million-selling live album, *Cheap Trick at Budokan*, having recently been released in the US this was never really a viable option. Arkush had then set his sights on The Ramones and flew to New York to meet with the band. Corman was coming round to the idea but had never heard of The Ramones and couldn't figure out why Arkush was pushing for them to be in the film.

"There's this bunch of kids in their high school," Joey told the *NME* during the filming. "They're all fans of the Ramones and they use the Ramones to sorta . . . rebel against the authorities. But like, there's a lot of gags, y'know, like in front of the ticket-line there's gonna be this Indian, and someone asks him what the hell he's doing here, and the Injun says, 'I'm a scalper' . . . y'know, kinda dumb, but it's funny."

The Ramones would record two tracks for the film's soundtrack: the title track and "'I Want You Around', which were both subsequently remixed by Phil Spector. Spector would produce The Ramones' 1980 album, *End of the Century*.

Plastic Letters had stalled at #72 on the US chart yet scored

Blondie a UK Top 10 hit. The follow-up album, *Parallel Lines*, however, would finally give the band their first significant homegrown success in reaching #6 on the *Billboard* 200 following its September 1978 release. The album also gave Blondie their first UK #1 album. Chrysalis had already issued three singles from *Parallel Lines*: "Picture This", "I'm Gonna Love You Too" and "Hanging on the Telephone" with mixed fortunes so the decision was made to release "Heart of Glass" as a fourth single from the album was something of a bold move by the label.

Disco may well have been sweeping across America, yet some 90,000 rock fundamentalists had recently convened at a Chicago baseball field to witness the detonation of a crate filled with disco records. To their collective myopically unimaginative mind, Donna Summer, Gloria Gaynor, the Bee Gees, Chic et al could release as many disco records as they saw fit, but supposedly bona fide rock bands such as Blondie were expected to keep to a 4/4 balls-to-the-floor beat. "People were furious," Debbie reflected. "People were like, [hissing] 'Death to disco! How could you do that?'"

"We planned to release 'Heart of Glass' as a single but we wanted to hold it back because we knew we were gonna get tagged with the disco thing," Stein added. "We didn't want to release it as the first [single] from the album."

Somewhat amazingly, Clem Burke says Chrysalis didn't see any hit singles on the multi-platinum selling *Parallel Lines* at the time "Heart of Glass" was released in February 1979. "Picture This" and "Hanging on the Telephone" had both charted in the UK (#12 and #5 respectively) yet surprisingly neither would trouble the *Billboard* 100. "I'm Gonna Love You Too" had also failed to register on the US chart but would prove a hit in both Belgium and Holland. "Heart of Glass became a hit and the album went back up the [US] charts," says Burke. "It took around 35 weeks to get into the Top 10. Until the Go-Go's, we were the band to take the longest to get an album into the Top 10. *Parallel Lines* is a classic album. I think when people think of Blondie they think of *Parallel Lines* and 'Heart of Glass'"

John Lydon's idea to list Public Image Limited as a limited company was totally out of leftfield, but of course, the ex-Pistol had already proved himself the ultimate nonconformist.

Rather than risk a second helping of shoddy mismanagement,

Lydon called upon Brian Carr's assistance to ensure PiL would be "completely free of all attachments and dictations." All sums of money accrued in recording royalties and song publishing were to be split equally between the four band members. "We produce equally, write equally, and share the money equally," Lydon brazenly declared. "There will be no Rod Stewarts in this band. This is the beginning of a huge umbrella organisation."

Lydon's insistence that there would be no pecking order in PiL was a magnanimous gesture on his part. After all, he was the face of PiL. "It was announced in a very grandiose way that PiL was going to be run along egalitarian lines," Wobble reflected. "A new way of doing things was the order of the day; it was going to be a democracy. I just wanted to be playing and would have preferred a more straightforward situation where I knew exactly where I stood, as well as enjoying a realistic wage. Instead, we had this convoluted arrangement where we all became directors of Public Image Limited."

Lydon's circumstances were somewhat different to those of Wobble, walker and Levene owing to his having signed a publishing deal with Warner Bros whilst in the Sex Pistols. The 50/50 publishing split with Virgin didn't sit well with the rest of the band, however. Wobble says he believes the 50/50 split was due to Brian Carr's wanting a larger advance from Virgin to enable Lydon to continue his ongoing legal battle with Glitterbest. Instead of receiving an equal share of the £30,000 publishing advance, Wobble, Walker and Levene were put on £60 weekly wages. To add insult to injury, John blithely used the vast majority of the publishing advance to purchase the downstairs annexe flat at 45 Gunter Grove.

The monetary grievances that were to cause irreconcilable differences within PiL's founding line-up were as yet in the future, and in early July the group – with Brian Carr's assistance – bought the name "Tinkascus" off the shelf and registered it at Companies House.

(The company name would be changed to "Public Image Limited" on December 31, 1978.)

Jim Walker says he was already unhappy with how things were going in PiL but that it was the band's shambolic approach to playing live that ultimately brought him to the point of no return. "We'd all got along brilliantly during the first few months of PiL. There was never any money to speak of, so we had nothing much else to do

Chrysalis records didn't forsee
any hits on Blondie's *Parallel Lines*.

but work. And we worked hard! We wrote most of the first album during those glorious months, plus other stuff – some of which was better than what ended up on the album. It was a fantastically creative period. Each of us gave PiL a dimension that spurred us all on. One of us would play something, and everyone else would pick up on the vibe. John was without question the greatest frontman of his generation. He was also a great laugh to be with when he was in the right mood. It's difficult to explain – at least without sounding big-headed - but Wobble and I really were one of these miraculously perfect drum and bass combinations. Whereas Keith had the best musical brain I have ever worked with.

"I didn't like the finished mix of 'Public Image' because I thought it wasn't good enough. I honestly thought we were going to re-record it. I thought we could do it better, but we didn't. And as for the flip side . . . well, don't get me started. It was one decent track for the price of two. PiL were in effect mocking those who were feeding us . . . Our fans! I hated that sort of crap. John had written a beautiful Irish ballad. We only played it once with that wonderful lyric. The thing was I'd come up with the idea for that song one morning. I was trying to rip off the theme song for Bonanza and I can only think that's how 'The Cowboy Song' came about. Another strong song that would be dropped without explanation was called 'You Stupid Person'. It was a fantastic song and much better than 'Public Image'. It would have been impossible to keep it from being a number one hit and would have probably broken PiL in America all by itself. I was fooling around on the kit when Keith suddenly jumped up and shouted to me to repeat whatever it was that I was playing. It was just some hi-hat thing. Anyway, I repeated it and Wobble instinctively came up with this awesome bass line. Then Keith jumped in and played the most blistering guitar part I think I ever heard him play."

Walker remembers being Bob Regehr flying over from LA just to watch the band rehearsing. He was this huge bear of a guy in a Stetson. He told us that Warner Bros. was willing to give us a million bucks for promotion in America if we delivered the album by the end of October in time for the Christmas market. But we couldn't even manage that! Bob had recognised our potential from that one rehearsal. We didn't have a manager. Instead, we were all directors of Public Image Limited. It sounded revolutionary, but the contracts were so one-sided that John was holding all the cards. Unlike Keith and Wobble, I came from a mercantile family. I saw instantly that we were being swindled. I tried to stand up and tell everyone that we were making a mistake giving John majority ownership in the company, but I was shouted down by Keith and Wobble."

Walker says that money was beginning to come in by the time PiL got around to talking about playing some live dates, but that the band was "three-quarters down the rabbit hole of personal abuse, professional incompetence and outright chaos." The situation was getting so out of hand that Virgin were worried as to whether PiL were ready for going out and playing live. "They had every right to worry because we'd stopped rehearsing as well as writing by this point. Our relationship with Virgin had also plummeted by now. The Christmas shows at the Rainbow had already been booked and I was looking forward to them. I've heard it said that Virgin were keen to arrange a European tour whereby we'd play a couple of dates in cities in West Germany, Holland, Belgium, and France. I don't remember things that way, but that's not to say it wasn't so. If we were going to tour anywhere before the Rainbow shows – and that's a big 'If' – we would surely have played some shows in Britain as that's where our core fan base was."

Amidst the ongoing chaos, it was agreed PiL would make their live debut in Brussels at the Théâtre 140 on Wednesday, December 20, 1978, with a second European show being booked at Le Stadium in Paris two days later. "In the run-up to Belgium John and I were enjoying a pint in The Man in the Moon pub on the King's Road not too far from where SEX/Seditionaries was," Walker continued. "Sitting at the next table was none other than Peter Grant, Led Zeppelin's tough, no-nonsense manager. He was a colossus of a guy and I knew he cast an even bigger shadow in the music industry. Peter had obviously clocked John, and, sensing an opportunity in the making, went out of his way to come across and say 'hello'. John was polite but his aversion to managers meant nothing was ever going to come from the encounter. I can honestly say I've spent the last forty years kicking myself for not following Peter out onto the street, introducing myself, and seeing about the possibility of his managing me. After all, I was a director in PiL wasn't I? from having Peter come along to meet the others. Having Peter as a manager would have presented untold options.

"The Christmas shows at the Rainbow were horrible. The

The story of The Runaways told in
picture-book style from the pages of *ZigZag* magazine

organisation was like a ten-year-old kid running Microsoft. We kept the fans waiting till nearly midnight before going onstage with no thought as to how they were going to get home afterwards. By the time we actually managed to play those shows we were already on our last legs as a cohesive unit. Being a drummer is pretty much like being an athlete in that you need to stay in shape. By the time December came, we had virtually stopped rehearsing. I was in terrible shape. All I could do was fake it. I knew I was leaving but was worried that I was making a mistake so I kept trying to find something good about PiL. I couldn't. I originally joined a band of four brilliantly talented and young musicians - not the 'Johnny Rotten Band', which to my mind is what PiL turned into very quickly. I'd have never joined to start with had I known what was going to happen.

— Staring At The Rude Boys

"John's inspiration for the lyric to 'Poptones' came in part during a nocturnal car ride through the Oxfordshire countryside one evening in a roadie's car. As usual, the sulphate had been caned in the days previous and the comedown beckoned. No one was saying much, and the roadie had one of his dodgy cassettes playing. The lines about 'foliage and peat and losing my body heat apparently referred to a kidnapping/murder case John had read about."

Jah Wobble

By 1979 punk was well and truly on the wane in London yet conversely, it was still thriving in the provinces. The Coventry-based Automatics had moved into The Clash's rehearsal space in Camden Town the previous summer, living under the auspices of Bernard Rhodes. They'd also accompanied The Clash on the Out on Patrol Tour, having to undergo a hurried name change to Special AKA on the eve of the tour owing to there already being a band called Automatics that had recently signed with Island Records and were about to release their debut single: "When the Tanks Roll Over Poland Again".

Opposite: Jah Wobble rose to fame in Public Image Limited

The Camden Market of today is one of London's "must-see" locations, with thousands of tourists flocking to marvel over such artisan creativity on any given day. Many of those same tourists seek out the iconic stairwell that once led up to The Clash's rehearsal space. The Clash had been operating out of the dilapidated two-storey end-of-terrace railway storage shed for two years but the amenities hadn't improved any by the time Special AKA took up residence. There were a toilet and a sink, but no hot water. Aside from the one-bar electric heater upon which Paul Simonon had famously cook the leftover flour and water paste from one of The Clash's fly-posting forays, there was no form of heating and the majority of the soot-encrusted windows broken were still stuffed with scrunched-up newspaper to keep out the chill. "It was a shithole, but it was the Clash's shithole," says Roadent. "I was looking at having to doss on the streets when I arrived in London, so any port in a storm and all that. But I can imagine it coming as something of a shock to Jerry and a couple of the others."

"Rehearsals was very basic," The Specials' guitarist Roddy "Radiation" Byers confirms. "There was nowhere to sleep bed-wise, there was the legendary electric fire and a sink, which I remember as having hot water, but my memory could be playing tricks after all these years. Bernie would pop in occasionally and give us enough money to buy fish and chips. We sometimes toasted slices of bread on the electric fire. I remember a rat running over Silverton (Hutchinson)'s chest one night while he was sleeping in the rehearsal space. Most of us slept on the floor in the upstairs office. I couldn't have cared one way or the other. We were young, and it was all an adventure.

"Bernie would ramble on about this and that at times, but he was the Clash's manager. I was very impressed by that because I was a fan of the Clash. Bernie wasn't with us all that long in the scheme of things so I'm not sure if he influenced us all that much. I remember him saying something about how we didn't look united, didn't look like a band. So maybe that's where Jerry got the idea to have us wear tonic suits and pork pie hats because Paul Simonon was wearing stuff like that at the time."

According to 2-Tone folklore, in the run-up to the Clash tour, The Automatics/Special AKA founder and keyboardist, Jerry Dammers, met up with Roadent in London and handed the latter a cassette tape containing some demos The Automatics had recorded earlier in the year to pass on to John Lydon in the hope he might be swayed to front the band. Such a scenario seems improbable seeing as Lydon had already unveiled Public Image Limited to the waiting world. "I don't remember Jerry handing me any cassette tape for John," says Roadent. "I'm not denying it, only that I don't remember it happening. I knew Jerry of old, of course, so I suppose it made sense for him to sound me out. I did introduce him to Bernie, however. So, despite what you've read elsewhere I'm the one who actually discovered the Specials. Just one of my 'fifteen minutes' of fame, I suppose . . ."

Roddy Byers remembers Dammers mooting the idea of Lydon's joining during a rehearsal: "Jerry did talk about wanting John to front the band, but whether he said it in jest or was serious who knows?"

As mentioned earlier, Rhodes' days as Clash manager were numbered owing to his stubborn refusal to post bail for Simonon and Headon over the pigeon-shooting fiasco. "We didn't have any idea as to what was going on between The Clash and Bernie," says Byers. "And we didn't know anything about Bernie's scheme to replace Mick Jones with Steve Jones from the Pistols. Bernie thought of musicians as though they were football players that he could put together in any team. There was a story doing the rounds that he wanted to put Terry with the Black Arabs (Another band Rhodes was managing at the time and who would feature in *The Great Rock 'N' Roll Swindle*). Not sure how that would have worked with Terry being white, though."

Touring with The Clash had given the Special AKA a national exposure of sorts. They'd made a few connections and managed to get the odd write-up in the music press. They imagined their being invited out on the road with other named acts, hopefully as the main support. Yet as the weeks slipped by, self-doubt and despondency inevitably began to set in. Rhodes' management offer still held, however. Although it would mean the band relocating to London permanently, doing so was surely better than being left to wither on the bough in Coventry. "The problem was not everyone in the band was happy with Bernie's offer," Byers continued. "I know me and Lynval wanted to sign. We were all on the dole, and the money Bernie was offering was more than we were getting for signing on. Of course, we were living in the moment. Luckily, Jerry said no, otherwise we would have been on a meagre wage forever."

Rhodes must have sensed the in-house wavering. As a means of bringing the doubters in line, he arranged for the Special AKA to play a five-night residency at Le Gibus in Paris, commencing Tuesday, November 14. The Paris trip would rapidly descend into a folly worthy of an Ealing comedy and brought the band close to breaking point. In hindsight, however, it was to prove one of the defining weeks of The Specials' career as it inspired the lyric to 'Gangsters', the song that is credited with giving rise to the 2-Tone movement.

Several of the Out on Parole Tour dates had been marred by violence, and Dammers, having sensed a coming wind of change ever since the inaugural Rock Against Racism carnival at Victoria Park, was looking to take The Special AKA in another direction. "I idealistically thought, 'We have to get through to these people,'" he told *The Guardian* in 2018. "It was obvious that a mod and skinhead revival was coming and I was trying to find a way to make sure it didn't go the way of the National Front and the British Movement. I saw punk as a piss-take of rock music committing suicide. It was great and really funny, but I couldn't believe people took it as a serious musical genre which they then had to copy. It seemed to be more healthy to have an integrated kind of British music, rather than white people playing rock and black people playing their music. Ska was an integration of the two."

In early September 1978, Rat Scabies formed Les Punks for what was intended as a one-off show at the Electric Ballroom in Camden Town. In essence, the show served as a quasi-reunion of The Damned as the line-up featured Dave Vanian, Captain Sensible (switching to guitar) and Motörhead's Lemmy Kilmister filling in on bass. The following month saw the ad hoc outfit play the reopening night of The Mayflower in Manchester. On this occasion, they billed themselves "The Doomed" to avoid getting any potential legal entanglements with Brian James.

In the run-up to a December '78 mini-tour of Scotland – again billed as The Doomed – Vanian pulled another of the "vanishing acts" he was fast becoming renowned for and was temporarily replaced by Gary Holton of the Heavy Metal Kids. Holton, who would die of a heroin overdose in 1985, is perhaps best known for playing cheeky chippy Wayne Winston Norris in *Auf Wiedersehen, Pet*, and yet the Heavy Metal Kids are regarded as being the unsung heroes of punk. The "Kids", as they were known, had started out in

othing* | Maggie's Farm | **THE SPECIALS**

NEW SINGLE

45 RPM

1972 as The Speakeasy's house band after their co-manager, Laurie O'Leary (who was the club's promoter) secured them a residency. By 1976 they'd recorded two albums for Atlantic Records and one for Mickie Most's RAK without achieving the recognition many pundits felt they deserved. Indeed, *Melody Maker* and *Sounds* championed them from the off. Conversely, the *NME* treated the band with disdain, slating them at every opportunity.

The Damned were huge fans. During a Kids show at the Rainbow Theatre, Sensible and Scabies engaged Holton in a realistic pre-staged fight, dragging him off screaming into the wings. At the band's farewell show at The Speakeasy in late-1977, Rotten was seated in the front row, loudly and theatrically pronouncing: "boring, boring, boring" to anyone within earshot. It was to prove a different scenario when Rotten and Holton came face to face at the Roebuck pub a few weeks later. "Gary was holding court with me and a group of others by the fireplace, when the atmosphere suddenly changed," Kids' bassist Ronnie Thomas revealed on *www.daveling.co.uk*. "Rotten had walked into the room with two big bouncers – he always had to be protected because he was such an obnoxious little cunt. There was a deathly silence. Finally, Rotten undid this huge gold safety pin and put it on Gary's lapel. He then patted his cheek and said, 'You've been ripped off, Holton. How does it feel?'" Keyboardist, Danny Peyronel still feels the Kids were cheated. "What happened to the Pistols in '77 should have been us. We were one of the first bands to have the term 'punk rock' used to describe us."

The Vanian/Holton situation was still only spoken of in hushed tones when former Eddie and the Hot Rods bassist, Paul Gray, joined the band in 1980: "Vanian had pulled one of his disappearing tricks I believe, so at the last moment Rat called Gary. En route to Glasgow, the first stop was an off-license. It's a fair old trot from London to Scotland, and lyrics went flying out of the window along with empty cans. When they arrived, Gary could only remember the title of one song, which happened to be 'Neat Neat Neat', repeated ad infinitum until, unsurprisingly, bottles started flying."

Lemmy would remain with The Doomed for a clutch of dates in early 1979 and even accompanied them into the studio to record some demos before returning to outstanding Motörhead commitments. Multi-instrumentalist, Henry Badowski, filled in temporarily before being replaced by Algy Ward, formerly of The Saints.

Having signed with Chiswick Records they played their first gig as The Damned in early April 1979, the same month they released "Love Song"; the first single to be released from the parent album, *Machine Gun Etiquette*. Chiswick's clever marketing ploy in issuing the single in four variant picture sleeves, each one featuring a member of the band, coupled with continuous radio airplay and a national headline UK tour, helped propel "Love Song" to #20 on the UK chart. However, the second single from the album, "Smash It Up", was perceived by the BBC to advocate violence. As a result, the single stalled at #35.

The Damned recorded the majority of *Machine Gun Etiquette* at Wessex Studios at the same time The Clash were there recording *London Calling*. In a show of punk bonhomie that had been sadly lacking on the Anarchy Tour, Joe Strummer and Mick Jones would make an uncredited vocal guest spot on The Damned album's title track. *Machine Gun Etiquette* would stutter to a halt at #31 on the chart, despite receiving favourable reviews at the hands of the music press.

Supporting The Damned on the Machine Gun Etiquette Tour were The Ruts, a Middlesex-based quartet that were signed with Virgin and promoting their debut single for the label, "Babylon's Burning". Aided by an appearance on *Top of the Pops*, 'Babylon's Burning' would crack the UK Top 10, reaching #7.

The reggae-influenced Ruts made their live debut in September 1977, playing three songs during a set break by another band their guitarist Paul Fox was playing at a pub in Northolt, Middlesex. Fox and Ruts' frontman, Malcolm Owen, had known each other from school. The two had formed a short-lived band with future Ruts founding drummer, Paul Mattocks, whilst they were living in a commune on the Isle of Anglesey during the early Seventies. Mattocks' tenure in The Ruts was to prove equally transitory; his being replaced by one-time record shop owner, Dave Ruffy. Fox and Ruffy were also acquainted from their playing together in a funk band called Hit and Run. Following Mattocks' departure, Ruffy resorted to drums and John "Segs" Jennings was brought in on bass. Jennings was working as a Post Office telephone engineer and had had little understanding of the emerging punk scene, but his interest was piqued by the Ramones T-shirt Ruffy was wearing at the time of their encounter.

The Ruts were now beginning to incorporate reggae and dub elements into their songs. John Peel was an early admirer of the band and booked them for a Radio One session in January 1979 around the time they released their first single, "In a Rut" via the People Unite label. (David Jensen would also showcase The Ruts in a session in February 1979, while Peel booked further sessions in May 1979 and February 1980.) People Unite was Misty in Roots' record label. The Ruts had become acquainted with the south London reggae outfit owing to their shared support of the Rock Against Racism movement. The B-side to 'In a Rut' was an anti-heroin tirade called 'H-Eyes'. The irony here, being that Owen would die of a heroin overdose in July 1980 aged just 26.

The rabble-rousing 'Something That I Said' was released as the lead single from the band's debut album, *The Crack*. The Ruts' debut long-player has since been declared a classic owing to its blindingly-original amalgam of punk, roots reggae, dub and hard rock meets hardcore. The album reached #16 on the UK chart following its October 1979 release.

The Ruts had been working on their second album, *Grin & Bear It*, at the time of Owen's death. As a result, the posthumous album consists of singles, B-sides and live performances recorded at the Marquee.

In July 2007, Ruffy, Jennings and Fox reunited as The Ruts for a benefit at the Carling Academy in Islington to raise funds for Fox, following his being diagnosed with terminal lung cancer. Henry Rollins stood in for Owen. The following year would see Ruffy and Jennings return to both studio and stage as Ruts DC.

X-Ray Spex's debut album, *Germfree Adolescents*, was released in November 1978 and reached #18 on the UK chart. Despite EMI sending the band over to New York for a two-week residency at CBGBs, the album would remain unreleased in the US until 1992. Except for 'Identity', which is said to be based in part on Poly's witnessing Bromley Contingent member Tracie O'Keefe slash her wrists in the girls' toilets at The Roxy, the album tackles feminism and anti-consumerism. "I chose the name 'Poly Styrene' because it's a lightweight, disposable product," Poly said in a January 1979 BBC special on X-Ray Spex. It sounded alright. It was a send-up of being a pop star -plastic, disposable. That's what pop stars are

meant to mean, so therefore I thought I might as well send it up."

Poly always viewed herself as an "anti-star" – going so far as to shave her head at John Lydon's Gunter Grove home in response to one of the music papers proclaiming her a sex symbol. She wouldn't be diagnosed as bi-polar until 1991, but the signs were there for all to see. Whilst on the road promoting the album she had a vision of a pink light in the sky and felt objects crackling when she touched them. Thinking Poly was hallucinating, her mother took her to see a doctor. She was misdiagnosed with schizophrenia, sectioned, and told she would never work again. Although she missed playing at the time, in hindsight, she felt that getting out of the public eye was good for her. "I wasn't mad but I went into hospital after that," she later reflected. "They used to lock her up occasionally . . . She'd break out and always make a beeline for my house," says Lydon in *Anger is an Energy*. "She was good fun until the ambulance turned up for her." Unable to cope with the demands of touring, Poly would quit X-Ray Spex in 1979. She would embark on a solo career, releasing three albums and a clutch of singles. During this time she became a devotee of Hare Krishna and recorded some of her solo work at the in-house recording studio at Bhaktivedanta Manor, a Gaudiya Vaishnava temple in Hertfordshire where she was also living. Whilst recording her third solo album, *Generation Indigo*, Poly revealed in a February 2011 interview with *The Sunday Times* that she was being treated for breast cancer, and that the cancer had since spread to her lungs and spine. Poly would succumb to her illness within two months of giving the interview.

By 1979 Buzzcocks were ever-presents on the UK charts. Their follow-up album, *Love Bites*, gave the band their second Top 20 album following its September '78 release, while 'Promises' 'Everybody's Happy Nowadays' and 'Harmony in My Head' had resulted in further appearances on *Top of the Pops*. Buzzcocks' third album, *A Different Kind of Tension*, was another accomplished body of work and revealed how much Buzzcocks had matured in terms of their songwriting over the past few months. Though failing to emulate the success of its predecessors, the album reached a semi-respectable #163 on the *Billboard* 200. Somewhat surprisingly, both of album's attendant singles – 'You Say You Don't Love Me' and 'I Believe' would fail to chart.

To Promote *A Different Kind of Tension* Buzzcocks embarked on a 27-date UK Tour (also taking in Dublin and Cork) with Joy Division in support. When reflecting on the tour, Peter Hook said how Joy Division had a great time "blowing the Buzzcocks off every night". This wasn't strictly true as the author can testify. Though it's undoubtedly true that Joy Division were the new flavour of the month by the autumn of 1979, Buzzcocks proved they were more than capable of holding their own against their brash young fellow Mancunian upstarts.

Joy Division had released their debut album, *Unknown Pleasures*, earlier in the year. The hype surrounding the band saw some 5,000 copies in the first two weeks of going on sale. However, it wasn't until Joy Division appeared on *Something Else* on September 15, 1979 - performing 'She's Lost Control' and non-album single, 'Transmission' – that the remainder of the initial 10,000 pressing sold out. It's said that Tony Wilson's arrangement with Joy Division was to divide the profits from *Unknown Pleasures* in a straight 50/50 split. Although the band members were able to quit their jobs before embarking on the Buzzcocks tour, Wilson would ultimately divert much of the album's profits on other Factory-related projects.

'She's Lost Control' centres around a young woman experiencing a violent epileptic seizure. However, the lyric could be said to be semi-autobiographical as by this juncture Ian Curtis had been diagnosed as an epileptic.

Jim Walker's grumblings about the shoddy quality of *Public Image: First Issue* were to prove prescient as Warner Bros. deemed the album too uncommercial for a US release. PiL consented to record revised versions of certain tracks sometime between March and May 1979, and yet the album was to remain unreleased in the US. PiL were as yet without a drummer following Walker's departure, but with Virgin pressing for a follow-up single and new album, rather than place another ad in the *Melody Maker* classifieds they called upon Dave Humphreys, the percussionist with a jazz fusion outfit called Seventh Seal who were also rehearsing at Rollerball.

Following an ad hoc rehearsal at Rollerball, the 19-year-old Humphries accompanied PiL to The Manor in Oxfordshire to lay down demos of the new songs the band had been working on intermittently since the release of *First Issue*. One of the new songs was "Death Disco", which had been earmarked as the follow-up to "Public Image". Lydon had penned the lyric as a lasting lament to his dying mother, Eileen. "I've never come to grips with death but through music, I kind of found a way of dealing with it," he reflected in *Anger is an Energy*. "It's me howling in bitter agony. Grief, grief, grief, but at the same time you've got to give joy for those you've loved. Not wallow in the self-pity of it, but rather celebrate the good things about them when they were alive."

Eileen Lydon had asked her firstborn son to write her a song in her honour. As soon as the band had laid down a rough demo at The Manor, Lydon returned to London and rushed to the hospital to play her the song. "I had to curtail it a bit because what I wrote is very directly about death, so I wanted her to feel it was more about the challenge of an illness."

"The person he was singing about, 'Seeing in your eyes' was his mother dying," Levene told the *Perfect Sound Forever* website in 2001. "That's what John was singing about very passionately, I might add. From my point of view, I was just trying to do something with the music. I didn't know what he was singing about at the time – he was just, 'It's "Death Disco" Keith, that's what it is!'"

While the sentiments behind "Death Disco" are to be lauded, releasing it as a single threw everyone into confusion. Speaking about the reaction to "Death Disco" with the *NME* in February 1980, Lydon said that he'd deliberately gone against the tried-and-tested verse/chorus/verse/chorus/middle-eight progression. "To be forever and ever exactly in the same genre would never be what I ever wanted to do. And if I'm writing a song about my mother dying, believe me, I ain't gonna be following no three-chord progression! That's anger and fear, and rage, and it goes all over the place. It's formless by nature."

Levene, of course, had long-since viewed three-chord progressions as anathema to his way of making music. "People don't realise there's thirty-two levels of different things you can get off in PiL music. If you listen to it three times you think it's a good disco track, but if you listen to it thirteen times you think fucking hell, there's a whole spectrum of stuff that you can draw from it. PiL's music doesn't meet the eye or ear on first appearance or listening."

Validation was probably the last thing PiL were seeking and yet it came with 'Death Disco' reaching the UK Top 20 following its release in June 1979 with no daytime radio airplay whatsoever. PiL had shot a promotional video that was as dark and despondent as the music, but when the BBC invited the band to appear on *Top of the Pops*, Lydon set his loathing of the show to one side and agreed to appear in person. Rather than mime along to a pre-recorded near-identical version of the single, however, PiL pre-recorded an alternate version over which Lydon sang the vocal live. "I was determined to do *Top of the Pops* even though it was pure hell,' Lydon said in a *Record Mirror* interview around the time of the *TOTP* performance. "There's no point hanging onto principles and morals if nobody in the world can hear you. Now they don't play our record on the radio except in the chart countdowns on a Sunday afternoon – and that I don't like! I want that record to be heard."

The irony surely wouldn't have been lost on Lydon, Wobble and Levine that whilst PiL were striving to break down the constrictive barriers of rock 'n' roll, their old compadre Sid was sitting pretty at #3 on the chart with his souped-up version of Eddie Cochrane's 'C'Mon Everybody'.

With The Manor being owned by Richard Branson/Virgin, Lydon and Levene took full advantage of the copious free food and booze the label laid on for them. For Wobble, however, the novelty of living a debauched version of the *Downton Abby* lifestyle soon began to wear thin. The bassist had recently passed his driving test and whenever things got a bit stale at The Manor he'd jump in his newly-purchased cheap runaround and zip back to London and Gooseberry Studios to work on various ongoing solo projects. His occasional late-night forays to Gooseberry were being viewed with suspicion and matters were brought to a head when Levene and Jeannette Lee – who was dating the guitarist but yet to be brought in as a band member - stopped him en route to his car and told him they didn't approve of his moonlighting. Wobble dug in his heels and told them in no uncertain terms that he'd quit PiL rather than give up his solo work. The two warring factions stood facing each other for what seemed like an age before Lydon – who'd been furtively watching developments from an upstairs window – broke the deadlock by hocking a gob of nicotine-flecked phlegm into the ornate birdbath situated a few feet from where the trio were standing. Then, with the casual flick of his head, Lydon summoned Levene and Lee back inside.

The underlying reason for Wobble's hurried departures was that away from the writing and recording his relationship with Lydon and Levene was becoming increasingly poisonous. "It's often said that it was because of the darkness and confusion around PiL that *Metal Box* was such a classic recording," the bassist later reflected. "However, I now think that the reverse is true: *Metal Box* was an artistic success in spite of massive problems in and around the band."

Humphries was no longer around by this juncture; his having been shown the door for steadfastly refusing to quit Seventh Seal. Virgin had posted another *Melody Maker* ad, yet despite Lydon, Levine and Wobble trying out a variety of candidates, none it seemed, could meet the jazz-infused bar set by Jim Walker. "Most of them felt ill at ease," Lydon explained. "They'd be noting the tensions going on between Wobble and Keith, me and Keith, Wobble and me, between all three of us at once – a very hard thing suddenly to be in the middle of. You're walking into the lions' den, and the lions all know each other."

Humphries' eventual replacement in PiL was Richard "Snakehips Dudanski" Nother, whom Lydon, Levene and Wobble knew from his time in The 101ers. Up until recently, Dudanski had been keeping the beat in his own outfit, Bank of Dresden, but was at a loose end when Levene made his approach. With Virgin growing ever more impatient for the finished album, Dudanski was expected to hit the ground running. "Over the next ten days at Townhouse Studios we recorded five songs," says Dudanski. "The tape was just left running. Basically, me and Wobble would just start playing, and maybe Keith'd say something like double-time. But it was a bass/drum thing which Keith would stick guitar on and John would be there and then write some words and whack 'em on once we'd got the basic tracks.

"I think the first day we did 'No Birds Do Sing' and 'Socialist'. Then we did 'Chant' and 'Memories, but the whole thing ground to a halt. Wobble wanted to do something. We'd try and set something up, but it would just not happen because Keith wouldn't turn up. It could have worked, but we seemed incapable of actually doing it.'

"We messed around with Dudanski but he really wasn't up to it," Lydon countered. "He was too soft and gentle to really cope with our lack of fear."

Wobble's own "lack of fear" saw him serve as a one-man rhythm section in laying down the drums on 'Careering', while another example of his dexterity came with 'The Suit'" – both of which were set for inclusion on *Metal Box*. "The drums are actually an analogue loop that I made at Gooseberry with Mark Lusardi (Gooseberry's in-house engineer). I played the drums and we mixed it down to quarter-inch tape, cutting it to length and then using editing tape to connect the ends. As soon as I'd finished my own mix I nipped up to the Manor with the multi-track. I remember cajoling John out of the telly and video room to check it out. I suspect he hated using stuff that I was originating elsewhere, but when stuff was as good as 'The Suit' what could he say?"

Considered to be by far and away the best of the new songs PiL were working on at The Manor was 'Poptones'. Indeed, Wobble regards it as being "the jewel in the PiL crown"; the song being partly inspired by the octave runs he was hearing on disco records of the period.

Dudanski's ongoing struggle to get his drumming to everyone's specifications was again proving problematic, however. So much so, that Levene would end up taking the job on.

Lydon fell instantly in love the tune's laidback groove and set to work on completing a lyric that he'd been toying with. When

Many regard *Metal Box* as a classic recording and a high point for PiL

subsequently giving his account as to how the harrowing lyric to "Poptones" came together, Lydon said the thing that had leapt out from the page whilst reading about the case in the newspapers, was how the girl in question could remember very little about her abductors other than the song playing on the car's in-built cassette player. And that when the police eventually traced the car, the cassette had still been in the tape deck.

"They never mentioned in the media what the tune was but I actually found out that it was a Bee Gees song. Having a great love and affinity for the Bee Gees I found that even more interesting. So, hence the line in the song: 'And the cassette played poptones....'"

The *Metal Box* sessions were still ongoing when Lydon was invited onto *Juke Box Jury* to offer his verdict on the latest pop offerings alongside ageing Radio One DJ Alan 'Fluff' Freeman and actresses Elaine Page and Joan Collins. Hosted by Noel Edmunds, the show's format was a rehash of the original *Juke Box Jury* that ran from 1959 to '67. Of course, what made for popular televisual fare back in the day didn't necessarily translate a decade or so on. Inviting an obvious loose cannon such as Lydon onto the show was stage-managed as Edmunds introduces him as 'Johnny Rotten' while mentioning PiL as something of an afterthought. Given Edmunds' known loathing for anything remotely connected to punk rock, the metaphorical battle lines were drawn before nary a word was spoken.

The new releases selected for that week's show – broadcast Saturday, May 31, 1979 -included 'Sweet Little Rock 'n' Roller' (Showaddywaddy), 'Angel Eyes' (Abba), 'Ain't Getting' Any' (The Monks), '"Bad Girls' (Donna Summer), 'C'est Sheep' (Adrian Munsey), '"Playground Twist' (Siouxsie and the Banshees) and "We All Need Love' (Domenic Troiano).

Lydon looked suitably bored throughout the proceedings and lived up to everyone's expectations by caustically dismissing each of the new releases in turn – including the Banshees' PiL-esque 'Playground Twist'. Ever the miscreant, Lydon had smuggled a bottle of his favourite tipple onto the set and even lights up a cigarette at one point. Realising the audience are hanging onto Lydon's every caustic putdown; Edmunds tries turning the tables by asking him to give an example of music he prefers listening to. "Well, my own stuff, for a start," Lydon shot back with perfect timing. "I set out to end that programme and I thought I succeeded," he told *ZigZag* later in the year. "They didn't like me at all. I was meant to look a fool. They cut the bit where I was talking to the audience. Didn't like that!"

Several weeks later, PiL appeared on Tyne Tees TV's new late-night youth-orientated show *Check It Out*. The episodes were recorded on a Monday afternoon and broadcast the following evening at 11 p.m. "At first we were only to do a live set but later we said an interview was on provided they didn't just want more prattle about the Pistols – which, as you know, they're all absolutely sick to death of reliving," Jeannette Lee subsequently bemoaned to the *NME*. "Well, Tyne-Tees said they only wanted to talk to John so we kind of guessed the kind of thing they were hoping for and said it wasn't on. Eventually, they consented to interviewing the whole band but still only posed the same old questions to John."

PiL performed 'Death Disco' and 'Chant' on the *Check It Out* stage but when the band came across to conduct the interview they found just two chairs had been set up. Not to be outdone, Levene perches himself on the chair arms betwixt Lydon and Wobble. Dudanski has little option but to crouch down behind Lydon to get in the shot. From their edgy expressions, the band were fearing the worst. Their suspicions were soon confirmed when the show's presenters – Chris Cowey and Lyn Spencer – fired off one inane question after another. "We do not like cheap publicity, pseudo gimmicks, condescension, and crawling," Lydon spat, finally tiring of the charade. "And that's what was expected from us tonight. Was it not? After all, you would only interview me and Wobble at first until we refused point-blank."

The interview surprisingly cuts to a pre-recorded film clip of Cowey interviewing Angelic Upstarts' guitarist Ray 'Mond'" Cowie, during which Cowie launches into a tirade about Lydon saying he was finished as a musical force, and that PiL were the "worst band that ever came about."

"Look, I don't have to explain myself to anybody and I ain't gonna really bother,' Lydon seethed when the studio interview resumed. "Now, I was asked here, right, to interview with the band here – PiL – but now like, we're facing a cheapskate comedy interrogation act and it just ain't on, pal. It's a joke. It's a farce. I don't need to explain myself. Sooner or later somebody will open their fuckin' eyes. Oh, sorry, rude word,' he added with a mock roll of his eyes. Instead of asking for the "next question" as he had of Bill Grundy on *Today* back in December '76, Lydon unhooked his mic and tossed it at Cowey before walking offset. He was closely followed by Levene, Dudanski and Wobble, but only after the latter had vented his spleen at Cowey. Wobble had already removed his mic beforehand but the continuous bleeping leaves little to the imagination.

A spokesman for *Check It Out* would later claim PiL were manhandled out of the building by security, but Jeannette Lee is insistent that no such eviction took place. "There was no question of being 'escorted out'," she said in the same *NME* interview. "In fact, they became pathetic and couldn't apologise enough, saying how they'd get us a drink. You can understand that the whole cheap affair was an attempt to goad John into doing his nut and giving the show a great deal of publicity. It was sickening."

"It was like a big set-up," Lydon seethed to the *Record Mirror*. "All about how glorious the Pistols were and us bad boys and then the Upstarts waffling on about how we sold out to the working classes. I thought it was diabolical. If I'm asked to do something then I'll do it, but I don't like to be set up. I mean, I'll talk about PiL, but not about the past and other people.'

Metal Box was set for an October 12 release, with 'Memories' the lead single. It wouldn't be so much an album as three 12" singles – with an aggregate playing time equivalent to that of a normal LP - and packaged in what the music press described as being a "cross between a film can and a biscuit tin."

"We were unanimous that it had to be a completely different sort of presentation," Wobble reflected. "Various materials were discussed, as was the potential cost of getting vinyl-sized containers made up. For reasons of an aesthetical, practical and financial nature, wood, plastic, glass and cloth were rejected. We kept coming back to metal – I'm pretty sure it was John who said that it should be called '*Metal Box*'."

The Fall's Karl Burns had taken over from Dudanski but his tenure with PiL barely lasted a month owing to Levene and Wobble's supposed bullish behaviour towards him. Virgin were once again forced to place an ad in *Melody Maker*. Daunted at the prospect of endless hours wheedling the wheat from the chaff, Lydon, Wobble and Levene decided to extend an olive branch to Jim Walker.

Walker had spent much of the year traversing Israel with his girlfriend Carol, their going so far as to join a kibbutz. Picking fruit or vegetables for hours on end under the hot Israeli sun soon lost its allure, however, and upon their return to London, Walker had joined The Pack, the punk-orientated outfit fronted by Kurt Brandon that would evolve into Theatre of Hate.

Though deeply sceptical as to Lydon's motives, Walker agreed to a face-to-face meeting to see if they might iron out their differences. When Walker arrived at the designated meeting place the following afternoon, however, he discovered Lydon's idea of a "face-to-face meeting" was somewhat different to his own. "If Brian Carr was dragged along to intimidate me it certainly didn't work," he says. "I said the same thing I'd thought of when Lydon called the night before, 'Sure, I'll come back, but I want the twenty-five per cent I was promised. I don't care about the other suckers. You can go on paying them sixty quid a week for all I care but I want my twenty-five per cent in writing. And that's it - take it or leave it!'"

Much to Walker's astonishment, Lydon agreed to his demand, saying Carr would take care of the necessary legalities. Somewhere betwixt the meeting and the coming dawn, however, John had undergone a rethink. Rather than the written confirmation that his percentage stipulation had been met, Walker instead received a letter chastising him for his "ludicrously greedy demands". This was to prove Walker's last-ever direct dealings with Lydon.

Whatever the cause of Lydon's change of heart, Virgin's *Melody Maker* ad was to provide dividends. Nuneaton-born Martin Atkins was just 20-years-old and yet had already made two fruitless attempts to join PiL. "I tried to join PiL when John first left the Pistols," he revealed on the *Fodderstompf* website. "I came down from Durham (where he was playing in local covers outfit, The Hots) for the auditions, which I read about in the music papers but I had to go back early and so I fluffed that one. I tried again when Richard Dudanski joined, [and] when he left I called Keith who said, 'Come along'. It was just me pestering, really."

Such was Atkins' pestering; that a wearisome Jeannette Lee took to calling him "that Northerner" whenever he called. His persistence ultimately paid off with Levene inviting him to an audition at Townhouse Studios in Shepherd's Bush. Levene told Atkins that he, Lydon and Wobble would be at the studio from 4 p.m. onwards and to expect a call. Atkins dutifully stayed at his digs all afternoon, but no call was forthcoming. When the phone did eventually ring it was around 4 a.m. By the time Atkins had scrambled out of bed and down the three flights of stairs from his attic room to the payphone on the ground-floor the caller presumably (Levene?) had rung off. Atkins didn't have the Townhouse's number to hand, and with no second call coming, he must have thought he'd blown yet another chance to join PiL.

The *NME*'s Danny Baker proclaimed 'Memories' his Single of the Week, but with Radio One having wilfully limited PiL's previous 45s to once a week airings on the weekly chart countdowns, there was little likelihood of the station changing tack. However, PiL's unwillingness to cut the song's playing time could be construed as a self-inflicted coup de grâce. "'Memories' didn't do well commercially because it was nearly five minutes long and we knew it wouldn't get any airplay because of that," Lydon reflected. "Keith and I were in

Jordan making freinds with the cops. Photo Ray Stevenson

total agreement on this: neither of us knew where you'd cut it, or what you'd cut out ... and what was the point? It was the length of it that got the true emotions across."

'Memories' would stall at #60, but much to the relief of everyone at Virgin the parent album would do much better following its belated release in late-November 1979, reaching #18 on the UK Album chart.

By and large, the critics remained apathetic towards PiL, but two of the three main music weeklies – *Sounds* and *NME* – were both fulsome in their praise for *Metal Box* - the latter paper going so far as to put the band on the front cover of its November 24 issue despite no interview to support it. Spiralling budget costs had forced PiL to shelve plans to include a lyric sheet in *Metal Box*, but such was their determination not to be outdone the band took the novel approach of placing a full-page advertisement in that same issue of the *NME* featuring the lyrics in their entirety.

"The whole punk scene is, of course, responsible for the Go-Go's ever getting created. Because before punk rock happened, you couldn't start a band if you didn't know how to play an instrument. But when punk happened it was like, 'Oh, it doesn't matter if you can play or not. Go ahead, make a band.' And that's exactly what the Go-Go's did."

Jane Wiedlin

In recent months the LA scene had been rent asunder with the arrival of hardcore punk acts such as Vicious Circle, Fear, Circle Jerks and Black Flag. These hardcore bands and their fanatical followers were younger in the main and looked upon the older "artsy" Hollywood punk scene with disdain. "It was more LA County being invaded by Orange County," says Theresa Kereakes. "It certainly wasn't a rivalry, as a 'rivalry' would imply an equal playing field. It was more like the European conquest of Native Americans: Manifest Destiny! Nobody slam danced before that. We all pogoed like we learned from England. Shows were fun and peaceful except for an occasional squabble. But then these . . . let's call them 'Orange County yahoos' . . . showed up and slammed and started the running circle, shoving and hitting people, and spitting. Stuff they learned from watching

TV. They totally ruined the scene! We had the Hermosa Beach church punks, San Pedro punks, Redondo Beach punks, Marina Del Rey punks; none of whom would call you a 'poseur' or they'd beat you up. I was seriously beaten up by some girls at a Siouxsie and the Banshees show. We had to run away down the street and the owner of a liquor store let us hide in his back room." (Penelope Spheeris's 1981 documentary, *The Decline of Western Civilization*, chronicles the period when the older LA punk scene was being completely taken over by hardcore and features performances by bands from both scenes.)

The Go-Go's surprisingly don't feature in Spheeris's documentary – this despite the girls having made their live debut at The Masque while the film was being made. Imbued with the punk spirit of "don't think, just do", the nascent Go-Go's jumped at the opportunity to get up onstage during what has since been described as a "going away party" for The Dickies in late May 1978. The Dickies had recently signed with A&M Records and were heading over to the UK ostensibly to promote the release of their debut single – a souped-up version of Black Sabbath's 1970 hit, 'Paranoid'. They didn't even stop to consider they had only had two completed songs to their name . . . or that they were missing their drummer.

"I remember meeting up with the others and us all going over to the Masque that night for the Dickies send-off," says Go-Go's' founding drummer Elissa Bello. "The Dickies weren't playing of course, as they'd already left for England, so I'm not really sure how or why it came to be regarded as a 'send-off'. But anyways, there were a whole bunch of other bands getting up and playing a few numbers. It was all very casual. That's most likely how it came about; you know, someone seeing us in there and saying why don't you get up and play?

"It could also just be that the others just decided 'what the hell!' and jumped up on stage between the other bands and borrowed some equipment. I know for a fact that my drums stayed locked away in our rehearsal space at the club that night. I'd also been working all day, and whenever I worked I just wanted to get home and grab a shower. And you have to remember that if what happened hadn't have happened then no one would probably even remember anything about that night. Like I say, the Dickies weren't there so it would have most likely been quickly forgotten. Just another crazy night at the Masque, you know. And there were lots of those, I can assure you.

"As you can imagine, the girls were all pretty stoked I when I next met up with them at the Masque for a rehearsal. I'm pretty sure it would have been the following night as we were rehearsing regularly by then. They were all like, 'Guess what; we played the show last night. You should have stayed!' And I was like, 'Wow, that's great an all, but I just wanted to be clean.' I might be getting things a little bit messed up a bit here, but I'm pretty sure Terry Graham played the drums with them that night. Terry played drums with the Bags for a time, and later with Gun Club."

Terry Graham had arrived in LA from his native Dallas in early 1977 with little more than the clothes on his back, the two hundred dollars that his mother had given him, a contact number for a cousin, and copy of *Ramones*. He was 19-years-old at the time, his intention having been to attend film school. Instead, he fell into the West Hollywood scene. His highly amusing and insightful memoir, *Punk Like Me!: Liner Notes For A Revolution That Almost Happened*, was published in November 2017. "I did play with the Go-Go's that night at the Masque," he acknowledged. "I already knew the girls really well by that time of course. And I also knew the songs – all two of them - because I would rehearse with them when Elissa either couldn't make it or hadn't shown up for whatever reason.

"It was some event to do with the Dickies, and they were all excited and obviously didn't want to pass up the opportunity to get up and play. I don't know whose drums I used, or whether Margot (Olivarria) played her own bass, but Jane had her guitar with her onstage. She was still learning, of course, and she'd painted the letters on the guitar's fretboard to denote where to place her fingers to form the chords. The first song ("Robert Hilburn") went okay, but we got a bit mixed up on the second song ("Overrun") as Jane forgot the chords, I think. Not that it mattered much. We just played the song again. It was a fun night, and I was all too happy to help them out; happy to be part of their vaginal history."

As Elissa Bello says, The Dickies send-off was merely another of the Masque's ad hoc free-for-alls, with one band jumping onstage to replace the last and sharing the instruments. Pleasant Gehman happened to be in the audience and remembers the occasion well. "As it was the going away party for the Dickies our whole gang was there. Because I was friends with Belinda and Jane I knew all about the Go-Go's before they even started practising. They might not have come up with the name 'the Go-Go's' by then, but I was one of the first people to know they had a band going. I don't think they'd gotten as far as getting any instruments. But that was what everyone was doing at that time - forming a band first, and then seeing if they could get instruments or a place to practice.

"They only played three songs as I remember - and two of those were the same song. We all loved the girls as people, and we all loved our friends' bands even if they were terrible -like the Go-Go's' first show was. We just adored it that people were getting up to play. It was the energy that counted, basically, not the music. And the Go-Go's definitely had that energy."

Punk aficionado, Gabi Berlin, was another who caught The Go-Go's debut. "I wouldn't say we were friends or anything, more like acquaintances. I was probably closest to Margot from the band's founding line-up. I remember going over to her apartment at the Canterbury a couple of times. Her apartment was so different than most of the rat nests at the Canterbury. She had actually painted it bright lime green and it was so neat and clean. She was just adorable.

"When the Go-Go's played the Masque that first time, I'll always remember when they were done as everybody cheered. We were all so pleased and wanted more, but Belinda shouted out, 'But that's all we know!' Was it only three songs? I always thought it was four songs they played. I actually had a tape recording of that night for years afterwards. My sons got into punk and ended up destroying most of my stuff. They were second-generation punks though. I was the coolest mom in town. Gosh, I wish I still had that tape because it proved the Go-Go's could actually play. You have to remember nobody could really play back then, but the girls could really play! They practised relentlessly. If anything, I actually got kind of annoyed by their poppy sound. I mean it wasn't like they were playing the Greek (Theatre) or anything; just a tiny stage in a basement. What did surprise me most that night was that Belinda managed to sing. She was always so out of it. I can't remember who was playing drums, but it makes sense for Terry to stand in for Elissa, he was Jane's boyfriend at the time."

"We only played the two songs because that is all we knew well enough so far," Margot Olivarria confirmed. "For a first gig, it was not that intimidating because we knew just about everyone in the audience. I wonder if there is a recording of that gig out there someplace. I'm sure we sucked, but 'A' for effort!"

Belinda Carlisle would subsequently enthuse about the Masque show; the club being packed to the gills while they were up onstage; the crowd being in their faces as they played, and of everyone telling them how great they were. She then goes to say that while she and the other girls had recognized their limitations, they were all agreed they couldn't wait to get up onstage again. If Carlisle is to be believed then the girls got the opportunity a week or so later when they were invited onto a Masque bill that included The Bags and The Plugz, but again Elissa Bello has no recollection of it. "Belinda says that? It's possible, I suppose, but I honestly don't remember us playing the Masque till much later . . . or maybe I needed a shower that night too? I do remember some of the other early shows we did, however. Playing the Whisky for the first time was pretty cool. Everybody's ambition was to play the Whisky, and we played there very early on . . . like our fifth or sixth show.

"Another early show came at a club called the Rock Corporation, which was out in the valley someplace. Someone told me afterwards that David Bowie was in there that night. I certainly didn't see him; you tend to remember those kinda things. And my brother and sister, who were over on a visit, didn't see him either. It was just what we got told. The other really cool clubs to play back then were the Troubadour on Santa Monica Boulevard, and Club 88 down on Pico. The Starwood was another great place to play, but there were also horrible places that would literally stuff the people into there. Like, screw the fire regulations! And everyone or nearly everyone smoked back then. So the air would be filled with cigarette smoke. There was never any air conditioning in those kinda places, and it was so hot-infested that it was really hard to breathe - especially when you're the drummer!

"I particularly loved the shows we did at the Fab Mab. Those shows came later on, of course; early '79 I think. We were all really excited when we got booked to play the Mab. Playing your first out-of-town dates is always a thrill for any band, and those memories stay with you. That trip was the first time I learned about the rivalries between the LA and San Francisco punk scenes. We'd heard all the stories of course, but we hadn't played anywhere outside of LA up to that point. Some of the people we met were great, but I remember we were setting up our gear on the first night and the guy that ran the place, a guy called Dirk Dirksen, kept coming over and shouting things like, 'Hurry up, you LA people! Get a move on!' We were being all nice and polite and he was just a total asshole. Eventually, I got tired of his crap. The next time he said it I shouted right back, 'Hey, I'm not from LA. I'm from Buffalo, New York, so fuck off!' He didn't come over again."

Whether the purists would consider their doing ten-minute freebie without their drummer a proper gig, The Go-Go's were at least now up and running. Energy and enthusiasm had carried them thus far, but if the girls were ever to progress beyond being regarded as a Masque novelty act they would seriously need to raise their game. The obvious solution was to augment the line-up by bringing in a bona fide musician, preferably someone with plenty of experience in the recording studio as well as on the live circuit. Of course, the only viable roles that were available within the Go-Go's' set-up were those of lead guitar or keyboards. Ordinarily, this wouldn't have proved too much of a problem had The Go-Go's not been keen to maintain their "all-girl band" identity. Fortunately, Olivarria knew exactly where to turn.

Charlotte Caffey says she was working on a song idea backstage at The Starwood where her band, The Eyes, were playing when she was distracted by two pairs of spiked heels click-clacking across the floor towards her. Caffey looked up to see two girls dressed in matching thrift store vintage attire, their heavily-made up beaming faces framed by haphazard multi-coloured hair. "It was me and Belinda that went backstage," says Olivarria. "I didn't know Charlotte personally, but I knew who she was because the Eyes were already a well-known group on the LA circuit. All the girls thought it was a brilliant idea when I suggested we approach Charlotte. Sure, she was a bit older than us, but who cared! All I was concerned about was that she knew how to do the things that we didn't at that time. And there were plenty of them, I can assure you."

"Yeah, Charlotte definitely made a difference to the band when she came on board," Bello acknowledges. "When Margot first suggested our approaching Charlotte I was like, 'Yeah, good luck with that one!' Charlotte might not have been a 'name' if you catch my meaning,

but she was definitely someone other musicians respected so you can imagine my surprise when she agreed to join us. I think a lot of other people were caught by surprise as well. Who cared if she told a fib about being able to play lead guitar? She'd studied music for one thing; got the degree and everything. All we had were a few okay songs at that time.

"Charlotte was very kind to everyone; always careful not to hurt anyone's feelings; very diplomatic. That's what I remember most about her from my time in the band. And she and I got along very well. Despite having to learn our material, she was always willing to help out - especially with Margot who was of course still learning to play bass. And unlike Jane, Charlotte was happy to let me show her little pieces on the guitar that I knew would help her. That was what really sealed the deal for me."

Carlisle had also never spoken to Caffey before that night at the Starwood, but nonetheless felt a connection. Caffey was dating Dickies' frontman Leonard Graves Phillips, (she'd accompanied the Dickies over to the UK so missed the Go-Go's Masque debut), and Carlisle had dated the band's drummer, Karlos Kaballero.

Bands were forming daily in LA, and if The Go-Go's were going to be counted amongst the wheat rather than the chaff they needed an identity. The main players on the scene had their gimmicks and trademarks. Darby Crash was wont to smear his torso in peanut butter and red liquorice, The Bags would take to the stage with bags over their heads, Black Randy and the Metrosquad had a penchant for covering seventies porn movie themes, and The Plugz' line-up were all Latinos. These bands, as well as every other band on the scene, were either all-male or male/female line-ups. A band consisting of five female firebrands would standout from the crowd just as The Runways had a few years earlier.

"The difference between the Runaways and the Go-Go's was that the Go-Go's did everything themselves," says Terry Graham. "There was no Kim Fowley 'Mr. Burns' type figure lurking in the background pulling the strings. There was a lot of resentment towards them on the West Hollywood scene simply because they were an all-girl band. People were like, 'Oh yeah, the Go-Go's; they're just copying the Runaways.' But that just wasn't the case at all. The Go-Go's had total conviction in what they were doing, and you have to admire the courage it took for them to do what they were doing; and more power to them for that."

The Dead Kennedys hailed from San Francisco, and yet are viewed as being major players on the LA hardcore scene. Fronted by Jello Biafra, the Dead Kennedys had formed in June 1978 when guitarist East Bay Ray advertised for potential bandmates after seeing a ska-punk show at the Mabuhay Gardens. Owing to their provocative name, the band often played under pseudonyms such as The Sharks, The Creamsicles, The Pink Twinkies or simply The DK's. In the run-up to a show at the Fab Mab on November 22, 1978 – the fifteenth anniversary of John F Kennedy's assassination in Dallas - The *San Francisco Chronicle* columnist, Herb Caen, wrote: "Just when you think tastelessness has reached its nadir, along comes a punk rock group called 'The Dead Kennedys'" Contrary to popular belief, the band's name – according to Biafra at least – wasn't meant as an insult to the Kennedy family, but rather to "bring attention to the end of the American Dream".

In June 1979, the Dead Kennedys released their debut single, "California Über Alles" on the band's own independent Alternative Tentacles label. Though the single didn't chart in the US, it reached #4 on the UK Indie Chart. The parent album, *Fresh Fruit for Rotting Vegetables*, would rightly go on to achieve critical acclaim.

The Clash spent much of the spring of 1979 holed up at the long-since demolished Vanilla Studios in Pimlico working on the follow-up to *Give 'Em Enough Rope*. Vanilla was a cramped low-ceilinged, rectangular windowless womb, but was possessed of a six-inch platform running down one wall and across the far end that could serve as a stage. Stung by the unfair criticisms levelled at *Give 'Em Enough Rope*, The Clash remained determined to make the music they wanted to make and not what they felt they had to deliver. "By the third album we were still learning, still developing and we developed our musical style," Mick Jones reflected. "There was a point where punk was getting narrower and narrower in terms of what it could achieve and where it could go. It was like painting itself into a corner and we wanted to do anything and everything. We thought you could make any kind of music."

Sandy Pearlman had proclaimed Topper a "human drum machine" owing to his unerring ability to play any style or mode without dropping a beat. Topper's dexterity, coupled with Mick's unerring knack for finding a melody, allowed The Clash to experiment with any musical genre that took their fancy. Having shaken off the shackles of their self-imposed restraints, the songs were coming thick and fast. "I don't think the first American tour was the inspiration for *London Calling*, Jones continued. "A few of the songs on the second album had talked about that but I think by this time the lyrics were actually the spur to start doing different kinds of music."

The Clash were scheduled to headline the second of two Rock Against Racism-orchestrated benefit shows over consecutive evenings at the Rainbow in Finsbury Park on July 13/14. Itching to see how the new songs would go over with their fans, they decided to book a couple of low-key shows at the Notre Dame Hall the week before the Rainbow date. Both shows sold out within hours of word hitting the street, the new material largely being greeted as enthusiastically as the old.

It was generally assumed within the Clash camp that Sandy Pearlman would be recalled to duty for the new album. Indeed, it was only the producer's taking himself out of the equation owing to the death of his father that the band were forced to look elsewhere. CBS had a list of seasoned producers at their disposal, so the news that Strummer was out trawling the darkest recesses of Soho in search of Guy Stevens would have surely had everyone at Soho Square reaching for the smelling salts. A compromise would soon be reached, however, whereby The Clash could have their man on the proviso that CBS could nominate a third party capable of grabbing the tiller should the mercurial Stevens stray off course. The "third party" CBS called upon was Bill Price, whom The Clash were already familiar with from the *Cost of Living* EP sessions back in January. Price's appointment surprisingly didn't get everyone's vote, however. Strummer was supposedly keen to record the new album on two Teac machines at Vanilla to reduce studio costs and in turn, keep the album's retail price at a minimum. On this occasion, however, he was outvoted and The Clash block-booked Wessex's Studio One for a calendar month.

After several months of seemingly aimless meandering in the wake of Bernard Rhodes's dismissal, The Clash appeared to have their career firmly back on track. They'd written enough new material for two albums and Epic were keen to get them over to America at the earliest opportunity to promote the US-friendly version of *The Clash*. Another unexpected boon came with their being approached with a last-minute, cash-in-hand support slot at the Ruisrock Festival in Turku, Finland; the £7,500 fee going a long way to easing any immediate personal financial worries they may have had.

The Clash opted for Stevens because they believed he was still imbued with that indefinable talent for recognising a hit record when he heard one. Stevens's unorthodox approach to producing has since become part of the *London Calling* legend. The first hint that he had scant regard for normal recording procedures came with his insisting The Clash's cover of Vince Taylor's 'Brand New Cadillac' was a wrap after a single take – regardless of it speeding up towards the end.

Further mad-cap behaviour came with his wrestling Bill Price to the floor over a fader, pouring a bottle of wine into the studio's prized Bösendorfer Grand piano to improve the sound. He also lay prostrate in front of a visiting Maurice Oberstein's Rolls Royce, refusing to get up until Obie had declared the album to be "magnificent". On another occasion, he had the cab driver charged with delivering him to the studio sit in on the sessions with his meter running.

Diversifying into different musical genres had worked well enough at Vanilla, but it soon became obvious that some of the new songs would require a broader format than guitar, bass, and drums. With The Clash now signed to Blackhill Enterprises, it was easy enough for them to call upon their new PR guru, Kosmo Vinyl (born Mark Dunk), to call upon Ian Dury and the Blockheads' organ player Mickey Gallagher seeing as both bands were signed to Blackhill. Vinyl's previously working for Stiff also allowed him to call upon Graham Parker and The Rumour's brass section – credited as the "Irish horns" on *London Calling* – to further flesh out the sound.

Bringing in outside help meant The Clash would overrun their allotted time at Wessex. Working to their usual six-week turnaround, CBS had been aiming for a mid-October release date. To have the album in the shops by that juncture, the label needed the finished album in the can by the end of August at the latest. The Clash, however, were on a roll and had little interest in working to corporate mandates. In keeping with Strummer's *Melody Maker* proclamation that "there will be no six-quid Clash LP ever!", the band, first of all, got CBS to agree to release the album at £5 (the lowest UK price category for a single album at that time), and then inveigled the label into including a free two-track seven-inch single, which was subsequently augmented to a four-track 12" EP. The wheedling wasn't finished there, however. With CBS having conceded that a 33rpm twelve-inch cost no more to manufacture than a 45rpm four-track 12" EP, The Clash hoodwinked the label into giving them what they'd wanted all along – a double album retailing for the same price as a single. The Clash had scored a value-for-money victory for their fans, but the sting in the tail came with CBS insisting the proposed double album counted as a single album.

While Bill Price busied himself with mixing the tracks slated for *London Calling*, The Clash flew out to California for the Tribal Stomp II Festival before commencing their 23-date Take the Fifth Tour' in

Saint Paul, Minnesota, four days later. The tour was by far The Clash's biggest live undertaking, yet despite the ever-present lack of funds, the band insisted on a bigger entourage. Joe, Paul and Topper also brought along their respective lady friends. Having recently split from Viv Albertine for good, Mick invited Rory Johnston along to serve as his personal tour manager. The rest of the group saw Johnston's inclusion as yet another show of their guitarist's increasing diva-esque behaviour – especially seeing as he hadn't thought to discuss the matter beforehand. The *NME*'s resident cartoonist, Ray Lowry (who'd befriended The Clash after seeing them at the Electric Circus in Manchester on the Anarchy Tour), and photographer Pennie Smith would be covering the tour for the paper.

"Taking the Fifth" is the colloquial term for when an American citizen invokes the Fifth Amendment of the US Constitution which protects against abuse of government authority in a legal procedure, but The Clash's use of the axiom could well have applied to their recruiting Mickey Gallagher as a temporary fifth member. Gallagher had been thinking of taking the wife and kids on holiday when Strummer called him out of the blue on the eve of the tour. Gallagher explained his predicament and was told to bring the wife and kids with him.

The Tribal Stomp II Festival was the brainchild of Chet Helms, a charismatic Bay Area music promoter who'd made his name promoting a wide range of artists in San Francisco during the mid-to-late-sixties. Helms had also managed Big Brother and Holding Company and was largely responsible for turning the psychedelic rock outfit's mixed fortunes around by bringing in the then-unknown Janis Joplin. Helms was hoping the festival would recreate the mystique of the legendary Monterey International Pop Festival of June 1967. Despite repeated assurances the festival would be a resounding success, Helms's aspirations weren't quite live up to everyone else's expectations as only 500 of the 12,000 tickets available had been sold. The Clash were included in the festival's opening afternoon bill along with Soul Syndicate, the Chambers Brothers and Joe Ely, whom the band had befriended the previous summer while he was in London promoting his second album, *Honky Tonk Masquerade*. Somewhat surprisingly, given The Clash had spent the last six weeks or so playing and listening to the songs intended for *London Calling*, the only one to

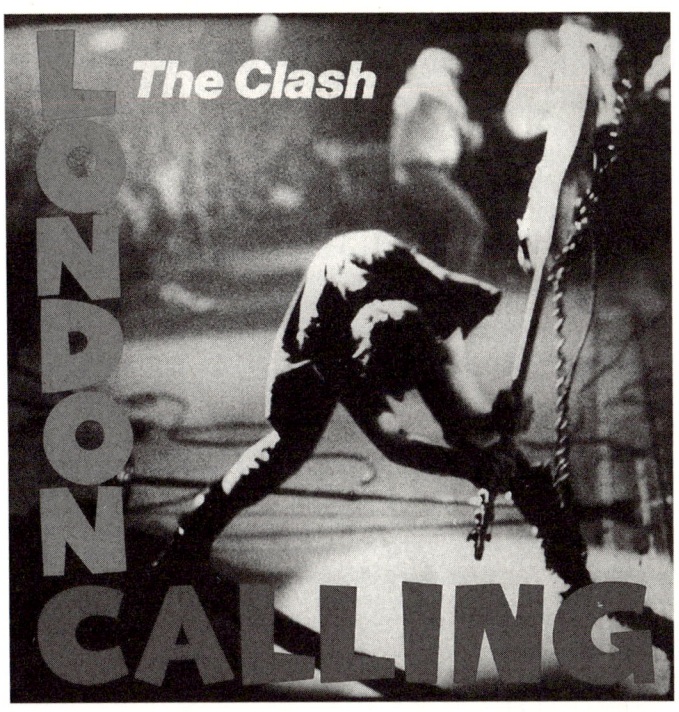

The cover image by Pennie Smith was inducted into the Rock 'n' Roll
Hall of Fame as the ultimate rock 'n' roll rock picture

feature during their performance was the title track.

Aside from his single-handedly bringing Rory Johnston onto the
tour, Mick Jones distanced himself further from the rest of The Clash
by rejecting the tour backdrop that Simonon had conceived back in
London. The backdrop - depicting WWII American B52 bombers
raining their cargo of death down on Topper's kit – had set The
Clash back £1,500. Ray Lowry was charged with finding a suitable
replacement and was to spend a frustratingly fruitless couple of days
dashing hither and thither about Manhattan with a huge canvas
under his arm. His efforts were to prove in vain, however, for as
soon as he mentioned which band the backdrop was intended for,
the artist invariably bumped up the price. As a result, the multi-flag
backdrop that was first unfurled at the Harlesden Roxy shows the
previous October was hurriedly flown over and pressed into service.

The Clash's mood wasn't improved when the tour rolled into Chicago two days to discover Epic hadn't as yet stumped up the $20,000 Blackhill had requested the label contribute towards the tour. What had initially seemed an administrative oversight was soon seen for what it was when CBS suggested they be allowed to release the US version of *The Clash* in the UK and advance them money from the royalties they could expect to earn to finance the tour. The Clash refused point-blank, and it was only when they threatened to pull the tour that CBS relented.

The tour saw Clash would return to New York's Palladium for two sold-out shows over consecutive evenings (September 20/21). Although Pete Townshend has the honour of the first accredited onstage guitar-smash – trashing his Rickenbacker at the Railway Hotel back in September 1964 – its Pennie Smith's snap-photo of Paul Simonon slamming his Fender Precession bass into the Palladium stage at the second Palladium show that would subsequently be inducted into the Rock and Roll Hall of Fame as the "ultimate rock 'n' roll rock photo".

Smith had no idea what was going on, of course, but sensing Simonon's onstage frustrations she focused her lens on him "I remember thinking something was wrong, realising Paul was going to crack - and waited," she explained. "The shot is out of focus because I ducked - he was closer than it looks"

Before The Clash left for America, Kosmo Vinyl had entered into negotiations with the *NME* to look at repeating the 'Capital Radio' flexi-disc single idea that had proved so successful with *The Clash*. By the time an agreement was reached, The Clash had just 24 hours to come up with a new song that didn't appear on *London Calling*. It was a big ask in anyone's book – especially as The Clash were busy overseeing the mixing at Wessex. Mick Jones returned the following afternoon, however, with both the tune and finished lyric to a funky, soul-pop ode to Viv Albertine called 'Train in Vain'.

"Mick used to cry and cry about Viv," Johnny Green revealed. "She was quite hard on him. He rarely behaved like that with other women. He played the rock star normally, but with Viv, no. It's the only time I've ever seen him like that. She broke his heart. He was in love with her."

Cut had hit the record shops whilst The Clash were in America. The Slits' debut album contains the track, 'Ping Pong Affair', with a lyric centring around a female protagonist who leaves her jilted lover sulking in his room while she heads off down Ladbroke Grove to have some fun. Though careful not to mention Mick Jones by name, it's obvious as to who the song is about. A far more personal revelation on Albertine's part came via the publication of her 2014 award-winning autobiography, *Clothes, Clothes, Clothes, Music, Music, Music, Boys, Boys, Boys*, in which she confesses to having aborted Mick's unborn child sometime during 1978.

Bill Price would always maintain that the tune to 'Train In Vain' – if only as a backing-track – was laid down at Wessex before The Clash embarked on the Take the Fifth Tour. Even if this were true, it's still an exceptional effort on Mick's part as 'Train in Vain' is one of the standout tracks in The Clash canon. Vinyl's flexi-disc strategy would come to nought, however, as the *NME's parent company, IPC, rejected the idea out of hand. No one would have pointed a finger at The Clash had they saved 'Train in Vain' for a later day. However, as the initial idea had been to give the fans a freebie, the decision was made to tag "Train in Vain" as an uncredited track at the end of side four of London Calling.*

— Degenerate The Faithfull

"Everything I do, writing, touring, travelling, it all comes from the punk and hardcore attitudes, from the expression -from being open to try things but relying on yourself, taking what you have into battle and making of it what you will, hoping you can figure it out as you go. Make some sense of it."

Henry Rollins

As 1980 and a new decade dawned, punk was fast becoming a parody of itself – helped in no small part by Kenny Everett's ageing punk character, "Sid Snot". When new exciting bands such as U2, Echo and the Bunnymen, Teardrop Explodes and The Smiths – all of whom had been influenced by punk one way or another – broke through to achieve chart success, punk itself was by and large regarded as passé. Indeed, punk wouldn't become "fashionable" again until 1986 and the tenth-anniversary festivals such as the one at Manchester's GMEX arena. Which Bill Grundy even deigned to attend, speaking openly about the fateful three minutes that had irrevocably altered the British musical landscape while sending his career into a tailspin. In the interim, however, we had Oi! (the term being coined by *Sounds'* Garry Bushell, who in turn lifted it the garbled "Oi!" Cockney Rejects' frontman, Stinky Turner [born Jeffrey Geggus a.k.a. Jeff Turner] used to introduce songs at the band's live shows.) Other

Opposite: Henry Rollins *Gets In The Van* with Black Flag

primary exponents of Oi! were Cock Sparrer, The Business, The 4-Skins, Peter and The Test-Tube Babies and The Exploited. Sham 69 would also find themselves associated with Oi! owing to the skinhead elements attending their shows.

Skinhead, of course, was a subculture of its own, having originated among the working-class youth of mid-sixties London before expanding to other parts of the UK. They incorporated elements of mod and Jamaican rude boy fashion. A noticeable overlap existed between skinhead, mod and rude boy subcultures – all three openly interacting and socialising with each other. The unnerving rise of the National Front from February 1976 onwards – following Martin Tyndall's restoration as party leader – gave rise to a "second wave" in skinhead culture. Unlike their predecessors, however, these skinheads eschewed anything and everything connected with Jamaican culture. In August 1977, some 500 NF members – many of whom were skinheads - attempted to march from New Cross to Lewisham in southeast London in protest of the then Labour government's agreement to allow Malawian Asians into the UK. The Anti-Nazi League and other left-wing organisations rallied to thwart the rally. This resulted in violent clashes between the two factions and the police. The media would dub this the "Battle of Lewisham" owing to it being the first occasion that riot shields were used on mainland Britain.

Not all skinheads promulgated violence, of course, but the more extreme elements began targeting punk shows. Sham 69 would suffer more than most. Speaking with *www.punk77.co.uk*, Jimmy Pursey reflected about how this calamity came about. "Somebody in the audience shouted out at one of the gigs at the Roxy, 'Skinheads are back', to which me, being a little skinhead from 1967 where it lasted for about six months, and if you didn't go to fuckin' school with a shaven head you would get the crap kicked out of you and which 90 per cent of kids at that particular time had, you would then understand that someone shouting that out in 1977 would bring a sarcastic reaction from me, as normally things like that do. As 'Yeah mate, yeah sure they are . . . blah, blah, blah', to which someone took it upon them to say that I was saying 'Yeah, they are back aren't they.'"

"What actually happened was at an early gig when we were drawing a crowd of about five, an old friend of Jimmy's who had been an original skinhead the first time around was in the crowd,"

Dave Parsons added. "Jimmy spotted him and said (tongue in cheek), 'Skinheads are back.' The next time we played, the place was packed with people queuing to get in, all with freshly cropped heads."

"Why did Sham experience such a meteoric rise?" Bushell wrote in the October 28, 1978 issue of *Sounds*. "Sham are a working-class and fitting in neatly with working-class teenage gang mentality. Skinheads were a working-class phenomenon, encompassing two main types of kids. The ex-punk disillusioned with the middle-class element of punk and the rip off fashion scene side, and kids who at other times might have stayed happy with football and gang fights."

With more and more of their shows being disrupted by violence, Sham 69 had openly aligned themselves to the Rock Against Racism movement. "I thought I could get them thinking the same way I was thinking," Pursey told *Sounds*. "When they started those Nazi salutes I thought I could bicker them down about it. They know exactly what I'm about. In the early days, the National Front sent someone to see whether we'd work for them and I said 'You must be fucking joking. NO WAY!'. So when the skins start all that I say 'What are you doing? You want to do that. Why come here and do that? You know I don't believe so why do it? I don't beat around the bush. I'm a figurehead and they know I'm having a go at them . . . I think I'm winning if I can get someone aged sixteen just thinking about politics so they're not just going down the road and voting for the National Front . . . and it's hard when you're out on stage to put it across like that.

"I feel that we're the only band trying to do something and everybody else is shitting on the kids around us. When I last saw the Clash, Joe Strummer said to me, 'Y'know, we're not really a punk band anymore, we're trying to get away from that type of thing.' That's what gives 'em their bread and butter! It gives me my bread and butter and I'm not ever gonna deny I'm in a punk band. We're in a punk band that's it. If the band's gonna die, it's gonna die as a punk band, not as a fuckin' pop group."

It's said the prevalent ideology of Oi! was a working-class rebellion owing to the lyrical topics centring around unemployment, police harassment, government oppression (Margaret Thatcher's recently elected Tories). "Oi! played an important symbolic role in the politicization of the skinhead subculture," says Timothy S. Brown in *Subcultures, Pop Music and Politics: Skinheads and "Nazi Rock" in England and Germany*. "By providing, for the first time, a musical focus for skinhead identity that was "white" – that is, that had nothing to do with the West Indian immigrant presence and little obvious connection with black musical roots - Oi! provided a musical focus for new visions of skinhead identity [and] a point of entry for a new brand of right-wing rock music."

Bushell, as was his wont, tried arguing down the overtly right-wing elements that had infiltrated Oi!: "[They were] totally distinct from us. We had no overlap other than a mutual dislike." Mutual dislike or no, the writing was on the wall – quite literally as it was to prove. A show featuring The Business, The 4-Skins and The Last Resort at the Hambrough Tavern in Southall on July 4, 1981, erupted into five hours of rioting. 120 people were injured in the rioting and the venue was burnt to the ground. In the run-up to the show, the surrounding area was daubed with NF slogans, while local Asian residents were also targeted. In response, local Asian youths set the tavern alight with homemade Molotov cocktails.

In the aftermath of the riot, many Oi! bands openly condemned racism and fascism, but said condemnations were largely met with cynicism; the flames already having been fanned with the release of the *Strength Thru Oi!* compilation album a couple of months earlier. Not only was the title a blatant play on the Nazis' "Strength Through Joy" slogan, but the front cover featured British Movement activist Nicky Crane, who was currently serving a four-year sentence for racist violence.

Bushell, who compiled the album for Decca Records, disingenuously insisted the title was a pun on The Skids' September 1980 album, *Strength Through Joy*, and that he'd been unaware of the Nazi connotations. He would also try denying knowing that it was Crane adorning the album's cover – at least until a *Daily Mail* expose later in the year.

Though Oi! lost momentum in the UK, the movement found fertile ground elsewhere – most notably in the US where it mirrored the hardcore Orange County punk scene of the late-Seventies with bands such as The Radicals, U.S. Chaos, Iron Cross, and Agnostic Front.

Post-punk, or "new musick" as it's also known, has been described as being more a musically experimental form of punk, yet no less angry or political. Though imbued with punk's DIY spirit, emerging bands such as The Pop Group, Cabaret Voltaire, Gang of Four, Wire,

Birthday Party and Manicured Noise saw little point in replicating the Pistols, Clash or Damned and instead forged into more experimental territory, often taking cues from Bowie (notably the "Berlin Trilogy" albums: *Low, Heroes* and *Lodger*), disco, dub and Krautrock. Indeed, it could be argued post-punk served as the precursor to the alternative rock scene of the mid-to-late-eighties.

PiL's 1981 album, *The Flowers of Romance* (by which time Jeannette Lee had replaced Jah Wobble), saw Lydon and Levene push against the boundaries of conventional rock with the heavy use of percussion and various tape and processing effects. In stark contrast to the axis of throbbing bass and guitar slashings of *Metal Box*, *The Flowers of Romance* is centralised around haphazard percussion – although Atkins's razor-sharp drumming features on three tracks - and Lydon's typically lecturing vocals. Becoming increasingly disenchanted with the guitar, Levene's increasing infatuation with synthesizers was also at a crescendo around this time.

The album brought praise from an eclectic mix of admirers. Kurt Cobain would go so far as to include *The Flowers of Romance* in his all-time favourite 50 albums, while Phil Collins praised its strident sound. PiL's efforts were somewhat less appreciated by Virgin, however; the label believing PiL had delivered the least commercial record ever made.

Virgin's disillusionment with *The Flowers of Romance* saw them contemplate re-releasing "Public Image" in an attempt to generate interest in the new album. Virgin's continuing reticence regarding the album's commerciality would result in a five-month delay in getting it out into the shops. Even then, only pressing 30,000 copies. "They (Virgin) have the finance but no ideas," Lydon bemoaned to the *NME*, '[while] we have the ideas but no finance. That's where the arguments begin and end."

"The way round [it] is to make PiL the Company but it's a company that doesn't exist because you need a massive cash injection to give it a boost," Levene added. "We need people to invest in us on a contract basis, which Virgin are doing in terms of music in Britain, as are Nippon Columbia in Japan and Warners in America. We've suggested our ideas to all three companies, and all the problems that amounted were the same: 'We can't do that. It won't sell. There's no market for this, there's no market for that.' The market probably won't exist for another seven years and they're waiting until the market exists instead of inventing one."

Virgin's misguided obstinacy towards *The Flowers of Romance* would soon be exposed with the album reaching #11 on the UK chart. The single of the same name – aided by an appearance on *Top of the Pops* - peaked at #24.

The Pop Group, whose founding line-up included future PiL drummer Bruce Smith, had formed in Bristol in 1977. They released just two albums - *Y* (April 1979) and *For How Much Longer Do We Tolerate Mass Murder?* (March 1980) – before splitting in 1981, but with their overt fusion of funk, free jazz they are viewed as post-punk pioneers.

Gang of Four's December 1978 debut single, 'Damaged Goods' was released on the Edinburgh-based independent Fast Product label would top the UK Indie Chart – largely thanks to the auspices of John Peel, which resulted in the band subsequently delivering two Radio One radio sessions. Such was the interest both at home and abroad that EMI snapped them up.

Their debut album, *Entertainment!*, was released in October 1979. It would only reach #46 on the UK chart but has since come to be regarded as a classic of the post-punk genre. The lead single, "At Home He's a Tourist" failed to crack the Top 40 yet Gang of Four were nonetheless invited to appear on *Top of the Pops*. Their refusal to replace the risqué "rubbers" with "rubbish" in the lyric led to their being replaced on the show and a BBC ban. The Beeb would also take offence to Gang of Four's follow-up single, 'I Love a Man in a Uniform', would also receive a BBC censor owing to its being released at the height of the Falklands War in May 1982.

Reflecting on 'At Home He's a Tourist' during a September 2009 interview with *Clash* magazine to commemorate the thirtieth anniversary of the release of *Entertainment!*, Gang Of Four's frontman, Jon King said: "Sometimes you get lucky and a line comes that makes everything easy. Suddenly getting the answer to a question when you turn off and think about something else. Thrownness - if that's a word at all – was something we puzzled over. Why, if everything like it is, do so many things seem ersatz, phoney. But it's not phoney if you know it's phoney. So, with this present from nowhere, (guitarist Andy) Gill was inspired and created the perfect existential squawl, different every time it's played.

"This is what happened that afternoon in a single take. No

assemblage, pro-tools confection, just the strings being hit and screaming in pain as they're bashed and cajoled into a beautiful anti-solo that is all about the now and no about the maybe. We thought this song was a mutant disco thing, at a time when it was not done to like dance music when funk and rock had to be kept in separate rooms for fear of miscegenation. But the genie was out of the box now!"

Goth rockers, Bauhaus, fronted by the androgynous Pete Murphy, brought a hard-edged collage of cool glam to the early-eighties post-new wave wasteland, incorporating a heady cocktail of angular rhythms over electro, funk and avant-metal. But as dark and brooding the atmosphere was at Bauhaus shows owing to a large number of their devotees adopting a funereal dress sense, many others were still sporting Pistols, Clash and Buzzcocks button badges.

Formed in Northampton in late-1978, Bauhaus (originally called Bauhaus 1919 in homage to the inaugural operating year of the German art school Bauhaus), released their debut single, "Bela Lugosi's Dead" via Small Wonder Records in August 1979 – despite the song being some nine minutes in length. John Peel played the song incessantly on his evening show and resulted in the band being invited into the studio. Bauhaus subsequently signed with 4AD, releasing 'Dark Entries' in January 1980. Their much-anticipated debut album, *In the Flat Field*, would be hailed by the *NME* as "Gothick-Romantick pseudo-decadence" following its October 1980 release. The band signed off from 4AD with an eerie version of the Marc Bolan classic, 'Telegram Sam', before signing with Beggars Banquet Records, with whom they would enjoy a modicum of chart success with 'Kick in the Eye' and a cover of Bowie's 'Ziggy Stardust'.

Cabaret Voltaire had formed back in 1973 but their experimentation with sound creation and processing largely remained under the radar until the arrival of punk brought the Sheffield-based trio a more appreciative audience; their often sharing a bill with Joy Division.

They signed with Rough Trade in 1978 and would go on to release several highly-acclaimed albums, including Three Mantras, The Voice of America and Red Mecca. The *NME* were staunch supporters, going so far as to declare that Cabaret Voltaire "will turn out to be one of the most important new bands to achieve wider recognition this year. Wait and see."

Over the intervening decades, Cabaret Voltaire have been

acknowledged as one of the key instigators of the electronic music scene

Several acts that emerged from punk's first wave would make a successful crossover into the pop mainstream during the Eighties and beyond. Elvis Costello's *Armed Forces* album and lead single, 'Oliver's Army' both reached #2 on the respective UK charts in 1979. The Jam would benefit immensely from Jeffrey Munday's telling a "little white lie" at the Polydor pressing plant when 'Going Underground' went straight in at #1 on the chart in March 1980.

"There was great anticipation and a terrific buzz within the company surrounding The Jam," he says in *Shout to the Top*. "Like 'David Watts', we released ["Going Underground"] as a double A-side single with 'Dreams of Children' as the alternate. Polydor had 500 promo copies pressed with 'Underground' clearly marked as the A-side and I told the boys (The Jam) the factory had made an error but nothing could be done and we would do everything to get 'Dreams of Children' airplay. This was one of the few times I was dishonest with the band. It was a necessary deception as if you want to have a big hit you can't afford to split the airplay between two tracks. No matter how good 'Dreams' was, 'Underground' was *the* big hit record."

'Start!' would give The Jam their second consecutive #1 in August 1980, while the parent album, *Sound Effects*, narrowly missed out on the top spot, peaking at #2. The band would enjoy several more Top 10 hits and score two further no. 1s with 'Town Called Malice' and 'Beat Surrender' before Weller stunned the music world and fans alike in calling time on The Jam in December 1982.

1982 would prove the year The Clash finally enjoyed significant mainstream chart success on both sides of the Atlantic with the *Combat Rock* album peaking at #2 in the UK and #7 on the *Billboard* 200. Two of the album's attendant singles, 'Should I Stay or Should I Go' and 'Rock the Casbah', would help cement the band's standing in the US. Topper Headon, who single-handedly wrote "Rock the Casbah" was no longer in the band, his having been dismissed because of his spiralling heroin habit. His replacement in The Clash was Pete Howard, the 23-year-old, Bath-born drummer having beaten off fierce competition that included SLF's resident stickman, Steve Grantley.

Bernard Rhodes had been reinstated as the band's manager by the time of Headon's departure. Indeed, he insists he was largely responsible for turning around the band's fortunes. That is a matter of conjecture, of course, but he was instrumental in Mick Jones' sacking the following year. The Clash would soldier on with two relatively unknown guitarists – Nick Shepherd and Vince Taylor – resulting in the execrable album, *Cut the Crap*. By the time of the album's November 1985 release, however, The Clash were a band in name only.

"Should I Stay or Should I Go" would provide The Clash with a posthumous UK #1 in March 1991 following its featuring in a Levi jeans commercial. "It wasn't about anybody specific and it wasn't pre-empting my leaving The Clash," Jones revealed in the 1991 *Clash on Broadway* box set. "It was just a good rockin' song, our attempt at writing a classic. When we were just playing, that was the kind of thing we used to like to play." Jones would have the last laugh and further chart success with Big Audio Dynamite (BAD), which included Don Letts on keyboards.

Siouxsie and the Banshees' second album, *Join Hands*, was released in September 1979. The band were only several dates into a national tour in support of the album when drummer Kenny Morris and guitarist John McKay quit after an argument at an in-store signing in Aberdeen. The simmering tension between Siouxsie and Severin and Morris and McKay had been mounting for some time. Polydor had only sent a small number of copies of the new album – released that very day - to the Other Record Shop, forcing the band's management to sell the shop owner a couple of hundred promo copies to satisfy demand. Much to the shop owner's dismay, Morris and McKay began handing out copies for free. McKay also removed *Join Hands* from the shop's turntable and replaced it with The Slits' album, *Cut*. It was this that finally pushed Siouxsie and Severin over the edge; the latter reportedly physically attacking McKay. Somewhat ironically, it was The Slits' one-time drummer, Budgie (born Peter Clarke), who replaced McKay. As The Cure were supporting the Banshees, their frontman, Robert Smith, volunteered his services for the remainder of the tour. Morris's eventual replacement was John McGeoch, formerly of Magazine.

Join Hands peaked one place lower than *The Scream* on the UK chart but the Banshees third album, *Kaleidoscope* (released in August

1980), which saw the band experimenting synthesizers, sitars and drum machines, would reach #5. By the time of the Banshees' fourth album, *A Kiss in the Dreamhouse* (November 1982), Siouxsie and Budgie were doing plenty of kissing of their own. They also formed the side project, The Creatures, releasing their debut EP, *Wild Things*, in September 1981. The Banshees would go on to enjoy a successful career before splitting up in 1996 – coincidentally, the same year the Sex Pistols reunited against all the odds.

Rumours had been mounting about a possible Pistols reunion from the start of the year, but on June 18 the four founding Sex Pistols staged a press conference at the 100 Club where they unveiled plans for the Filthy Lucre World Tour, set to commence at the Messila Festival in Finland three days later. In *No Irish, No Blacks, No Dogs*, Lydon was adamant that there would never be a Pistols reunion as he was content to let sleeping dogs lie, but by 1996 PiL were floundering. Cook would subsequently reveal the band had mischievously approached McLaren offering him his old job back. McLaren had recently likened the reunion to that of "dray horses out for one last ride before being put out to pasture", yet surprisingly accepted. He was told to "fuck off".

Creation Records' head, Alan McGee, was so overawed by the Pistols' performance at the Shepherd's Bush Empire that he paid £20,000 to secure the back pages of several music magazines extolling their worth. The Pistols would come together again in early June 2002 to celebrate the twenty-fifth anniversary of the release of 'God Save the Queen' at the Crystal Palace National Sports Centre where they opened proceedings with Hawkwind's 'Silver Machine'. They also performed 'My Way' just as Sid had recorded it. Lydon would forget the words, leaving Matlock to finish the song much to the bemusement of the crowd. That same year they headlined the KROQ Inland Invasion. The festival was celebrating "25 Years of Punk rock', and also had The Damned and Buzzcocks on the bill.

During the summer of 2003, the arthritic anarchists embarked on a US tour, and November 2007 – a year on from telling the Rock 'N' Roll Hall of Fame where they could shove their induction - they played five nights at the Brixton Academy, two more at Manchester's GMEX Centre and the Glasgow SECC in celebration of the thirtieth anniversary of *Never Mind the Bollocks*. The following year saw them undertake the Combine Harvester Festival Tour 2008, which included the Isle of Wight Festival. Following on from their festival frolics the Pistols played the Hammersmith Apollo in early September 2008.

A year on from the Sex Pistols' Filthy Lucre reunion, Virgin released John Lydon's debut solo album, *Psycho's Path*. Despite Lydon's dexterity in playing an array of instruments on the album, Psycho's Path would fail to excite either the critics or Lydon's fan base and as a result, quickly disappeared without trace. Lydon ultimately laid the blame for this squarely at Virgin's door saying how he'd misguidedly agreed to the label's proposition to put the album on hold so they could concentrate on maximising the momentum surrounding the reconstituted Sex Pistols in return for their setting aside a larger promotional budget for *Psycho's Path* than they might otherwise have done.

It appeared that Lydon had set himself up for another mauling at the hands of the UK media when it was announced in January 2004 that he'd agreed to appear in the third series of ITV's *I'm A Celebrity . . . Get Me Out Of Here!*. However, his total lack of guile, coupled with a genuine fascination for all things nature, endeared him to the armchair millions watching at home – this, in spite of his calling the TV audience "fucking cunts!" for not voting him off. Indeed, there's every chance Lydon would have been proclaimed "King of the Jungle" had he not walked out midway through the series. His appearing on *I'm A Celebrity . . .* would, however, lead to his being invited to present *John Lydon's Megabugs* on the Discovery Channel. Other wildlife escapades included his going in search of gorillas in Central Africa and swimming with Great White Sharks in the waters off South Africa.

In the autumn of 2008, Lydon sent the naysayers and finger-waggers that had openly criticised him for anything he did away from either PiL or the Pistols into overdrive when it was announced that he was to become the 'face' of Country Life butter in Dairy Crest's latest TV advertising campaign. But once again the British public warmed to Lydon's eccentric style, and sales of Country Life reportedly shot up a whopping 85 per cent in the wake of the first ad (broadcast Wednesday, October 1, 2008). Aside from bolstering British industry, the fee Lydon pocketed meant he had the cash to splash when LA-based promoters Live Nation sounded him out the following summer about the possibility of his reconstituting Public Image Limited for some live shows.

Reactivating PiL, of course, had never been far from Lydon's thoughts, but with Virgin having shown neither the interest nor inclination to assist him in his ambitions it had seemed as though the unrealized dream would tease him like an itch he couldn't scratch. It's not as if he didn't have the money, but his self-esteem would have taken a bruising had he been forced to put his hand in his pocket to put a new line-up together. The Country Life cash enabled him to book a rehearsal room, as well as hire a road crew.

As a result of the negotiations with Live Nation, three dates were tentatively lined up for December 2009 at the Brixton Academy. This was subsequently expanded to a mini UK tour – billed as ALiFE 2009 - taking in shows in Birmingham, Leeds, Glasgow, Manchester and concluding with a show at the Brixton Academy. Lydon had already pencilled in Lu Edmonds and Bruce Smith for the new PiL, and although bringing in a fellow founding member hadn't been a Live Nation prerequisite, he'd approached Jah Wobble.

Wobble's solo career had hit the skids in the mid-eighties, largely, it has to be said, because of his fondness for the bottle. However, with his blurry Bacchanalian past behind him, the newly-sober Wobble reformed the Invaders of the Heart and saw his career take a sudden yet deserved upturn in fortunes. According to sources close to Lydon, Wobble was said to have been delighted at being approached; his only stipulation being that he couldn't work with Levene. This wasn't a problem as far as Lydon was concerned as he'd long-since washed his hands of Levene. Negotiations would ultimately break down, however, when the subject of Wobble's wages was broached. "His (Wobble's) manager had extra-special ideas about Wobble's big bad self and how important he was to the whole thing, and that he should get more than everybody else," said Lydon at the time.

Lydon's "big bad self" believed Wobble should have been sympathetic to his having to work at putting a PiL line-up together ing on a finite budget. Three decades had passed since Wobble had quit PiL, and the memories of Lydon's shoebox-under-the-bed accounting at Gunter Grove were still fresh in the memory. The wages Wobble was seeking for returning to his former post (which he disclosed during a conversation with John Robb at the 2014 Louder Than

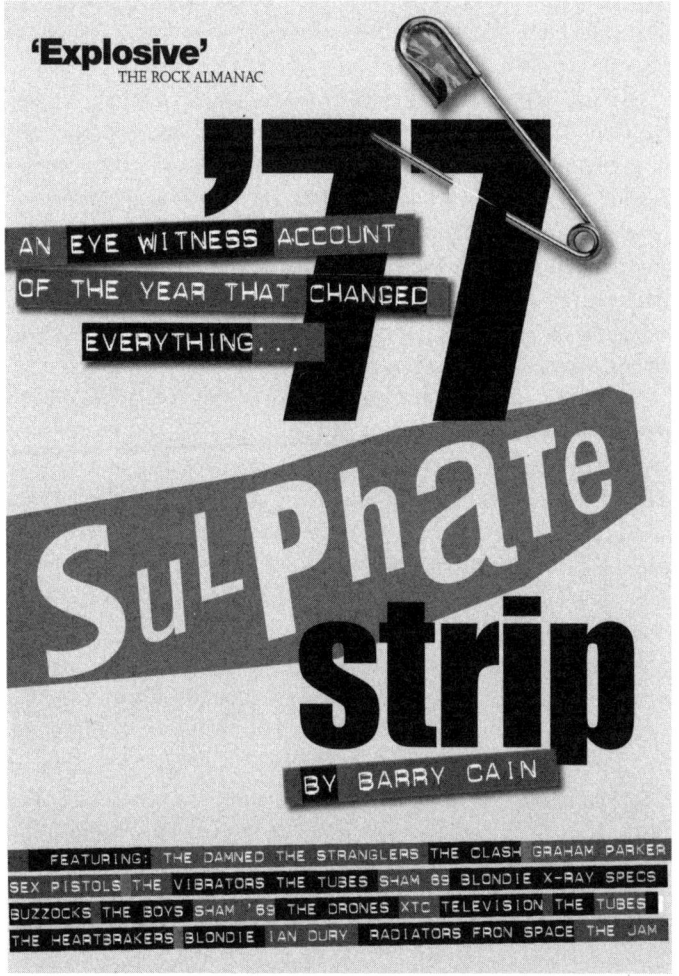

'Explosive'
THE ROCK ALMANAC

AN EYE WITNESS ACCOUNT
OF THE YEAR THAT CHANGED
EVERYTHING...

'77

SuLPhaTe
strip

BY BARRY CAIN

FEATURING: THE DAMNED THE STRANGLERS THE CLASH GRAHAM PARKER
SEX PISTOLS THE VIBRATORS THE TUBES SHAM 69 BLONDIE X-RAY SPECS
BUZZOCKS THE BOYS SHAM '69 THE DRONES XTC TELEVISION THE TUBES
THE HEARTBRAKERS BLONDIE IAN DURY RADIATORS FROM SPACE THE JAM

Barry Cain's book *77 Sulphate Strip* covers all the major bands
and captures the spirit of the year 'that changed everything'

Words Festival in Manchester) were well within reason – especially
as his being a founder member of PiL would have surely proved an
added draw when the tickets went on sale.

With Wobble now a no-go and Allan Dias still on Lydon's shit-
list owing to his jumping ship following a PiL's show at Alton
Towers in July 1992, Lydon approached the Liverpool-born multi-

instrumentalist, Scott Firth; the kicker coming with Firth's being to play the double bass.

Lydon leaked the news about PiL and the new tour in an interview with The *Sun* in early September 2009. By then, however, rumours were abounding on social media owing to the sudden appearance of the holding page for an official PiL website, *www.pilofficial.com*, bearing the readily-identifiable PiL logo, coupled with the tantalizing communiqué: "I could be right. I could be wrong. It's coming some time maybe . . ."

PiL's 2009 reformation shows wouldn't just be marking the 30th Anniversary of the release of *Metal Box*, but rather to showcase the band's entire career. On the day the tickets went on sale the demand was such that a second Brixton Academy show had been added for December 22. This, however, would subsequently be amended to two shows at the Electric Ballroom in Camden Town. "I've always loved doing this more than the Pistols," Lydon told the *NME* in the run-up to the shows. "PiL is from the head - deeper, darker, more fun, and more angst. I'm only doing a few gigs with this. That's it. This is an act of pure joy . . ."

A decade on and the "act of pure joy" shows little sign of diminishing as PiL have recorded two new studio albums – *This is PiL* (2012) and *What the World Needs Now* (2015) – and toured the US, Europe and beyond several times over. 2018 saw the release of *The Public Image Is Rotten* documentary, in conjunction with *The Public Image is Rotten - Songs from the Heart*, a CD/DVD compilation box set celebrating PiL's fortieth anniversary.

The Police had enjoyed chart success both in the UK and America with their debut single, 'Roxanne' following the single's re-release in April 1979. The band's debut album, *Outlandos d'Amour*, would reach the UK Top 10 despite receiving mixed reviews. The band's follow-up album, *Reggatta de Blanc*, was to prove the first of four consecutive UK No. 1 albums, spawning two No. 1 singles in the process: 'Message in a Bottle' and 'Walking on the Moon'. Further UK hits included the Grammy Award-winning 'Don't Stand So Close to Me' 'De Do Do Do, De Da Da Da' (both lifted from *Zenyatta Mondatta*).

After touring the *Ghost in the Machine* album in 1982, The Police took a sabbatical, with Sting, Andy Summers and Stuart Copland all pursuing outside projects. Taking a year out would have an adverse effect, however, as when the trio reconvened to record the multi-million-selling transatlantic smash, *Synchronicity*, (which featured the Ivor Novello Award-winning 'Every Breath You Take' and 'Wrapped Around Your Finger') they were barely speaking and reportedly recorded their parts in separate rooms.

The Police would go into hiatus again in early 1984 to allow Sting to record his debut solo album, *The Dream of the Blue Turtles*. The idea being that they would reconvene again once Sting had finished touring his solo debut to record a sixth studio album, but Sting was for going solo – despite The Police being proclaimed the "biggest band in the world" at this point. By the time the appropriately-titled 'Don't Stand So Close to Me '86' was released in October 1986, The Police had effectively gone their separate ways.

Following the release of *Dirk Wears White Sox*, Adam Ant approached Malcolm McLaren to act as the band's manager. McLaren readily agreed, only to coax the Ants - guitarist Matthew Ashman, bassist Leigh Gorman (who'd recently replaced Andy Warren and drummer Dave Barbarossa – to defect and form Bow Wow Wow with the then 13-year-old Annabella Lwin. Adam remained undaunted, however, and called upon his friend Marco Pirroni to assist in re-recording 'Cartrouble Pt. 2' – one of the tracks from *Dirk Wears White Sox* – to fulfil the Ants' contractual obligations for the Do It label (with Jon Moss helping out on drums). The truncated 'Cartrouble' was duly released by Do It in March 1980 and reached #1 on the UK Independent Singles Chart. Ant and Perroni then brought in Kevin Mooney on bass along with drummers Terry Lee Miall and Chris Hughes (a.k.a. Merrick) to give the Ants the Burundi-beat sound for which they would become known for and which McLaren had suggested during his brief tenure as manager.

Having recorded a new Ant/Perroni composition, 'Kings of the Wild Frontier' to tempt prospective record companies into signing the band, the revamped Ants embarked on the 'Ants Invasion' UK tour courtesy of a £500 advance from one-time X-Ray Spex manager Falcon Stuart. Adam had undergone a makeover, hiring the light cavalry jacket worn by David Hemmings in the 1968 film *The Charge of the Light Brigade*, along with black leather trousers and boots. He also painted a Comanche-style white stripe across the bridge of his nose, with braids and feathers in his hair.

Out of the several record companies that showed interest in the demo, the Ants went with CBS. While the Ants were in the studio recording their first CBS album, *Kings of the Wild Frontier*, the label rush-released 'Kings of the Wild Frontier' as the band's debut offering in July 1980. The single would stall at #48 on the UK chart, but owing to the subsequent success of further singles '"Dog Eat Dog' (#4; October 1980) and '"Antmusic' (#2; January 1981), CBS re-released 'Kings of the Wild Frontier' in March 1981. This time around the single reached #2. The parent album would go one better in claiming the top slot on the UK album chart in January 1981. ('Antmusic' and 'Kings of the Wild Frontier' surely only being denied the top spot by John Lennon's 'Imagine' following the ex-Beatle's murder on December 8, 1980.) The Ants' new-found success saw both Decca and Do It Records reissue the band's previous recordings. As a result, 'Young Parisians' reached #9 following its release in December 1980, while Dirk Wears White Sox would reach #16 the following February. 'Zerox' and 'Cartrouble' also charted in February 1981, peaking at #33 and #45 respectively.

Adam had been dating Jordan for some time but unbeknown to him she'd started seeing Mooney on the side. When Adam found out he was understandably less-than-pleased. Mooney was summarily sacked and replaced by Gary Tibbs. When Jordan and Mooney married soon thereafter, Vivienne Westwood's wedding present to Jordan came in the form of a P45 – this after some seven years of faithful service.

Jordan says Mooney wasn't bothered about being kicked out of the Ants as he – as did Jordan herself – believed Adam had made a mistake in continuing with the teen market. The band's fans were of a different opinion, however, with more and more of them emulating Adam's warpaint look at shows. Indeed, the band's popularity was such that their next single, 'Stand and Deliver' would debut at #1 in April 1981.

'Prince Charming', the second single from the album of the same name, would also Reach #1 and remain there for four consecutive weeks, while 'Ant Rap' also reached the UK Top 3 in January 1982. The album itself would narrowly miss out on the top slot following its release in November 1981.

'Ant Rap' was still on the UK when Adam and the Ants won the BRIT Award for Best Album for *Kings of the Wild Frontier*. By this juncture, some of the Ants were beginning to believe themselves as important as Adam. Speaking with the author in 2005, Perroni said that the others went so far as to hire their own management. "It was ludicrous. They'd had a taste of the five-star lifestyle and believed it was going to go on for some time to come. But they didn't know Adam as I did. He was always thinking three steps ahead and already plotting a solo career. I didn't mind too much as I was done with touring by that point. And I knew I'd be staying on as Adam's songwriting partner if nothing else."

Sure enough, Adam disbanded the Ants in March 1982. Speaking with the media at the time of the announcement, Adam said the split had been amicable. Once he'd embarked on his solo career – scoring another UK #1 with "Goody Two Shoes" in May of that year – Adam said he'd felt Miall, Merrick and Tibbs had lost interest: "[It] just wasn't there anymore. It might have been Adam and the Ants on the billboards but not on stage."

Despite suffering mental issues throughout his career – having been diagnosed as Bipolar aged 21 – Adam has continued performing to the present day.

Stiff Little Fingers are another band still flying the flag (pun fully intended). Burns and Co. would release two further albums for Chrysalis, *Nobody's Heroes* (March 1980; UK #8, which contained the single 'At the Edge' which reached #15 on the UK chart) and *Go for It* (April 1981; UK #14), as well as the four-track *Now Then . . .* EP (September 1982; UK #24), before calling it a day in 1983. They came together again in 1987 – the idea being to raise the cash to enable them to return to Belfast for the Christmas holidays. Realising their fans hadn't forgotten them, SLF reformed permanently with ex-Jam bassist Bruce Foxton replacing Ali McMordie in time to record the *Flags and Emblems* album. McMordie would in turn return to replace Foxton in 2006. Henry Cluney left the band in 1993 to be replaced in the long-term by Ian McCallum, who was singing for his supper in Burns' Newcastle local at the time.

U.K. Subs have released 26 studio albums – each beginning with a different letter of the alphabet (Their most recent being 2016's, Ziezo) – since their 1976 formation, and their charismatic frontman, Charlie Harper, has engaged nearly as many guitarists, bassists and drummers in that time. They signed with RCA subsidiary GEM Records in May 1979. And released their debut album, *Another Kind of Blues*, in September of that year and narrowly missed out on reaching the UK Top 20. The album's attendant singles, "Stranglehold" and "Tomorrow's Girls". The follow-up album, *Brand New Age*, would succeed in breaking into the Top 20, peaking at #18, and give the U.K. Subs another Top 30 single with "Warhead". Proof of the band's burgeoning popularity came with the live album, *Crash Course* (recorded at the Rainbow Theatre on May 30, 1980), peaked at #8 on the UK album chart.

Crash Course was to prove the high water mark for the U.K. Subs in terms of chart placings, but their core fan-base would remain steadfastly loyal over the proceeding years. Though 75 at the time of writing, Charlie Harper shows little sign of hanging up the mic and the Subs have continued gigging to the present day with many of the band's early fans bringing along their offspring.

Over in the US, Blondie would continue to build on the success of *Parallel Lines* with their fifth studio album, *Autoamerican*. The album went Top 10 on the *Billboard* 200 following its November 1980 release and gave them two more US #1s: the first being a cover of The Paragons' 'The Tide Is High' and the rap-tinged 'Rapture' – the first song to feature rapping to top the US chart. (*Autoamerican* peaked at #3 on the UK chart). While enjoying a break from Blondie to pursue various solo endeavours, Chrysalis released *The Best of Blondie* compilation album (UK #4; US #30). The band were said to be far from happy at what they saw at Chrysalis's blatant cash-in.

Blondie's next album, 1982's *The Hunter* (UK #9; US #33) was poorly received at the hands of the critics and didn't fare as well on the charts as everyone had anticipated. The album's poor showing merely served to heighten tension within the band. Whether Blondie could pick themselves up off the canvas was rendered a moot point when Stein was diagnosed with pemphigus, a life-threatening autoimmune disease that affects the skin and mucous membranes. Despite having sold millions of albums around the world, years of fiscal mismanagement had seen a sizeable share of the royalties that should have gone to Blondie going elsewhere. As a result of this, Harry and Stein were forced to sell their five-story Manhattan home to pay off creditors and meet Stein's medical bills. Stein would recover in time, but the constant strain would ultimately bring about a separation. The two would continue their working relationship, however, most notably on Harry's solo projects.

With various Blondie compilation albums never failing to chart, Stein and Harry began the process of reuniting Blondie with Burke, Destri, and Valentine. Nigel Harrison and Frank Infante were not invited to participate in the reunion and would launch an unsuccessful lawsuit to prevent the reunion under the name Blondie.

1999's *No Exit* album saw a very promising return to form, especially with the lead single 'Maria' giving Blondie their sixth UK #1. Their most recent album, Pollinator, saw the band invite outside writers such as Johnny Marr, Sia, Nick Valensi (The Strokes) and Charli XCX, to pen songs in a "Blondie style". The album stalled at a desultory #63 on the Billboard 200 but went Top 5 in the UK.

The Ramones would go on to release a further nine studios albums before disbanding in 1996. Regardless of their pulling power as a live act, however, The Ramones were destined never to have a bona fide hit record in their homeland. The band's Phil Spector-produced strings-laden cover of The Ronettes' 'Baby, I Love You' – lifted from the *End of the Century* album – provided a Top 10 hit in the UK following its January 1980, but this was to prove something of an illusory dawn. 1992's Mondo Bizarro being certified Gold in Brazil upon selling 100,000 copies was the first Gold certification The Ramones were ever awarded. Even the news they were going their separate ways following the release of *Adios Amigos* failed to engender much of a reaction amongst America's record-buying public.

The Ramones brought the curtain down with a valedictory show at The Palace in LA on August 6, 1996, featuring guest artists/fans such as Lemmy, Eddie Vedder, Chris Cornell, as well as Rancid's Tim Armstrong and Lars Frederiksen. Dee Dee would also make a "guest appearance some seven years on from his quitting the band to pursue an ill-advised career in hip hop as "Dee Dee King". Dee Dee would soon return to what he did best, however; releasing three solo albums. He would also continue writing songs for The Ramones. His replacement in the band was C.J. Ramone, who remained with the band throughout the remainder of their career. Marky had been fired and rehired after winning his fight with alcoholism. His replacement, Ritchie Ramone, would quit acrimoniously in 1987 after a five-year tenure owing to mounting frustrations at his being denied a share of the lucrative merchandising money. Ritchie was in turn replaced by Clem "Elvis Ramone" Burke. The Blondie stickman would last just two shows, however, due to his inability to keep pace with The Ramones' frenetic onstage tempo.

Johnny Ramone ran the band along similar regimented lines he'd experienced at military school as a teenager. Such was the in-band discipline that the story of Johnny and Joey's love triangle feud didn't emerge till after the split – despite the two not speaking to each other for many years. Joey had started dating the then 18-year-old Linda Danielle from 1978 onwards, the two having first met at a Ramones show at CBGBs a couple of years earlier. Speaking with The *Sun* newspaper in August 2016 to mark the band's fortieth anniversary, Linda said that when she first began travelling with the band, Johnny would barely speak to her and made her sit at the back. But that would soon change, however, and Linda would leave Joey for Johnny, the two eventually marrying in 1994.

The four founding Ramones were last seen together on July 20, 1999, when Joey, Johnny, Dee Dee, Johnny, Tommy, Marky and C.J. at the Virgin Megastore in New York's Times Square for an autograph signing. By the time The Ramones were inducted into the Rock and Roll Hall of Fame in March 2002, Joey had succumbed to the lymphoma he'd been first diagnosed with in 1995. Green Day, who, ironically, have sold millions of records imitating The Ramones' trademark style, played a three-song tribute: 'Teenage Lobotomy', 'Rockaway Beach' and 'Blitzkrieg Bop'. The ceremony would prove one of Dee Dee's last public sightings as the bassist died of a suspected heroin overdose at his Hollywood apartment on June 5. Johnny was to follow two years later, dying from prostate cancer in September 2004. Tommy would sadly lose his battle with bile duct cancer in July 2014.

Speaking with *www.theartsdesk.com* in March 2014, Belinda Carlisle would pay tribute to Buzzcocks saying how The Go-Go's had modelled themselves on the Manchester punk/power-popsters when first starting out. "[We were] so very much pop, but you couldn't hear what it was because no-one could play. As we became more proficient, people were like, 'Oh my God, it's a pop band, not a punk band.' Then, of course, we were one of the first to get a record deal. The Go-Go's came from the punk scene but we were punk-pop. People around us changed more than we did, but attitudes towards us changed more."

When The Go-Go's signed with I.R.S. on April 1, 1981, the consensus amongst the LA cognoscenti was that the label's supremo, Miles

Copeland, had fallen victim to a practical joke of his own devising. All this did do, of course, was make the girls doubly determined to make those same naysayers eat their words. By the time of the signing, Margot Olivarria and Elissa Bello had been replaced by Kathy Valentine and Gina Schock respectively.

The Go-Go's debut album, *Beauty and the Beat*, was released in early July 1981, alongside lead single "Our Lips Are Sealed". Copeland had estimated that album sales of around 100,000 would prove sufficient for the label to recoup its advance and cover all recording costs. 'Our Lips Are Sealed' would prove something of a slow-burner on the *Billboard* Hot 100 but would eventually creep up to #20 and remain on the US chart well into the following year. *Beauty and the Beat* received a lukewarm reception from the US music media, with *Rolling Stone* setting the median tone in saying The Go-Go's' debut was a "solid, likeable debut." Unsurprisingly, the album entered the *Billboard* 200 at a desultory #187. Copeland's decision to have The Go-Go's go out on tour with his brother's band, The Police, on the latter outfit's Ghost in the Machine Tour, in support of the album of the same name, was to prove a masterstroke, however, as it jumpstarted *Beauty and the Beat* steady climb to the top of the US chart.

Since the fabled "'Class of 76' first exploded onto the UK music scene, punk has since splintered into a myriad of diverse subgenres: Anarcho-punk (Crass, Conflict), Christian punk (MxPx, Dogwood), Crust punk (Hellbastard, Discharge), Garage punk (Mudhoney, Hives), Glam punk (. Mötley Crüe, Poison), Horror punk (Misfits, Balzac), Skate punk (Offspring, Pennywise), Ska punk (Less Than Jake, Mighty Mighty Bosstones), Street punk (Dogs in the Fight) and Punk metal (Rage Against the Machine, L7) to name but a few.

By the advent of the twenty-first century, punk had long-since been absorbed into the mainstream. As the cliché goes, even bank managers now have spikyish hair, while Ramones, Pistols, Sid Vicious and other punk-themed T-shirts can be found in a plethora of high street fashion boutiques. But they do say that no matter what you throw at capitalism, it will absorb it and sell it back to you. The irony being, of course, that bands such as Green Day, Rancid, NOFX, Sum 41 and Blink 182 are left to reap the dividends, playing sold-out arenas around the globe and selling records by the bucketload, while a good number of the musicians from the punk bands that

Blondie's Debbie Harry and Chris Stein at Dingwalls
Dance Hall, London in 1979. Photo: Ray Stevenson

inspired them to pick up an instrument are living in near-penury.

No one anticipated punk lasting beyond its initial short, sharp shock of the mid-to-late-seventies – least of all the bands themselves. Elvis, Little Richard, Chuck Berry and the other rock 'n' roll pioneers were ultimately overshadowed by The Beatles, who in turn were eschewed in favour of the Stones and The Who by those who preferred something edgier.

Mod has since been proclaimed the "new religion", but since its mid-to-late-sixties, new converts have proved few and far between. Prog rock and pub rock were both made by serious-minded musicians for serious-minded music lovers yet were ultimately hampered and hoisted by their own petards. Glam rock was undoubtedly a precursor to punk but was aimed at the teen market and therefore ultimately condemned to brevity. Many of those that could affect the shifting trends and had lived through mod, glam, prog and pub rock were most likely already looking beyond punk by the time the Sex Pistols released 'God Save the Queen', and yet here we are four decades on with the revolution still evolving.

These days, any band playing high-energy rock 'n' roll while copping an attitude in front of the camera can expect to be labelled "punk", of course, but isn't that what happened back in 1976/77?

—Top 100 Punk Tracks

"It's never easy compiling a top 100 list of any musical genre. If I had my way, I'd do away with the placings and say these tracks struck more of a chord than others while writing the book."

Mick O' Shea

001	Pretty Vacant	*– Sex Pistols*
002	Complete Control	*– The Clash*
003	God Save the Queen	*– Sex Pistols*
004	Bored Teenagers	*– The Adverts*
005	Blitzkrieg Bop	*– The Ramones*
006	(White Man) in Hammersmith Palais	*– The Clash*
007	Into the Valley	*– Skids*
008	Ever Fallen in Love (With Someone You Shouldn't've?)	*– Buzzcocks*
009	Alternative Ulster	*– Stiff Little Fingers*
010	Public Image	*– Public Image Limited*
011	New Rose	*– The Damned*
012	Down in the Tube Station at Midnight	*– The Jam*
013	Shot By Both Sides	*– Magazine*
014	Hong Kong Garden	*– Siouxsie and the Banshees*
015	Brickfield Nights	*– The Boys*
016	Stay Free	*– The Clash*

017 When Them Tanks
     Roll Over Poland Again   – *Automatics*
018 Your Generation   – *Generation X*
019 London Calling   – *The Clash*
020 Orgasm Addict   – *Buzzcocks*
021 Holidays in the Sun   – *Sex Pistols*
022 Gary Gilmore's Eye   – *The Adverts*
023 Smash It Up   – *The Damned*
024 At the Edge   – *Stiff Little Fingers*
025 The Saints are Coming   – *Skids*
026 Flying Duck Theory   – *The Vibrators*
027 The KKK Took
     My Baby Away   – *The Ramones*
028 Nasty Nasty   – *999*
029 Gimme Danger   – *The Stooges*
030 White Riot   – *The Clash*
031 No More Heroes   – *Stranglers*
032 In the City   – *The Jam*
033 Don't Dictate   – *Penetration*
034 Action Time Vision   – *Alternative TV*
035 Questions and Answers   – *Sham 69*
036 Rich Kids   – *Rich Kids*
037 Thick as Thieves   – *The Jam*
038 Typical Girls   – *The Slits*
039 Oh Bondage Up Yours   – *X-Ray Spex*
040 Poptones   – *Public Image Limited*
041 My Mind Ain't So Open   – *Magazine*
042 I Wanna Be Me   – *Sex Pistols*
043 Personality Crisis   – *New York Dolls*
044 Rockaway Beach   – *The Ramones*
045 Why Can't I Touch It?   – *Buzzcocks*
046 Atmosphere   – *Joy Division*
047 Safe European Home   – *The Clash*
048 Radio Radio   – *Elvis Costello*
049 Venus in Furs   – *Velvet Underground*
050 Smash It Up   – *The Damned*
051 Staring at the Rude Boys   – *The Ruts*
052 Johnny Was   – *Still Little Fingers*
053 Search and Destroy   – *The Stooges*

054	Jet Boy	– *New York Dolls*
055	You Can't Put Your Arms Around a Memory	– *Johnny Thunders*
056	Emergency	– *999*
057	No Time To Be 21	– *The Adverts*
058	What Do I Get?	– *Buzzcocks*
059	Holiday in Cambodia	– *The Dead Kennedys*
060	Teenage Kicks	– *The Undertones*
061	Barbed Wire Love	– *Still Little Fingers*
062	Neat Neat Neat	– *The Damned*
063	Masquerade	– *Skids*
064	Sheena Is a Punk Rocker	– *The Ramones*
065	Denis	– *Blondie*
066	Born to Lose	– *The Heartbreakers*
067	1977	– *The Clash*
068	She's Lost Control	– *Joy Division*
069	I'm Stranded	– *The Saints*
070	(Get A) Grip (On Yourself)	– *The Stranglers*
071	Babylon's Burning	– *The Ruts*
072	Raw Power	– *The Stooges*
073	One Chord Wonders	– *The Adverts*
074	Goin' Steady	– *The Heartbreakers*
075	Kick Out the Jams	– *MC5*
076	Love You More	– *Buzzcocks*
077	Ready Steady Go	– *Generation X*
078	Bodies	– *Sex Pistols*
079	Death or Glory	– *The Clash*
080	On the Roof	– *The Adverts*
081	Detroit 442	– *Blondie*
082	I Wanna Be Your Boyfriend	– *The Ramones*
083	Janie Jones	– *The Clash*
084	Doesn't Make It Alright	– *Still Little Fingers*
085	Angels with Dirty Faces	– *Sham 69*
086	Press darlings	– *Adam and the Ants*
087	Another Girl, Another Planet	– *The Only Ones*
088	Heroine	– *The Boys*
089	12XU	– *Wire*
090	See No Evil	– *Television*

— Sources

Books:

Please Kill Me: The Uncensored Oral History of Punk, Legs McNeil, and Gillian McCain **(Grove Press 1997)**

Parallel Lives, Dick Porter and Kris Needs **(Omnibus Press 2012)**

Defying Gravity: Jordan's Story, Jordan Mooney, with Cathi Unsworth **(Omnibus Press 2019)**

There's No Bones in Ice Cream: Sylvain Sylvain's Story of the New York Dolls, Sylvain Sylvain with Dave Thompson **(Omnibus Press 2018)**

'77 Sulphate Strip: The Year That Changed Everything, Barry Cain **(Red Planet 2008)**

Lonely Boy: Tales from a Sex Pistol, Steve Jones **(Windmill Books 2017)**

England's Dreaming: Sex Pistols and Punk Rock, Jon Savage **(Faber & Faber 1991)**

I Was a Teenage Sex Pistol, Glen Matlock with Pete Silverton **(Reynolds and Hearn 2000)**

Rotten: No Irish, No Blacks, No Dogs, John Lydon with Keith Zimmerman **(Hodder & Stoughton 1994)**

Anger is an Energy: My Life Uncensored, John Lydon with Andrew Perry **(Simon & Schuster UK 2015)**

Sex Pistols: 90 Days At EMI, Brian Southall **(Bobcat Books 2007)**

Spirit of '76: London Punk Eyewitness, John Ingham **(Anthology Editions 2017)**

The Clash: Return of the Last Gang in Town, Marcus Gray **(Hal Leonard 2004)**

Sniffin' Glue: The Essential Punk Accessory, Mark Perry **(Sanctuary Publishing Ltd 2000)**

The Wicked Ways of Malcolm McLaren, Craig Bromberg **(Omnibus Press 1991)**

The Roxy Our Story: The Club That Forged Punk in 100 Nights of Madness Mayhem and Misfortune, Andrew Czezowski, and Susan Carrington **(Carrczez Publishing Ltd 2017)**

Vivienne Westwood: An Unfashionable Life, Jane Mulvagh **(HarperCollins 2011)**

Hey Ho Let's Go: The Story of the "Ramones", Everett True **(Omnibus Press 2005)**

Sid Vicious: No One is Innocent, Alan G Parker **(Orion 2008)**

Clothes, Clothes, Clothes. Music, Music, Music. Boys, Boys, Boys, Viv Albertine **(Faber & Faber 2015)**

Losing My Virginity, Richard Branson **(Virgin Books 2009)**

We Got the Neutron Bomb: The Untold Story of L.A. Punk, Marc Spitz and Brendan Mullen **(Three Rivers Press 2001)**

Live at the Masque: Nightmare in Punk Alley, Brendan Mullen with Roger Gastman **(Gingko Press Inc 2007)**

Lips Unsealed: A Memoir, Belinda Carlisle **(Three Rivers Press 2011)**

Under the Big Black Sun: A Personal History of L.A. Punk, John Doe with Tom DeSavia **(De Capo Press 2017)**

Stiff Little Fingers: Song by Song, Jake Burns and Alan Parker Alan **(Sanctuary Publishing Ltd 2003)**

The One & Only: Peter Perrett, Homme Fatale, Nina Antonia **(Thin Man Press 2015)**

Memoirs of a Geezer: Music, Mayhem, Life, Jah Wobble **(Serpent's Tail 2009)**

The Jam: Shout to the Top, Dennis Munday **(Omnibus Press 2008)**

A Riot of Our Own: Night and Day with The Clash and After, Johnny Green **(Orion 2003)**

Subcultures, Pop Music and Politics: Skinheads and "Nazi Rock" in England and Germany, Timothy S Brown **(Gale Group 2004)**

Magazines, periodicals & TV documentaries:

Melody Maker
Sounds
NME
Record Mirror
Rolling Stone
Punk magazine

Mojo
The Independent
The Sun
Austin Chronicle
Helsingin Sanomat
San Francisco Chronicle

Punk Britannia
Clash on Broadway booklet
Uncut magazine
Manchester Evening News
ZigZag
The Guardian
Clash magazine
The Sex Pistols - Never Mind the Sex Pistols
London Evening Standard
London Weekend Programme
Classic Albums: Never Mind the Bollocks
The Filth and the Fury
Punk Rock Movie
Never Mind the Baubles – Christmas '77 with the Sex Pistols

Websites & Podcasts:

www.philjens.plus.com
www.paulgormanis.com
www.cbgb.com/history-by-hilly
www.noclass.co.uk
www.tinymixtapes.com
www.magictramps.com
www.jonesysjukebox.com
www.thestranglers.co.uk
www.rnz.co.nz
www.fodderstompf.co
www.punk77.co.uk
www.songfacts.com
www.daveling.co.uk
www.perfectsoundforever.com
www.thebaker77.wordpress.com
www.x-rayspex.com
www.billboard.com/charts/billboard-200
www.officialcharts.com
www.the-skids.com
www.theartsdesk.com

Professional thanks:

Mark Neeter, Winlong Hong, and everyone at Red Planet Books. Very special thanks to Bernard Rhodes, Leee Black Childers, Steve Diggle, Stephen "Roadent" Connelly, John "Boogie" Tiberi, Glen Matlock, TV Smith, Gaye Advert, Jordan, Henry Cluney, Mike Thorne, Andrew Czezowski, Susan Carrington, Jonh Ingham, Roddy "Radiation" Byers, Rory Johnstone, John Holmstrom, Roberta Bayley, Bob Merlis, Barry Cain, Chris Salewicz, Pleasant Gehman, Theresa Kereakes, Margot Olavarria, Elissa Bello, Kathy Valentine, Terry Graham, Gabi Berlin, Helena Roessler (a.k.a Hellin Killer), Lamar St. John, Freddi Griffin, Doreen Cochrane, Peter Perritt, Lynn Stroud, Sharon Powell, Margaret Moser, Ken Hoge and Jesse Sublett III for taking time out of their schedules to share their reminiscences.

Special mention to:

Tasha "Bush" Cowen, Shannon "Mini B" Stanley, Lisa "T-bag" Bird, Ayesha Plunkett, David Fairness, Ziggy P & Zoe, Paul Young (not the singer), Mick Drain, Tony Makin & Pads, Drezzie & Catherine, Rand "Mad Swede" Winch, Luke Dillon (and Delia and Willow), Gemma and Donna (a.k.a. "The Girls"), Dan Carter and Claire Kingsley, "Blowback Annie" Chamberlain, Adam Larn, Johnny Diamond, Dan, Jeannie & "Pinks", Roop & Deb, Rob and Debs, Tiler Dan & Steph, "Scouse Mark" Rudge, Adam Larn, Andy Cole, Stuart Furlonger, Rob Gill, Mel King, Simone Jackson, Joel & Aggie, everyone at The Old House at Dorking and The Star, Faye and Richard and everyone at the Kings Arms, Winkleigh.

And last, but by no means least, here's to the "Accy Punks" (at least those whose names I remember): Kev Gray, Dave Heap, Neil "Nidge" Collinge, Mark "Gibby" Gibson, Tommy "Vomit" Crookston, Paul Stockton, Craig "Cunny" Cunliffe, Mark Heys, Dave Ward, Andy Gray, Paul Whalley, Brian and Phil Counsell, Tommy O'Kane, and Waz Brazendale.

Stiv Bators of The Dead Boys Photo: David Arnoff

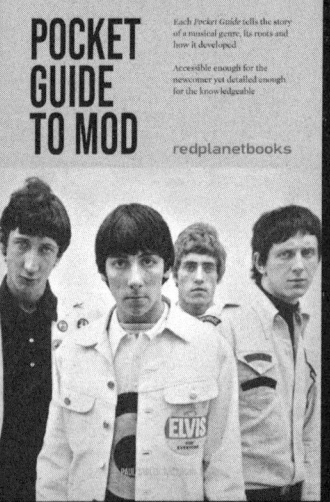

POCKET GUIDE TO MOD
AUTHOR / PAUL 'SMILER' ANDERSON
PRICE / £12.99 / $14.95

POCKET GUIDE TO SKA
AUTHOR / MICK O' SHEA
PRICE / £12.99 / $14.95

POCKET GUIDE TO PUNK
AUTHOR / MICK O' SHEA
PRICE / £14.99 / $19.95

POCKET GUIDE TO GLAM ROCK
AUTHOR / MICK O' SHEA
PRICE / £14.99 / $19.95

POCKET GUIDE TO METAL (COMING SOON)
AUTHOR / MICK O' SHEA
PRICE / £14.99 / $19.95

First published by Red Planet Books in 2021

Text © Mick O' Shea 2021

This edition copyright © Red Planet Books 2021

ISBN: 978 1 9127 3390 3

Printed and bound by TJ Books, Padstow

redplanetbooks

redplanetbooks.co.uk / PO Box 355 Falmouth TR11 9ER
Design Winlong Hong / info@redplanetbooks.co.uk
Cover: Gus Stewart Back cover: Jorgen Angel/Redferns